Saigon's Edge

Saigon's Edge

On the Margins of
Ho Chi Minh City

Erik Harms

University of Minnesota Press | Minneapolis | London

The University of Minnesota Press gratefully acknowledges financial assistance provided for the publication of this book by the Association for Asian Studies First Book Subvention Program.

Photographs in the book were taken by the author.

Published by the University of Minnesota Press
111 Third Avenue South, Suite 290
Minneapolis, MN 55401-2520
http://www.upress.umn.edu

Library of Congress Cataloging-in-Publication Data

Harms, Erik.
   Saigon's edge : on the margins of Ho Chi Minh city / Erik Harms.
      p. cm.
   Includes bibliographical references and index.
   ISBN 978-0-8166-5605-9 (hc : alk. paper)
   ISBN 978-0-8166-5606-6 (pb : alk. paper)
   1. Urbanization—Vietnam—Ho Chi Minh City. 2. Urban anthropology—Vietnam—Ho Chi Minh City. 3. City and town life—Vietnam—Ho Chi Minh City. 4. Sociology, Urban—Vietnam—Ho Chi Minh City. I. Title.
HT384.V52H634 2010
307.7609597'7—dc22

                                                                2010044695

Printed in the United States of America on acid-free paper

The University of Minnesota is an equal-opportunity educator and employer.

22 21 20 19 18 17 16   10 9 8 7 6 5 4 3

To Isabella,
to Mom,
and to Dad and Chris,
two triangle men in a land of squares

Contents

Acknowledgments ix

Glossary xiii

Introduction: Saigon, Inside Out 1

Part I. Social Edginess

1. Bittersweet Transitions:
Urbanization on the Fringe of the City 29

2. Power and Exclusion on the Edge:
The Conflation of Rural and Urban Spaces 61

Part II. Space, Time, and Urban Expansion

3. Future Orientations in the Country of Memory:
Social Conceptions of Time 89

4. Negotiating Time and Space:
Household, Labor, Land, and Movement 121

Part III. Realizing the Ideal

5. The Road to Paradise:
Building the Trans-Asia Highway 155

6. The Problem of Urban Civilization on Saigon's Edge 193

Conclusion: What Edges Do 221

Notes 239

Bibliography 261

Index 281

Acknowledgments

My warmest thanks to the people of Hóc Môn district, who tolerated my presence among them, answered my questions, and posed a lifetime of new questions. In particular, I thank our neighbors, who introduced me to the craziness of life on the edge and who exposed the nitty-gritty realities of "renovation." Trí and Liêm showed me the intricacies of getting goods to market and sending their young daughters to a better education. Phương introduced me to the loving family life behind the struggles of a lottery ticket seller. On the Tân Thới Nhì People's Committee, the hard work of Đỗ Thị Kim Tuyến forever challenged all unflattering misperceptions about Vietnamese civil servants, and her genuine compassion and friendship made my wife and me feel welcome in the community. The police in Tân Thới Nhì kept careful watch over us but never treated us unfairly; I later learned that "surveillance" has its advantages: it kept the thieves away when we were out of the house (by the thieves' own admission!).

I received support from Nguyễn Văn Tiệp at the University of Social Sciences and Humanities, Ho Chi Minh City, then under the able leadership of Ngô Văn Lê. I developed deep friendships with many people, especially anh Chí, anh Tùng and his family, em Ngọc, all my friends on Phạm Ngọc Thạch street, and Tiffany and Lộc, who gave me a window into the vibrant world of Vietnamese art and music. Matt Masur, Damon Hill, Benny Tran, and Howard Henry Chen were great interlocutors in Saigon while parts of this research were being conducted.

At Cornell University, Terence Turner nurtured my study of Marxism and all things anthropological; I learned something new from him every time we met. Viranjini Munasinghe proved a model teacher, and her insightful comments and unflagging support carried me through the most difficult periods of my work. I am convinced that Keith Taylor knows more about Vietnam than any living person, and I thank him for offering me a model for scholarly precision and intellectual dedication.

Jakob Rigi has proved a veritable intellectual sounding board on all the topics in this book and beyond. In addition to my committee members, Andrew Willford has always been a model teacher, Southeast Asianist, and anthropologist who has taught me more than he imagines. I still miss A. Thomas Kirsch, who first welcomed me into the anthropology department, and I thank Yohko Tsuji for keeping his memory alive.

I am indebted to the Cornell Southeast Asia Program (SEAP), the tight-knit intellectual community then directed by Thak Chaloemtiarana, run by Nancy Loncto, and held aloft by Wendy Treat. I especially thank my fellow students Jane Ferguson, Jen Foley, Tyrell Haberkorn, Doreen Lee, Johan Lindquist, Amanda Rath, Rick Ruth, Made Supriatma, Lisa Todzia, Christian Lammerts, Chie Ikeya, Alex Denes, and Worrasit Tantinipankul. Within SEAP we had our own little Vietnam subdivision. Special thanks to Keith Taylor, Thuy Tranviet, Tracy Barrett, Hồng Bùi, Audrey Cedeno, Nina Hien, Martin Loicano, Jon McIntyre, Bình Ngô, Brian Ostrowski, Vu Pham, Christophe Robert, Naomi Steinberg, Allison Truitt, and Wynn Wilcox. Another student, Steve Graw, was really my teacher; his spirit lives on with every word I write about Vietnam.

Brenda Maiale, Parvis Ghassem-Fachandi, and Anna Pandey made anthropological studies in Ithaca inspiring. I owe special intellectual debts to Christophe Robert, who showed me what it means to be a true scholar, unflinching, provocative, and always on the edge of new ideas, and to Sasha Newell, who is always an inspiring anthropological sounding board.

Christian Lentz and Adriane Lentz-Smith first helped ease the transition back to Ithaca after fieldwork, did it again by easing the transition to North Carolina, and then did it once again by helping us settle in New Haven. In North Carolina, Dan Duffy showed me that Vietnam studies can thrive from the back of a barn. Joe Harris and all the folks in the University Writing Program at Duke University were a great support as I juggled teaching with the final chapters of this book. In New Haven, my new home, my colleagues in the Department of Anthropology and on the Council on Southeast Asian Studies not only welcomed me with warmth and kindness but provide a stimulating intellectual environment within which I finished this work and embark on new projects.

I have an age-old debt to the California public schools, where Laura Nader first introduced me to anthropology while I was an undergraduate at Berkeley and offered a model of critical inquiry whenever her "anthropological antennae" went up. Her students Jay Ou and Roberto J. Gonzalez made me appreciate what could emerge from the combination of social consciousness and hard work.

My research in Vietnam was financed by a Fulbright–Hays dissertation research fellowship, and I received support for language study from the Foreign Language and Area Studies program, the Southeast Asian Summer Studies Institute, the Vietnamese Advanced Summer Institute, and the Blakemore Foundation. I thank Hy Van Luong and an anonymous reviewer who offered stimulating comments on the manuscript, and I give special thanks to my editor at the University of Minnesota Press, Jason Weidemann, who offered encouragement, patience, and keen advice. Nancy Sauro and Marilyn Martin improved the prose on every page with careful copyediting.

Scott Moir has always stepped in to make everything possible, and Bonnie has always kept me balanced. My mother convinced me to pursue higher education, and my father made it clear that writing is worth many times more than the effort. They have both supported me in my quests for knowledge and exploration, and I offer this book to them both with love and respect.

Finally, writing this book would have been impossible without the unflagging support of my wife, Isabella Fiorentino, who managed to keep my spirits up through many years in icy Ithaca; a year and a half in Vietnam filled with leaky roofs, termite infestations, dangerous highways, and inscrutable landlords; and another year and a half of dissertation writing. Even after all that, she still managed to give me time to rewrite this book in between moving through two academic jobs and the births of our two amazing daughters, Lena and Giulia. Isabella is, as our neighbors in Hóc Môn always reminded us, unmistakably "dễ thương"—lovely.

Glossary

âm and dương	Yin and yang, cosmological opposites. Âm, as opposed to dương, is associated symbolically with the moon, the female, the outside, rurality. Dương, as opposed to âm, is associated symbolically with the sun, the male, the inside, urbanity.
désakota	An Indonesian term used in academic studies of Southeast Asia to designate rural–urban interface zones
Đổi mới	Literally, change [to the] new; renovation; reform. Used to identify Vietnamese political and economic reforms instituted in 1986.
huyện	A classifier meaning "district" in rural provincial districts or outer-city districts, e.g., *huyện ngoại thành*
ngoại thành	Literally, outside the walls; outside the city; outer-city district
nội thành	Literally, inside the walls; inside the city; inner-city district
nông thôn	countryside, the rural
phát triển	development
phường	Ward, quarter; also known as a "subdistrict" in inner-city areas

quận	A classifier meaning "district" in inner-city areas, e.g., *quận nội thành*
thành phố	Literally, walls and streets; city
thành thị	Literally, walls and markets; city
thoải mái	To be at ease, relaxed, unencumbered
văn hóa	Culture; also refers to a level of education
văn minh	Literally, a compound of the words for "literature" *(văn)* and "light" *(minh)*. Commonly translated to mean civility, civilization, or civilized, and at times glossed as modern or modernity.
văn minh đô thị	urban civilization, urban civility, civilized urbanity

Introduction
Saigon, Inside Out

One can easily imagine Baudelaire . . . writing a poem about a slag-heap.
But the beauty or ugliness of industrialism hardly matters. Its real evil
lies far deeper and is quite ineradicable. It is important to remember this,
because there is always a temptation to think that industrialism is
harmless so long as it is clean and orderly.

—George Orwell, *The Road to Wigan Pier*

From the Outside In

If you ride a motorbike to work from Hóc Môn district into central Ho
Chi Minh City, take a change of clothes. In the dry season, the dust will
turn your clothes a dull reddish brown. In the wet season, you are bound
to be splashed with mud—assuming, of course, that you are lucky enough
not to fall headlong into a brackish, water-filled ditch.

I was offered this advice by Vân, one of Hóc Môn's lucky residents,
a young woman with an office job in the city.[1] The daughter of a vegetable merchant, she commuted by motorbike between the outer-city
suburb of Hóc Môn and an air-conditioned office building in the inner
city, where she worked part time as a bookkeeper and office aide. Five
days a week she joined the many thousands of commuters who navigate
the intersection of Highway 1 and National Highway 22 at An Sương,
who take a leap of faith each time they cross the unregulated diagonal
crossover at the intersection of the Boulevard of the Republic and the
Boulevard of the August Revolution, and who enter the notoriously pell-
mell intersection at Bà Quẹo on their way to the crowded streets of downtown Ho Chi Minh City.

With her extra clothes in her bag, a scarf wrapped tightly around her
face, and long gloves on to block the dust and sun, she made this daily
commute between "the outside of the city" and "the inside of the city"—
from *ngoại thành* to *nội thành* and back. In addition to navigating the
harrowing traffic, she was also navigating a key symbolic divide. Both
on city maps and in terms of the way people describe it, Ho Chi Minh
City has a bifurcated structure, divided into an inside and an outside.

Furthermore, Vietnam as a whole is also described as divided, between the country and the city.

The symbolic oppositions between the inside and the outside and between the country and the city act as both a model of and a model for a very real material divide as well. Among the people I came to know during a year and a half of fieldwork in both Hóc Môn and Ho Chi Minh City, these oppositions were incessantly used to explain and categorize a whole litany of social experiences. The ideas of country versus city and inside the city versus outside the city acted as key indexes of social difference and were used to codify everything from different social types and lifestyles to poverty indexes and living standards, from differential access to health care and education to general quality of life.

For those who live there, the social experience of life on Saigon's edge—the term I use to describe the anomalous interface of the rural countryside and the urban fringe of Ho Chi Minh City—makes the symbolic divide appear quite real indeed. If Vân was lucky to have an office job in the city, there were many, many others who were not so lucky. For a large majority of Hóc Môn residents, life on the "outside" proved constraining and marginalizing. Many people experienced their spatial position on the outside of the city as representative of their position outside of the networks of power and opportunity associated with the economic development of Vietnam during the contemporary "open door" period of market reform. They experienced life "outside" in much more than just spatial terms.

Ideal representations of inside and outside, as well as the rural and the urban in Vietnam today conflict with the practical spatial–temporal organization of the rural–urban fringe in contemporary Ho Chi Minh City. In the ideal model, social order depends on an organic unity of pure opposites in which a traditional and past-oriented rural countryside stands in complementary opposition to a modern and forward-moving urban core. Furthermore, the symbolic meaning of *inner-* and *outer-city* districts is infused by and made meaningful in relation to distinctly Vietnamese notions of kinship relations, which are also organized in terms of inside and outside lineages. These orderly, seemingly elegant models and local idioms, however, mask a much more complex reality. In practice, country and city blend with each other, forming a hybrid space that does not fit into acceptable categories people use for understanding the world.

This book is about how Hóc Môn residents like Vân navigate the apparent disconnect between ideal cultural models of the space they live in and the everyday realities of their actual lives, which so often transcend or contradict those models. My most direct goal is purely ethnographic. I detail the ambivalence Hóc Môn residents associate with the current urbanization process in Ho Chi Minh City, linking this to the ways that great numbers of people living on the fringes of the city fall between the spatial and temporal categories used to imagine the city. People living on the edge are neither rural nor urban, neither wholly inside nor outside, but uncomfortably both. Viewed through the lens of widely accepted pure sociospatial categories, the fringe zone appears as a wasteland *(đất hoang)* hindering the "modernization" of the city.

There are no Vietnamese poems about Hóc Môn, which is littered with construction materials, marked by the "creative destruction" of global industrial expansion and unbridled urbanization. From a critical perspective, the landscape represents the material manifestation of laissez-faire global capitalism, which Mike Davis has shown to produce the meteoric growth of the world's poor megacities, the rapid differentiation between the urban rich and devastatingly poor, the deterioration of urban environments, the dismantling of social services, and the general collapse of state capacities to provide for increasingly large portions of their populations. As Davis so clearly demonstrates, the postcolonial world order is increasingly urban and increasingly destitute.[2] Although George Orwell could "easily imagine Baudelaire . . . writing a poem about a slag-heap," he also added that such a search for beauty is largely misguided.[3] For the people I encountered, the ugliness of social space and the difficulty of life are still too closely entwined to step back and ponder the ironic beauty of industrial debris and rampant urbanization. Poverty is not beautiful, and the landscape it produces smashes ideal categories against the concrete realities of lived life.

Yet ideals do not always vanish in the face of processes that defy them. I describe how idealized categories describing the relationship between inner city and outer city persist, even in spaces like Hóc Môn that seem to render them irrelevant. The multiple manmade wastelands of marginal space throughout Vietnam would seem to undermine the state socialist mythology of progress in the nation. Yet the celebration of seemingly utopian ideals and the fervent hope that development will reshape the world to fit them persist. The ideal of man over nature and the celebration of urbanization as a universal trajectory to social advancement persist in spite of the acknowledged "other face of economic development," in spite of the growing differential between rich and poor.[4]

To explain this persistence of ideal categories in the face of spatial landscapes that contradict them, I develop the concept of "social edginess" to explain why people might hold onto concepts that would appear to exclude them. Unlike the concept of marginality, which struggles to account for active agency, has no active verb form, and can be written only in the passive voice, the semantic fluidity implied by the English word *edge* more accurately conveys the way many Hóc Môn residents deploy their edginess to complicated effect. Like the double-edged blade of a knife, this edginess cuts both ways, sometimes cutting back against structures of power and sometimes cutting the very social agents who wield it. Sometimes people actively edge their way into opportunities created by their position on the urban fringe; at other times they are edged out by processes beyond their control. The edge in Saigon's edge operates as a verb and a noun, and edgy is an ethos, a set of actions and attitudes as much as an adjective.

Social life in Hóc Môn both challenges and reproduces simplifying schemes for understanding Vietnamese spatial organization. Delving into the specifics of life on the edge in Hóc Môn, this book both critiques and seeks to understand the persistent use of binary frameworks such as rural versus urban and inside versus outside to understand complex urban processes. In doing so, it offers a model for thinking through a wide range of troubled "neither/nor" categories that proliferate in Vietnam. Neither wholly Eastern nor Southeast Asian, Vietnam follows the neither completely socialist nor capitalist political and economic policies of a "market economy with a socialist direction." The politics of neither/nor defines Vietnam's attempt to refashion its national identity as it seeks aid from foreign development organizations, enthusiastically entering into the World Trade Organization while fervently defending its proclaimed socialist economic and political orientation. Just as Hóc Môn lies between the constructed social categories of country and city, inner-city district and outer-city district, Vietnam as a whole finds itself as a country on the edge. Vietnam itself is both capitalist and socialist, an agrarian nation constantly marked by an emphasis on urbanization and industrial development. The case of Hóc Môn shows, through the lived experience of people who live there, the conceptual and practical difficulties that arise when a place and the people who inhabit it must straddle symbolically opposed concepts. It is not just people in Hóc Môn who must negotiate this predicament; in so many different ways, the entire nation of Vietnam is engaged in a similar form of symbolic and practical fence-sitting. It is an uncomfortable position; at times the fence seems to have barbed wire on top. But it is also a strategic position, enabling social actors to oscillate between contrasting social models for strategic effect.

Instead of taking social categories such as rural and urban or inside and outside at face value as elements of Vietnamese culture, I demonstrate what these categories do, how people deploy them to achieve material gain, construct meaningful identities, and carve a space for themselves within society. Following the tradition of Roger Keesing and William Roseberry, I see culture not simply as a set of symbols and meanings but also as a system of power.[5] Inspired further by Laura Nader's work on the processes of social and cultural control that underlie central dogmas, I examine the oppositions of rural and urban and of inside the city and outside the city as more than just a system of cultural meaning; they also organize political and economic relations among people within society.[6] As Nguyễn-võ Thu-hương has shown, essentialized conceptions about "true" Vietnamese society and culture often buttress economic disparities and legitimize unequal access to resources.[7] Although it may well be that the distinction between the country and the city has an important symbolic meaning in Vietnamese society, using this meaning to explain contemporary social relations fails to fully explain how these distinctions came about and the way they are so often transcended or strategically deployed in everyday life. Although the ethnographic description of Hóc Môn drives the book, I also challenge the reader to rethink the oppositions between the country and the city that are so often used to explain social difference in Vietnamese cities today and, by extension, in cities elsewhere.

The Universal Particularity of the Country and the City

Idealized descriptions of Vietnam's rural–urban divide invite comparisons with a wide range of ethnographic contexts from diverse places around the globe. Writing of English depictions of the country and the city during the transition to industrial capitalism at the turn of the nineteenth century, Raymond Williams describes how a very labile language of exultation and denigration hinged on the structural oppositions of these two binary categories. The fount of national culture was to be found alternately in the city or the country, and so were the seeds of the Fall.[8] Furthermore, in the England of that time, as in today's Vietnam, the interpretation and valuation of these structural opposites must be understood as politically charged symbols in debates over what counts as "true" culture and what stands as a threat. In both cases "certain images and associations persist" about the clear-cut distinction between country and city, and they persist despite the fact that such clear-cut distinctions are actually quite difficult to pin down in everyday experience.[9]

The superficial simplicity of this comparison of the present situation in Vietnam with bygone English history, however, challenges the usefulness of this universalizing rural–urban distinction. Certainly something must be amiss if the social relations of Ho Chi Minh City at the turn of the millennium can be explained with the same categories used to describe England at the dawn of the industrial age. Vietnam is no England, and the Industrial Revolution shares only a family resemblance to the ongoing industrial transformation of Vietnamese society. The Vietnamese government's decision to move away from its failed experiments in collectivization toward export-oriented production of market goods may recall the social changes experienced during the historical shifts toward market mechanisms in other societies. But these resemblances are only superficial. In the English case, the move away from production by family households and direct producers and toward industrial agriculture and factory work regulated by the clock emerged when new market imperatives compelled producers to increase productivity and profit.[10] Competition forced direct producers into new class relations and disembedded the economy from its role within society and culture.[11] Vietnamese decollectivization since the 1980s and the gradual dismantling of state-run industry, by contrast, has led to a move away from centralized production and toward a resurgence of household production.[12] In England the national economy moved from household production to capitalist industry and industrial agriculture; in Vietnam it has gone from centralized socialist industry and industrial agriculture to a mix of centralized and privatized industry underscored and supplemented by an increasingly important sector of household production.

These are very different trends. The primary similarity between the two cases is the increased role of the market economy in organizing production. But even the market is different. Modern "just-in-time" methods of post-Fordist flexible accumulation that now organize large-scale commodity production for rapidly fluctuating world markets depend on diverse production regimes organized around networks of small producers in ways inconceivable to the nineteenth-century captains of industry in the West.[13] Indeed, new forms of industrial production all depend on the maintenance of "place-based" differences within a global industrial division of labor.[14] The prime universal in today's global economy is that each place be *different* and constantly adaptable. Processes of globalization that would seem to obliterate the distinctiveness of local social formations have actually produced new and highly particular regional relationships between the city and the country in different spaces. The binary distinction between country and city may seem universal, but the particularity of each situation is also universal. Williams himself recognized this: "Whenever I consider the relations between country and city . . . I find this history active and continuous: the relations are not only of ideas and experience, but of rent and interest, of situation and power; a wider system."[15] To political economy I would add the importance of people's stories and everyday lives.

The fixed poles of the binary opposition between country and city reveal very little themselves. More important are the ways that people in different social and historical contexts move between these poles, as well as the ways that people attempt to shift the parameters of this symbolic opposition in order to maximize their positional advantages within different levels of social relations and exchange. In Zambia, James Ferguson has shown how an idealized opposition between the country and the city was undermined by economic changes resulting from Zambia's faltering copper mining industry. What seemed to be deep cultural precepts proved to be tied into material relations and political economy.[16] As Ferguson wrote: "'The Country' as imagined locus of moral purity and wholeness is today increasingly in tension with "the Country" as the seat of actual and antagonistic social relations."[17] In Latin America, William Roseberry has shown how the social production of "the rural" and "the urban" does not follow a linear historical trajectory. Rather, the specific relationships between urban capital and the rural hinterlands condition the way the country and the city interact.[18] And as Michael Kearney has shown, concepts such as rural and urban emerge from the strategic agency of social actors as well as larger-scale structural transformations.[19]

Akhil Gupta shows how the very same global economic transformations that threaten the status of rural Indians also incite them to articulate their own interests *as a peasantry*.[20] The same assertion of "the rural" as a set of instrumental meanings informs Ramachandra Guha's description of the Chipko (hug the trees) movement in Uttarakhand, where peasant protests for land and grazing rights invoke the responsibility of the nation-state to fulfill its role as protector of peasant interests.[21] As Philip Huang has shown in China, the narrative of Chinese communist revolution deployed a notion of the shared interests of a universal class of exploited peasants that oversimplified the reality of diverse peasant interests.[22] And Patricia Pelley and Kim Ninh have both clearly demonstrated the same process in Vietnam.[23]

Just as the persistent binaries of rural and urban shift meanings according to context, so do the meanings of rural–urban peripheries. Daniel Goldstein's important work on the outskirts of Cochabamba, Bolivia, shows how structural adjustment programs have radically altered the symbolic meanings of rural–urban peripheries, which are increasingly left out of social services and where local residents are forced to "take justice in their own hands" through acts of vigilante justice.[24] Viewing reactions to similar structural economic processes from a different vantage point in the class hierarchy, Teresa Caldeira shows how privileged Brazilian citizens increasingly seclude themselves in fortified enclaves guarded by privatized security forces, a phenomenon witnessed in cities around the globe.[25] The meanings of rural–urban zones on the margins of cities constantly change in ways that are both linked to global trends and reworked by local permutations of those trends.[26] As Li Zhang has shown in the spatial outskirts of Beijing, as James Holston has described regarding the production of São Paulo's "peripheries," and as Michael Leaf has shown on Hanoi's "Urban Edge," the transformation of space on urban margins is tied into complex networks of politics at the interpersonal, local, provincial, and national levels.[27] As a result, even large-scale trends are always reconfigured by the micropolitics, economic maneuvering, and identity management of local actors navigating extralocal fields of power.

In Vietnam, as in Raymond Williams's England and the other examples given, the distinctions between the country and the city and the contested meanings of rural–urban margins represent more than inert objective descriptions of geographical fact. Conscious actors invoke these distinctions as if they constitute the universal organizing feature of social life, but they do so in order to carve out spaces of social action. National myths of eternal fixity make the relations of rural and urban seem legitimate, as if they were unchangeable, founded in the roots of culture, the spirit of a people. But such narratives obscure the ways in which these claims emerge out of particular historical circumstances. The symbolic power of rural–urban relations may well be universal, but each case is particular—universally particular.

Hóc Môn District: On the Edge of the Rural–Urban Ideal

Vân's daily motorbike commute begins and ends in Hóc Môn district, which straddles the constructed oppositions of the country and the city. In 2002, Hóc Môn was one of five outer-city districts *(huyện ngoại thành)* in the Ho Chi Minh City administrative zone.[28] Positioned just northwest of the seventeen inner-city districts that comprise central Ho Chi Minh City, it borders District 12 to the south, Long An province to the west, and the outer-city districts of Củ Chi and Bình Chánh to the north and southwest. The eastern border of the district is separated from Bình Dương province by the Sài Gòn River, which winds past the main ports of the city in District 1 before connecting with the Nhà Bè River, the main shipping route connecting Ho Chi Minh City to the Pacific Ocean.

In 1997 Hóc Môn was divided into two districts. Half of the district retained the name Hóc Môn and continued to be administered as an outer-city district *(huyện);* the other half of the district was redesignated inner-city District 12. Prior to the split the district consisted of seventeen *xã* (a term that can be translated "village" or "commune"). Following the split, the remaining portion of Hóc Môn was subdivided into seven *xã*, each divided into several *ấp* (hamlets). By contrast, District 12 was reclassified as a *quận* (inner-city district) composed of *phường* (wards). Following the split, Hóc Môn district occupied a total area of 16,952 hectares, which accounted for 5.23 percent of the total area of Ho Chi Minh City. Figures published in 1999 divide the total areas devoted to different activities as follows: 8,069 hectares devoted to agricultural production (73.68 percent of the total area), 855 hectares to "special use land" (7.8 percent),[29] and 1,250 hectares to residential land (11.41 percent), with 777 hectares unused (7.1 percent). For this district that was previously agricultural yet is rapidly urbanizing, predictions at the time forecast that the area of land devoted to agriculture would decrease to 7,279 hectares in 2000 and further decrease to 5,124 hectares by 2010.[30] Figures published in 2000 indicate that Hóc Môn was home to 205,419 people living within 109.5 square kilometers, yielding an average population density of 1,876 people per square kilometer.[31] By contrast, Districts 5 and 11, the two densest in Ho Chi Minh City, burst at the seams with densities of 51,392 and 47,864 persons per square kilometer, respectively, and the historic center of downtown Ho Chi Minh City (District 1), with its grand tree-lined colonial boulevards, monumental public architecture, and cosmopolitan feel, had a population density of 29,983 persons per square kilometer.[32]

It is not density but the incongruous mix of residential, industrial, and agricultural activities that marks outer-city districts like Hóc Môn in the local social imaginary. In popular discourse this mix of activities appears ugly and uninviting; indeed, Hóc Môn (see Map 1) is even described by many Vietnamese as "uncivilized" *(không văn minh)*. Zones like Hóc Môn—with their new factories, industrialized agriculture and animal husbandry, cheap land, and vulnerable labor force making the transition away from a largely agricultural economy—play a central role in the transformation of the economy that so clearly marks Vietnam's oft-cited development success. Yet, although places like Hóc Môn make the economic development associated with Vietnam's open-door economy possible, they are places that many people hope to forget. On my last night in Hóc Môn, Tân, one of my neighbors and by then a close friend, told me that I should not include any of my neighbors in my writing about Vietnam. My neighbors (who happened to be Tân's closest friends and whom he considered fictive kin) were underemployed, prone to heavy drinking, and fond of the vulgar joking typical of residents on the rural–urban fringe. *Go home to America and forget all of them,* he told me. *I want you to write the best book. But don't let those guys spoil your impression of Việt Nam. Forget them.*[33] Such sentiments were not isolated. In the interviews and the analysis of social interactions I conducted during eighteen months of fieldwork in Hóc Môn and in inner-city districts of Ho Chi Minh City, people on the outskirts were described as unrepresentative of Vietnamese society and culture. "They do not have culture," some would say. Others told me not to write about people living in the outer-city districts because they were not good examples of the "true Vietnam." At worst, such people and the spaces they lived in were described as dangerous, a threat to society. Theirs was a zone of "social evils," to borrow the language of the press. The disconnect between ideal cultural models of spatial-temporal order and the actual lived lives of people in this space profoundly affected the way these people and the space they lived in were conceived by others and, at times, by themselves.

The Edge in History

Even largely forgotten Hóc Môn has a history. When Nguyễn Hữu Cảnh established the *phủ* (prefecture) of Gia Định in 1698, Hóc Môn comprised six original villages: Tân Thới Nhất, Tân Thới Nhì, Tân Thới Trung, Tân Phú, Thuận Kiều, and Xuân Thới Tây.[34] Vietnamese scholars guess (with some uncertainty) that the name Hóc Môn most likely refers to the *môn nước* plants (Indian taro, called *dọc mùng* in the north) that grew in the many *hóc* (swampy zones) that once existed in the region before it was drained for agriculture by the French; a place with lots of *hóc* filled with *môn* became known as Hóc Môn.[35] French colonial reports indicate that Hóc Môn did indeed contain several large marshy areas, making travel difficult. Lucien De Grammont, one of the first colonial officials to administer Hóc Môn after the French captured Saigon in 1859, had much to say about the poor condition of the roads (which he viewed as a sign of native laziness and often cited as evidence of the great need for the French *mission civilisatrice*).

For de Grammont (whose language foreshadows recent Vietnamese thinking), building roads was one of the first steps required to civilize the countryside around recently conquered Saigon:

The importance attributed to waterways in Lower Cochinchina, combined with the apathy of the inhabitants, prevents them from devoting much care to the upkeep of terrestrial routes; and the grand roads which one has until now conferred the name of royal routes, are themselves quite far from being in the state we see our own in France. One hardly recognizes them in the middle of a perpetually green countryside, except for the denuded quality of the surface that they occupy, which is sufficient indication of the habitual passage of pedestrians and vehicles.[36]

De Grammont also mentioned the Mandarin road that led from Sài Gòn to Tây Ninh, which traced the same route that today leads from downtown Ho Chi Minh City through Hóc Môn to Tây Ninh province, then

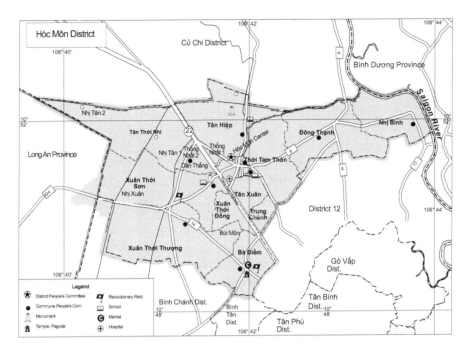

MAP 1. Hóc Môn district. Top is north. Highway 22, recently upgraded to part of the Trans-Asia Highway, runs diagonally through the district, connecting Ho Chi Minh City with Phnom Penh, Cambodia. Fieldwork for this book was conducted in xã Tân Thới Nhì, located in the northwest portion of the map.

cuts through Cambodia toward Phnom Penh (Nam Vang). The Sài Gòn–Tây Ninh road, he said, was one of "only two roads worthy of mention in Gia-dinh and My-tho." Most of the other roads turned to mud with only the slightest bit of rain. But this route was an exception:

The Gia-dinh road, departing Saigon from the center of the city, passes the Bar-bet pagoda on the right and fort Testard on the left, crosses the canal extension of the *arroyo de l'Avalanche* [now known as the Thị Nghè canal], the old lines of Kiloà and the Bahôm canal at the Tam-luong bridge, creates a junction at the forts of Tuân'Keou, and then a bit further, in Hoc-môn, Binh-long sub-prefecture, it enters the marshes at the rach Tra fort, comes to the Trang-bang post, and then reaches Tay-ninh; after covering a total distance of 80 kilometers, it joins with the border of Cambodia and turns to the West, where it goes on to connect with Nam Vang. The land it runs through is, most certainly, the driest portion of Gia-dinh province, with the exception, however, of the passage between Hoc-môn and

Phuc-my, where the line between the watersheds is interrupted by the marshes of Binh-long.[37]

Everywhere on this road was dry but Hóc Môn. Nonetheless, de Grammont, a committed civilizer, was far from modest about his ability to teach the natives to understand the importance of transforming the natural environment. Although his own oversight of public works projects in Hóc Môn lasted for only one year (1861), he confidently explained that the locals were nonetheless able to build roads through several of the swampy areas in Hóc Môn even after his departure from Indochina: "When you have shown them the utility of something, they always manage to complete it well themselves."[38]

As I detail more carefully in later chapters, this commitment to imbuing outer-city districts with utility is not a French invention. It has a pre-colonial Vietnamese precedent in the notion of a walled city *(nội thành)* functionally linked to its hinterlands *(ngoại thành)*. More important, this civilizing rhetoric has also continued to define official constructions of the rural–urban margin as a functional handmaiden to the city in ways that crosscut the many ruling ideologies that have come and gone through the history of Vietnam's southern region. The many iterations of the functional connection between the inside and the outside of the city have appeared in colonial conceptions of the "garden city," postcolonial nationalist imaginings of the outer-city districts as a productive greenbelt, American wartime notions of the outer-city districts as protective buffer zones, socialist experiments with periurban collectivization, and, more recently, functionalist forms of urban planning. In all of these different periods, the outer city has long figured in the minds of administrators as a place to control by making it a productive complement to the inner city. As Đ. H. Liêm has shown, official conceptions of developing the outer city have most often entailed finding ways for it to serve *(phục vụ)* the inner city.[39]

Hóc Môn Today

Today the land in northwest Hóc Môn remains conducive to agriculture and is regulated by sophisticated irrigation works that radiate from the important An Hạ canal, which forms the district border with Củ Chi and runs west through Long An province on a path that connects the Saigon

River with the Vàm Cỏ Tây River. Although the names have changed, the position of this now drained and irrigated area indicates that this must have been the site of the swampy *marais de Binh-Long,* which de Grammont referred to in the Hóc Môn of 1861. And today the roads de Grammont described still lead into the city from Hóc Môn, carrying a combination of agricultural products, industrial goods, small handicrafts, processed foodstuffs, and laborers. From the city to Hóc Môn flow newspapers, factory managers, land speculators, imported goods, industrial foodstuffs, and other manufactured goods.

With its combination of cultivable soils and its position so close to the dense urban center of Ho Chi Minh City, Hóc Môn has long served as an important part of the city's agricultural "greenbelt." Before dawn, Hóc Môn's central market still serves as an agricultural distribution center where farmers from the agricultural zones northeast and northwest of the city converge and trade their goods before loading them onto motorized carts and motorbikes that carry them farther away to the various markets scattered throughout the central districts of the city. Also mostly before dawn, but not as early, buses are loaded with ambulant traders who carry homemade snacks for sale in the city. On their way into town, the buses take circuitous routes, stopping to accommodate various small-time textile weavers who load their poly-cotton-blend blankets into huge

TABLE I. Land use in Tân Thới Nhì

Land category	Area (hectares)
Agricultural land, including rice and vegetables (525 ha.), long-term crops such as trees (395 ha.), and household-use gardens (57 ha.)	1,397
Historical vestiges	66
Residential land	79
Transportation land	50
National security	5
Factory and industrial land	10
Cemetery land	11
Unused land	52
Rivers, canals	50
Total land area	1,720

Source: Statistics office in *xã* Tân Thới Nhì.

TABLE 2. Population in Tân Thới Nhì

Population category	% of total	Number of households
Agricultural households	18	713
Industrial households	13	500
Trading households, service professions	25	1,000
Other occupations	44	1,727
Total population		3,940 (17,864 persons)

Source: Statistics office in *xã* Tân Thới Nhì. I received other numbers from the vice chair of the local People's Committee. She said there were 3,300 families and a total population of 18,647. I have listed the other numbers in the text because they are "official" statistics, given to me by the head of the statistics office in *xã* Tân Thới Nhì. But it seems prudent to think of them as estimates only. The category "Other occupations" includes a wide range of diverse economic activities such as unregulated piecework, waste recycling, selling lottery tickets, working as motorbike taxi drivers, carrying goods for hire, operating impromptu repair shops, and providing temporary manual labor in construction, agricultural, and other work. This category also includes less legal but financially important livelihood strategies such as small-scale smuggling, running gambling operations and secret karaoke rooms, engaging in small-time drug trading, and other money-making schemes too numerous to list.

woven plastic sacks that are strapped to the roofs of the buses. It can take between one and a half and two hours for one of these buses to make this trip from Hóc Môn to the large markets at Bến Thành and Bình Tây in Saigon and Chợ Lớn. The distance is less than twenty kilometers.

In addition to these products produced by small-scale producers operating out of their homes, larger industries send shoes, garments, corrugated metal, cigarettes, bricks, rattan and bamboo furniture, industrial webbing, and other goods into the city using their own modes of transportation. The diversity of economic activity in Hóc Môn can be seen in microcosm through the statistics for one of its subdivisions, *xã* Tân Thới Nhì, where most of the fieldwork for this study was concentrated (see Tables 1 and 2).

Tân Thới Nhì, like Hóc Môn as a whole, has a complex, diversified economy. As the population and employment figures listed in Table 2 indicate, seven hundred households are primarily engaged in agricultural activity, which primarily consists of double-harvest rice production and vegetable growing but also includes the raising of some industrial crops such as tobacco and peanuts, as well as the processing of bamboo for a significant bamboo furniture enterprise. The five hundred households engaging in industrial labor are employed by one of Hóc Môn's 196 registered companies, located either in their own walled compound or in one of six industrial zones at Xuân Thới Sơn (fifty hectares), Đông Thạnh (sixty hectares), Đông Thạnh (forty hectares), Bà Điểm (sixty hectares), Thới Tan Thôn (fifty hectares), and Tân Hiệp (thirty hectares). Some 20.2 percent of total production in all of these industries is devoted to food and foodstuff processing, 29 percent to textiles, 10.8 percent to wood products, 6.73 percent to plastics, 9.84 percent to paper products, and 23.35 percent to a variety of other goods ranging from cigarettes to bamboo furniture.[40] The one thousand households engaged in trading and service professions run everything from cafés, small restaurants, and sundry shops to barbershops, building supply shops, and household services (which include everything from water delivery to laundry services). These figures themselves indicate the kind of mixed economy that develops as a formerly agricultural area urbanizes and shifts toward industrialization.

Even more important, however, are the 1,727 households engaged in "other occupations," the largest single category of households, comprising close to 44 percent of the total. During my fieldwork, such other occupations included a wide range of diverse economic activities—everything from selling lottery tickets to engaging in unregulated piecework for local handicraft enterprises to working as motorbike taxi drivers and carrying goods for hire, including loads of dirt from the rice fields to serve as foundation fill for new construction in the city. People labor as itinerant laborers in construction or agricultural work, sift through recycled waste, and run impromptu motorbike repair shops on the side of the highway, and male laborers in the area's numerous roadside cafés are prepared to engage in any kind of labor that pays well enough to coax them away from their conversations. Less scrupulous people sell illegal drugs, smuggle cigarettes from Cambodia tax free, run numbers games, conceal secret karaoke rooms behind their houses,[41] and organize illegal brothels (sometimes out of cafés, sometimes out of homes). Ambulant bicyclists offer massages and moxibustion, other roaming salespersons sell trinkets, and a group of enterprising migrants from the Mekong Delta even set up unregulated late-night outdoor massage stations for tired workers coming out of factories and truck drivers and travelers coming into the city from distant destinations (sometimes with smuggled cigarettes from Cambodia). One must also include the unnamable category I will call "scheming," which includes a host of activities that come and go as opportunities arise—selling information about urban plans to speculators from the city, offering to marry daughters to foreign males, hatching plans to pay foreign men to engage in fake marriages, looking for things to buy cheap and sell dear. As this partial list indicates, although this part of Hóc Môn can be considered part rural and part urban, a large number of residents engage in a complex mix of economic activities. This diversity contributes to the district's symbolical ambiguity, combining in one place symbolic elements that are normally juxtaposed as opposites and other elements that fit into no category at all.

Spatially, the *xã* of Tân Thới Nhì is divided into seven hamlets, or *ấp:* ấp Dân Thắng 1, ấp Dân Thắng 2, ấp Thống Nhất 1, ấp Thống Nhất 2, ấp Nhị Tân 1, ấp Nhị Tân 2, and ấp Tân Lập. The first four are primarily organized along the Trans-Asia Highway, and the other three are more agricultural, organized along smaller roads leading off from the highway into the rice, vegetable, peanut, and tobacco fields. This division within Tân Thới Nhì itself represents a more general division in Hóc Môn district as a whole, where the spaces closest to the road are generally more urban in outward character and the spaces off of feeder roads tend to be more agricultural. The exception, however, is that garment factories tend to be located off the main road as well, so the most "agricultural" of the hamlets also tend to have the highest concentration of newly built factories, industrial operations, and associated migrant housing compounds.

The population itself comprises a mix of long-term residents whose families have lived in the area for several generations; a significant number of predominantly Catholic northern transplants who moved into Hóc Môn after 1954 onto land granted to Catholic parishes by Ngô Đình Diệm's government; and, in more recent years, streams of migrants who have come from regions across the country in search of employment in the district's many industrial zones. The ethnic makeup is relatively homogenous; 98.23 percent of the population is ethnic Vietnamese (Kinh), 1.67 percent Chinese Vietnamese, and 0.49 percent Khmer. According to official statistics, 79.15 percent of residents do not claim to follow any officially recognized religion, 12.75 percent are Catholic (mostly clustered together into parishes spatially organized around large churches), 7.62 percent are Buddhist, 0.28 percent follow Cao Đài, 0.19 percent are Protestant, and only 14 people in the entire district claim to follow Islam.[42] Although such a large number of people claim to follow no religion, most of the "agnostics" I met during fieldwork participated in syncretic practices not unlike those described by Léopold Cadière as being part of "the Cult of Spirits";[43] most families set incense outside their doors at night to protect them from malevolent spirits, tend to shrines in symbolically potent sites, enjoyed visiting pagodas and temples, had their fortunes read, hired ritual specialists for weddings and funerals, and went on pilgrimages to potent sites such as Núi Bà Đen in Tây Ninh and other places farther afield.[44]

Symbolic Ambiguity and Liberation on the Edge

Uncomfortably straddling both country and city, Hóc Môn undermines binary ideals that divide space into discrete rural and urban complements. As Huỳnh Văn Giáp notes, the agricultural sector is increasingly compromised by the way it mixes with urban development: new pests, including feral urban animals and infectious rats, along with changes in the microclimate and air quality brought by urban development, have plagued harvests, and agricultural land is threatened by encroachment, having diminished at a rate of two hundred hectares per year since 1998.[45] Rising land prices and industrial pollution have made agricultural activity both more expensive and less profitable than it was in the past, and the poor regulation of land use makes farmers reluctant to invest in agricultural production and also causes land disputes among formerly amicable neighbors.[46]

Residents in downtown Saigon describe Hóc Môn as a manmade "wasteland" *(đất hoang)* of unfinished roads, polluted fields, piles of construction rubble, factories surrounded by vegetable gardens, dusty roads in the dry season, muddy roads in the wet. The landscape emerges as a collection of juxtapositions: buffalos bathe in front of factory gates, rubber cutout soles from the local shoe factory line the dirt roads leading to rice fields, people dry rice paper and plant crops for personal household use in the extra spaces of cemeteries (see Figure 1), and fancy multicolored concrete-covered aluminum-trimmed multilevel brick houses with gingerbread rooftops rise up next to shacks made of scrap metal and plywood. The city dump is in Hóc Môn, and so is the newest water treatment plant serving all of Ho Chi Minh City. There are no karaoke songs about Hóc Môn. It cannot represent the kind of idealized space such sentimental songs require.

FIGURE 1. Vegetable cultivation in a cemetery. Hóc Môn district.

Despite its contradictions, however, Hóc Môn proves intellectually productive precisely because it is a Vietnamese place that defies all of the idealized categories that supposedly organize Vietnamese social space and life. Like the historian Keith Taylor, who studies the "surface orientation" to life of Vietnamese speakers in different times and places, Hóc Môn reveals the "surface of fluid human experience in time and terrain, which softens and fables the coherencies of historicized regions and nations." Taylor metaphorically speaks of the archival traces historians confront as a form of debris that resists the categorizing schemas of nationalist ideology. Hóc Môn district strikes the observer as a field of debris as well, "a beautiful confusion"[47] (see Figure 2).

The "True Vietnam" as System and Order

This beautiful confusion disrupts both Vietnamese and foreign depictions of Vietnamese cultural order and challenges simple stereotypes about what it means to be Vietnamese. Since at least the founding of the Indochinese Communist Party in 1930, Vietnamese scholars have expended great

FIGURE 2. The spray-painted sign on the side of this building reads "contested land." Hóc Môn district.

intellectual effort in order to define what counts as culture within the Vietnamese people themselves.[48] In an important work on the historical and political roots of the concept of culture in Vietnam, Kim Ninh documents the concerted efforts of revolutionary theorists between 1945 and 1960 to develop a politically effective theory on the meaning of culture. Early intellectual debates about the meaning and role of culture eventually congealed around a politicized interpretation that led to the formation of the Ministry of Culture, established in September 1955, in order "to coordinate and shape cultural activities," to control publishing, and to establish structure down to the village level.[49] Ninh describes how, as the revolution solidified its ideological framework, cultural cadres came to insist that revolutionary culture and popular culture were one and the same.[50] But this top-down insistence on the equivalence of political culture and mass culture comprehended a key contradiction: culture supposedly came from the masses, but the masses needed to raise their cultural level in ways that conform to an ideologically rigid construction of true culture. This amounted to a "state-constructed popular culture" in which the masses "were rendered both active and passive."[51]

Although Ninh's work locates the concept of culture squarely in the political realm, these discourses have not simply floated around in the texts of socialist revolutionaries and scholars. Today people at all levels of society express a keen fluency in and affinity for a set of simplifying schemes that describe what counts as Vietnamese culture in highly reductionist terms. The traits of "true Vietnamese culture" that people repeat on the streets, write in books, and instruct others about at every available opportunity closely resemble the description Trần Ngọc Thêm offers in his textbook on Vietnamese culture, which is now used in introductory college courses throughout Vietnam. In *Cơ sở văn hóa Việt Nam* (Vietnam's Cultural Basis), Professor Thêm distills a long postcolonial history of culture theory into a contemporary treatise on Vietnamese culture. Thêm explains to Vietnamese students of culture that *văn hóa* (culture) has the "function of organizing society" *(được chức năng tổ chức xã hội),* that "it increases the level of stability in society" *(làm tăng độ ổn định của xã hội),* and that it is a "basis, or foundation" of society. Here *văn hóa* represents a set of value traits *(tính gía trị)* that can be used to separate the valuable from the valueless in both material and mental or spiritual terms. Cultural traits have value; those that do not may as well be classified in the same realm as "natural disasters, the mafia."[52] Culture is orderly. Disorder and chaos have no connection to culture.

Always emphasizing this sense of order and coherence, Thêm further describes the Vietnamese cultural system as operating along a coordinated system of structural relationships between cosmological conceptions of time and space. Thêm elaborates how the oppositions of *âm* and *dương* (yin and yang) create a structured ordering of the cosmological system that appears throughout the Vietnamese cultural landscape and pervades and informs a wide array of social relationships. Translated to the human world, this cosmology forms the essence *(bản chất)* of a cultural system of proper action based on hierarchical roles and structural oppositions. In this system, opposites produce each other: "the pole of *âm* gives birth to *dương,* the pole of *dương* gives birth to *âm.*"[53] As Thêm presents them, the antithetical concepts of *âm* and *dương* combine with each other to form a powerful synthesis with productive capacity. They form the motor for cultural production and reproduction and constitute the basis of a harmonious, truly Vietnamese culture.

Thêm's orderly system of cultural precepts closely mirrors the framework for *Understanding Vietnam* offered by Neil Jamieson, which argues that "*yin* and *yang* were complementary dimensions of a single cultural system that was essentially shared by all Vietnamese." Jamieson's approach usefully adds that neither yin nor yang "was more 'authentic' or 'legitimate' than the other."[54] Aspects of everyday life—market behavior, street life, disputes—find their place in the system because they can be reconciled through their more formal, complementary opposite. There is great allure to this approach, which avoids attempts to set cultural elements in hierarchical relations to each other and clearly resonates with Vietnamese depictions of culture like that of Thêm. Many of these traits appear quite clearly in Vietnamese literature, folktales, popular songs, and, as I detail in this book, official and popular representations of rural–urban spatial relations. An analyst of folktales, for example, may accurately claim that Vietnamese folktales follow "an ideology known as 'dual cosmos,' which dictates that life exists through the competing powers of opposing forces," as the articulate Bui Hoai Mai does in describing "The Anger of the Waters," a story within a collection of tales he illustrated.[55] But anthropologists are not literary critics, and it is important to remember the difference between a collection of folktales and social action. Although analyzing and describing symbolic elements within artistic creations often does reveal these kinds of "deep" underlying structural logics, even this folklorist and artist calls them "ideology," not a reflection of everyday reality. This ideology of generative oppositions is useful for studying myth because it is a form of myth-making itself.[56]

Such myth-making emerges in multiple realms of cultural production and also influences important ideas about urban spatial order, where the oppositions of rural and urban, as well as outside and inside, are mapped onto this framework of *âm* and *dương*. As Michel de Certeau has shown with his searing critique of expert knowledge, the very practices of urban planning and governance must also be understood as a form of discursive myth-making. The "utopian city" of planners and government bureaucrats founds its "own space" of rational organization, represses disruptions, and replaces the everyday actions of individuals with functionalist representations that dispense with deviance and abnormality and reduce all social action to a compressed, universal, anonymous subject.[57] In Vietnamese planning practices, official ideas about the city and its relationship to the rest of the country amount to a set of pronouncements designed to describe an ideal image of true culture to which all people should aspire. James Scott has developed a similar critique of top-down visions of urban planning that prioritize rationality, order, efficiency, and elegance over the messy realities of everyday city life.[58] As Scott shows through concrete comparative examples and de Certeau shows through philosophical critique, these totalizing strategies seek to homogenize difference by creating legible, governable subjects. Yet they inevitably fail: "Beneath the discourses that ideologize the city, the ruses and combinations of powers that have no readable identity proliferate; without points where one can take hold of them, without rational transparency, they are impossible to administer."[59]

Official representations always have political intent. Among Western intellectuals, socialist nationalists, and even American military experts struggling to understand their adversary, the idealization of the Vietnamese peasant as the source of Vietnamese tradition became further reified during the Vietnam War. The very notion of the "Vietnamese people" seemed intricately bound up with images of a "peasant nation" that was in some versions pure and innocent and in others wily and unpredictable, docile on the surface yet possessed of an inexplicable hidden dimension beneath the surface. On the one hand, North Vietnamese propagandists and sympathizers in the West painted the war in broad strokes as a "peasant war."[60] On the other hand, the concept of the idealized peasant also played a role in the American and South Vietnamese effort to win the hearts and minds of the Vietnamese masses, categorized mainly as peasants and rural villagers who were susceptible to the populist ideas of the Việt Cộng and the National Liberation Front. The whole idea of Ngô Đình Diệm's "strategic hamlet program" or Nguyễn Văn Thiệu's "land to the tiller" program involved keeping the peasants squarely in the Republican camp, either through encirclement or through seduction with the promise of land and financial security. In retrospect, U.S. failure in Vietnam was repeatedly chalked up as a failure to "understand" Vietnam. The postwar writings of Nguyễn Cao Kỳ reveal persistent examples of this logic, while those of James Scott move more toward a recantation of his own "romantic" view of the Vietnamese peasantry.[61] But in the formative crucible of war, the search for the "real Vietnam" began with a search to unlock the hidden mystery of rural Vietnamese society.

In the West, it seemed that if academics could understand the Vietnamese peasantry and their relationship to urban centers of power it would become possible to understand the real Vietnam, to get to the truth behind the masked realm of urban life. The sociology of Paul Mus, translated and highly simplified by one of his American students who sought to understand the Vietnamese during his country's own military debacle, was reduced to sound bites: "Vietnam is a certain way of growing rice," a place where peasants are blindly guided by the "Mandate of Heaven."[62] Seen within these frameworks, designed to make Vietnamese culture understandable, the idea of the rural–urban relationship emerges with explanatory force, as a way to understand that country and city are fundamentally different yet ultimately linked in a cofigured relation of mutual self-production and self-realization. This explanation purported to have an almost magical ability to escape from surface distractions and get to the "true" cultural logic of the relationship between country and city. Yet tall tales often lie in the telling of cultural truths. The deep-rooted logic of the "true Vietnam" grows from the seedbed of myth; by conflating myth with reality, ideology masquerades in the guise of authentic culture, assuming the pose of the real.

On Social Edginess and the Structure of This Book

This book describes how national tropes and cultural stereotypes about rural–urban relations persist in places like Hóc Môn despite the constant disruptions of an everyday existence that seems to depart so dramatically from the ideal. For those who fall between the cracks of the rural–urban and inside–outside opposition, these powerful ideals have very material effects. In the first part of the book, "Social Edginess," I describe the uncomfortable position of people living in the outer-city district as a form of "social edginess," a term I use to clarify how spatial marginalization translates into a sense of being left outside the normal institutions of social life and being left out of the future-oriented trajectory of urban development.

But edginess can be empowering as well. My ethnographic project in this book explicitly engages in what de Certeau calls "walking in the city," seeking encounters with the "innumerable collection of singularities" that he imagines will reveal, through their practices of everyday life, a form of "antidiscipline" that unravels the myth-making of the state. Yet de Certeau's simple opposition between singular individuals and top-down impositions of ideology itself elides the role that individuals themselves play in the reproduction of larger ideological systems. As I came to realize through long-term fieldwork, the social actions and "tactics" of these everyday people could not always be simply cast in opposition to state ideologics. Everyday people also use highly reductionist, idealized terms to explain the differences between the country and the city. These categories, in turn, structure many of their interactions with each other. Urban anthropologists have made great strides in unraveling the conceit of planners who have for so long imposed fictional order on the blurry and messy realities of urban life. But a new false binary unwittingly appears in these efforts to pose the ideals of planners against a fictional notion of everyday reality populated by "the people." Planners are people, too, and "the people" also have plans, ideals, and mental models of their own. They are not always disconnected.

Instead of opposing "the people" and "the state" to each other, I detail the intertwined relationship between idealized myth-making and practical reality. As Michael Herzfeld has done with the marginal island populations of modern Greece, I detail the identity of nonstandard, economically marginalized, "un-Vietnamese Vietnamese" living on Saigon's edge. I examine what Herzfeld called the "the effects of state attempts to control and reshape the refractions of that identity in social life."[63] But rather than pose the hegemony of the state in strict opposition to a resistant counterhegemony of some abstract undefinable category called "the people," I show the ways in which the ideal categories of "Vietnamese culture" are simultaneously contradicted and reinforced through everyday social life. Although ideal categories suffer descriptive deficiencies when faced with the elements of actual social life, they have tremendous staying power. Myth and symbol profoundly condition social life within the so-called real world.[64] The confrontation of a set of ideals with a seemingly contradictory reality does not directly threaten the production of cultural ideals but rather enforces them in surprising ways. The edginess I describe, then, is double edged, such that the relationship between ideal categories and what de Certeau calls the practices of everyday life are intertwined.

The second part of the book, "Space, Time, and Urban Expansion," develops this idea by showing how the same temporal and spatial relations that resist officializing ideologies also reproduce them, not out of capitulation but often as a means of fashioning spaces of agency and autonomous social action. The reproduction of ideals actually creates the possibility for a powerful kind of practical social action that I call "spatiotemporal oscillation." This concept describes how, on the one hand, the binary poles of the ideal spatiotemporal categories produce the conditions within which everyday social action takes place and how, on the other hand, everyday social action can produce a space of meaningful action by moving productively between ideal categories. Vân's motorbike ride between the inside and the outside of the city illustrates this concept well. She deploys ideal constructs when explaining that she is moving from the outside in and from the inside out. But as she oscillates back and forth between these spaces, she also transcends those very same ideal categories. Her social oscillation ultimately depends on accepting the ideal notion of inside and outside as social facts. Yet moving between them both reproduces the categories and transcends them at once.

The third part of the book, "Realizing the Ideal," builds from the arguments of the first two parts. Understanding the intersection of space, time, and power and the interplay between cultural ideals and everyday practices helps me explain both the concrete history of a highway expansion project and the ambivalent reactions to it of most Hóc Môn residents. The exaltation of the kind of urbanization this highway project brings sets the context for the penultimate chapter, which shows how derogatory rural stereotypes have been buttressed by an ideology of "civilizing" the countryside and the people who live there, a rhetorical strategy that stands in direct contrast to the historical construction of the Vietnamese peasantry as a symbolic representation of original purity. The idealization of the peasant-based Vietnamese Revolution stands in stark contrast to the public denigration of rural life and the denigration of the countryside as the source of all Ho Chi Minh City's difficulties in achieving its campaign to "Build an Urban Civilization."

First and foremost, however, the chapters of this book are structured by the lives people lead, the stories they told me (and sometimes told me to forget). Their stories reveal how symbolic meanings associated with urban and rural space, as well as with inner-city and outer-city space, derive from and also reproduce an orderly system of seemingly elegant binary oppositions. They also reveal that objective spatial relations in the outer-city districts never fit comfortably into these idealized categories. To see what happens when reality and dream do not match, I invite you to Saigon's edge. To get there, join me as I hitch a ride on Vân's motorbike as she heads back home from work, following the same route that de Grammont once described, on a pathway that will lead us from the inside of the city to the outside in Hóc Môn.

Part I

Social Edginess

1. Bittersweet Transitions
Urbanization on the Fringe of the City

Today, the painter tossed his brush away
because Reality and Dream don't match.
Those vaporous strokes just shimmer in his soul:
his paltry art can't bring them onto silk.

—Vũ Hoàng Chương, *The Beau Ideal*

Inside and Outside on the Rural–Urban Edge

There is an edge to Saigon but no physical boundaries. Depictions of the outer-city district of Hóc Môn form a congeries of symbolic references and everyday realities rife with double-meanings. In history books, Hóc Môn's Bà Điểm commune is famous for the failed anti-French uprising led by Phan Văn Hớn and Nguyễn Văn Quá in February 1885. The name of the uprising, Uprising of the Eighteen Areca Garden Villages, indicates that this was a rural zone known mostly for its production of areca nuts and betel leaf and, as nationalist histories would have it, for its production of anticolonial resistance.[1] But Hóc Môn also hosted an infamous French execution range located at the "Giồng" triple intersection, where many anticolonial figures perished, including, most famously, the trio of Nguyễn thị Minh Khai, Võ Văn Tần, and Nguyễn Văn Cừ, who were put before the firing squads there on August 28, 1941.[2]

Today the images appear equally mixed. The map of this outer-city district *(huyện ngoại thành),* for example, reveals a wide-open expanse of apparent green space stretching toward the northwest district lines bordering *huyện* Củ Chi and Long An province. The map of this space, identified as "Second Springtime Farm," evokes idealized images of a rural greenbelt on the edge of the city. But this is not really a farm. It is a camp for heroin addicts sent from the city for reform. And nowadays the historic memorial to revolutionary martyrs executed at the "Giồng" triple intersection is threatened by development, land speculation, and unregulated building. The planning department has had to introduce new zoning regulations in order to formalize what has already become an active zone of industry and housing for several hundred workers newly arrived from poorer provinces throughout Vietnam.[3] There are also plans for a so-called green industrial zone to go in near Nhị Xuân, a euphemistic name for what amounts to a dumping ground for polluting industries slated to be moved away from sites closer to downtown.[4]

What once marked the rural fringes of the city is now a mixed-use zone of agriculture, industry, and newly platted real estate. The land has been subdivided to accommodate urbanites looking to find outer-city land investments and internal migrants seeking to gain a foothold in the city. On the one hand, this outer-city district is still described as green space, a lung to the city, a rural refuge from the ills and confusions of the urban world. Yet it is also uncontrollable, lacking structure and order. It is a space of contradictions: a historical site of anticolonial resistance and of colonial repression, a greenbelt and a refuse pit, an open space and a space of haphazard building and land speculation. The *idea* of the garden city on the edge retains symbolic power. Yet very few areca palms remain in the concrete-covered plots of the eighteen areca garden villages.

Hóc Môn residents living on this edge with no boundaries are *edgy,* both frustrated and optimistic; they are betwixt, between, and ambivalent about their position in the social and spatial hierarchy of the city. As I show in this chapter, the ideal representations of Ho Chi Minh City and its surroundings simultaneously conflict with and provide a framework for the social experience of everyday life in the outer-city districts of the city's administrative zone. Although the outer-city districts really have no definable edge, people continue to imagine spatiotemporal relations in terms of the strict differentiation of pure rural and pure urban types, as well as a distinction between inside *(nội)* and outside *(ngoại).* On the one hand, these ideal models are never complete or totalizing; real space never truly reproduces these spatial ideals, and people transcend these dichotomies through their acts, confounding categories as they make their way through everyday life. On the other hand, this chapter reveals some of the ways in which Hóc Môn residents reproduce and negotiate the parameters provided by ideal categories to strategic effect. Everyday social action emerges not as a simple rejection of false binaries but instead as a negotiation of the contours provided by the binaries themselves. While many Hóc Môn residents may be pushed to the edge by structural conditions beyond their immediate control, they also make use of the edge as a strategic position. I call this social edginess.

But first, what is it like to live on Saigon's edge?

Sucking the Soapberry

To understand what it is like to live in Hóc Môn, try chewing on the bitter peel of a soapberry *(bồ hòn)*.[5] Then smile and call it sweet. Underemployed Thành—whose main daily commitment consisted of driving his wife (and her pots of roasted onions and *bánh ướt,* wet rice noodle treats) on the back of his Chinese "Hongda" motorbike into Saigon's Phú Nhuận market—was having trouble describing his life in Hóc Môn. Thành's life represented a complex history of triumphs and struggles, good times and bad times. In earlier conversations, he had often waxed nostalgic about his youth in Quảng Ngãi province during the American intervention. When he was a child there, his family lived well off his father's generous and stable salary as an officer in the Army of the Republic of Vietnam. In his early teens he enjoyed following the American troops, who gave him candy, let him ride on the tanks, and made him their "buddy" as long as he agreed to fetch them goodies from the local market.

Despite the ravages of war in heavily contested Quảng Ngãi, Thành recalled that period as a time of material abundance and carefree joy. He contrasted this with the period that came after Giải Phóng (Liberation). His father was sent to various reeducation camps for ten years, and his mother had to sell the family house to afford provisions for his father, who risked dying of hunger in the camps, where internees "only ate rice with salt on it." The "liberators" took all of their family savings and their stored gold, and Thành went from being well off to being out of work and poor.

Immediately after Reunification, Thành, then in his mid-twenties, moved to Hóc Môn in order, as he explained, to "hide" himself and to try to start anew in the outer-city district where land was cheap and the authorities were less inclined to ask questions. He tried his hand at a wide range of jobs but was more focused on cultivating his reputation as a ladies' man. He was handsome and so skilled at playing the guitar and singing songs that "many girls followed" him. His new life in Hóc Môn allowed him to rebuild a sense of stability. His eventual wife, Phương, was beautiful, and many men followed her, too, but she had eyes only for Thành. Her family was more stable, having moved to Hóc Môn from the north in 1954 to settle on land granted to them as part of a "new economic zone." The handsome couple fell in love with each other, and, despite objections from her family, they married. In contrast to the patri-lineal ideal often associated with Vietnamese kinship, Thành now lives far from his side of the family, and social life revolves around his wife's family, which remains in the immediate area. His own family has spread out broadly; his mother remains in Quảng Ngãi, his father and his nephew live in Biên Hòa, and his sister is married with children and lives in Modesto, California. In many ways, Thành's circumstances embody the double meaning of the outer-city district. There he has found a place to rebuild his life, but it is fundamentally the place of an outsider—out-side the city, outside the patriline, and also outside the confines of his own inner family, which has disintegrated in the face of world-historical transformations.

Thành wanted to tell me about Hóc Môn. But he could not finish his sentences. At his request, I ordered him a beer ("to clear the mind"), poured over ice. His eyes were restless yet piercing, shifty yet concen-trated. He was searching for words to describe life in this outer-city dis-trict of Ho Chi Minh City. Beer would not help. He ordered a bottle of moonshine rice alcohol, *rượu đế*. We shared a few glasses.

A few moments passed; then came luminescence. Thành's mind started waking up. (*Sometimes,* he said, *I can't think clearly until I have a few drinks*). The Vietnamese have a saying for this: "Rượu vào, lời ra" (quite literally, Alcohol enters and words emerge): *in vino veritas.* How to describe life in Hóc Môn? He searched his mind for a sentence to describe his plight. He struck on another Vietnamese proverb: "Ngâm bồ hòn làm ngọt" (Suck the soapberry and call it sweet). This was how he wanted me to remember the social experience of living in Hóc Môn, as something bitter that people force themselves to see as sweet. To com-plete his point, he tweaked his face into a false smile that was not so much a smile as a mockery of a smile. In Hóc Môn, where social mar-ginalization often translates into high unemployment, even higher under-employment, poor housing conditions, and material deprivation, it is easy to locate the sources of his bitterness. But what about the "sweetness"; what would one say, and to what images would one turn, when calling the soapberry of life in Hóc Môn sweet? Perhaps there was sweetness in the factories sprouting up across the landscape like a winter–spring har-vest from the rice fields, in the new asphalt on the newly widened road. Perhaps it is more than a coincidence that *đường,* the word for "road," means "sugar" as well.

People like Thành offer a double image of the outer-city district as sweet ideal and bitter reality, a false surface of ideal appearances that masks the tribulations and difficulties of everyday life. On the level of ideals, the surface masquerades as depth, offering a sweet-sounding explanation for the logical structure behind the organization of city space in relation to its periphery, lending meaning to chaos. This is the tweaked smile, the sweetness. Everyday life, on the other hand, appears as chaos, pretending to revolt against the structure of ideology and false ideals—the bitter rind of the soapberry. But this distinction between a sweet ideal and a bitter reality is itself a false opposition; for order and chaos, like the ideal concepts of Vietnamese spatial order and the practical experience of life on the edge, turn out to be part of the same story, cofigured.

The bittersweet experience of social change emerges most clearly while one is cruising the mean streets of Hóc Môn. Outside of taking his wife to market each morning, Thành had much free time on his hands. To pass the days he often took me on the back of his "Hongda" through the different parts of Hóc Môn, almost always gravitating toward the most crowded parts of the district that lay in the direction leading toward the city center, where the roads were choked by people and increasing urban density. We would weave our way through foot traffic, dodging wobbly bicycles, erratic motorbikes, porters driving both foot-pedaled and motorized three-wheeled carts (and often carrying impossibly long bundles of lancelike metal tubing drooping under their own weight), minivans, dump trucks, and oversized buses; we would compete for the road with people zipping in and out of alleyways, narrowly avoiding patrons who darted in and out of cafés, motorbike repair shops, and store-front shops selling everything from peanuts to shampoo. Thành jumped on every opportunity to show me around—to ride around without direction, simply looking at the changing urban landscape. In Bà Điểm commune, the densest section of Hóc Môn district, people were cutting and welding metal at the side of the road, incessantly sweeping, breaking ice, sewing clothing, changing tires, carving wood, washing and cutting hair, roasting food, boiling food, and carrying goods, always carrying something somewhere.

When Thành directed these initial explorations through Hóc Môn, he rarely made for the fields that lay to the northwest in the direction of Tây Ninh and Long An provinces but instead headed for the crowds, where we would search out new cafés, stop in front of new factories, stop to urinate in irrigation ditches down small alleyways, and look enviously at the new houses replacing the old ones. When the new concrete overpass bridge opened over the intersection of Highway 1A and the Trans-Asia Highway (formerly Highway 22) at An Sương, he took me there just to ride across it. We stopped at the top of the bridge, where other groups of friends had stopped, huge trucks kicking up dust from the still unpaved and surprisingly sandy surface of the brand-new bridge. Despite the dust, Thành marveled at the cool wind. "Ở đây mát" (It's cool here), he said as we joined the small crowd standing next to their motorbikes on the edge of the bridge, staring down the road toward Saigon, enjoying the cool but dusty breeze. This was the edge of Hóc Môn, at the boundary of District 12, where Highway 22 turns into the Boulevard of the August Revolution, where the road commemorating Hồ Chí Minh's revolution becomes the road to Ho Chi Minh City itself.[6]

On the map, this marker between the inner-city district and the outer-city district appears substantial and seems to mark a divide. Move one direction and you will go in *(đi vào)* to the numbered districts of Ho Chi Minh City; the other way leads out *(ra)* to Hóc Môn. But the divide is more symbolic than real. Hóc Môn is also part of *(thuộc)* Ho Chi Minh City, and there seems no objective difference between the density or urban character of the streets on either side of the planners' arbitrary divide. In Hóc Môn, Thành and I found ourselves both inside of Ho Chi Minh City and outside it. To understand how this can be and the kind of social experience this produces requires that one understand the *ideal* constructs of the city as well as the everyday experience of life on its imagined edge. One must engage with Hóc Môn while sucking the soapberry with a smile, enjoying the cool air as cement trucks rumble past, clouds of dust rising in their wake, air horns blasting.

Social Edginess

Thành's description of life always revolved around a sense of living on the edge of the city. His fascination with the recently urbanizing section of Hóc Môn was tempered by a sense that his own area was getting taken over by a form of urban blight. On the one hand, he thrived on the excitement of increased population density and the new cafés, businesses, and modern houses popping up along with it. On the other, he explained that life was becoming *phức tạp,* "complicated." There were unsavory people moving into the area, social connections were increasingly distant *(xa lạ)*, and the area was increasingly beset by drug users, criminals, and prostitutes, problems he claimed were normally reserved for the city. Thành described the people in Hóc Môn as caught in the middle. He longed for an urban life and yet saw this very urban life as a threat to the existence he had created in Hóc Môn. When he said he felt as if he was "sucking the soapberry," he explained that it was impossible to critique the urbanization process because it was bringing jobs and new opportunities. Like many people in Hóc Môn, he felt that complaining about the negative aspects would somehow undermine the possibility of improving life in Hóc Môn. In contemporary Vietnam, *urbanization* is not simply a descriptive term; it is typically seen as an attempt to improve living conditions through development. As a plywood manufacturer who lost the front of his lot beside the Trans-Asia Highway project in the Tân Thới Nhì section of Hóc Môn, explained, "How can one have development without suffering?" He was willing to suffer through the process because he believed in the potential for a better future that would come through the transformation of the landscape brought by urbanization and development. This was life in Hóc Môn.

This double-edged sword of urbanization on the fringe of the city produces what I call social edginess. This concept of edginess unifies the social categories of spatial order with the experiential ethos of life on the imagined edge of a rapidly expanding city. In particular, this edginess itself emerges out of the material transformation of space and how it is refracted off of common social categories used to describe space and social relations. There is no actual edge of the city, but common spatial and social idioms of rural and urban, as well as inside and outside, inevitably produce the idea of an edge. The edge exists only as that which falls between the boundaries of these pure social categories. As a form of social practice, "social edginess" expresses the ambivalence of life between pure sociocultural categories and also offers possibilities to deploy those categories to strategic effect. It is the social meaning of such a spatial position, in turn, that guides the ways in which people experience spatial change. Unlike the important anthropological concept of "marginality," which implies a static structural position outside of centers of power, edginess emphasizes the possibility and the risks associated with moving into, outside, and across the boundaries created by discrete categories. Edginess involves a sense of teetering on a symbolic precipice; full of potential, full of risks, it is always a space of social struggle where spatial identity "takes place" through the active social construction of space.[7] For some, the "edge" that develops on the edge of pure categories enables new forms of creative action; for others, it constrains social action in significant ways, most clearly by relegating less advantaged social actors to the margins of social consciousness, the gray zone that lies between commonly understood categories of action and social status.

This edginess emerges in concert with the reproduction of ideal social categories that define it in opposition to what it is not. The practical experience of everyday life on the edge emerges as both a reiteration and a violation of those categories. Edginess develops out of a feedback loop among ideal sociocultural models, rational discourses of idealized space, and the everyday experience of lived life within and in contradistinction to such space. In Hóc Môn, social edginess is the experience of life between contradictory models of social hierarchy framed in the national opposition of rural and urban, as well as a familiar "inside" and "outside" idiom of kinship and social reproduction I will describe at the end of this chapter. These models give social meaning to material space, as well as political economic relations of power and influence within a rapidly urbanizing zone on the periphery of the city. The edge is not simply the byproduct of a set of false ideals; both these ideals and the experience of the edge are realized through social practice. Even people relegated to the edge of ideal social categories participate in the reproduction of the ideals that put them on the edge. Furthermore, all of these mutually intertwined relations produce and continue alongside objective transformations of space at the blurred interface of the city and the countryside, and this transformation itself enters the process as a new element in the social production of edginess itself. Just as pure cultural concepts become fetishized as cultural truths, the idea of the edge comes to appear as a material fact.

As David Harvey has demonstrated in other contexts, the physical space of a city appears as the apparent "thing" that crystallizes out of the process of historical change. In Hóc Môn, the edge is the "thing" that both constrains and grows out of social relations framed by the symbolic opposition between country and city, as well as idioms of inside and outside which parallel Vietnamese conceptions of kinship; it is the thing transformed by reform era Vietnamese commitments to privatization, urbanization and the move to capitalist relations of production; the thing that supports the resurgence of petty trading and privatized accumulation;

that gets transformed by urban planning, land speculation, and rural urban migration. It is this "thing"—this physical landscape—that in turn delineates the physical space of social relations.[8] And this thing is symbolically charged, imbued with socially meaningful boundaries and edges, which themselves crystallize out of a dialectical relationship between rural and urban, inside and outside, and cast the city's edge as a site of both power and danger.[9]

Rural–Urban Purity and the Ideal City

When one looks at the Ho Chi Minh City maps commonly available in bookstores and sold by magazine sellers at the side of the street, the distinction between country and city seems almost natural. By representing space in clear, discrete units, these maps normalize and lend an almost material sense of tangible reality to otherwise arbitrary spatial divides.[10] On such maps, the administrative borders of Saigon/Ho Chi Minh City appear perfectly contained, with primary colors carefully demarcating the city's twenty-two districts into an orderly system of seventeen inner-city and five outer-city districts. Looking even more closely at the colorful map of the city, the observer will note the apparent foresight with which planners have drawn in a ring road around the inner-city districts.[11] This offshoot of National Highway 1 forms something of a ring road, an almost perfect belt around the inner-city districts (called *quận* or *quận nội thành*), clearly separating them from the outer-city districts (called *huyện* or *huyện ngoại thành*) and accentuating what seems to be the most apparent distinction of space within the Ho Chi Minh City administrative zone.[12]

This distinction between inner-city *quận nội thành* and outer-city *huyện ngoại thành* recalls two of the primary binary distinctions in Vietnamese political and social organization: the opposition of the country *(nông thôn)* and the city *(thành thị, thành phố)* and the opposition of the inside *(nội)* and the outside *(ngoại)*. *Ngoại* simply means "outside." The second component of the word, *thành,* means "rampart," or, in this context, "city wall." The Vietnamese word for city, *thành phố,* combines the words for streets *(phố)* and ramparts *(thành),* forming a compound that corresponds with the historical origins of many Vietnamese urban centers. Although most sources identify the founding of what is now Ho Chi Minh City with the military occupation of the area, the naming of districts, and the establishment of administrative works by Nguyễn Hữu Cảnh in 1698, Professor Nguyễn Đình Đầu argues that it did not become a true "city" until Nguyễn Cửu Đàm built a citadel there in 1772 to protect against the danger of Siamese invaders. Before the citadel was built, "there had existed the urban areas of Saigon city [now District 5] and Bến Nghé city [now District 1] with many markets and bustling commercial transaction centers for local and external exchanges. [With the building of the citadel] this locality had turned into a real 'thành phố' (city), as it had both rampart (thành) and urban zones (phố)."[13] The very words that signify a city reinforce the idea that a city is a contained whole, surrounded by a wall or rampart. Likewise, the compound word for urban (đô thị) contains the roots for capitol (đô) and market (thị), a conjunction that also implies a bounded, identifiable center of administration and commerce. Although the parameters demarcating what counts as inside and outside have changed with the spatial transformations of the city since the building of this citadel in 1772, people today continue to assert that the idea of the city or of urban space emerges from a sense of boundedness, an idea that persists with the clean division on the map of inner-city (nội thành) and outer-city (ngoại thành) districts.

Symbolically, being outside the ramparts signals a certain sense of abandon and wild possibility, but it also signals vulnerability. People name this area not for what it looks like in terms of objective social science categories but by using common terms, as well as those depicted on maps and repeated in bureaucratic writing. Regardless of what it actually looks like, Hóc Môn is ngoại thành or ngoại ô, outside the city. Although scholars of urban Southeast Asia have developed terms to describe mixed rural and urban transition zones,[14] Vietnamese terms do not refer to mixed-use spaces in this way; spatial concepts of the city divide space into that which is inside and that which is strictly outside: ngoại. Every utterance of the term repeats the binary distinction.

Ideal depictions of the city also emphasize a spatial distinction between rural and urban, a distinction that is also anthropomorphized in the popular distinction between the rural peasant (nông dân, nhà quê) and the urbanite (thị dân, người thành phố), categories that have profoundly important symbolic meanings in the idealized conception of Vietnamese society and culture. Reproducing the ideal-typical terms of what the city *should* look like, the city map paints the picture of a central core made up of worldly and modern urban quận immediately surrounded by rural

outer-city *huyện,* which themselves act as a symbolic buffer between
the city and the country. The agricultural "rice basket" provinces of the
Mekong Delta lie to the southwest, arid and rural Tây Ninh lies to the
northwest, and the newly industrialized but formerly rural southeastern
provinces of Bình Dương, Đồng Nai, and Bà Rịa-Vũng Tàu stretch out
from the city along major highways in a development corridor extending
to the sea.

In the ideal scheme of cultural order, the city must have an edge. There
must be countryside as well. As pure categories, both the city and the
countryside have a role within a larger system of complementary oppositions. Trần Ngọc Thêm, extending his overarching use of *âm* and *dương*
(yin and yang) to explain all aspects of Vietnamese society, argues that
even the organization of national space reproduces (or should reproduce)
the philosophy of oppositions as a spatial division between country and
city. The space of rural village society is *âm,* and the space of urban
society is *dương.*[15] In this ideal of productive interrelations through the
maintenance of distinctiveness, the city emerges as the material embodi-
ment of a unique urban character that contains elements of the countryside but never fully blends with it. The city has a market reserved for
agricultural produce, and it has shoulder-pole vendors to feed the city
people, sell flowers, and deliver fresh goods, but these only feed the potential for urbanites to focus their efforts on political, intellectual, and artistic activity. The ideal countryside, by contrast, has its district seat *(thị trấn)*
with a post office, administrative offices, an agricultural bank, seed and
fertilizer stores, and sites of urban life (such as cafés, karaoke bars, and
shops), all of which support but do not undermine the primacy of agricultural activity. The latent city is always present in the country, and the
latent country is always present in the city, and although there is always
a risk that the city will be overtaken by the country, this possibility is
posed as a threat to order, not as a natural course of events.[16] The city,
scholars and planners warn, might "suffer from ruralization" *(bị nông thôn*
hóa). Such a blending of categories strikes these observers as an aberra-
tion, a problem to be avoided at all costs. In the ideal system, the difference between country and city should remain clear and distinct.

Even in cases in which the ideal distinction between rural and urban
areas does not materialize in actual practice, official pronouncements
insist that it certainly *should* be preserved. In a speech before the Second
National Congress on Urbanization in 1995, then–Prime Minister Võ Văn

Kiệt lamented the fact that administration for urban areas and rural areas was virtually the same. The urban areas, he implied in his speech, were clearly examples of Vietnam's forward-moving success in the modernization process. But these urban areas, he complained, were still administered using the same old-fashioned techniques used to administer the countryside. The prime minister spoke about the need to modernize the administration of urban areas and to maintain the distinction between the urban zones and the rural zones by implementing new administrative measures:

The organizational model for the government machinery in urban areas today is no different than the organization of that machinery in the rural districts and communes. . . . This situation cannot continue. . . . We are carrying out the Industrialization and Modernization of the country, but if we do not regularize *[chính qui hóa]* urban administration, the above goals can never be reached. It is necessary to have proficiency in administration, and also to modernize the level of administration, so as to prevent the evil of bureaucracy *[nạn quan liệu]* from becoming a fertile ground *[mảnh đất màu mở]* for the evil *[tệ]* of harassing and pestering *[những nhiễu]* all the people.[17]

Such a statement indicates the degree to which policy makers and planners see the need for a clear-cut administrative divide as self-evident. There is no need to argue about the desire to keep city and country separate, because city and country are different things; they require different forms of administration, and they need to be kept separate in order to preserve their functional roles in the larger order of things. Just look at the map. With its clear-cut divisions, the map appears to will this ideal of administrative separation into existence.[18]

This division is not purely urban hubris or political simplification. Scholars depict it as something on the order of a cultural fact. And this idea of the innate difference between rural and urban society appears with great force in cultural analyses of village Vietnam as well, where scholars have long argued that this idealized separation of pure types has a function within the larger social organization of society.[19] Emphasizing the internal coherence of "traditional" village organization conceptualized as a bounded unit, the rural view of the complementary ideal stresses how inward-looking village institutions create the potential for a productive national division of labor and authority. Traditional forms of social order within the village emerge as perfect complements to those of outward-oriented cities. Emphasizing a productive dialogue between the inward-oriented tradition of the countryside and the outward-oriented modernity of the city, authorities on rural tradition adopt the same assumptions as planners and development boosters in their assertions about how the differences between rural and urban society create the potential for large-scale unity. For example, Toan Ánh, the prolific author of at least ten books on traditional Vietnamese culture and festivals and a renowned expert on village social organization, argues that the rural village is both independent of and integral to the proper functioning of the nation. In this ideal depiction, the rural village maintains a certain form of independence from national affairs. But rather than undermining national unity, he argues that such independence strengthens the nation: "Only with village stability can there be national strength" (Làng có vững, nước mới bền).[20]

In the original Vietnamese, Toan Ánh's turn of phrase cleverly plays on the contemporary idea of "sustainability" *(bền vững),* which has such currency in the development world. At the same time, the sentence structure echoes a folk maxim, employing the six-syllable cadence of the first line of a traditional six-eight couplet[21] and playing on the rhetorical logic of uniting two words in a forceful compound to make the author's point. To achieve stability, *bền vững,* he argues, requires first that the village be *vững,* firm, steady, secure, and stable. Only then is national strength *(bền)* possible. This casts the whole idea of *bền vững* as an inherently logical extension of folk truths; it resonates as a bit of folk wisdom, and it displays the strength that emerges through the unity of organic opposites. Turning to the seemingly rational "cultural logic" of the way things seem to be, it appears entirely natural to assume that the independence of the village can be realized only through its integration in a larger whole, much as modernization theories once articulated the mutual importance of great tradition and little tradition, of village independence and national strength.[22] "The village," Toan Ánh continues, "is the smallest unit of the nation. But it is also the essential unit that unites the people, and accordingly, it organizes the people."[23] This organic vision offers national strength and local autonomy as simultaneous aspects of the same form of social order.

Complementing the ideal depiction of discrete rural spaces is an image of the city as a bounded whole, linked to but ideally differentiated from the surrounding countryside. On the map, the city appears as a circle of urbanity contained by the ring road. And the road itself separates the city from the countryside surrounding it at the very same time that it connects the city to a network of national highways and provincial roads that lead out to the idealized countryside in every direction. Visually reproducing these ideal relations of unity through opposition, the Ho Chi Minh City map places the city in the center, marks it as the unambiguous hub of the southern region as a whole, mediating the eastern southern region with the western provinces of the Mekong Delta and focusing the potential of the south into a powerful, outward-oriented entrepôt of commerce and exchange. In a recent critique of urban-centered development discourse, Philip Taylor clearly showed that cosmopolitan modernity can also be found in what planners often consider the rural margins of developmental space.[24] But if you look at the map, such possibilities are concealed by spatial representations of power that place modernity squarely in the city; it seems easy to understand where one might find city and where one might find countryside. Where is the countryside? Outside of the city. Where is the city? Right there in the middle.

The Stretched Ideal

Yet like the trouser belts of the city's *nouveaux riches,* whose bellies have expanded with the feast of new opportunities since the end of Vietnam's economic isolation, the belt that surrounds Ho Chi Minh City seems unable to contain the rapid growth that has come with the city's emerging role in the national, regional, and world economies.[25] The spatial edge of Ho Chi Minh City defies the colored boundaries on the map. The edge is in motion. Areas that once lay squarely in the countryside now often lie within the city itself. To accommodate the expansion of Ho Chi Minh City's urban center, the city's administration has had to change the names and boundaries of districts, adding five new administrative units since 1997. The formerly outer-city *huyện* Thủ Đức was divided into three new inner-city districts named *quận* 2, *quận* 9, and *quận* Thủ Đức. Hóc Môn was split into two districts, forming the present-day division of outer-city *huyện* Hóc Môn and inner-city *quận* 12.[26]

    One major cause of this urban expansion is rural-to-urban migration, which is described as blurring the pure categories of country and city in a process that threatens to break down the very structure of social order itself.[27] According to Nguyễn Văn Tài, for example, migrants from the countryside who come seeking work typically find temporary and unstable jobs. And with 72 percent of in-migrants settling in the inner-city districts, the *nội thành* is becoming overburdened while the outer-city districts remain only "thinly populated" with these new settlers. The strain on the inner-city districts is clear, Tài explains, because migration from the countryside has become a "force that makes the unemployed army in the city even more dense."[28] Although Tài implies that a more equitable distribution of migrants throughout the inner- and outer-city districts would help ease the strain on the city, he does not dwell on how the symbolic meaning of the inner city encourages this concentration on the inside. The problem results from the improper melding of urban and rural people. If the outer city has a role, it should serve as a buffer zone to protect the urban center from the infiltration of people from the rural hinterlands. The outer-city district is supposedly rural. Should not the rural migrants go *there?*

In depictions like this, the melding of country and city appear as a major crisis. The ideal city is described as a zone under threat. Migration transforms cities into "poverty traps" *(bẫy nghèo đói)* that become a "hell" *(địa ngục)* for poorly educated newcomers. These migrants are then left to scramble for the crumbs of life in "disintegrating" migrant areas, areas that turn into "gathering places for many social evils" *(nơi tập trung nhiều tệ nạn xã hội).*[29] Tài describes "rat-infested" houses *(nhà ổ chuột)* built on trash pits, along canals, and in cemeteries; he points to statistics from 1997 that claim that 41 percent of arrested criminals were born outside the city; he also points out the large number of children who are put to work as beggars; and he specifically refers to "the chicken-coop city" in Gò Vấp district, which gets its name from the prostitutes, or "chickens with red fingernails" *(gà móng đỏ)* who live and work there.[30] In such depictions, the mixing of rural and urban seems frightening indeed.

The "Extended Metropolis" Viewed from Afar

The poet Vũ Hoàng Chương proves to have been prescient when he wrote: "Reality and Dream don't match." From an objective perspective, the boundary between country and city is always blurred. Even when one claims to find what one might call an edge to the city and locates it in space, the edge itself moves in space as new projects come to completion, as settlements shift, as land-use regulations change, or as people buy and sell the use rights to land and divide and subdivide plots for housing, industrial parks, and so on. In morphological and demographic terms, when we look at the actual pattern of city growth and expansion, the whole idea of the rural and the urban obscures the emerging shape of Saigon/Ho Chi Minh City and the larger southeastern region as a whole. For much of this space is only space in the sense that it is neither rural space nor urban space.

Based on his demographic and geographical studies of other large Asian metropolitan areas, McGee argues that the distinction of rural and urban proves misleading. These are false categories clouding our vision of the city and its surrounding regions, making us look for something that is not really there. Instead of a pure edge marking the strict boundary between pure categories, McGee describes a hybrid spatial form characterized by mixed agricultural and nonagricultural land use, multiple forms of employment that are both stable and seasonal, and a fluid population with ties to the urban core, people from the countryside, and some people who have ties to both.[31]

To account for this new kind of space, McGee invented the term "*désakota* region," which he derived from the Bahasa Indonesian words for city *(kota)* and village *(désa)* and uses to describe "the situation where one or more urban cores are located in densely settled peasant rural areas."[32] With this term, McGee usefully moves away from a bias that attempts to read the Southeast Asian city with categories derived from the urbanization of European and North American cities in the nineteenth and early twentieth centuries. Southeast Asian cities cannot be read as simple circles expanding outward in concentric rings of decreasing density, as urban "cores" fading into the surrounding countryside. Instead their demographics are more complex, and human settlement and urban expansion are linked to internal migration policies, land values, urban planning policies, local-level authority relations, infrastructure development (or even underdevelopment), and cultural factors such as migration networks and kinship ties. McGee describes Southeast Asian cities and the areas around them as mixtures of urban and rural land use, with filaments of technology and agriculture interpenetrating each other in complex processes, always in motion, constantly reproducing new social spaces. The new Asian "extended metropolis" emerges from and itself constrains new relations of capital investment, agricultural transformation (mostly low-tech), and improvements in transport, as well as new spatiotemporal relations that impinge upon class and social identity.[33]

Spatial change always emerges out of distinctly human decisions, grounded in particular economic and local cultural frameworks. Take, for example, a newly married couple like Bình (the bride, who was from the city's central District 1) and Nam (the groom, who was from the border-ing outer-city district of Củ Chi). They chose to move to Hóc Môn because it lay between their two families and because it offered afford-able land where they could set up neolocal residence and open a business with frontage space. However, the parents of young Lộc brought their family of ten to Hóc Môn from the northern province of Nam Định after a period working as tenant farmers in Kiên Giang province. They chose the area because it was near a Catholic church and allowed the parents to continue working fields while the children exploited the economic potential of the city. While his mother tended to rice fields, Lộc sold lot-tery tickets in cafés and businesses along the Trans-Asia Highway, one sister worked in the Fuji film factory twenty minutes away by motorbike, another sold textiles in Bình Dương province, an hour away by motorbike, and the rest of the younger siblings helped out by assembling various piecework projects for a nearby bamboo furniture company. The dynamic of movement includes people coming from other provinces as well as moving among the various districts within the city's administrative zone. High prices in the inner city encourage families to move farther from the city center, and high unemployment in the countryside encourages oth-ers to seek affordable housing closer to the city. Industrial zones offering jobs and roadway projects improving the possibility of commuting in and out of the city create clusters of settlement along the highways lead-ing in and out of town.[34]

In large part, the expansion of the city looks quite similar to the urban-ization process in many of what McGee and Robinson describe as the "Mega-Urban Regions" surrounding Southeast Asian cities. Their snap-shot of this megaurban type reads as an accurate, albeit generalized, de-scription of contemporary urban growth in Ho Chi Minh City:

Metropolitan regional growth tends to sprawl along major expressways and rail-road lines radiating out from the urban cores, and leapfrogs in new directions, put-ting down new towns, industrial estates, housing projects, and even golf courses in areas hitherto agricultural and rural. In such areas, regions of dense population and mixed land uses are created, in which traditional agriculture is found side by side with modern factories, commercial activities, and suburban development.[35]

In Hóc Môn, like so many other Southeast Asian cities, the city cuts across the rural landscape and creates new forms of space that are both rural and urban at once.

Objectively speaking, this new mixed zone of multiple occupational activities and mixed land uses questions the usefulness of pure categories such as rural and urban. But this does not explain why such categories persist in social life; it does not tell us how people living there imagine this space, describe it, and negotiate social relationships within it, how people suck the soapberry and call it sweet. Instead, the language of this objective, outsider's description of megaurban regions gives agency to growth. Growth tends to "sprawl" and "leapfrog," "putting down towns." Regions of population "are created."

Yet growth itself is an abstraction; it has no real will or agency of its own. Outside of nature, only people have the power to transform space—even if it *appears* that such space magically produces itself. *Growth* is itself just another word for human activity, an abstraction of a social process; for growth grows out of society itself. In order to avoid this temptation to reify social processes, anthropologists must toggle between two analytical positions, moving from the objective analysis of spatial change outside Ho Chi Minh City to people's practical vision of that very space. A socially relevant understanding of social life as it is actually lived and experienced requires reconciling both of these perspectives, keeping in mind that objective change, ways of interpreting the world, and practical action are all part of a single process, always in motion.

The transformations that have made Hóc Môn into a classic example of mixed rural and urban space are by no means unique to Vietnam. As in the cases of other suburban fringes surrounding cities in agricultural nations, the emergence of this marginal space must be understood in the context of larger regional and international trade regimes; new regional exchanges of finance, commerce, and agriculture; and historically specific changes in each country.[36] "In essence," McGee explains, "the central processes that shape these regions are the dynamic linkages between agriculture and non-agriculture, and investment seeking to utilize cheap labor and land within a distinctive agroecological setting."[37]

In contemporary Vietnam generally and in Ho Chi Minh City particularly, this "distinctive agroecological setting" does not refer simply to a set of physical qualities or a location on the map. Instead, the symbolic meanings people attach to space frame the material reality of such space and contribute to the values such material realities come to represent. Both local Vietnamese and international investors commonly describe Ho Chi Minh City as a new economic *frontier,* using a spatial metaphor that really hinges on ideological changes in the orientation of the Vietnamese Communist Party toward the economy. Although the geographical position of Ho Chi Minh City has not changed, its emergence as a new market and a new source of cheap labor has certainly changed its position within the political and economic geography of world finance, industrial production, and commercial exchange. The outer-city districts, furthermore, attract foreign investors because they purport to combine the best elements of two worlds: rural land and labor (which, from the perspective of foreign investors, really means "cheap land and labor") and proximity to urban infrastructure, markets, and distribution. Hóc Môn proves alluring because it is a bargain not too far from the city. The frontier mentality underscores the actions of local and foreign commercial interests trying to take advantage of the epochal changes brought by post–*đổi mới* transformations in the Foreign Investment and Land laws, investor-friendly elements of "socialism with a market orientation," opportunities made available by the lifting of the U.S.-imposed economic trade embargo, the signing of the U.S.–Vietnam bilateral trade agreement, new tariff reductions that have come with Vietnam's integration into the Association of Southeast Asian Nations regional trade bloc, and construction and development projects financed by the World Bank, the International Monetary Fund, the Asian Development Bank, and other international lending institutions. All these other factors, in addition to simple location in geographical space, have contributed to the production of Ho Chi Minh City and its environs as a specific kind of "place" on the edge, even if it is not objectively on the physical or material edge of anything definable.

An interesting paradox has developed. The value of Saigon's edge emerges from its position "on the edge" as an untapped space, yet the very tapping of that edge leads to its own crisis. At the outer limits of the city, people seek the material manifestation of this edge in the form of cheap labor, inexpensive land, and room for expansion. According to Nguyễn Văn Tài, many of the new jobs being created are poor jobs that migrants will take but locals will not. Migrants earn, on average, monthly wages that are 50 to 100 thousand *đồng* lower than those paid local laborers. With 71,718 migrants in the city, this leads to a total wage difference of 3.5 to 7.1 billion *đồng* per month. Producing such low-skilled jobs, Tài argues, has actually become a drain on the Ho Chi Minh City economy because it keeps wages low.[38] Economic sustainability requires developing well-paying, skilled jobs and discontinuing the reliance on low-paying, dangerous jobs. Yet the quite reasonable desire to improve the living conditions of these low-wage laborers runs up against the fact that low wages are one of the primary draws enticing industry to the edge in the first place.

The existence of the edge, then, must be understood as a moment within a larger period of economic transition from labor-intensive to capital-intensive industry, a process that has occurred throughout many of the East and Southeast Asian economies. Many of the "Asian Tiger" economies began their path to development by first exploiting their own low-wage labor and then encouraging the development of high-technology infrastructure. In this way, the development of the edge should lead to its own transcendence as the exploitation of the edge blurs the edge itself. Objectively speaking, there is no real edge. This frontier mentality produces the edge as a mirage as it sends people off to the edge that disappears by virtue of their very presence. The edge begins to move at the very moment that interest in the idea of the edge grows stronger.

This is a classic example of how too much interest in a good thing transforms the good thing itself. Such an implicit contradiction becomes intensified on the rural fringes of rapidly expanding cities. The opportunities provided by open space and cheap land that make the fringes attractive come to be undermined by the very fact that they are attractive. This attraction brings people and construction that fills in the open space and drives up the price of land. This situation is not unique to Vietnam; Lewis Mumford described this process in his critique of Western suburbanization, where wholesale expansion into open space had a "fatal penalty attached to it—the penalty of popularity, the fatal inundation of a mass movement whose very numbers would wipe out the goods each individual sought for his own domestic circle."[39] On the rural–urban fringes around Ho Chi Minh City a similar process has swung into motion, fueled by multiple factors such as rural–urban migration of people looking for work in the city, outmigration from the city center to the periphery by people who cannot afford to live in the city center or who want to purchase larger middle-class homes, and the requirements of foreign investors who seek cheap land and plentiful labor for outsourced production.

The edge, then, is in motion, because its own attractiveness as edge makes it impossible to maintain the marginal utility of the marginal space itself. In countless interviews with small-scale vendors along major roads and in alleyways, I was instructed on the increased difficulty of preserving one's niche in the market. Café owners complained that business was slowing down because there were too many cafés popping up. People engaged in small-scale production and services—from the local *hủ tiếu* noodle makers and soup sellers to sandwich makers and even the proprietors of karaoke bars and illicit *café ôm* [40]—complained about how the oversaturation of the market made it increasingly difficult to turn a profit. When one runs the only café on a rural fringe, steady business flows in without much effort. But the economics of the edge are only temporary as the edge itself urbanizes.

With the edge of the city in this state of flux and movement, it would seem that the strict categories of rural and urban cannot account for actual spatial transformation. However, despite the fact that it appears as an element in a system of strict binary oppositions, the very idea of an outer city *(ngoại thành)* is actually more flexible than it first appears. In the next section I show how the binary oppositions of inside and outside, while seemingly static, actually open up the potential for significant flexibility in everyday practice. To demonstrate this, I draw on an analogous relationship in Vietnamese kinship. Like urban space, Vietnamese kinship is organized around a spatialized logic of inside and outside relations. While seemingly rigid in their ideal form, however, kinship relations are actually quite dynamic, oscillating between an idealized, seemingly rigid patrilineal model and a more flexible bilateral model that responds to the exigencies of everyday life. In Vietnamese kinship, life "outside" has potential, but it is often a double-edged potential. This double sense of both having potential and being at risk recalls the same ethos and attitude that frames social edginess on the urban fringe.

The Inside/Outside Dichotomy in Vietnamese Kinship

In the practical manifestations of Vietnamese kinship, the manipulation of the categories inside and outside both follows norms and transgresses them through the pragmatic manipulation of kinship terminology. [41] Hy Văn Lương demonstrates how two seemingly contradictory yet coexistent models of social organization and lineage structure in Vietnamese kinship allow for the active manipulation of associative and dissociative terms of address, depending on context and the conscious manipulation of person reference terms by social actors. Because kinship can be traced through both patrilineal and bilateral lines of descent with different effects, the possibility of semantic double meanings opens up in the course of everyday interactions. A quick look at this phenomenon helps clarify the ways in which social actors manipulate the meanings of being inside and outside a lineage, which in turn clarifies how people negotiate the meanings of being inside and outside the city.

On the one hand, Lương shows that kinship terminology, which enacts a relational hierarchy between interlocutors in virtually every discursive exchange, profoundly influences the ways in which people view social relationships: "In the metalinguistic awareness of virtually all native speakers, person reference constitutes the most salient domain through which interactional contexts are structured and partly in terms [in] which the native sociocultural universe is reproduced and transformed."[42] On the other hand, he demonstrates that the "structure" of kinship never wholly predetermines the nature of hierarchy in practice. Vietnamese can have it both ways, because two coexisting (and seemingly contradictory) male-oriented and non-male-oriented models of kinship give individual actors the opportunity to manipulate social interactions by drawing on different possibilities according to context and the conscious manipulation of ends. Although person references reflect the native model for seeing the universe, the "diversity of discursive practices . . . reflect opposing models of and for sociocultural reality."[43] There are formal rules of address, but there is more than one set of references from which to choose these rules to follow, thus opening up the potential for selective appropriation of the rules in the course of practical action and everyday encounters.

This ambiguity is clearest in the fundamental unit used to demarcate a "family line" *(họ),* which can refer to patrilineage, patronym, bilateral kindred, credit association, outer/distant relatives, and they/them.[44] In particular, the fact that *họ* can refer to both patrilineage and bilateral kindred shows the labile meaning of the category, which stems from this copresence of what Lương calls a "male-oriented model" of kinship and a "non-male-oriented model" of kinship.

The idealized and most commonly referred to form of standard Vietnamese kinship is organized around a "male-oriented model" that emphasizes patrilocality and patrilineal descent, which is traced back in time to a number of generations through the male line *(bên nội),* "the inside." This model emphasizes solidarity within the *họ,* a solidarity founded on hierarchal differentiation of members within it—all designated by age- and gender-specific personal pronouns such as those for older brother *(anh)*, older sister *(chị)*, father's younger brother *(chú)*, aunt *(cô)*, father's older brother *(bác)*, and nephew *(cháu)*. In this model, a strict separation of the sexes along a gendered division of labor corresponds with a strictly spatialized understanding of the patrilocal home as "the inside," *bên nội*. The wife marries in from the outside, focusing on the domestic domain, and the husband represents the lineage in public life.

The second, less commonly referred to, form of kinship is a bilateral model that is not bounded in space, has little historical depth, and includes both the "inside" (the husband's patriline, *bên nội*) and the "outside" (the wife's patriline, *bên ngoại*).[45] In this non-male-oriented model the extent of inclusiveness demarcated by the limits of the *họ* is not strictly localized in the same way that the *họ* is localized in the patrilineal model. In the bilateral model, the *họ* emphasizes the conjugal unit of husband and wife, a unit that is itself formed out of the unity of *họ nội* (inner *họ,* the father's patriline) and *họ ngoại* (outer *họ,* the mother's patriline).

In short, when one refers to one's family, one can alternately choose idioms of inclusiveness or exclusiveness. The referent family can either be highly localized in space, bound to the land and to a long connection to historical ancestors traced through patrilineal descent *(dòng họ bên nội),* or it can be widely expansive, extending outward to include both sides of the bilateral kindred extended through space but not very far back in time *(bên ngoại).*

The variable meanings of inside and outside in these two coexisting kinship models has important ramifications for understanding how social actors conceive of space in Ho Chi Minh City and its peripheral zones. Regarding person reference and the manipulation of kinship terms in everyday practice, Lương argues that "only in terms of the co-existence of two alternative kinship models can we fully understand the choice of kin terms and other linguistic/non-linguistic behavioral patterns in social interactions in general."[46] The ability to draw from two sets of appropriate kinship relations allows for a sense of agency in social interactions that would otherwise be prescribed and stultified by seemingly formulaic patterns of address. Evidence from fieldwork in Hóc Môn reveals the same manipulation of *nội họ* and *ngoại họ* in the ways people negotiate person references. At times, only patrilineal relations will be included in a reference to one's *họ*. On other occasions, a distant cousin on the mother's side living in the United States will be referred to as a member of one's *họ*. Indeed, demographic researchers have argued that assumptions about the patrilineal "Confucian" basis of Vietnamese kinship obscure the real-life kinship practices of many Vietnamese. Instead of a dramatic preponderance of male-headed households, researchers found that up to half of the households in cities were headed by females. Despite the persistence of the patrilineal family as the model for the ideal Vietnamese family, "the general pattern seems to be flexibility with residential location influenced more by economic opportunities and practical considerations than cultural prescriptions."[47] This explains the inclusion of a cousin in California in one's *họ*.[48]

In parallel fashion, the manipulation of *nội* and *ngoại* also informs different conceptions of the city in the ways in which people conceive of *nội thành* and *ngoại thành* as alternately separated and linked, depending on context. The labile meaning of these idioms of inclusion and exclusion color the map of the city and its surroundings. This flexibility makes it possible to construe Hóc Môn as both part of Ho Chi Minh City and outside of it. Like terms of person reference, the very meaning of *ngoại thành* changes according to context, such that a person living in Hóc Môn is both a resident of Ho Chi Minh City and an outsider to Saigon, even though Saigon and Ho Chi Minh City are considered interchangeable in some instances. Interlocutors simultaneously claim that they live in Ho Chi Minh City and make references to going into the city *(đi vào thành phố)*.

The fact that the center of reference changes indicates that the symbolic meaning of *ngoại thành* shifts in ways analogous to how the position of a wife's bilateral relations within a family changes according to context. Although I am not trying to claim that the outer-city districts are associated with a "female sphere," it is useful to consider the implications of this inside/outside construction of space by comparing it with oft-cited contradictions in the problem of patrilocal residence and the hierarchical distinction between *nội* and *ngoại*. Many scholars have commented on the impossible role of a new wife in a Vietnamese family. As an outsider charged with maintaining and reproducing the patrilineage, the wife is caught in a contradictory position between two worlds. On the one hand, a wife is a connection to the outer element of the bilateral line where her relations are construed as *bên ngoại;* yet the wife is seen in ideal terms as the master of the most intimate inner realms of the house-hold, the "general of the interior" *(nội tướng)*.[49] As Malarney puts it:

Confucian-inspired adages, useful for articulating male-centered elite ideology, in some cases obscure Vietnamese social reality. The position of women in the Vietnamese family is a case in point. . . . Women engage in production, are responsible for the family finances, and often have a voice in important family decisions such as the children's education or building a new home.[50]

The ideal of a male-centered household, which idealizes the "inner realm" as a wholly contained site of household production and reproduc-tion, conceals the full contribution of the wife and the "outer realm" in the production of the lineage. This leads to an important contradiction: while the home is the site of patrilocal residence and thus considered to be associated with the "inside" elements of the patriline, it is also con-sidered something of the "female" sphere in social relations writ large.[51] Paradoxically, the female sphere, which maintains contact with the "outer" *(bên ngoại)* sphere of bilateral relations, encompasses the site of resi-dence that defines the location of the "inner" *(bên nội)* patriline. Thus the man of the family is *in* the family, but the female originates *from the outside*. But at the same time, this same female is supposedly in charge of the home, the inner realm. The family ends up with an outsider in charge of the most intimate domains of the inside. And this outsider is charged with the responsibility of raising children in order to reproduce the lin-eage she is brought into only tangentially by virtue of marriage. Tradi-tional Vietnamese mythology, folklore, and song have much to say about this lamentable situation. For the most part, the elder females—mostly the husband's mother—are said to torment the new wife with insults, degra-dation, and lack of respect. Yet the new wife is expected to reproduce the male lineage.

Nội/Ngoại *and the City*

This contradictory dependence on the outer lineage coupled with insults, degradation, and lack of respect recalls the relationship of the outer-city districts to those of the inner city. Like Hóc Môn, all of the outer-city districts are both denigrated as "nasty" *(ghê quá)* and also idealized as an important greenbelt. The outer city is a "wasteland" *(đất hoang)* and also a source of vegetables, produce, meat, and poultry; the districts are denigrated as dirty and celebrated as lungs for the city. As places of "social evils" inhabited by romanticized (and also denigrated) peasants, they contain city dumps and also water filtration plants. In a way highly analogous to the uses of idioms of kinship, the inside of the city is understood as *nội,* with a long history located in a defined and bounded space that seems to reproduce itself by tracing its historical links to a founder. But this illusion of internal coherence and self-reproduction masks the vital contribution of the outer realm in this process of social reproduction. The spatiotemporal understanding of the social organization of *nội* and *ngoại* on the city map corresponds to the conceptual ideas of lineage relations and social hierarchies and inscribes them into geographical space and conceptions of time.[52] The symbolic relationship of inside and outside in the city combines with the spatial organization of the home to create a spatial representation of lineage relations that extends conceptually through historical time to the very founding of the city but becomes physically mapped into a space marked by its distinction from the outside. Manipulation of spatial inclusion and exclusion in conceptions of the city is very much like the manipulation of kinship terms designating the inside and the outside of a family (see Figure 3).

Ho Chi Minh City simultaneously refers to a city space distinguished from the outer-city districts as well as an administrative zone that requires those outer-city districts for its self-preservation and reproduction. People living in the outer-city districts must negotiate this sense of simultaneous

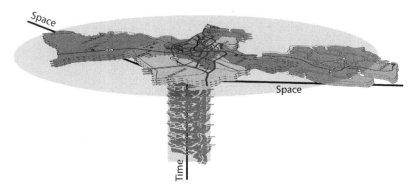

FIGURE 3. Conceptual image of inside and outside relations transposed on a city map. Like lineage relations, which depend on a spatial and temporal relationship between inside *(nội)* and outside *(ngoại),* the outer-city districts *(ngoại thành)* extend broadly across space with very little sense of historical depth. The inner-city zones of the city *(nội thành),* while spatially bounded, extend deep into historical time.

inclusion and exclusion in ways analogous to a new wife who marries into her husband's household. Like a wife, people in the outer-city districts are effectively charged with reproducing a form of social organization that keeps them in an outsider position. And like a wife in a traditional family organization, the outer city is "outside" but is supposed to be the place from which nourishment comes. Indeed many people in the outer-city districts literally feed the city but continue to maintain and reproduce their image as outsiders. In order to illustrate this by way of conclusion, I will turn briefly to the example of two female traders who constantly move between *nội thành* and *ngoại thành*. Their movements and performances of social identity show how this symbolic distinction colors the ways they negotiate the outer-city world they live in and the inner-city world where they work. Their relationship to the city embodies the social relationship of inside and outside, reflected by their manipulation of symbolic attire that changes according to their position in space and reflects an intimate understanding of space and subjectivity through material and symbolic practices.[53]

Producing the Edge

Mrs. Thúy and Mrs. Lan are both female traders from Hóc Môn who sell goods in central Ho Chi Minh City markets. They both mark the distinction between life inside the city and life outside the city with embodied performances of social identity that satisfy and play into received social expectations and stereotypes. Following the work of Judith Butler, it is important to recognize that these women "do" their bodies within a particular context of symbolic meanings, performing their identity as *"a corporeal style,* an 'act'" that both reproduces and actualizes their social position, which is both gendered female and associated with clear expectations about what constitutes an appropriately rural or outer-city presentation of self.[54] Both women independently described how they use and manipulate rural imagery as part of their sales strategies.

Mrs. Thúy is a shoulder-pole trader who earns the bulk of her family's income by walking around the city selling distinctive Huế-style pork sausages *(chả lụa Huế)*. Each day her husband and daughter would rise well before dawn to begin preparation of the sausages—pounding the pork, mixing the spices, wrapping the meat in banana-leaf packages, and then steaming the little green packages that would be sold to urban consumers.

When finished, the wrapped sausages looked like little gifts, wrapped in the green of the countryside. Then Mrs. Thúy would rise, still before dawn, help finish the sausages, and load them into two large aluminum covered pots suspended on either end of a bamboo carrying pole. When all was ready, she would dress up in the traditional *áo Ba Ba* identified with the Vietnamese peasantry, head for the road, flag down the Củ Chi–Saigon bus, and go into town to carry her pole around, selling as she walked from morning until late afternoon. Her labor was clearly intense, heavy, hard-to-bear work, and she would return home exhausted in the evenings with her pots empty and her pockets full of money.

Besides back-breaking labor, Mrs. Thúy's work included a performance as well. This became clear when I asked her if I could go with her and help her sell the sausages. I joked that the novelty value of a tow-headed American selling Huế pork sausages would surely contribute to swift sales. "Không!" (No!) she said emphatically, literally screaming out her objection to express how crazy she thought the idea seemed. It would never work. People like to know that the sausages are made in the countryside. My presence would ruin the act. She then left the room to change out of her *áo Ba Ba* into her everyday home clothes, which did not look like peasant clothes at all.

In Hóc Môn, traders who sell goods in the city don "peasant clothing" for their trips to the city and change back into city clothes when they return to Hóc Môn, the supposedly rural space outside the city in which they try to convince city folks that they live.

Another woman trader from Hóc Môn, Mrs. Lan, worked out of a stall next to the fishmongers in Saigon's Tân Định market in District 3. She sold sweet soy-based custard in addition to a selection of vegetables and fruits that varied according to the season. She told me that she once received a ticket from a friend to see a musical performance at the Ho Chi Minh City opera house. Because the market where she sells her goods was only a short *xe ôm* motorbike taxi ride from the opera house, she decided to go straight to the show from her stall at the market. She then started laughing as she described how she showed up in peasant clothing to this event with people dressed in suits and dresses. She was so embarrassed that she walked right out after taking only a few steps into the concert hall. The rural clothing that was appropriate, and indeed necessary, for the marketplace was utterly inappropriate for the exceedingly urban setting of the concert hall. She realized that the urban world of Ho

Chi Minh City outside of the market was guarded by a regime of fashion and distinction. Even though she worked inside the physical limits of the city, there was a distinctive urban boundary, a boundary that would require a change of clothes in order to cross. Of course she owned urban clothes, but they were back home in Hóc Môn; she rarely wore urban clothes into the city.

Regardless of what the demographic data tell us about the blending of country and city on the rural–urban fringe, there is, at least in terms of the practical negotiation of symbolically marked space, a definite distinction between urban and nonurban; the distinction emerges most immediately in the forms of the clothes people wear and the kinds of comportment appropriate for the space inside the city and the space outside it. It also emerges in the use of space, in the layout of homes, and in the economic activities of people in different zones. The two examples given here show how female traders wield the symbols of the countryside to give credibility to their position as sellers of food products. They show how this symbolism rests on an idealization of the countryside that is at odds with the actual place they live. They live in a space just outside the city, and while in that space they participate in many of the same urban pursuits that city dwellers do. But they have to play the role of country folk for their jobs in the city. Wearing the *áo Ba Ba* links the seller with the *idea* of the rural periphery from which fresh foods are supposed to come. It mediates between the imagined rural supplier and the urban consumer in market transactions, but it also makes the exchange possible by emphasizing the primacy of *difference*. In fact, the difference is what makes the exchange desirable. Urbanites want to buy from imagined peasants specifically because they link certain foodstuffs with imagined ideals of peasant purity.

Indeed, at the very same time that the pace of urbanization increases (and the blurring of the objective distinction between country and city intensifies), the production and reproduction of the ideal image of the pure countryside also increases, albeit in a sometimes stereotypical, theme-park-like fashion. Throughout the city center, new restaurants increasingly peddle rural stereotypes as a means of enticing urban customers. Some restaurants offer specialties such as "Mekong Delta–style field mice" *(chuột đồng),* or the servers dress in loose, country-style clothing. The restaurants have names such as "Hai Lúa" (Rice Picker) or "Hương Đồng" (Scent of the Fields), to name two of the most popular urban eateries in the Ho Chi Minh City restaurant scene.

The same processes that contribute to the intensive urbanization of Ho Chi Minh City produce a concomitant nostalgia for the countryside. Nguyễn-võ Thu-hương argues that this fascination with rural food provides a metaphor for national identity that stands outside of the neocolonial threat of the market economy. The outer-city districts figure prominently in this imagination of rural salvation from the ills of modernization. The outer-city districts themselves become a link to the rural pleasures of inner-city businessmen who seek avenues that will bestow "native-ness on Vietnamese men of status, distinct from the sexual/social presence/domination by foreign men."[55] The spaces along the highways leading out of the cities through the outer-city districts become coded as secret sexual zones of rural nativeness. Among its many associations, the rural fringe also becomes a place to find "secret pleasures accessible only to those initiated into a native way of being and knowing."[56] These secret pleasures are spoken of through the metaphors of rural delicacies *(đặc sản),* to be had by those "connoisseurs" who know where to find authentically Vietnamese foods and pleasures, on the "fresh" *(tươi mát)* rural fringes of the city.[57] The outer city, denigrated as dangerous and dirty in some accounts, is also covertly celebrated as a source of vitality that will regenerate the emasculated city businessman with good fresh (rural) food and possibly sex. In Hóc Môn's Bà Điểm commune, a whole section of "hotels" (in a place where few people would otherwise stay) complement the roadside restaurants that serve grilled snake meat, forest boar, and other exotic specialties. And if a man rides past these hotels after dark, prostitutes on motorbikes will follow him, advertising their own bodies as another form of outer-city specialty.

The social performance of the edge—itself dependent on reproducing the essential difference between the inner city and the outer city— realizes the ideal distinction depicted on the map. That is, it makes the ideal distinction seem real, so real that I simply could not follow my neighbor into town to help her sell her sausages, so real that Mrs. Lan could not bear to enter the opera house in her peasant clothes, so real that a well-dressed man driving through the district at night *must* be looking for sex. But the distinction between country and city is clearly not real, either; both of the female traders were performing according to expectations, dressing up for an expected role, so to speak. So are the prostitutes and the outer-city restaurants. As they "do" their gendered and spatialized identities, they produce what I describe as social edginess.

What Marx once called "the real basis of ideology" in the division of country and city is itself founded on a performance of the kind of reality that emerges from a set of idealized concepts.[58] People on the edge clearly play with the categories of inside, outside, rural, and urban in order to realize strategic ends. But in the process they also reproduce the spatial conditions of edginess that put them in the social position they find themselves in to begin with. They edge their way into possible modes of social action that cannot be divorced from the processes of social change that themselves contextualize the edge and lend it symbolic meaning.

Why would people edge their way into set of ideals that seem to conflict so directly with their everyday experience of space? Why does the outer city persist as edge when the edge has been blurred? To understand these issues, I now turn to look more carefully at the ambiguous social experience of life on the edge. The edge, it turns out, produces both power and exclusion.

2. Power and Exclusion on the Edge

The Conflation of Rural and Urban Spaces

> So many ideas of power are based on an idea of society as a series of
> forms contrasted with surrounding non-form. There is a power in the
> forms and other power in the inarticulate area, margins, confused lines,
> and beyond the external boundaries.
>
> —Mary Douglas, *Purity and Danger*

Mixed Categories and Fixed Ideals

Power and exclusion mark the edge. In contemporary Hóc Môn the
primary-colored distinction between city and country fades to gray. Yet
despite their fuzziness, and regardless of how they appear from a vantage
point above society, the categorical oppositions of rural versus urban
and inside versus outside persist. For better or for worse, these categories inform the stereotypes and mental maps to which people refer both
consciously and unconsciously as they make choices and live their lives
in relation to the space and time of immediate action as it is perceived.
This is not to say that people cannot see the material transformations and
social problems that develop out of the conflation of rural and urban space.
In this conflation, the vegetable gardens suffer from poisonous run-off
from the industries that surround them, and the rice fields are mined for
soil that is carted to various parts of the district and into the inner city
for use in filling the foundations of new construction projects. Farmers
walk their buffalos along the same newly paved roads traveled by blue-
shirted factory workers, fallow fields become soccer fields for laborers,
and ditches around factories become pools for bathing water buffalos or
ponds for planting Vietnamese water spinach. Cemeteries become gardens
and grazing plots, spaces in which to dry rice paper, and impromptu play-
grounds. What remains of the "rural" part of the so-called rural outer-city
districts is crammed into the interstices of urban expansion, tucked into
triangular patches of not-yet-developed land, squeezed in along the sides
of roads and in the gaps between homes.

Newspapers often fashion attention-grabbing headlines out of the more
egregious examples of unpleasant category mixing. And the outer-city

districts provide ample fodder for the editorial impulse to shock the reader. One article announces, "Many Ho Chi Minh City families are drinking water from cemeteries" and describes how families in the outer-city districts are living in close proximity to spontaneously built, unregulated cemeteries.[1] Another article, "HCMC: Worried Feelings . . . Superthin Houses," describes the strange new shape of houses in the cut-up spaces of the outer city: "A house on the corner of Phan Văn Hớn street and national highway 1A in Bà Điểm commune, Hóc Môn district has the shape of a sickle, but each end is uneven. One end is about 0.7 meters and the other is not even 2 meters. That is the depth of the house, and the length is probably over 10 meters."[2] The outer-city districts appear as secret spaces of escape, "hotels on the urban fringe—where couples meet."[3] But they also appear as sites where crafty, insincere people live. One reader sent in a complaint to the letters section of the newspaper *Tuổi Trẻ* that cried out: "The plague of spreading nails has returned to Hóc Môn," then went on to describe the appearance of unscrupulous motorbike tire repair shops that spread nails on the highway to create customers with flat tires.[4] Other stories are less shocking but imply discomfort with the conflation of seemingly opposed categories.

The implied shock of these headlines makes it clear that many people readily acknowledge the contemporary mix of land uses and social types in places like Hóc Môn. But this does not mean that ideal categories simply vanish in the face of objective changes in the landscape. In fact, part of the shock comes from an ideal expectation of what the outer city should be like. Thus, in order to understand what this space *means* we must recognize that there are "objective limits to objectivism."[5] The idealization of social categories cannot be ignored because they seem objectively flawed. Instead the city map represents an ideal representation of the city, a form of official knowledge that must be supplemented with an ethnographic understanding of what it is like to live in a space defined both by its position on a map and by its failures to fulfill an ideal. This reveals how it can be that the very people who live in Hóc Môn both describe it as a violation of all the categories they hold dear and continue to reproduce these categories as an idealized form of cultural truth. Understanding life on the edge, then, requires moving back and forth between the symbolic categories of space and the everyday experiences of lives lived within that space. Both the ideal categories and the everyday experience of space are objectively real—both are products of human interaction and creative agency—and both coexist. From the sky or in a satellite image, the processes of change in Hóc Môn may look like those in other places. But from the ground, in Vietnamese terms prescribed by the ideal expectations of social and spatial organization, the social space in Hóc Môn represents both opportunity and denial, power and exclusion.

Space as Social Process

Seen as a social process, the shape of the city and new development on its rural–urban fringes emerges as the totality of social negotiations and encounters, of deals and plans made among businesspeople and land speculators; members of district, city, and national government; as well as people living in the spaces in question. This notion of urban change as process shows that space is embedded both in social and cultural frameworks and in relations of power. Although cities and the areas surrounding them are obviously experienced in quite material ways—as sights and sounds; as clean, dirty, or dusty; as open or congested; full of potholes or smooth—they are more than just things. They are products of human endeavor; human beings built them and continue to build and give meaning to them as members of social groups. Although this may seem obvious, a birds-eye view of the city from on high, or a view constructed solely from maps and from demographic, social, and economic statistics can sometimes miss the fundamental interactive process between people and the world they create for themselves. Jane Jacobs, the great poet of urban analysis, argues, "It does not do to focus on "things" and expect them to explain much in themselves. Processes are always of the essence; things have significance as participants in a process, for better or for worse."[6] And this process is populated and driven by people.

Hybrid rural–urban zones, McGee explains (despite his insistence on their objective existence as *désakota* zones), "are to some extent 'invisible' or 'grey' zones from the viewpoint of the state authorities."[7] They do not fit into received categories of knowable space; they are not "legible," to borrow Scott's phrase.[8] But the evidence from the margins of Ho Chi Minh City shows that this is not simply a question of state authorities' inability to "see" such spaces. Those who live in these very spaces often see the world in the same categories that the authorities do, and what they see does not always fit properly into their categories, either. Furthermore, the most important question is not just whether people can "see" objective transformations in space but whether they like what they see, what they make of this failure to fit the ideal, and how they organize action around this perception of what this space looks like. In many ways, the failure to fit into ideal categories does not produce blindness as much as it shocks categories. But a shock to categories can mean different things to different people within a single social framework. Hebdige, for example, argued that the "meaning of style" among British youth subcultures construed shock as mixing familiar categories in unfamiliar ways: for youths it represented the "meaning of style"; for reactionary traditionalists it represented an affront to acceptable categories, a threat.[9] In the same way, the shock of Hóc Môn emerges out of the juxtaposition of familiar oppositions within a single social space. But the meaning of this juxtaposition depends on the point of view of different actors and their relation to the social space of Hóc Môn as well as to the social space that extends beyond it. The shock of the real most forcefully emerges out of the way it stands juxtaposed against an ideal. And, most important, the ability to act on the shock to categories represents the ability to negotiate the ambiguity of the edge. This ability, in turn, is directly connected to what it means to live on the edge. Because of this, "edginess" can be either debilitating and unpleasant or enabling and exciting. Depending on whom one asks, the idea of living on the edge can signal either opportunity or despair, power or exclusion.

Three Bombs and a Supermarket:
Despair and Opportunity on the Edge

A friend of mine in Hóc Môn, a man named Dũng in his late thirties, used to make the same joke over and over, almost every day when we drank coffee and read the morning newspaper. The papers informed us that Hans Blix and the United Nations weapons inspection teams were in Iraq. The Vietnamese dailies printed articles discussing how the U.S. military was building up for a possible attack. Reading this, Dũng told me he hoped they would bomb Hóc Môn. Instead of talking about real politics in either Vietnam or abroad, instead of making the parallels between the Vietnam War and Iraq that U.S. commentators were making at the time, he kept joking that I should tell President George W. Bush to finish off Hóc Môn. Dũng's joke started out with a single bomb, but grew to include two more bombs reserved for the points of administrative power in Vietnam as well. "Ba trái bom" (Three bombs), he would say, "one for Hanoi, one for Saigon, and one right here on this café in Hóc Môn." "Go report to Mr. Bush."

This was a common kind of half-joking, half-serious, and, more often than not, tormented comment people would make about living in the mixed-use rural–urban zone McGee calls a "city–village" *désakota* zone but Vietnamese people call *ngoại thành*. Of course, Dũng did not *really* want to suffer from an air raid. But he did not have very nice things to say about where he lived in Hóc Môn, either. He joked that bombing it would be the only way to start over. Day after day, looking around at the landscape as he told the joke, it seemed difficult to keep calling it a joke in the strict sense of the term. It seemed more like an expression of resentment and desperation, of his inability to do anything with this space he lived in.

Like many other men in Hóc Môn, Dũng was effectively underemployed. His wife's parents owned the café he spent his time in, which was in itself a symbol of his failure to live up to a patrilineal ideal, and he managed to make a small income using the café space to sell lottery tickets, to run a covert numbers game, and to collect bets during European soccer matches televised on the café television. Although he was never forthcoming about his exact income and the sources of his money, he and his wife had managed to build a small single-story brick home in a neighborhood of red-dirt alleys not far from the café. Dũng and his family had enough to live on but were not able to save much. As he described it, Hóc Môn offered no opportunity for advancement. Everyone was stupid, *dốt!* His choice of words was important here. He used the northern rather than the southern Vietnamese word for stupid to enforce his conviction that this was a certain stupidity imposed by northern cadres responsible for the recent developmental direction of Vietnam.

But Dũng had a friend—a Vietnamese American man who saw power and potential in the melee that was Hóc Môn. A former officer in the South Vietnamese army, Hoàn spent the postwar years in a reeducation camp along with Dũng's older brother Hùng. When he was released in the 1980s, he moved to the United States on a special visa that granted asylum to former allies of the Americans who had spent extended periods in the camps. In the United States he spent many years working at menial jobs in several East Coast cities until the late 1990s, when he received a large amount of worker's compensation in response to a claim he filed following an on-the-job accident in a Boston-area factory. With this money, Hoàn returned to Hóc Môn and bought a plot of land near the An Hạ canal. He then bought a thousand pigs and built a large warehouselike structure where he raised the pigs for slaughter.

Hoàn was a man of excess, combining extreme ambition and almost comical enthusiasm with an insatiable love for drinking, eating, and singing karaoke. In contrast to Dũng, he described Hóc Môn as a place of opportunity forged from its reckless abandon, a place where anything was possible. The same lack of order Dũng decried was for Hoàn exactly what made things possible. Hoàn used the example of his own success to underscore his optimism: where else could one use worker's compensation payments to buy a poor farmer's rice field and convert it into a successful slaughterhouse? He grew excited talking about such things, and his excitement increased as he began explaining his next big project: to convert his pigs into a supermarket. He already had the land, purchased with profits from his pigs. He offered me a ride down the highway to Hóc Môn's Bùi Môn commune in order to see the plot of land he had purchased to build his supermarket. He was so drunk on his motorbike that I made an excuse to meet him there later instead.

As we toured the L-shaped, thousand-square-meter plot of land, Hoàn described what the building would look like, explained the kinds of bricks he would use, talked about the tiles, mused about what he would sell there, and compared it to other supermarkets in the center of Saigon. Then he pointed to a locked gate near the back of the property that some hired hands were boarding shut with plywood, rusty wires, and other materials. Deep tire tracks led from the gate out to the face of the highway, indicating that it led to an access road to the space behind Hoàn's property. This, he said with a laugh, was the greatest thing about his new supermarket. When he finished construction, his supermarket would block the only possible entrance to a garment factory that lay behind the land. He shook the gate, emphasizing how sturdy it was. It was *his* land, and he was not going to let the factory traffic pass through any more.

He gave a little chuckle and rhetorically asked how they were going to get the goods in and out of their factory. "Airplane," he said, answering his own question with a laugh. There was no other way in and out. Hoàn could not stop laughing. He had offered to sell his land to the factory owners many years earlier, but they had refused to buy it. Now they were caught in a bind, he laughed, because he was going ahead with his plans to build his supermarket, and they would not have a road anymore. He said all this with a slight glimmer of excitement. He seemed happy to get back at them for not buying his property when they could have and for not selling him some property in the area earlier when he wanted to buy it. This was why he had invited me—to perform his triumph before me.[10]

I give the two contrasting examples of Dũng and Hoàn to emphasize the ways in which one's vision of space depends on one's position within the social order of things. These two friends were looking at the same kind of space: disorderly, unorganized space where a factory or a supermarket can grow out of a garden plot. Using purely objective concepts to describe the configuration of mixed rural and mixed urban space does not explain the diverging experiences of two friends like Dũng and Hoàn. Yet turning to simplifying "cultural logics" also fails to explain the differences between these two. On their own, neither objective descriptions nor cultural explanations can really say whether these spaces make sense both to the people who live in them and to the people who have the power to create policies about them. When people like Dũng and Hoàn look at places like Hóc Môn, they certainly understand and see the objective transformations going on, and ethnographic evidence also makes it clear that they refract their vision of such changes through cultural categories that idealize the opposition of space into pure rural and urban types. They read the same commingling of ideal categories in different ways; one of them loathes this space, while the other one thrives in it.

In an important sense, despite the divergent subjective feelings of these friends about Hóc Môn—whether it evokes optimism or despair, power or a sense of exclusion—both interpretations depend on the fact that it lies between categories. For Hoàn, this position outside of the established order of things offers powerful possibilities. For Dũng, this position signals failure to fulfill an ideal and stands as another example of the seemingly abstract processes that have produced his sense of being edged out of potential opportunities. Objectively, the binary categories of rural and urban may appear irrelevant to explaining the space as one or another of these idealized poles, but the categories still inform the way people imagine space. How does the persistence of these categories color the fact of living in spaces that lie between them? Why do spaces like Hóc Môn fall into the gray zone of consciousness for some and stand out as great sites of potential for others? The question is not whether they are "visible" but how it is possible that they are seen as both ugly and enticing. Why would it occur to Dũng to say that it would be a good idea to drop a few bombs there? Even if he was joking, why the *thought?* And what is it about the configuration of space that allows Hoàn to treat Hóc Môn space in such a way that its very disorder signifies possibility?

The Symbolic Political Economy of Social Edginess

The symbolic meaning of a space between categories is particularly shifty. In an important sense, Hóc Môn appears as a classic example of what Mary Douglas described as "matter out of place," a place that causes despair specifically for the ways it represents "that which must not be included for a pattern to be maintained."[11] Looking at representations of the outer-city district, the unpleasant mixing of categories appears as the greatest problem in Hóc Môn. It is, to borrow Victor Turner's classic phrase, "betwixt and between." Symbolically, this is like the problem of getting drinking water from a well in the cemetery. Or, following Durkheim, it epitomizes that kind of "social anomie" that comes when people no longer understand their role in the larger social order of things, when the division of labor in society becomes a divisive rather than a cohesive force.[12]

In large part, what Douglas would term the danger and what Durkheim might term the social anomie of the edge emerges from the fact that it falls between the strict categories used to conceptualize society in terms of rural versus urban and inside versus outside. Indeed, as the insights of Douglas and Durkheim reveal, the fact that Hóc Môn is both rural and urban, no longer outside the city but not yet inside, produces a sort of dissonance between the categories available for describing the world in ideal terms and the way the world actually works. In this way, Hóc Môn appears "dirty" or "dangerous," the perfect place to put the city dump and the camp for heroin addicts.

But clearly this anomie is not universal. Hóc Môn's marginal position on the edge of ideal categories produces different effects. As in the case of other marginal spaces (including physical, ritual, and symbolic margins) described in ethnographic literature, the meaning of this position in between dominant categories depends on context. As Douglas observes, margins can be "powerful" as well as dangerous.[13] In a similar fashion, Anna Tsing emphasizes the inherent ambiguity of margins, seeing them as "an analytical placement that makes evident both the constraining, oppressive quality of cultural exclusion and the creative potential of re-articulating, enlivening, and rearranging the very social categories that peripheralize a group's existence." Margins are "sites from which to see the instability of social categories . . . the zones of unpredictability at the edges of discursive stability."[14] People living in marginalized spaces may at times be excluded from social life, but they also pose a powerful threat to it or gain a certain potentiality from this position. Likewise, both the optimistic and the desperate approaches to space in Hóc Môn derive from the categorical otherness of its status as a space between the pure categories of rural and urban.

Yet these insights about the inherent danger or power of marginal spaces and the symbolic potential of space between categories do not explain the difference between those who feel excluded by this margin-ality and those who feel empowered by it. Although contemporary Hóc Môn can certainly be understood as a marginal space, this fact explains very little on its own. For the *meaning* of that marginal position depends on the context within which one construes social relations. The subjec-tive view of what that space means—whether it is seen as presenting opportunity or viewed with despair—depends on the hierarchical posi-tions of the actors in question. The way this experience of space effects social action depends on the ability of social actors to manipulate this ambiguity of categories. It depends on their ability to act within and upon the world rather than having the world act upon them. But this ability is not a simple question of "will." There are symbolic, political, economic, and social-structural constraints on the ability to manipulate the ambi-guity of categories.

The Outer-City Official and the Factory Manager

This became clear to me when I visited a shoe factory with Mrs. Tuyến, the vice chairwoman of the People's Committee in Hóc Môn's Tân Thới Nhì commune.[15] Confounding the stereotype of the self-interested party cadre, Mrs. Tuyến was a hardworking administrator, respected by the community and dedicated to serving its interests. She worked full days on the People's Committee and also regularly attended evening law classes in central Ho Chi Minh City, where she was trying to improve her under-standing of the new legal apparatus regarding land-use regulations and local administration. With her administrative duties, her legal studies, and her own work running a household, Mrs. Tuyến was constantly on the move and slept an average of only five hours a night. Everyone in the community knew her by name, and none of them had any complaints about her honesty. She was a local, dedicated to local interests.

We went together to meet with Mr. Tuấn, the Vietnamese manager of Lan Hương Enterprises, a Vietnamese–Korean joint-venture shoe factory that employed six hundred workers, five hundred on the sewing lines and one hundred on the cutting and gluing lines. Our conversation was very superficial, focusing on worker safety and wages, which were paid at a piece rate and ranged from 500 thousand đồng (US$33) per month for new employees to as much as 1.2 million đồng (US$80) during peak production periods for more experienced work-floor heads. Three Korean quality control managers also lived in apartments onsite and earned wages of between US$2,000 and US$3,000 per month.

This conversation was interesting because Mrs. Tuyến and I were able to engage the manager in only very superficial talk about the activities of the factory. Here was the vice chair of one of those feared Vietnamese People's Committees interviewing a shoe factory owner, and we spent most of our time simply learning about how the shoes were made. It was like a field trip to see where shoes come from. Mr. Tuấn evaded any pressing questions about worker safety and concentrated mostly on talking about how the presence of the factory was improving the local economy. He pointed out that locals have been able to open cafés, small housewares shops, and restaurants to serve the workers. And many locals have built additions to their homes that serve as dormitories for the workers.

When I asked about the waste produced by the factory, Mr. Tuấn diverted the question by saying that there was no chemical run-off from the production of the shoes because the constituent parts were all produced elsewhere.[16] He said that he, too, was concerned about pollution and immediately started talking about a different factory nearby, a rusted and rain-stained corrugated metal factory down the road that leaks chemicals and heavy metals into the vegetable fields surrounding it. "Was anybody going to do anything about that place?" he asked. Mrs. Tuyến explained that nothing could be done because "the City issued its papers." Everyone knew that the corrugated metal factory was ruining the local fields around it because the vegetable plants had first started losing their leaves and then stopped growing altogether. But then she added that the commune-level authorities did not issue the permit to build the factory there in the first place. It was issued by the central planning office and approved by the Ho Chi Minh City People's Committee. Local-level commune authorities can do nothing besides file an official complaint with the city.

At this point our discussion with the factory manager moved away from his factory to Mrs. Tuyến's own downbeat explanation of the fact that local officials have no power to regulate their own districts. It was a strange scene. The vice chair of the People's Committee was openly lamenting her lack of authority to the factory manager. Mrs. Tuyến described how orders about the organization of administrative divisions and the mapping of space emanate from the city center as directives to be simply implemented by the officials at the communal level. At the level of the communal administration as a whole, the local members of the People's Committees serve as little more than administrators charged with implementing pronouncements sent out as "instructions" from the center. The local cadres represent small cogs in the machinery used to carry out policy, but they seem to have a very limited role in influencing that policy as a whole.

The factory manager nodded in apparent sympathy. He said that Mrs. Tuyến really seemed to care about her district and that she was a very good official. Then, with a condescending smile, he asked, in a feigned compliment, "When will you become the head of the whole district of Hóc Môn?" She laughed and said that she could not dare to harbor such ambitions. She reminded him that she was just a local who did not have the education needed for such a position. What had started out as an attempt to interview the factory manager about working conditions devolved into a revelation of local-level political weakness. The talk about the other factory and the revelation of her own low status in the administrative hierarchy made it clear that it was the factory manager who was in control of our conversation.

After we left the shoe factory, Mrs. Tuyến and I continued talking. In addition to her lack of education, she said that the nature of politics really precluded a woman's getting involved with the actual decision-making process, which takes place in informal situations behind closed doors. She worked hard as vice chair, and she attended classes that improved her qualifications, but she explained that she would really never be able to know the way that decisions about the spatial dynamics of Hóc Môn are made because they are made in unofficial male realms such as karaoke rooms and in drinking sessions. No matter how much she advanced in the administrative apparatus, she could never become an insider in this gendered male space of political decision making. She had two strikes against her: she came from rural origins, and she was a woman.

As a female representing a commune in an outer-city district, Mrs. Tuyến was doubly outside. But her exclusion from the politics of planning the community extended to the entire commune-level administration. This is not simply about male cadres excluding female cadres from political decision making. Instead it is more about the relationship between the inside and the outside and how the inside exploits the symbolic ambiguity of the outside district for its own purposes. For all intents and purposes, decisions about land usage on the urban–rural fringe are not really based on the appropriateness of different uses to rural or urban space. Instead the politics of land usage depends on the manipulation of these categories in ways that privilege the reproduction of the "inside."

Hóc Môn is depicted as alternately rural or urban depending on how its classification fits the symbolic and economic message of the inner-city administration. For example, in the rhetoric used to promote new industrial zones in the so-called rural outer-city districts, planners and city boosters negotiate the ambiguous nature of the space to sometimes claim that the area is rural and sometimes claim it is urban. For Vietnam to compete on the international market and to attract foreign direct investment, it has to portray itself as a place with plentiful cheap labor and plentiful cheap land to construct factories. In both symbolic and real terms, the cheapest land is rural land and the best markets are urban markets. With these wide-open swaths of space designated as rural hinterlands within easy reach of downtown, the city is able to portray itself as an untapped frontier ready for new investment as well as a space with established markets. From the perspective of the urban center, maintaining the fiction that Hóc Môn is rural encourages the idea that it can provide the city with cheap foodstuffs, that the people there can live cheaply and therefore survive on low wages, and it provides a sort of escape valve for the unbridled expansion of the city. Rural imagery attracts buyers looking for cheap land and labor to build factories, as well as urban land speculators looking to purchase real estate at rural values in the hope that they will be able to capture the price differential by someday converting it to urban land uses.[17]

The notion that Hóc Môn is outside also places outer-city cadres in a submissive relationship to city-center decision makers. This is further exacerbated by questions of economic and political manipulation, where the very manipulation of administrative categories such as rural and urban intensify the distinction between *nội* and *ngoại* for clearly strategic ends. But *nội* and *ngoại* are themselves flexible categories that refer to spatial relations as well as to social relations and can be manipulated by social actors themselves. Because they are implicit to kinship as well as the city, the social experience of life cannot be divorced from the politics and economics of space in the city. This becomes clear in the following story of a marriage, where the submissive position of being outside also offers a chance to gain economic independence.

"Happy Happy, Sad Sad": On the State of Being Inside Out

The experience of the newlyweds Thu and Phong helps illustrate the connections between the symbolic meanings of inside and outside and the opportunity potentially afforded by life in the outer city. In their marriage, the wife's symbolic move "from the inside out" produced a certain sense of social exclusion. But she accepted this situation in order to negotiate the political-economic realities of contemporary Ho Chi Minh City.

When Thu married into Phong's family, she learned two lessons about the existential state of living on the edge. After meeting and falling in love at their workplace in the Saigon Hotel Equatorial, they decided to get married. After the wedding, Thu moved from her family's home in central Saigon to *xã* Tân Thới Nhì in the outer-city district of Hóc Môn, where Phong's family had arranged to buy a plot of land for them. In a sense, Thu was moving in two directions at once: from the inside out and from the outside in, in both cases becoming an outsider in relation to the inside. Physically speaking, she was moving from the inside of the city to the outer-city district where she would become an outsider in relation to the inner-city district she had come from. At the same time she was moving into the patrilineage of her husband Phong, where she would be an outsider living in the inside. Although they were moving outside of the patrilocal unit into a new home of their own, their land was part of the patriline's property because his parents had purchased it for them.

What was it like to be newly married? Thu laughed and sighed: "Vui vui, buồn buồn" (Happy happy, sad sad). Hóc Môn was "boring," she continually emphasized, but she also conceded that it was great to have a new home with her husband. She loved her husband but grew tired of the obligations to his family. At death anniversaries, she was relegated to the women's table in the kitchen, preparing food for the men in Phong's family to eat while they consumed massive quantities of alcohol. But the marriage also provided a new kind of economic independence. Because the couple's new home had an open doorway facing the highway running through Hóc Môn, they opened a business together selling canisters of cooking gas, bottled water, and gas stoves out of an addition facing the road.

As Thu described it, the home appeared to offer a great opportunity as well as a set of intense obligations. On the up side, this street-facing property enabled them to run their own business, no longer working for a wage at the hotel. On the down side, Thu explained that she could never leave the store because she had to stay and guard the business while Phong delivered the water and gas to customers in the area on the back of his motorbike. He was always in and out of the house, and she had to stay home. Not only this, but Thu claimed that she had made more money when she was working at the hotel than they were making now. And she also missed the chance to speak with foreigners at the hotel, where she could use the English she had studied so hard in school.

As Thu put it, they were living the dream of independence and suffering the consequences as well. Although they had their own home and still had the same interests and desires they had when they lived and worked in central Saigon, she explained that they felt trapped out in Hóc Môn, bored, tied to this shop. They were propertied but bound to that property as well. Although they had the financial means to take a vacation, she could not imagine going anywhere. "Who would watch the shop?" she asked. When she found out she was pregnant, she had to ask her brother from Saigon to come out for the day to watch the shop while Phong took her on the back of his motorbike to the downtown clinic for tests.

Thu's experience helps clarify some of the affective aspects of social edginess by indicating how the idiom of being outside generates a sense of subservience to the inside at the very same time that it produces a sense of new potentials. There was a very clear connection between the way she felt as an outsider in her new family and the way she felt as an outsider in relation to Ho Chi Minh City itself. Moving to Hóc Môn, Thu worried about her relationship with Phong because she was bound to the house and he was able to move around the area, meeting people and making connections. Yet this moving around and making connections was essential to the reproduction of the inner realm of the home, for that was how Phong could do business and accumulate the resources necessary to support the home itself. Thu's role was also important, because staying home allowed Phong to move about delivering their products and developing a new customer base. The stereotypical complementary relationship of husband and wife actually underscored their business strategy, and the form almost directly mimicked the ideal complementarity of country and city seen in descriptions of rural–urban relations. The very fact that they had a strong localized home/business grounded in space allowed them to consolidate resources accumulated through Phong's expansive forays into the community.

However, although this ideal of a symbiotic relationship between inside and outside seemed functionally sound as a business theory, it produced certain contradictions. Although the couple had met each other in central Ho Chi Minh City, Thu was really an insider to the city and Phong was an outsider. He was from Củ Chi district (the *ngoại thành* district farthest from the center of the city, just beyond Hóc Môn), and she was originally from central Saigon, decidedly *nội thành*. In this sense, she was the insider in relation to the city and he was the outsider. But in their move to Hóc Môn, he became the insider in two ways and she became the outsider in two ways. Phong's move put him in contact with a wide range of social relations throughout the community, while Thu became effectively confined to her home. She constantly worried about her neighbors, whom she barely knew, who she openly told me were "talking" about her, gossiping. Phong ignored such concerns; he had good relations with people throughout the area. He did not see his neighbors as suspicious at all.[18]

Here spatial mobility and the ability or inability to extend one's social relations across space have become key factors in the interpretation of social relations. The husband, Phong, effectively gained spatial free reign at the very moment that he solidified his position within the inner patrilineal realm. Furthermore, by marrying Thu and moving to Tân Thới Nhì, he established connections closer to the city while maintaining those in his home in Củ Chi, effectively expanding his spatial domain. Thu, by contrast, became increasingly bound spatially, and she expressed it readily as the sadness that came despite her apparent happiness at getting married. *Happy happy, sad sad.*

This double sense of the edge as both liberating and suffocating— of being "happy happy, sad sad"—most clearly identifies the ambiguous effects of social ediness. This ambiguity emerges from the way relationships among people themselves hinge on contradictory idioms of inclusion and exclusion cast in terms of the spatialized notion of inside and outside. For Thu, the move to Hóc Môn represented a move outside of the city center, putting her outside of Ho Chi Minh City at the same time that she became decoupled from her own patriline in the center. In her new marriage she felt the same sense in inverted form; she moved to the inside of her husband's lineage but entered it as an outsider. Her connection to her own patriline in Saigon was converted from an insider's relationship to one that could be maintained only through the bilateral model of kinship.

The ability or inability to move between these different levels of inside and outside connections both maps kinship idioms onto space and emerges as a key indicator of social power in the relationship. Phong held the power to move about; Thu had to negotiate to attain it. Even the act of inviting her brother to watch the shop was an appeal to her own bilateral social relations, which in turn enabled her to leave her spatially constrained position in the shop, if only temporarily. Nevertheless, even though her marriage seemed to put her in a spatially constrained position, these sacrifices made sense to Thu because they offered an alternative form of economic independence that she had crafted together with her husband: private homeownership and an independent business with frontage property. Social edginess describes the experience of marginal and indefinable existence in between pure categories—of being both inside and outside as Thu was. But unlike simple marginality, edginess implies negotiation and decision making, with social actors recognizing how seemingly pure categories are shifty symbols, with meanings that change according to context.

Space and Power

The example of Thu and Phong indicates two key points. First, it shows that the power of a spatial position depends on the differential ability to move through and across space. Second, it shows that spatial positions are both symbolic and material. The idiom of inside versus outside provided by Vietnamese kinship is a cultural construction, but the symbolic meaning embedded in this relationship produces very real effects that constrain action in the real world. The ability to manipulate ideal categories, therefore, depends on the ability to navigate different levels across both symbolic and material space. This ability is both material and socially constituted; political and economic constraints on action work in feedback with the power of symbolic representation and meaning to organize the social world.[19] The real materiality of physical space as well as the socially produced oppositions of rural versus urban and inside versus outside are all sociologically important aspects of the landscape that mutually influence each other. In this way, material reality itself exists in dialectical relationship with ideology and social action, what Marx called "praxis" and what Lefebvre refers to as "social space" composed of both mental space and physical space.[20] Ideal concepts of space and actual physical space produce the conditions for each other.

It is not only the Vietnamese state that enforces binary categories that obscure the rural–urban *désakota* or the hybrid social forms produced on the rural–urban fringe.[21] Although the state often does indeed simplify the contours of everyday life for the sake of bureaucratic legibility, everyday people also continue to imagine space in terms of such strict contrasts, even though this other kind of hybrid mix of rural and urban space sits before them, right there before their eyes. The ways that people speak of the categories rural and urban depends on whom one asks and on their socioeconomic position. For example, a young man I shall call T, who worked on his family's farm and rarely left the area immediately surrounding his family land, described the distinction between city and country as more than a false ideal. He experienced this distinction in the material fact that "city people" were buying land, but people in Hóc Môn were working it:

ERIK HARMS: Do you know anyone in this area who worked the fields in the past but now has switched to another profession?

T: Here? There's probably no one who does anything else, [people here] just work these fields. . . . There are some people who come up from the city and buy land but they don't work the fields. The people around here just work the fields, don't do anything else.

EH: What do the city people do? Buy land and work the fields, or . . .

T: They buy the land and leave it.

EH: Leave it?

T: They let us work it.

EH: Let you work it? . . . So the city people are like landlords?

T: They become landlords, because they buy it, they live down there [in the city], come up here, we sell it, they buy it, then they hire people to work it.[22]

In this exchange, the binary categories of country and city became mapped onto the social relations differentiating Hóc Môn residents from "the city people" with great clarity. For this young man, the distinction between country and city is quite real and clarifies why he works the land while city people buy it and hire others to work it. His structural position as an agricultural laborer leaves him very little room to negotiate and play with the symbolic difference between country and city.

A sixty-five-year-old woman whose extended family compound was devoted to making *bánh ướt* (a wet rice noodle) clearly underscored the difference between the country and the city but also noted how these distinctions can and do change when a person moves across space:

I'm a country bumpkin, how can I be a city person! Country folk must be happier, must be cleaner than city people. They must work the vegetable gardens, the fields. . . . You can only tell the difference between country folk and city people when they speak. Because country folk are also refined . . . a lot of times you can't tell the difference. When I go down to the countryside people see me . . . they say I'm a city person. [Ha! Ha! Ha! Laughter.] How can I be a city person! But I dress in clean dry clothes, respectable things . . . they think I am a city person. But me here . . . what kind of city person is this?[23]

A forty-year-old woman who worked as a state official but whose husband was a rice farmer also argued that the distinction between country and city depended on social context: "I am a city person when I'm in between the city, a city person when I return to my *quê* [home province] in Long An . . . a country person when I go to study or for some other kind of work in the city."[24]

For individuals who have the ability to move across social space, the distinction between country and city changes according to context. These two women do not, however, challenge the categories of country and city themselves; instead they reflect on what happens when they move between them. For the farmer, however, the distinction is not so easy to navigate and remains quite fixed. These examples show that there are clear political-economic relations that underlie who is seen as a country person and who is seen as a city person and that the ability to play with the categories is ultimately tied to the ability or inability to move across them. Furthermore, the spatiotemporal understanding of the social organization of inside and outside on the city map inscribes cultural understandings of social relations into geographical space. For the farmer, the ideal of rural and urban complementarities indexes a one-way relation of extraction and exploitation that denigrates the outside while reproducing the inside. Although rural and urban are socially constructed categories, this form of organizing space nevertheless appears quite real in terms of the ways in which it appears to resonate with the social relations and relations of production in which he lives. The meaning of these ideal categories is forged in relation to the material circumstances of those who interpret them.

The Political Economy of Spatial Relations and Ideal Categories

In some cases, reproducing the categories of rural and urban enables people to benefit from the marginal qualities of life on the edge. In other cases, it seems to push them further into a relationship of subordination. This becomes clear when comparing Hoàn (the pig farmer who wants to turn his pigs into a supermarket) with Dũng's older brother Hùng. Their contrasting experiences illustrate the difference between people who see marginality as opportunity and those who see it as despair. The differences are simultaneously symbolic and material.

Hoàn, the successful Vietnamese American pig farmer, often invited pessimistic Dũng's pessimistic and depressed older brother Hùng out for beer and a feast of hot pots and fish soup. Hoàn and Hùng had a special bond because they were old friends who had served together in the southern Vietnamese Army of the Republic of Vietnam and they had both been in reeducation camps following the war. Hoàn had managed to gain asylum and eventually made it to America. Hùng, by contrast, was not in the camp long enough to qualify for the automatic asylum program. He stayed in Hóc Môn, lived in poverty for many years (despite his high level of training, his skills as a mechanic, and his command of English), and had only recently begun steady work again in the Walls ice cream factory in the Củ Chi export-processing zone. Like his brother Dũng, Hùng was not very optimistic about life in Hóc Môn. He worried about making ends meet. He did not like working in a walk-in freezer; emerging from the icy cold at the end of a long workday only seemed to intensify the oppressive heat of Saigon itself. And like his brother Dũng, he certainly did not like Hóc Môn, despite Hoàn's constant insistence that "anything is possible here."

The most apparent difference between someone like Hoàn and someone like Hùng is access to money. Thanks to his access to American dollars, Hoàn is rich. Hùng, by contrast, is relatively poor, and this fact completely determines the degree to which their position on the edge gives them the potential to transform society or puts them at risk of feeling excluded by it. But where does Hoàn's money come from? It comes from outside. This is crucial.

The ability of someone like Hoàn to find potential in the pure binaries of the rural and urban dichotomy depends on the ways in which he can exploit them, which depends not so much on his positive attitude as on his hierarchical relationship to society within Hóc Môn. Thanks to his dollars and, more important, to his American citizenship, Hoàn is effectively able to move inside and outside of Hóc Môn with relative facility. He is able to set down roots and buy land-use rights in Hóc Môn, but he is not bound by the social relations of Hóc Môn itself.

This appears in even the most mundane interactions between these two friends. Hoàn smokes Kamel Red cigarettes, which he buys in bulk at duty-free shops when he travels in and out of Vietnam. When these run out, he buys more in Saigon. He readily offers these cigarettes to anyone who will take them and encourages his friend Hùng to help himself. Normally Hùng, like his brother Dũng, smokes cheap local Bến Thành cigarettes. This small difference in what they smoke immediately shows that Hoàn has money and Hùng does not. But, more important, it also references the source of Hoàn's power. The very fact that a pack of cigarettes from outside the country can create a symbolic hierarchy of consumption indexes a more important form of power that emerges through the crossing of spatially construed boundaries. Although Hoàn claims that his success stems from his positive attitude and his belief in the possibility of self-improvement, it is Hoàn's time in America and his access to capital from outside the locally circumscribed social system that have made all the difference. For a man like Hoàn the trick is quite simple—he has used this money from his worker's compensation payments to buy land when it was cheap agricultural land and is waiting for it to become urban land. In the meantime he raises pigs for slaughter. Hoàn knows that the value of the land itself will increase exponentially as Hóc Môn becomes more and more urbanized over time. This is why he now plans to turn his pigs into a supermarket.

For Hùng, who has no access to outside capital and rarely has occasion to leave the outer-city districts, rising real estate prices simply represent another example of his inability to capitalize on new opportunities.

Transformations are happening all around him, but he has no means of actively participating in them. The difference between these two friends is not simply about a lucky person like Hoàn; it is a political-economic reality that underscores the hierarchical nature of the rural–urban relations of Vietnam today. The difference between them emerges as a difference of mobility between spatially demarcated scales of social space. This structural position is emphasized, wittingly or unwittingly, every time Hoàn pulls out his pack of Kamel Reds.

The pack of cigarettes stands as an unspoken allusion to the classic formula of capital, M-C-M', and Hoàn's structurally advantageous position related to it. In this formula, money (M) begets commodities (C) that can become realized as more money (M'). As Hoàn demonstrates with his business plan in Hóc Môn, one has to spend money to make money. But the money has to come from somewhere. Ultimately, this is the difference between the two friends, for people recognize that money (like the pack of Kamel Reds) has more value when it comes from outside the spatially bound social system. Hoàn's money comes from outside, and he is able to accumulate resources according to the standards of the inside, but Hùng's money comes from the inside, while his labor power produces surplus capital that will be accumulated by the outsiders who own the Walls ice cream company.

There are numerous schemes to access this money outside the system, and they all depend on the ability to control the movement between levels of social relations spatially construed. We can understand this if we take apart the relationship of M-C-M', focusing specifically on the process embedded in commodity production, through which money becomes more money. That is, what do people do at point C to make money magically grow? In this formula, C stands for "commodity." In the simplest sense, money becomes more money when some sort of value is added to the commodity. A classic, "traditional" means of doing this in Hóc Môn is to buy a bag of rice; grind it up; add water, heat, sunshine, and labor; and produce several bags of rice noodles *(bún)*. A kilo of rice sells for about the same price as a kilo of rice noodles.

Effectively, the difference between money (M) and money (M') in the rice noodles emerges through the labor it takes to inject the rice with water. Pound for pound, the bags of noodles that emerge are nothing more than watered-down versions of the original bag of rice. In this case, M-C-M' is the process through which water is injected into the rice before it is resold to produce more money. The water and sun cost almost nothing (depending on whether the water is drawn from a well by hand or by electric pump). Making the fire to cook the batter incurs some fuel costs, but the main source of increased value is the labor of the people who grind the rice, cook the batter into sheets, carry it out to dry in the sun, cut it into noodles, pack it into bags, and then carry it to market. Their reward for these herculean efforts is the difference between M and M', the difference between what it costs to buy a bag of rice and what they can get for selling these water-logged rice grains shaped in the form of noodles.[25]

Now imagine that one could transform money (M) to more money (M') without suffering through the agony of the middle passage from M to C. That is, imagine that one could produce more money without carrying around sacks of rice, grinding the grains, and standing over boiling cauldrons. What if one could make the passage from money to more money without engaging in production, if one could add value without adding one's own labor (or the labor of somebody else)? A passage is still required, but this is a passage not through labor but through and across social space. This is what Hoàn does with his American money, which magically turns into more money when it crosses the border into Vietnam. It is what the Walls ice cream company does when it uses European money to buy Vietnamese labor power.

It is clear that the ultimate source of Hoàn's success is his fortunate access to foreign capital and his ability to cross socially produced boundaries that make his American money more valuable in Vietnam. Hùng cannot do this. This political-economic difference itself transforms the symbolic meaning of space for each of these men. Yet the symbolic meaning of space also makes it possible for this different relationship to exist in the first place. The very fact (even though it is symbolic, it is still a social fact) that Hóc Môn exists as this edge space and that Vietnam exists as a peripheralized marginal economy makes this transformation in the relative value of money possible. The difference between Hoàn and Hùng socially embodies the classic production of a structurally imbalanced relationship between core and peripheral economies.[26]

This extreme example that extends to the level of global finance and capital flows should not obscure the ways in which analogous relations are produced and reproduced at all levels and scales of social life. As I have already shown, the subservient hierarchy of inside to outside is also enshrined in official representations of the city. The relation of the inner city to the outer city itself provides a miniature version of the larger global relation of core and peripheral economies. We see this in a whole variety of economic schemes. When everyday people pass from the city into the countryside, often as part of a daily routine, they are effectively trying to capitalize on the persistence of two alternate spatial regimes of value that allow for the increase of capital while minimizing the application of labor power. The trick is to earn money according to the standards of the city and spend it according to the standards of the countryside. The economy of remittances, to cite another obvious example, works only because it enables one to cross a significant social-spatial divide by conveying the medium of money. What might be an insignificant amount of money in the social circumstances of the United States becomes a fortune in Vietnam. This can also be seen in the ambulant economy of shoulder-pole vendors who live and produce their products on the rural margins of the city and carry them in for sale throughout the city. They live in the outer city, but by selling their goods in the inner city they effectively seek to generate capital in an area where the money is relatively more valuable. In the process, they effectively do what Hoàn does, albeit on a much more modest scale: they obtain money from outside the social space they live in but use it to reproduce their means of subsistence within Hóc Môn. The economic function of the outer city emerges in symbiosis with its relation to the larger Ho Chi Minh City, national, and ultimately international division of labor that produces profit specifically through this process of crossing socially produced boundaries that spatially demarcate different regimes of value.

This relationship thus provides the foundation for the economic logic that underlies everything from large-scale factories and industries to outer-city vegetable gardeners who sell goods in the city and on down to those people who commute to work in the city but live according to the standards and prices of the outer city. On varying scales and to different degrees, with more or less success, they are all doing the same thing that Hoàn does with his American money. And, like Hoàn, they require the passage from one space to another, a passage that itself rests on a socially produced notion that these spaces are *different.*

In the end, the difference between people who see the edge as a space of desperation and those who see it as a space of potential depends on whether they can manipulate the economic and symbolic potential of the edge or whether they are manipulated by their position on the edge itself.

The difference lies in the degree to which people are able to transcend the limitations of the localized spatial relationships of Hóc Môn to Ho Chi Minh City itself. Edginess, crafted in relation to a set of idealized binary categories, becomes empowering when one can transcend the categories themselves by escaping the bounds of the social system constituted by them; it becomes imperiling and alienating when the categories themselves define the limits of social action. For Hoàn, Saigon's edge is a temporary position within a larger field of social relations that extends beyond Ho Chi Minh City and even beyond Vietnam. For Hùng, Saigon's edge constitutes his total field of social relations. Hoàn is empowered; Hùng claims to feel powerless and excluded.

Power and Exclusion on the Edge

There is no real physical edge to the city, no point where the city stops and the countryside begins. But the categories of country and city and inside and outside themselves seem to demand such a strict division. The ambivalent conflict between the sense of power and the sense of exclusion that people feel toward their surroundings—what I call social edginess—emerges from the fact that people cannot readily define the edge of the city in practice, while ideal conceptual categories lead them to expect that such an edge exists. Objectively speaking, these categories and associations of rural and urban cannot be physically located on the landscape in any fixed manner. Yet people continue to reproduce them as if they were utterly real, tangible, seemingly material truths. These categories form what Bourdieu has called "officializing discourses," idealized paradigms that define the bounds of the thinkable, even when every case in practical action seems to break the paradigm.[27] But the official also permeates the everyday. The fact that these conceptions of rural and urban persist as categories for the proper organization of people across accepted conventions of space, time, and social hierarchy does not disappear with the development and transformation of the landscape. As a result, people look at the world using these categories, regardless of whether anyone really fits them.

The potential power these categories offer softens the threat of dispossession, and people often play into the reproduction of imperiling ideals that ultimately relegate many of them to the margins of the city. I argue that the double sense of potential power and exclusion inherent to social edginess as both a political-economic and a symbolic position of living in between pure social categories helps explain why people living on the edge contribute to the reproduction of this edginess. Although it is clear that a sense of permanent marginality between categories seems to produce a sense of despair for some, many people also manipulate the very potential of marginal space in order to manipulate the categories that purportedly organize the world. This social edginess can thus represent the cutting edge of possibility or the edge that cuts, the possibility of social advancement or the sharp edge of social marginalization.

The next two chapters expand this analysis by looking at the temporal dimensions of this same process. The double edge of space on Saigon's edge builds from and emerges out of a social oscillation between the future and the past in a temporal orientation that elides the spatial ambiguities of the present day with a belief in the salvation politics of the future. Because there is no limit to Saigon's edge, the future can seem limitless as well.

Part II

Space, Time, and Urban Expansion

3. Future Orientations in the Country of Memory
Social Conceptions of Time

There is no fairyland where people experience time in a way that is
markedly unlike the way in which we do ourselves, where there is no past,
present and future, where time stands still, or chases its own tail, or swings
back and forth like a pendulum. . . . There are only other clocks, other
schedules to keep abreast of, other frustrating delays, happy anticipations,
unexpected turns of events and long stretches of grinding monotony.

—Alfred Gell, *The Anthropology of Time*

Future Orientations in the "Country of Memory"

Ten years ago there were hardly any houses here, said "Red-Faced" Minh
"Mặt Đỏ," the *xe ôm* motorbike driver who often gave me a ride to my
field site from the end of the inner-city bus line. *Just vegetable gardens
and rice fields, a scattered bunch of leaf-roofed shacks (nhà lá).*

The air-conditioned Saigon Star bus with cheap fares subsidized by
the city stopped at the An Sương bus station in Hóc Môn's Bà Điểm commune. *Xe ôm* drivers would take me the final eight kilometers out to my
field site in Tân Thới Nhì commune at the far edge of Hóc Môn district.
As we rode, motorbike drivers like Minh would often point toward the
dusty haze of cement block buildings lining the road that leads from central Ho Chi Minh City to the outer-city district of Hóc Môn. They would
say that these brothels disguised as hotels were once part of a U.S. military depot and that they were now the property of northern Vietnamese
(Bắc kỳ) who had served the revolutionary cause. They would lament
the slow progress of road construction, curse the dust and scattered rocks,
dodge the obstacle course of construction materiel left strewn about the
road, and repeat the common gossipy pun about corrupt construction company heads: they do not just "build" *(xây cất);* they "build in order to
take" *(xây để mà cất).*[1] Some assured me that the road would be finished
soon. Others had no idea if it would ever be finished. It had been three
years already.

They spoke into the wind. They told me these things over one shoulder as we sped down the road. Amid the rumbling thunder of passing

trucks, the sounding of air horns on the half-finished highway, and the whipping wind of our own motion across the landscape, the motorbike drivers would help me try to imagine the changing look of this once rural area now set within the current whirlwind of rapid development and a growing city.

This section of National Highway 22 was being upgraded into the Vietnam section of the Trans-Asia Highway, the *Xuyên Á*. It continued past Củ Chi to the border post at Mộc Bài in Tây Ninh province and eventually on to distant Phnom Penh, Cambodia; but we would stop at the Lam Sơn intersection in Tân Thới Nhì, exactly eighteen kilometers from the heart of Saigon's District 1. Over sweetened iced coffee at the café Lam Sơn, we would talk about Hóc Môn, about the landscape we had just traversed by motorbike. These conversations about space always ended up as discussions about social change; spatial transformation gave clues to history, to the political distribution of power in the here and now, and led to anticipatory ideas about the future and what it might hold.

As we cleaned the accumulated dust from our nostrils and the cracks of our eyes, it became clear that these discussions about change held delicate double meanings that always had to be read in several ways at once. The voices of people I spoke to in Hóc Môn alternately held an air of triumph and a wisp of nostalgia. Proud comments about progress and excited statements about the potential promises of national development were often tempered by a sense of loss, a longing for a mythologized past. In these kinds of discussions, the transformation of Hóc Môn appeared as a double edge. People described the district as if it lay on the edge of the city, but this was not a purely geographical description of where it lay in space. More important, descriptions of Hóc Môn marked the edge as a mixture of orientations to time, a sensibility that combined a distinct future orientation with a symbolically charged form of nostalgia described by scholars who have taken to calling Vietnam "the country of memory."[2] As local residents described it, Hóc Môn lay somewhere in the middle of this temporal mix of present, past, and future; descriptions of the here and now oscillated between a vanishing rural past and the vanguard of modernization. The sense of place implied a sense of time as well as space. Where Hóc Môn was and where it was going always evoked a sense of *when* it was; the question of where it lay in space was also a question of where it was in time.

And yet where it was in time was a key indicator of what kind of place it was. This question of time, this double sensibility of nostalgia and longing, this "future orientation in the country of memory," I argue, provides an important explanation of why people reproduce the categories of country and city that seemingly keep them "on the edge" and exclude them from the full benefits of urban citizenship. Even people exceedingly critical of the Communist Party often turned toward pure concepts of the future and the past as a means of transcending the imperfections of the present and to elide the failure of space to fit into ideal categories of cultural order. Today Hóc Môn is neither rural nor urban, but a future orientation allows one to imagine what it will be like once it becomes urban, and an emphasis on memory allows one to imagine a time when it was marked by a certain rural purity. This oscillation between orientations to the district's imaginary perfection in the future and the past allows a sort of escape from the imperfect present. Yet it also hones the sharp divide between categories and contributes to the reproduction of the categories as binary oppositions. Reproducing such categories perpetuates the state of social edginess. For the present is never really either of these things, and social life as experienced in the here and now is almost always inauthentic when viewed against these pure poles.

This process amounts to a form of what Gramsci calls domination through consent, the everyday acceptance of cultural ideology in the face of circumstances that would seem to undermine it. People often critique the Communist Party, but they seem to agree, wittingly or unwittingly, with the party's teleological ideals of progress and tradition. Looking carefully at time orientation on Ho Chi Minh City's rural urban margin gives us an understanding of how political legitimacy builds upon a notion of "urbanization" *(đo thị hóa)*, "development" *(phát triển)*, and progress *(tiến bộ)* that promises a forever-arriving better future *(tương lai tốt đẹp)*. Examining these concepts of forward advancement through time also gives us a clue to the operation of power through the manipulation of access to different temporal modes. I begin with this movement across a road both scarred by development and given hope by development, with people like Minh cursing space as we traverse it and yet idealizing progress all the while. This experience serves as an introduction to the double bind of a development dream that hinges on an idiom of sacrificing the present for the hope of a better future and a celebration of the past.

The Politics of Time Orientation

In speaking about this mixture of orientations to time in Hóc Môn, I am not interested in a metaphysical question about what time itself might be. Instead I am interested in questions of time use, of what people do with time (the subject of the next chapter) and time-orientation, how people experience the passage of time through the lens of collective categories and subjective ideas about their relationship to social action and to the past, present, and future (the subject of this chapter). In Vietnam I never encountered a fairyland of different time sensibilities.[3] But the idea of time came up in myriad ways, and there were many socially construed ways of interpreting it. Although my friends and acquaintances in Hóc Môn held ideas similar to mine about what time *was*, we had infinite discussions about what people (should) do with time and how different people relate to it. When I speak of "social time," then, I am not trying to argue for a fundamentally different understanding of how time works or for a mystical other understanding of causality but am interested in what Gell calls "the manifold ways in which time becomes salient in human affairs."[4] I show that Hóc Môn residents conceive of their social space in terms of temporal categories associated with (mainly urban) development and a (mainly rural) sense of preserving the past during a period of rapid spatial transformation. The sense of time I refer to is thus both concrete and relative. My conversation partners and I all agreed on the idea of such things as history *(lịch sử)*, the past *(quá khứ)*, the future *(tương lai)*, the present *(hiện tại)*, and time itself *(thời gian)*. In this chapter I describe what people in Hóc Môn make of these ideas and how orientations to them inform social action in the here and now.

Time, Space, and Social Change

Social change is itself a temporal concept, and we can begin to understand what social change means only if we look at how social actors give meaning to simultaneity, sequence, interval, duration, change, and other aspects of what Dilthey calls the "lived experience of time."[5] Although scholars of a religious bent intent on proving the existence of God may ultimately be correct when they argue, as Saint Augustine did, that time is purely an ideal with no "real" content, Dilthey argues that the social experience of time must guide the "human sciences," for time and temporality have very real effects in "the life actually lived."[6] Even a metaphysician like

Saint Augustine agreed that people use conventions in speaking about time, that they must turn to common expressions in order to express a socially accepted understanding of time. Although these conventions elide what religious thinkers see as the ultimate mystery of time, they allow for social action. We speak of time as if it exists, as if it were a thing, despite the Augustinian argument that "past" and "future" simply do not exist as physical facts. Even Augustine conceded that "we say these things and listen to them, we are understood and understand."[7] In this chapter I am interested not in whether time exists but in what happens when concepts about time are understood to mean things and how this understanding affects lived reality and social relations. Although time itself may not have material content, the effects of time can be quite material indeed.

That is why I began this chapter on the back of a motorbike, speaking of time as Minh and I traveled across space. As we rode down the highway we were engaging with time first in a temporal idiom of change that unfolded over an expanse of linear historical time that is directed forward in a process of development. The prefatory remark *Ten years ago . . .* actually prefigures an inherently historicized commentary on how the present came to be, which itself prefaces speculation about the future. Development takes time; ideally it moves forward in step with time. When development is impeded, time continues to move forward; development thus falls behind, and the task is to "catch up."

Second, reflections on the space of Hóc Môn were couched in terms of a spatial-temporal model that associated different kinds of spaces within a double hierarchy of temporality. On the one hand, the hierarchical valuation of places was framed by the linear notion of progress forward through time on the path toward modernization *(hiện đại hóa)*. On the other hand, there was an alternative hierarchy of place that stressed antiquity and origins. Both conceptions hinged on the linear notion of time, but the valuation of social life within that linear scheme varied according to context. In general terms, rural space was traditional *(truyền thống)*, and urban space was modern *(hiện đại)*; the task for those living in the present was to discover which of these Hóc Môn was and what it meant to be one or the other.

Third, the very idea of the city developing and expanding across space implies a temporal relation. It quite literally takes time for the city's edge to move across the landscape. You can almost feel the city growing on its edge. This feeling leads to a situation in which people associate spatial difference with a sense of separation and movement in time. But even this practical understanding of how time and space relate to each other takes on symbolic meaning. For the relationship between time and space is itself subject to change; Hóc Môn is thirty to forty-five minutes away from District 1 by motorbike, an hour or two by bus, half a day by bicycle. The idea of a forward-moving triumph over the problem of spatial separation through technical advances in time-space compression signified a temporal orientation of its own. The material manifestations of what David Harvey calls the tendency of contemporary capitalism to "annihilate space through time" were seen by many Hóc Môn residents as markers of progress linked by a generalized framework of associating technical with social advancement.[8]

Fourth, this idea that certain spaces can be associated with certain moments in social evolution rests upon a whole range of symbolic associations about the connection between space and time in everyday life. These associations link temporal practices with certain kinds of people who live in certain kinds of places—modern urbanites rushing around to meet the demands of the workaday world and rural laborers rising at the crack of dawn, sleeping during the hot noon, and following the patterns of the agricultural calendar rather than the tick-tock press of the clock. That is, people held deep beliefs about how rural space could be associated with a kind of rural time orientation and urban space could be associated with a kind of urban time orientation. Again, people living in the present often tried to explain what kind of time orientation existed in Hóc Môn, for this was intricately connected to the understanding of what kind of place it was. And this constant struggle to place Hóc Môn within temporal categories persisted even when the practical reality of experience defied the linear categories used to associate certain times with certain spaces.

These four temporal lenses are all entangled with each other. They all inform and emerge from the idea of space, and they illuminate the subjective experience of social transformation in a time of socialist market reform.

Teleology and Social Change:
Spatial Transformation Unfolding through Time

There are places in Hóc Môn where it almost seems possible to watch the city's edge crawl outward in space (see Figures 4 and 5). The built

FIGURE 4. Platted subdivisions. The brick grid lines mark the outlines of houses to be constructed on subdivided land. Hóc Môn district.

FIGURE 5. New construction along the Trans-Asia Highway. Hóc Môn district.

landscape shows the traces of this movement; one sees it in the brick grid lines of foundations marked off for homes yet to be built on subdivided land; in the odd triangular plots of paddy land hemmed in by new buildings, gas stations, and new roads; in the fresh tarmac, new flyovers, the pavement rollers. One senses change in the workers breaking stones to fill dirt roads, in the demolished houses on the shoulders of newly widened roads, in construction shops along the highway where one sees brand-new colored tiles and plaster molds of eagles and laurel wreaths that will soon be mounted on the new houses being built. There is a sense of movement, and the images and associations give it the feel of an *advance—Việt Tiến* (Viet Advance), the name of the Vietnamese line of brand-name clothing advertised on shops along the highway. The leaf-roofed houses give way to angular brick and cement homes with aluminum roofs, cement walls painted in fresh pastels, shiny tile floors, Inox metal fixtures, and glamorous plaster moldings. There is no mistaking the fact that these houses are new, the houses they will replace old.

"Real Time" and "Social Time"

In a visceral sense, one can almost feel the change; the transformation of the material landscape in Hóc Môn appears to be only a matter of time. But what is this "time"; how is it possible to feel its movement? Cultural anthropologists have long protested that there is no universal form of "real time" against which to measure this kind of movement and change. "Time," writes Carol Greenhouse, "is cultural."[9] Edmund Leach claims that human beings "*create time* by creating intervals in social life. Until we have done this there is no time to be measured."[10] Norbert Elias argues that "the idea that people have always experienced the sequences of events which one now experiences as time-sequences in the manner which predominates today—namely, as an even, uniform and continuous flow—runs counter to evidence we have from past ages as well as our own."[11] Greenhouse further argues that ethnographic writing on time mistakenly (and ethnocentrically) naturalizes Western assumptions about linear time and human action as unfolding in time and place.[12]

In short, according to these arguments, we cannot assume that linear time is "natural"; the apparent movement of time emerges from socially situated mechanisms for marking intervals and organizing social action in relation to those markings. Nonetheless, evidence from Saigon's edge indicates that people experience the outward expansion of the city limits in exactly this way, as a linear process of advancement that puts them on the edge of two temporal moments—the traditional rural past and the modern urban future. As people describe it, the city unfolds outward in space along a trajectory of history that unfolds in time. But we cannot take this feeling of movement for granted. We must stop for a moment, take stock of the notion of change and progress expressed by people in Hóc Môn, and try to understand the larger circumstances that frame this kind of talk about linear development and progress proceeding forward through historical time.

The idea of a standard, linear concept of time has been criticized as a technology of capitalism imposed on peasant economies by the advance of the capitalist world system.[13] In the case of Vietnam, historians have speculated about an utterly different, precapitalist, precolonial understanding of time. "For ordinary Vietnamese," before the colonial era, Patricia Pelley argues,

the linearity of "universal" time and the relentlessness of the clock had no special merit; they were content to regulate their lives according to the phenomena of sunrise, sunset, the stages of the moon, equinoxes and solstices, and seasons—the events by which pre-industrial peoples traditionally demarcated time. Just as colonial administrators restructured personal archives by recording specific dates of birth or death, they also reshaped popular notions of history in a broader, collective sense. Dismissing traditional conceptions, they began to emplot the Vietnamese past in the framework of universal time; where dynastic chronicles recorded cycles of power and decay, colonial historians saw linear developments.[14]

The evidence for this viewpoint extends the generalized and largely sensible observation that a preindustrial mode of production exacts of labor specific requirements that are organized in time according to temporal markers more appropriate to the needs of agricultural production. Indeed, before clocks and industrial time discipline, life was certainly regulated by different temporal markers. But does this necessarily mean that people had a fundamentally different view of time itself? It surely means that they acted within time according to different schedules and that they tracked time according to different methods. But there is no evidence that time itself was somehow different.[15]

Taking the relativistic position regarding time to the extreme has led some scholars to attribute—under the guise of a sensitive cultural relativism—an irreconcilably different (and physically impossible) kind of time to the peasant "other."[16] Gurvich, for example, claims that the peasant class "tends to remain faithful to traditional patterns and symbols which supports the peasant's inclination to move in retarded time turned in on itself, because traditional patterns and symbols unfold in this time."[17] In positing this retarded, slowed down time, scholars like Gurvich invent an impossible scenario that puts the "peasant class" in another world that defies the possibility that peasants can coexist in the same temporal universe as nonpeasants.[18] It is physically impossible for time to actually move slower in a peasant world: even if a peasant's day *appears* to move slower than a "New York minute," it still takes the equivalent of twenty-four hours for a day to pass, regardless of whether the peasant has any use for or conception of "hours."

When we speak of time in a relative sense, then, we must be careful to distinguish the *perception* of passing time from the actual passing of time; we need to distinguish what we say about what people *do with time* from assertions about what time itself is. The real question, then, is not whether "linear" time itself represents a fundamentally new mode of consciousness but how the ways social people organize their action within time affects their consciousness of social relations writ large and how that relates to symbolic systems used to conceptualize time. Time passes at the same rate everywhere, regardless of whether people use the same technology for marking it. These arguments about fundamentally different notions of time do not speak about different metaphysical understandings of what time is as much as they speak about different technologies for recording the passage of time, different orientations to that passage of time, different ways of giving meaning to the fact that time passes, and ultimately, different ways of organizing social action in relation to that fact.[19]

Furthermore, in Vietnam today the philosophical point about time conceptions—about whether people have a concept of time passing or whether they understand the notion of a day broken up into hours—is itself largely inconsequential, for even farmers who do not always follow the strict clock of industrial time have a clear conception of clock time. Even if they do not "clock in" to work, they can speak about hours with relative facility. A farmer in the fields of Hóc Môn, to cite one example fortuitously caught on tape, described the process of planting, tending, and harvesting cucumbers:

FARMER: On a day like that [planting cucumbers] . . . there's about five or six hours, not so much.

ERIK HARMS: How many people?

F: The two of us people, yeah?

EH: Two people.

F: Work about six hours.

EH: Morning and afternoon?

F: Uh, morning and afternoon together about six hours.

EH: So you just rest in the afternoon?

F: Yeah, just in the afternoon. It looks like from seven in the morning we work until ten, ten-thirty, then go rest for the afternoon, and only about two p.m. we go back out and work because this weather here is so hot that its not possible to come out too early. So we don't come out until two or two-thirty.[20]

The cucumber farmer here describes what seems like a "peasant mode of production" intricately linked to a rhythm of the agricultural cycle very similar to the stereotype depicted by Gurvich and not much different than the one Pelley used to describe a "pre-industrial," nonlinear time sense. Yet even though the farmer begins work early, sleeps during midday to avoid the heat, and never skips a day due to the needs of the plants he tends, there is no indication that he does not understand linear time or that the idea of clock time is in any way at odds with his understanding of time. He articulates so-called peasant time using hours.[21]

Scholars will protest. Clearly our cucumber farmer can be articulate about hours because he is drawn into articulation with a capitalist mode of production. Indeed, this is the point; he can conceive of the passage of time in two ways without developing a fundamental metaphysical crisis. Of course he will have to integrate the notion of hours and days into his schedule and rethink the steps of his work that constitute a full cycle of production. The cucumbers are produced for sale in the market; consequently he has to coordinate his labor with the needs of the market middlemen. As the farmer explained it, vegetable buyers come directly to the fields and buy his produce. He said that he can find a better price if he carries the cucumbers directly to market but that it eventually turns out to be easier to sell to middlemen right there in the fields. A good portion of the extra money he might earn with a better price in the market would be wasted on transport costs anyhow. Even if he was able to squeak out a slightly better price after expenses, it would not be worth the extra effort, because the buyers who come straight to the fields "buy at a price just a little bit lower." The farmer is sophisticated about markets and makes calculations based on price and weighs these considerations against his own expenditure of labor. But he must still tend his cucumbers. And he calculates the marginal utility of carrying everything to the market not purely in terms of profit margins but against the more subjective idea of the "drudgery of labor."[22]

The theoretical question we must consider is this: how do these two conceptions of time interact with each other? The cucumber farmer has a relatively clear "capitalist" conception of clock time and of market prices fluctuating in time. But in spite of this, his understanding of the clock and his conception of the market do not mean that he is fully subordinated to the clock. His economy of time is oriented to both a "moral economy" and a rational "market economy," open to diverse interpretations, and intimately related to conceptions of value.[23] He uses a certain time orientation to mark time for certain aspects of life and social interaction, but it does not compete with the time orientation necessary to do a good job planting, tending, and eventually selling his cucumbers.[24]

Even more important in terms of our question about linear time, we see that the cucumber farmer has an understanding of historical transformations occurring over time, and these transformations are themselves intimately connected to changes in the sense of everyday time experience. In our discussion about how he waters his vegetables, he talked about alterations in the labor process by referring to a temporal frame marked by technological changes associated with how he pumps water to the hose he uses for watering. This led to a comparison of the time "before liberation" with the time "after liberation" in 1975:

In the period before liberation there wasn't any electricity at all. . . . At that time I bought a "Kole" engine.[25] In that time before I'd use gas, then I'd pull-start it, then I'd water, then only after that was there electricity in the countryside here [. . .] This was about 1980 . . . 80 . . . 83, 84 when there was first electricity.[26]

In this example, he talked about a significant change in the process of agricultural production and subtly indicated several temporal frames. First, electrification was a historical event mapped onto the temporal idea of "before liberation" and "after liberation." Second, even though he could not remember the exact year of electrification, he had a general idea of when it occurred and certainly indicated that it did occur in a specific, historically verifiable year, which he tried to recall by thinking out loud—"80 . . . 83, 84." Third, he linked this temporal understanding of historical change with the temporality of everyday life. Electricity makes it much easier to pump water; he does not have to lug out the Kohler generator, buy the gas, and so on. Yet despite all of this, he still follows the rhythm of the agricultural cycle, the rhythm of the cucumbers.

Clearly, even a "peasant," like any person, can think through several temporal models at once. Linear time does not necessarily pose a direct contradiction to cyclical time. One can think historically about things that unfold in time without compromising one's ability to think about repetitive cycles. Thus, when we talk about Vietnamese notions of cyclical time or when scholars speak about the difference between "sacred" and "profane" time or the time of myths,[27] we must be careful with our assumptions about how these are fundamentally incompatible with linear time. In Vietnam, the calendrical system of "heavenly stems and earthly branches"[28] sounds quite mystical and foreign, but this lunar calendar can in fact be translated quite simply into a Western calendar year with a formula and a chart.[29]

This does not mean that specific ways of referring to time do not have symbolic importance but rather that a cyclical notion of time reckoning does not in and of itself prove the absence of a conception of linear time or the inability to conceive of the past. It is easy to ask, as I did: "When do you use the Western calendar, and when do you use the lunar calendar?" Following are some of the answers I received.

When I go to work in a company or do all of the certification papers in society I follow the Western calendar. In regards to the lunar calendar, then, in the family there are the festive days like death anniversaries, weddings, processions.[30]

I have the habit of using the lunar calendar to calculate the days.[31]

I usually think in terms of the Western calendar. The lunar calendar is only used for festivals.[32]

And so on. The lunar calendar marks time in relationship to festivals and cyclical occasions that recur each year or each month (such as Tết, the midautumn festival, or days in the Buddhist calendar, such as the midmonth fast on the day of the full moon, *ngày rằm*). Even the woman who said she tended to use the lunar calendar more often than the Western calendar said she had the "habit" *(thói quen)* of doing so. Like the others, she was comfortable using both calendrical systems, but she worked in a market, where much of the seasonal produce as well as the kinds of foods people would seek to buy depended on the ritual calendar more than the Western calendar. But the Western calendar was by no means foreign to her.

The presence of a form of time reckoning in and of itself does not say very much about the social experience of time. That experience of time depends more on social action and the distribution of agency within time, for what time "means" really depends on how "we make, through our acts, the time we are in."[33] Indeed, this is the point; time orientation is not mystical or magical in any sense, but the social effects of time depend on acts that are situated within but also create relationships of power, legitimacy, and authority. In relation to the transformation of space on the outskirts of Ho Chi Minh City, the idea that the city develops through time is nothing strange, for "chronotopes" frame social narratives in many highly divergent cross-cultural settings.[34] What is particular to each historical moment or social context, however, is the relationship of people to the authoritative interpretation of time, to the people who give *meaning* to time.[35] Time does not fundamentally change; the idea of how one *relates* to time does.

To return to the patient cucumber farmer, then, his sense of time reveals two forms of power at work, two systems that regulate his malleable social relationship to time: one is the relation to time imposed by those peaceful-looking cucumbers themselves (if he does not follow their schedule, they will die and he will lose his investment); the other is the social relation to time imposed by the people he has planted those cucumbers for (if he does not have fresh produce when they come to buy it, he will also lose his investment). We can quite easily understand his relationship to the cucumbers. His relationship to the other people is much more complicated. But this is the most important relationship for any understanding of time and social transformation, for there is a whole society involved in social change, not just relations between people and cucumbers but social relations between people and other people. And these relations are embedded in fields of power and hierarchy, status and authority.

In the larger Vietnamese social relationship to time, the cucumber farmer becomes associated with the past. Somehow the fact that he tends to cucumbers grown according to a natural cycle allows people to assume he is not modern. This assumption is based on an imagined separation between cyclical and linear time. Yet cyclical patterns of agricultural activity do not actually stop the passage of historical time (just as the fact that the reader celebrates a birthday each year or follows a cyclical weekly routine will not, I am afraid, stop her from growing older each year). Yet in contemporary Vietnam the idea of urbanization has become associated with forward, linear movement. And the idea of agriculture has become associated with the past, as if the cyclical process of planting and harvesting has sent time itself into a spiral. The cucumber farmer is just as present as everyone else. But at best, people like him are rarely considered modern; at worst, they are relegated to an eternal past. What makes it possible to associate a person one meets in the fields with the collective past? It is not a linear conception of time that does this, but an ideology of rural–urban difference that maps space onto time.

Party Time for the People: Propagandistic Understandings of Socialist Time, Teleology, and the Laws of Urban Development

When Pelley argues that postcolonial Vietnamese "internalized colonial notions of 'universal time,'" we need to be clear about what we mean by this internalization of linear time reckoning.[36] As I have been arguing, there is nothing new about linear time in and of itself. This internalization of new forms of time reckoning really corresponds to public discourse, in which revolutionary uses of history attempted to legitimize the forward march of antiimperialist struggle and the improvement of society under the guiding hand of the rational, scientific principles of the Marxist–Leninist Vietnamese Communist Party. Yet although it seems clear that universal time and an infatuation with progress are sensible to everyone in postcolonial Vietnam, it is not so clear that everyone agrees on the mechanisms that organize social action within this linear concept of time.

The evidence from contemporary Vietnam corroborates the view that universal linear time is almost universally accepted throughout Vietnam. In this mode of time orientation, people for the most part articulate an idea of history as forward movement, a kind of accumulation of "progress" that builds up toward "development," and this interpretation of progress and movement underscores all interpretations of urban development. The city, for all intents and purposes, grows outward across space in a movement forward in time. For the purposes of this chapter, it is not important whether this historical mode stems from indigenous or "foreign" categories of time reckoning; it is simply the way people see the world. But at the same time, we cannot assume that everyone agrees with state-centered concepts of historical materialism emphasized by the Marxist–Leninist party-state simply because the party and the people both stress the linear trajectory of history in clear, unambiguous ways. The question here is not whether people really have internalized this linear conception of time but whether they have internalized a party-centric conceptualization of how social action occurs within time.

Party Time

The Communist Party narrative of the passage of time in Ho Chi Minh City is rather straightforward. It makes the party itself the motor of the city's recent historical successes and posits itself as the solution to its problems, problems that are cast as either historical vestiges of previous eras or nefarious influences from abroad. This narrative reconciles the development of the contemporary city with a larger national narrative of the forward march of history toward socialism. Not so much a radical philosophy of time, this narrative is really a political stance, an interpretation of action within history designed to legitimize the central role of the socialist state. That is, Vietnamese Marxism–Leninism reinterpreted what drives social change and offered a thesis on how to control it but did not meddle with the idea of time itself. Indeed, Vietnamese socialist time claims a sort of scientific rationality that looks more like Herbert Spencer's social Darwinism and the idea of the survival of the fittest than like Marx's own complicated dialectical ideas of historical materialism of the non-"vulgar" sort.

This approach to city history is not just used to speak of urban development but resonates with a larger philosophy of history that emphasizes the unified consciousness of party and people as the motor of social action and the vanguard of progress. Such a way of conceiving change was already evident in the emphasis on linear historiography promoted by the party and party-sponsored historians in the years immediately following Vietnamese independence from France. The rhetoric of socialist teleology was originally deployed as a weapon in the ideological battle against imperialism itself. As Pelley notes, the prominent historian Trần Huy Liệu told members of the Executive Committee of the party's Central Committee that "History is a combative work, always active. . . . Historian cadres . . . must not only live with the history of the past, they need to live right in the middle of the history of the present; they must not only write history, but contribute to its construction."[37] The linear model of historical materialism, with its emphasis on social evolution and progress, provided postcolonial historians with a scientific form of Marxist history that "made it possible to codify the 'laws of historical development' *(quí luật phát triển lịch sử);* these 'laws' in turn illuminated the 'laws' of combat."[38]

These laws, it seems, also inform the official understanding of urbanization itself as a marker of progress and development. In 1975, during the period immediately following the Liberation or Fall of Saigon, the theme of socialism driving history emerged as the fundamental explanation for urban history and development. With the conquest in April 1975 and the subsequent renaming of Saigon as Ho Chi Minh City in 1976, the new leadership was confronted with the task of bringing the city into line with the historical trajectory of the rest of Vietnam. The debate about what to do with Saigon and the south in general needed to unify the idea of urbanization as a process guided by forward-thinking policies of the party with the generalized party line on its own relation to history, "development," and the march to socialism.

After some debate following their military victory in 1975, the Vietnamese Communist Party leadership in Hanoi decided to move rapidly toward unification and to quickly begin the collectivization of agriculture in southern Vietnam. Debates within the party leadership centered around whether socializing the south so soon after military victory corresponded with their linear, historical-materialist interpretation of the stages in the advance to socialism. Postwar confidence fueled the ambition of rapidly implementing the socialist transformation into the south, and the leadership implemented Vietnam's second five-year plan in 1976 throughout the newly unified nation. In this plan, Hanoi aimed to firmly engage the south in the three revolutions of production relations, ideology and culture, and science and technology by 1980.[39] The party leadership's commitment to rapid unification and to bringing the south in line with the goals of the socialist revolution highlighted a general confidence in the socialist project despite the clear obstacles presented by the war-ravaged economy.[40] This confidence stemmed, in large part, from the belief in progress—the teleological, inevitable march toward socialism—and from what Turley describes as a particularly Vietnamese enthusiasm for the role that urban centers could play in the development of socialism:

One of the most important ways Vietnamese Communism always has distinguished itself from that of China is the greater favor with which the Vietnamese consistently have looked upon their cities in relation to the revolution. . . . For economic and security reasons, in addition to the imperatives of dogma and party mythology, the Socialist Republic of Vietnam seeks to integrate southern cities as bulwarks not backwaters or pariahs of the revolution.[41]

The party-centered narrative of urban development thus reconciles the urban development of Ho Chi Minh City with this linear concept of history, with the party as guiding force. The general emphasis of this narrative has continued up to now. On the occasion of the three hundredth anniversary of the founding of Ho Chi Minh City (1698–1998), the editorial board for a commemorative volume explained the significance of the city's urban development in the following way:

In line with the Vietnamese nation's tradition of industrious labor, those people who went to "open the country" *(mở cõi)* [in the seventeenth century] opened up a region of wild wasteland, forbidding forests, and poisonous water, progressively transforming it into a populous and wealthy place. [. . .] After passing through more than 116 years under the yoke *(ách)* of colonial aggression and domination, the people of the city united in continuous struggle for the independence of the nation/people, for democracy and social advancement, most especially since the leadership of the Vietnamese Communist Party and the City Party Committee [here the text cites the 1982 decision number one of the Politburo, which recognizes the importance of Ho Chi Minh City within the national struggle for socialism] [. . .] with the whole country, for the whole country, the city led and brought up the rear in the two wars of resistance against French colonialism and American imperialism, dynamic and creative in revolution—building—renovation—development. Truly deserving of its reputation as a heroic City.[42]

In this sweeping introduction to the commemorative volume, the authors map the entire history of urban development in what is now Ho Chi Minh City/Saigon into a linear progression of consistent development and triumph over natural and unnatural odds. This simplified rendering begins mythically with worthless "wasteland" brought under cultivation by the genius and hard labor of the Vietnamese people/nation, moves swiftly through anticolonial resistance, and reaches its pinnacle with the guiding leadership of socialism that solidified in the ultimate liberation of the people/nation.

The formulaic pattern of such statements can be found repeated in countless introductory sections of countless books on a wide range of topics. But to what degree do people believe this intellectual simplification of urban history? Can we assume from these party-sponsored documents that Vietnamese have internalized the idea of linear time?

Everyday Notions of Linear Time and Development

There is no pure and simple way to prove whether everyday people fully internalize or reject party-centered interpretations of history, for many people will repeat this story in public and in formal contexts, regardless of whether they believe it. During one of several official interviews I conducted in the presence of members of the Fatherland Front, an elderly man who practices traditional medicine offered me this statement:

What is industrialization—modernization of the county—like, from liberation until now, how is it? . . . How much I know, I'll tell you that much, so my dear Erik, here, um . . . in the past, well, around here in the countryside, then about agriculture. Agriculture, I can say a lot, speaking of agriculture, in the past there was only enough to live on, but one couldn't save anything, then thanks to the country, since liberation to this time right now, then the leadership of the party, of the government, has brought out this calm and tranquility for the people. One aspect is regarding life *(đời sống),* the second is about material goods *(vật chất),* as for my fellow countrymen *(đồng bào)* around here, generally speaking in Hóc Môn district specifically, and in Tân Thới Nhì commune generally, about that then, from Liberation day up until today things have changed a lot. Before this area was called just a bunch of brushwood *(rừng rú),* trees and plants *(cây cối),* roads were all ruined, you couldn't go anywhere, like in this month you wouldn't have been able to come in here at all, it was totally swampy *(sinh lầy),* but from Liberation Day to today then the leadership of the party and the government has spoken of developing the countryside.[43]

Even though this man said these things in real life, and even though he clearly cited the central role of the party in developing the outer-city district, it is not actually possible to decipher the truth value of these statements. First of all, observers from the Fatherland Front were sitting in on the interview. And most Vietnamese people I met in less formal encounters, if they read this interview or the introduction to the commemoration volume cited earlier, would privately find fault with the overly grandiose pronouncements in this argument. In fact, most of them would skip these platitudes and move on to the "facts," if there were any. But even if we disregard the propagandistic veneer of the "guiding hand" of the Vietnamese Communist Party, a substantial majority of people do believe in the idea of progress and social advancement. The very basic idea that development will occur over time and that "industrialization, modernization, and urbanization" are inherently positive indicators of progress and advancement certainly hold sway in contemporary Vietnamese society. The notion that the party itself is responsible for any advancement produces muffled criticism, but the idea of advancement itself is rarely criticized.

Alternate Conceptions of Social Action within Time

It is easy to be skeptical about the party notion that development will proceed in distinct stages and that all the good things mentioned came as a result of party policies. We cannot take these dogmatic statements about history as evidence of a deep, underlying cultural sentiment about time. Such pronouncements about time are thinly veiled mechanisms of power; categories of social time are actually arguments about the source of social agency. As Greenhouse has written, "Time's many forms are cultural propositions about the nature and distribution of agency across social space."[44] Accordingly, when we cite these official pronouncements of socialist teleology as we have done up to this point, we can not assume that official time really speaks for the people. Rather, this depiction of linear progress itself attempts to construct a vision of history guided by the enlightened policies of the party. Thus, like Greenhouse, "I assume that elites attempt to speak *to* their constituencies, but I do not presume their success in speaking *for* them or even convincing them."[45]

In less formal contexts, for example, many people actively contest official depictions of the party as the motor of urban development; they scoff at statements that history moves forward in a teleology guided by the wisdom of party policies. The most striking example was the comment from a young girl who speculated on what the fate of Vietnam would have been had the Americans stayed: *Daddy, if the Americans never left, we'd be ahead of Thailand right now, right?*

The girl was not saying that time has stopped in any mystical, magical sense since the Americans left. She knows that she has grown older over time, as has her father, who was her age during parts of the American War. She is repeating an argument she has heard from her family about the distribution of agency and social power within society. The government, according to this argument, was misguided in its understanding of society and economics; it failed to distribute the means of production in an effective way, the relations of production it instituted were naïve and counterproductive, and a lot of people simply did not get much work done. Party leaders simply were not as effective as the Americans were at organizing production and development. After the Americans left, bridges were not built, roads were not maintained, and the country did not develop. History continued, of course, but development slowed down. In fact, the very conception of past and present enabled the girl to make a statement that implied that time has continued to move forward while Vietnamese society has failed to keep up.

Such statements creep out in a wide range of informal situations. In the previous chapter, Mr. Dũng at the café joked in resignation about how he hoped President Bush would bomb Hóc Môn, implying that the area needed to start over. This does not mean that he thinks time itself will go backward but rather that people in the area may as well undo what they have done up to this point because social action within time up to this point has been poorly organized. On another occasion, Dũng repeated the same kind of story as the young girl just mentioned, this time adding visual aids. In order to illustrate the problem with contemporary Hóc Môn, he depicted the wartime North/South divide at the seventeenth parallel with cigarette boxes laid out on the table between us. One box represented the north and one represented the south, and he explained that South Vietnam had been "ahead" of all the countries in Southeast Asia at that time. Even South Korea was "behind" the southern cigarette box back then. Then, with unification, the divide was eliminated and the boxes became one. Dũng put them together briefly and explained how this new unified country fell behind the other countries in the region. Even Thailand surged ahead. And then he smacked at the boxes, sending them sliding in haphazard spirals away from each other across the table, as if to show the apparent chaos of social life since Liberation.

These comparisons of present-day Ho Chi Minh City with American-backed wartime Saigon are themselves narrative constructions that silence certain elements of the past in order to make a commentary on the present state of affairs. People select elements to construct stories in ways that become signifiers of a present that would have been, a future that remains to be achieved, a dream that is only now beginning to take shape. These stories are no less constructed than the propagandistic counterparts offered by the state media and historical publications, but they offer an alternate interpretation of how social life might have been organized within history.

Sometimes these comments offer clear political jabs at the government. Other times they simply provide commentary with no overt political critique. Even government sympathizers can sometimes marvel at the technical ingenuity of the Americans (just as American veterans often marvel at the ingenuity of the Củ Chi tunnels, the Hồ Chí Minh Trail, or the "genius" of General Võ Nguyên Giáp's military strategies). While sitting drinking rice wine mixed with fresh snake blood, a retired, well-to-do man with family connections in the local People's Committee told a story about a short stint he had spent working with the Americans. He compared the slow progress of the highway project through Hóc Môn with the technological achievements of Americans during the American War:

> Americans could do all sorts of things. . . . I remember when I was at Cam Ranh [Bay]. . . they saw that you had to drive around the peninsula to get to another point of the bay. They studied it [he said this holding his chin, his eyes fixed on an imaginary horizon to mimic the action of an American surveyor], and then within 48 hours they had built a bridge.[46]

As he recounted this anecdote of American ingenuity, he was enjoying retirement in Hóc Môn, reveling in the peace of the last remaining fields where he had built himself a sort of back-to-nature leaf hut on the edge of the rice fields. Although he openly supported the current government-initiated modernization schemes, he could not help laughing about the ineptitude of contemporary Vietnamese builders. This little story itself was his response to a discussion about the progress of road building in Hóc Môn. Building the road is not in and of itself a bad idea, he said. The people doing it were simply not very good at it. After his time at Cam Ranh he switched sides in the war and considered himself sympathetic to the Communist Party. Yet he challenged the dogmatic teleology of socialist triumphalism and harbored no illusions that Vietnamese engineers (socialist or not) were superior to those he had seen in the U.S. Army. And all his sympathies for socialism would not correct his laughter at the ineptitude of the urbanization process currently stumbling through his corner of Hóc Môn. "Uống tiếp đi" (Drink some more), he said. "I made this rice wine myself," using rice from the same fields that he was slowly selling, parcel by parcel, to investors from the city.

The stories people tell are not critiques of the *ideal* of progress or wild interpretations of alternate concepts of time. They are really stories about social action, how different ways of organizing people produce different material effects on the world.

All sorts of social and historical facts can be called upon to create alternative visions of how action could be organized within time. Some people look at the steady stream of migration from the north into Ho Chi Minh City as "evidence" that the party's economic policies can not compare with those of what is described as a naturally more capitalist south. Some read the development of consumer capitalism as a symbolic renunciation of socialism, referring to important dates in the way they express the history of development. The years 1975–86 were largely silent years, a period of deprivation and struggle; 1986 was the year of renovation; 1993 marked the adoption of the new land law, which allowed people to gain long-term use rights and transfer the titles of land-use permits; 1994 was the year that President Bill Clinton lifted the embargo; and so on.

The relative absence of talk about the years between 1975 and 1986 indicates a significant silence, but it is a public silence more than a private silence. Off-the-cuff statements made in private space illuminate the contested interpretations of historical change and contradict official visions of how economic and social development has unfolded over time. But they do not contradict the idealization of time itself as a linear progression of history, moving forward on the path of development. And although many people contest the party's interpretation of the success of the regime's development scheme, this does not mean that they have a fundamental existential disagreement about the nature of time itself. For critics, the general progression of events is still described as a kind of linear process of development and improvement, but this linear path itself seems to correspond to a gradual dismantling of socialism rather than a vindication of the party's role in guiding the nation.

Agreements between the Party and the People about Linear Progress

Linear concepts of time do not in and of themselves translate to support for the Communist Party. Different statements about the role of the party in history represent two different interpretations of the distribution of agency in society. But they do not represent a fundamental disagreement about the nature of time. Even in the disputed versions of Hóc Môn's recent historical (under-)development, the very idea of time holds that development is supposed to take place over historical time. *Phát triển,* the Vietnamese term for development, implies a kind of generation and emission of prosperity, a process of transformation and growth. Similarly, the ideas of urbanization *(đô thị hoá),* industrialization *(công nghiệp hóa),* and modernization *(hiện đại hóa)* are, in public, all propagandistic statements used to support the party notion of its role in history. But these terms also resonate with a populist notion of social development. I never heard anyone criticize the idea of *đô thị hoá,* although many criticized the Communist Party's ability to guide it. For urbanization is linked to progress, not to the party. Even though the party tries to assert its guiding role in the process, people have ways of imagining progress with or without the party within it.

When speaking about the transformation of space on the outer fringes of Saigon, people adopt a naturalized temporal frame. It takes time to build a road, to create infrastructure, and to build the infrastructure to support a city. This building is a process. And, despite the persistence of different forms of temporal orientation that coexist within society, the general consensus seems to hold that there is an objective form of linear historical time, that development unfolds over time, and that progress follows a straight path forward. This path can be blocked by historical events or poor decisions, and it corresponds to an understanding of time shared by Western modernization theorists since at least Max Weber. The debate in Vietnamese society is thus not about the nature of historical time itself but about what has been done through the course of time. In all discussions of development, people assume that development should naturally move forward through time. When development stops, time continues, and the task is to catch up.

This belief that infrastructure development represents a movement forward through time is itself connected to the valuation of infrastructure development as a marker of civilization within an idiom of social evolution that proceeds through time. Just as U.S. Air Force General Curtis LeMay could claim in 1964 that bombing campaigns could send Vietnam "back to the Stone Age,"[47] many contemporary Hóc Môn residents feel that the years of war and the subsequent mistakes in collectivized agriculture and centralized bureaucratic planning have prevented them from moving forward in time. Hóc Môn is obviously not in the Stone Age, but they speak as if it has been held back. The idea of its being "behind" itself implies a fundamental understanding that history has itself moved forward. Time has continued; development has failed to keep up. Just as LeMay's statement was really a metaphor for destroying infrastructure that has been built over time, the popular idea held by people in Hóc Môn is that their section of space in Vietnam is not yet developed, an idea that hinges on the practical understanding that it takes time to build infrastructure and that historical circumstances have interceded and stalled this process in Hóc Môn. Infrastructure thus stands as an iconic marker for the passage of time, where the amount and level of infrastructure development can thus be used to judge where Vietnam stands in temporal relation to a universal notion of historical progress. Using these criteria, Hóc Môn is backward in time; it is behind, "not yet developed" *(chưa được phát triển)*. Vietnam, too, is backward in relation to other countries in the world and in the region. In this equation Vietnam is to Thailand as Hóc Môn is to Ho Chi Minh City. But the signs of building, the constructive destruction all around, and the sense that the city is expanding outward in space over time serve to give the impression that Hóc Môn is catching up.

This notion of movement, of catching up, recalls the visceral sense of movement one feels on the edge of the city, the feeling that the city is growing outward in space. In this sense, the urban sphere of influence expands as time passes, and spatial expansion seems to follow linear time. The city cannot expand in a spontaneous moment. It does not expand while time flows backward. In fact, time never flows backward. But the reason for the expansion is really what is under debate. Expansion occurs because of human productive activity. With effective productivity, a lot of expansion can occur in a short span of time.[48] With ineffective productivity, very little expansion will occur. Perhaps, even, counterproductive activity will occur in the form of a war, postwar repression of adherents to the previous regime, misguided ideas about economic programs, some form of natural disaster, or even ill-conceived urban development projects.

This expansion is further marked by changes in administrative status. Rural outer-city districts become reclassified as inner-city districts—*huyện ngoại thành* become *quận nội thành.* I would sometimes encounter groups of friends debating when their section of Hóc Môn would become reclassified as a *quận.* Their speculations were informed by the facts that the part of Hóc Môn lying closer to central Saigon had been reclassified as an inner-city district just a few years earlier and that they could see construction everywhere around them. The experiential relation of inside to outside becomes mapped onto time such that the trajectory of linear movement makes it seem clear that the outside will be incorporated into the inside over time.

And these spaces on the edge—where the cucumber farmer stood, where the girl spoke about what it would have been like if the Americans had stayed, where I drank rice wine with the retired man, where I sat with motorbike drivers in a café along the Trans-Asia Highway—are physically farther from the center of the city. City growth is mapped onto time, and this movement seems to extend outward in space toward the vegetable gardens or to the rice and peanut fields, where new factories are being built, new roads are being graded, dirt roads are getting paved. So even though the narrative of the party's role in history may be critiqued or ignored, the idea of moving forward through time appears to people living on the edge as if it were a concrete reality inscribed on the face of the land itself. The spatial expansion of the city over time makes people associate different spaces with different times. Time takes on the material attributes of the growing city itself. Urban development becomes linked to the future; the space it swallows up *seems* linked to the past. In this mode of logic, the cucumber farmer who lives there seems part of the past as well.

On Being Behind, Catching Up, and the Promise of Development

The visceral feeling of development and spatial transformation, coupled with a linear conception of time as forward progress into a more developed future, contributes to the idea that healthy development can be understood as a form of *advancing forward through time.* In this idiom that measures development over time, those spaces that lack the attributes of other developed spaces appear behind in time. In this conception, it is not time that has stopped but social action within time. Time continues; people either do or do not keep up. In terms of urbanization, the idea of time as a forward march of progress seems to emerge from the idea of spatial expansion occurring over time. That is, the march of time seems to take on a material reality because it builds from a spatial metaphor of urban expansion that seems to objectively mark the progress of time. The statistics of urban growth are mapped onto time, and this idea of expansion over time turns back onto space as well, inscribing it with the symbolically charged meaning of time. If historical time moves forward and the city "grows," urbanization appears to represent forward movement. The flip side of this is the assumption that urban space is modern and rural space somehow belongs to the past. This translates to social categories that associate different people with different places mapped onto time.

The anthropologist Philip Taylor has summarized with remarkable clarity what he recognizes in southern Vietnam as "the widespread use of temporal categories to rank social or cultural differences," in which the orientation toward the future is often posed in opposition to a socially denigrated notion of being "backward" *(lạc hậu)*.[49] People in urban areas often look down on rural people as uncivilized and crude, lacking restraint, and uneducated, all implicit signs of being backward. This is by no means unique to Vietnam. Raymond Williams famously describes this in his classic work on the country and the city in Britain, and Rigg demonstrates the extension of this form of "temporal exclusion" throughout Southeast Asia and goes on to argue that it represents the "hegemony of the development discourse" that emphasizes the modernity of development and the backwardness of agriculture.[50] In many ways, Rigg is entirely correct, and the previous discussion of the linear assumptions of development proceeding forward through time clearly corroborates his view.

But the hierarchical relationship of the rural and the urban does not always remain fixed. Although the emphasis on the *difference* between social spaces such as country and city seems long-standing, the relative valorization and denigration of the two seems to shift according to context. Taylor, for example, quite carefully reminds the reader that rural Vietnam is not only denigrated as underdeveloped but it is also often celebrated as the font of "tradition" *(truyền thống)*, a designation with clearly temporal associations but without the negative connotation of backwardness.[51]

Temporal orientation does not in and of itself designate a static relation of hierarchy. Rather, the hierarchical relationship shifts according to context, and the value of "the past" depends on the function that the past can serve for action in the present. The "hegemony of the development discourse" has at times been replaced with a countervailing tendency to interpret what Taylor calls "neo-colonialism as poison," to fear the city as a space of corruption, "social evils," and cultural loss and vulnerability.[52] In moments when it stands in contrast to the evil of the city, the countryside provides a foil for purity. Although Nguyễn-võ Thu-hương has argued that Vietnamese public discourse depicted the rural areas as either "wronged or forgotten" or as "the neglected cesspool of oppressive backwardsness," she adds that both sentiments comprehended an implicit nostalgia in which "the rural remained a source of strength and renewal for the national consciousness."[53] Even though the Vietnamese national narrative has turned increasingly toward the promise of urban development, Nguyễn-võ argues that this narrative

> could also take with it such an imagined place as the rural, that clump of earth with the nation's metaphorical roots attached, a source and resting place, a depository of a national soul. This temporally mobile geographical source was not a particular place. It was an imagined (rural) heartland (seen from a plane as watery emerald expanses), which though particular enough in its edible commodities of food and sex, was ultimately carry on luggage as the nation flew toward some modern and foreign future.[54]

This idea of "the rural" as a "temporarily mobile geographical source" reveals a great deal. Nguyễn-võ clearly shows that "the rural" works mainly as an idea. And this idea has some function in the larger narrative of the nation's flight to the future. Because this idea is symbolically associated with "roots," "sources," and "resting places" for the national soul, it appears as the antithesis of the "modern and foreign future." This passage describes a movement between the ideal of the rural as a grounded "clump of earth" and its opposite, which is ungrounded (like an airplane), spatially expansive, and foreign. The movement between grounded national soul and ungrounded foreign corresponds to the movement between *nội* (inside) and *ngoại* (outside). As I showed in the previous chapters, the practical oscillation between these spatial categories enables people to manipulate categories of inclusion and exclusion for strategic purposes. Yet these are not simply spatial categories. The movement between the denigration and the celebration of rural and urban space enables a kind of temporal oscillation as well.

Two-Timing and Social-Temporal Oscillation

Philip Taylor usefully describes this shifting valorization and denigration of rural and urban space as a historical shift between discursive poles, a movement that alternately tries to associate different elements of society with modernity according to the changing exigencies of shifting historical moments. He critiques scholars who describe Vietnam's "relationship with the wider world over time as one of perennial confrontation between 'tradition' and 'modernity.'" In this schema, according to Taylor, "tradition is forever renewing itself, while 'modernity' is always just arriving in Vietnam. Time is ambushed and meaning eroded in a rhetorical tradition which offers the reader less of a fix on Vietnam's place in the world than a readout of different theorists' imagined relation to it."[55] Although Taylor's critique is certainly correct for a large body of Western scholarship, his most important point is how this rhetorical oscillation between tradition and modernity actually describes the very shifting between discursive poles that occurs in Vietnamese discourse itself. His own survey of Vietnamese thoughts on modernity in southern Vietnam, for example, emphasizes "how 'modernity' has been allocated to and displaced from various places in postwar Vietnam."[56] "Vietnam's extreme South," Taylor writes, is "a region incorporated relatively recently into the Vietnamese polity, with a history of intense engagement with the capitalist world." Offering fragments rather than reproducing official narratives allows Taylor to explore but not reify the history of Ho Chi Minh City and southern Vietnam through time, postwar experiments in socialism, and late socialist renovation policies. In doing so, Taylor convincingly describes a history of the alternating symbolism and meaning of modernity. The differential attribution of modernity to different social spaces results from the pragmatic negotiation of social actors who linked their interpretation of the ups and downs of spatial identities to the political and economic situation at hand. As one Vietnamese social scientist described it, leaders in the south were "pragmatists" particularly adept at manipulating the symbols of modernity in order to legitimize their own agendas by continuing to "exploit deviously the vocabulary of socialism while pragmatically pursuing their own ends."[57] Taylor himself tries to avoid this judgmental tone by letting the voices of his informants speak. But in the end, his analysis shows that it was not just the leaders in the south who pragmatically sought to play with the idea of modernity. Just about everyone does this. "Modernity" and "tradition" are shifting concepts that change according to the exigencies of social life. And images of rural and urban become key symbols in this conceptual debate.

The use of the past itself changes according to the needs of the present, such that the temporal association of an area with the past can mean different things in different periods or even according to different contexts within the same period. The very meaning of space in Hóc Môn is thus intimately tied to the changing understanding of what this so-called rural past represents. A peasant home, for example, can alternately represent a backward, old-fashioned, unsophisticated eyesore or it can represent a quiet retreat to traditional values, a safe haven away from the corrupting influences of the city. Both of these "meanings," however, emerge from the same sense that it is fundamentally something other than what one would find in the city. To visit such a home is portrayed as a movement back in time—but the nature of circumstances always affects whether this imaginary time travel is construed as a return to a golden age or a throwback to ignorance.

The meaning of the past depends on what people in the present want to do with these representations of the past. Calling this the "presence of the past," Trouillot thus helps us understand the pragmatic *uses* of history and temporality as themselves historically constrained phenomena.[58] And this shifting meaning of the past, in turn, transforms the way in which people choose to associate certain spaces with the past or the future. Together, future orientations and the exaltation of the past are inherently political, providing alternative modes of legitimizing the hierarchies of the present.

As Taylor shows, however, we can never presume whether the signifiers *rural* and *urban* represent tradition or modernity without a careful understanding of the context in which the symbols are used. In one reading of the complicated opposition of *nội thành* and *ngoại thành,* the center of the city appears to represent tradition; it is the place with the long history, where the original settlements were. In this sense, the *nội/ngoại* opposition unambiguously claims the center of Saigon as the center and casts the *ngoại thành* as a new, unbridled frontier. But in an alternate yet equally plausible opposition of *country* and *city,* the *ngoại thành* is associated with the countryside and traditional forms of Vietnamese cultural origins, while the city is seen as dangerously linked to the foreign and the modern.

Temporal Oscillation

The shifting means of depicting Hóc Môn as a place on the edge of both modernity and tradition validates Taylor's observation that modernity itself is a fluid category. But in addition to seeing the changing meanings of modernity as taking place over historical time, I argue that competing models of temporal hierarchy also coexist *within a condition of simultaneity.* The problem is one not only of *historical* oscillation back and forth between two forms of valorization but also of *simultaneous oscillation,* in which social actors exalt the past and the future all at once. This is a kind of temporal two-timing in which two apparently contradictory temporal associations coexist, offering different possible interpretations of the same event. The oscillation occurs because both interpretations of tradition and modernity are simultaneously plausible.

In other words, the two-timing rhetoric of Hóc Môn allows one to imagine the district both as a site of underdevelopment that needs more development and as a site of tradition that is threatened by development. The temporal idioms of reference between the country and the city reproduce each other in a process quite similar to what Kirsch has called "social oscillation," a form of movement between two idealized extremes of social organization that each have marked disadvantages and advantages and represent different possible alternatives for organizing society.[59] But social oscillation cannot take place solely in the realm of ideas. It involves a very real negotiation of ideas with everyday life. It is one thing to vacillate between an ideal of the past and the future, but it is another to perform this shift between ideals in one's everyday actions. It is here that conflicts between ideals take on material forms, because the idea of being modern and traditional is as connected to what one does with one's time as it is to what one thinks about time. In the next chapter I turn to the everyday use of time and space on Saigon's edge and show how this relates to the opposing ideals of inside and outside, urban and rural.

4. Negotiating Time and Space
Household, Labor, Land, and Movement

Outside and inside form a dialectic of division, the obvious geometry of
which blinds us as soon as we bring it into play in metaphorical domains.
It has the sharpness of the dialectics of *yes* and *no*, which decides
everything. Unless one is careful, it is made into a basis of images that
governs all thoughts of positive and negative.

— Gaston Bachelard, *The Poetics of Space*

Spatiotemporal Oscillation

The constructs of rural and urban Vietnam and of the inside and the outside in Ho Chi Minh City fashion images and expectations of distinct
spatiotemporal worlds bifurcated into discrete, opposed categories. As
idealized asymptotes, the inside is understood as having a certain urban
time orientation regimented by the clock and the outside as having a certain rural time orientation regimented by cycles of agricultural production. Both poles in this set of oppositions have potential advantages and
disadvantages. If one could somehow harness the potentials and escape
the limitations of both idealized poles, one could become a master of
time and space; one could be traditional and modern, sentimental and
sophisticated, carefree and efficient, attached to the land and yet spatially
mobile. These conceptions recall the way that Vietnamese kinship idioms
about the inside and the outside relate to time and space. The inside
extends deep in time but is bounded in space. The outside does the opposite—it has no history but extends outward across a wide area of social
catchments. What if one could combine these two? Then one could be
unbounded in both time and space, rooted in the land but also able to
reach outward into the outer world of exchange and capital production, a
traveling businessperson with a strong sense of family and a permanent
home address. One could wield the legitimate authority of tradition and
embrace the rationalized wisdom of the future.

The oppositions of rural versus urban and inside versus outside produce and maintain a sense of fundamental difference. But in doing this,
they also create the possibility for a type of movement between discrete

categories. This movement produces a socially constituted form of spatiotemporal power that accrues to those capable of harnessing the advantages and minimizing the disadvantages of each idealized asymptote. Producing these discrete spaces also creates the potential for a level of transcendence, a powerful space that straddles both realms.[1] The ability to oscillate between different spatiotemporal modes of social relations represents a form of power that is both symbolic and material at once. In this chapter I show how Hóc Môn residents deploy their position within spatialized urban–rural and inside–outside dichotomies as a means to harness the advantages of two competing forms of spatiotemporal organization that give them the power to reproduce themselves as social persons.[2]

Symbolic representations of space have potential material effects on the different socioeconomic positions of social actors within space. But this works the other way as well: the way people interpret and attach symbolic meaning to space depends on their different socioeconomic positions. On the one hand, a form of social, economic, and political power emerges from one's relative ability to negotiate social relations situated in both space and time. The degree of movement between rural space and urban space influences the degree to which people see these categories as fixed or flexible. As Harvey has written, "The assignment of place within a socio-spatial structure indicates distinctive roles, capacities for action, and access to power within the social order."[3] Yet, on the other hand, the negotiation of these categories is not fully open to the limits of imagination and free will. This negotiation is constrained both by historical transformation and by the political-economic, status, and power relations between social actors, who in turn assert their own competing visions of spatial relations and temporality. The contest over the meaning of time and space is thus political and economic, connected to the very practical reality of how people hope to organize social action and relations of production within society. "Unless one is careful," Bachelard warns, analysts risk mistaking the geometry of inside and outside for the basis of existence, such that "it is made into a basis of images that governs all thoughts of positive and negative."[4]

The complex, ever-contested relationships between inside and outside rest not on unmediated geometry but on social negotiations that transcend the materiality of the oppositions themselves. Furthermore, the tangible, physical reality of the spatial order enacted by these negotiations itself circumscribes the ability to oscillate between spatiotemporal ideals. The spatial meaning of the land and the ability of different people to move across it (both physically and symbolically) fundamentally change over time, and these changes limit the free reign of ideas to fully construct the social order. Thus, although life in Hóc Môn can be described as a negotiation between labile categories such as rural and urban or inside and outside, actual changes in the landscape over time gradually constrain the possibilities for such negotiation. Although most people understand and play with the fluid nature of these categories, they must nonetheless negotiate their own sense of self in relation to others in terms of flexible symbolic categories *and* the changing material reality of their social-spatial world. In this "intersubjective space-time," social relations and material transformations in the lived world unfold within "a spacetime of self–other relationships formed in and through acts and practices."[5]

In the simplified ideal scheme that opposes rural to urban, the outer-city district falls in the middle of these categories, cast as a meetingplace of two distinct social worlds where rural time orientations come into conflict with urban time orientations. The linear conception of social change leads to the expectation that the time orientation of rural folk will give way to the time orientation of the city, because the progressive spatial expansion of the city through time literally maps the urbanization process in time and space. This conception of bringing peasant time consciousness into the urban space-time of civilization rests on the fundamental assumption that rural time orientation is not only different from but incompatible with urban time orientation because rural people are bound by the rhythms of the agricultural cycle and urban people are bound by the tick-tock of the clock. This linear teleology implies that the organization of social action will become more rational and organized through the forward advance of history, insinuating that the organization of work and labor will necessarily lead to the triumph of rational, modern time, organized by the clock. But the poetics of lived space constantly thwart simplified notions of reciprocity and linear change. In actual praxis, according to Bachelard, "the dialectics of inside and outside multiply with countless diversified nuances."[6]

Oscillation between Rural Time and Urban Time

In contrast to simplified schemas positing foreordained relations between inside and outside, the actual diversity of experience within the outer-city districts makes it difficult to identify any clear-cut differences of time experience and time discipline that correspond in any consistent way with the spatial differentiation of country and city. Instead people engage in and manipulate multiple temporalities that sometimes appear to fit the image of a cyclical, non-clock-oriented "peasant" mode of production and at other times seem to fit urban time orientations more generally oriented toward the clock, linear progression, and a temporal stance that favors the accumulation of capital. Successful people are able to straddle both time orientations, whereas socially marginalized people remain symbolically and physically relegated to one time or the other. Ultimately, the power of spatiotemporal oscillation depends not so much on expressing a distinctly rural or urban time orientation but on the ability to move, according to contingent social circumstances, between states. In Hóc Môn, individuals constantly seek to oscillate between a spatiotemporal orientation subordinated to the generation of capital and regulated primarily by the clock and a seemingly incompatible state in which one's sense of time is gauged in terms of social reproduction. Confounding stereotypes, seemingly urban-oriented people often exhibit the so-called peasant indifference to clock time more than do so-called peasants. And people identified as peasants often exhibit a formal submission to the demands of the clock in ways much more striking than that of most urbanites. In order to explain this, I argue that the most relevant social division in Hóc Môn time orientations is not a division between "clock-oriented-time" and "non-clock-oriented-time" or even between "peasants" and "urbanites" but between people who can transcend and manipulate the dichotomy of inside and outside and those for whom the dichotomy becomes a real, constraining force in their lives. Both types of time orientation can exist within a single family and even within individual persons at different points in the course of their lives. The people who can negotiate these multiple temporal orientations seem able to act upon the world; others seem to be acted on by the world.

In the practical realities of lived time experience in Hóc Môn, there is no consistent correlation between "progress" and the adherence to clock time and industrial work discipline. Instead a set of double ideals develops in which clock time is associated both with progress and with exploitation and time disassociated from the clock is sometimes valorized as an alternative ideal, sometimes denigrated as "backward." Because clock time itself symbolically represents two opposing poles of progress and repression, successful, "powerful" people oscillate between two forms of time orientation. One form resists the clock and subordinates the accumulation of resources to the larger project of reproducing social relations. Another submits to the clock, subordinating social relations to the larger project of generating symbolic and material capital. The practical manipulation of inside *(nội)* and outside *(ngoại)* relations discussed in previous chapters creates the field within which the spatial and temporal elements of this oscillation play out. *Nội* emphasizes linear history and spatial boundedness in an idiom of reproducing the family unit in space and over time. *Ngoại* emphasizes short, repetitive durations of clock time and spatial expansion. The movement between inside and outside both generates capital and provides space in which to accumulate it.

To understand the way spatiotemporal oscillation generates effects of power, it helps to pause for a moment and imagine the kinds of people able to negotiate these two spatiotemporal realms associated with *nội* and *ngoại* most powerfully. The most famous case was Hồ Chí Minh, who is remembered for believing he had to "leave the country in order to save it." A less famous example might be someone like Hoàn, the Vietnamese American pig farmer who received workers' compensation payments in America and then took the money to Vietnam and converted it into a fortune (see chapter 2). And this is also the struggle of contemporary Vietnamese "socialism with a market orientation," simultaneously engaging with the outside international world of capital accumulation and preserving a fiercely bounded sense of nationalism, oscillating between the temporality of the market and the temporality of national self-reproduction. In the following more localized examples, the ability to move between different socially construed spatiotemporal modes underscores popular understandings of how to fashion a life worth living.

"The King" Reveals a Theory of Space-Time

Visits with the heads of the People's Committee in Tân Thới Nhì commune and with the heads of each of the seven hamlets *(ấp)* that comprise the commune typically turned into triumphal lectures on social change and development in the area, emphasizing progress and economic development within Hóc Môn. Commune leaders cited statistics on their efforts to increase the number of children in school and arrange job training programs, and they highlighted the steadily improving income levels of people in the community. They pointed out new roads and other infra-structure improvements and spoke of renovated hospitals. On one visit, Mr. Long, the head of a neighborhood association, had been assigned to show me around his section of the district. Part of his assignment in-cluded showing me the success stories of the area and introducing me to people doing well in the community—people whose success would highlight material progress and tangible signs of advancement. He showed me the newly restored community altar, talked about the road-widening project that would ease traffic on the road leading to the district seat, and even spoke of what he called local-level "democratic" institutions such as the neighborhood associations, including the one through which we were walking, of which his neighbors had elected him head.

On this tour we stopped first at an ethnic Chinese noodle soup *(hủ tiếu)* vendor's house for a discussion over tea. The soup seller waxed positive about his own successes and talked about how four years earlier he had been able to purchase use rights to the land upon which his house was built, which, he said, was very fortunate because land values had recently increased. He spoke glowingly about anticipated improvements to the district road that ran past his shop from the urbanized *thị trấn* cen-ter of Hóc Môn district. The widening of the road would not reach the edge of his restaurant's seating area, and the improvements would be sure to make his land even more valuable.

Then Mr. Long and I stopped in to speak with a small-scale merchant who sold everyday housewares out of the front room of her house. She enjoyed a brisk business and was doing well, with an income of about 4 to 5 million *đồng* (US\$267–334) per month (in a district with a reported average income of 2.2 million *đồng,* or US\$147, per month). The mer-chant also talked about the good fortune she had to have several children working abroad as export workers in Korea, Japan, and Taiwan, thanks in large part to programs organized by the district labor and training office. For the most part, hers was a story of progress, of slowly moving toward economic prosperity. Yet she was somewhat less enthusiastic about the road expansion, because she worried about what might happen to her business. The shopfront part of her house lay rather close to the shoulder of the district road already mentioned as being slated for widening. She held back her complaints but emphasized that she was somewhat con-cerned about where she would put her wares after the front of her shop was demolished. Sensing that Mr. Long wanted to put a more positive face on development, she then added that she would probably rebuild her house with the compensation payments she expected to receive. Mr. Long urged her toward optimism: with the compensation, surely she could build a two-story home and keep the shop on the ground floor. In the end, he convinced her to agree that she would have a more modern home, effectively paid for through land compensation payments.

Here were two successful business owners, evidence of a kind of forward-moving success linked to modernization, development, and urbanization. Even the necessary difficulty of the road-widening project would be overcome by what were described as fair and just land compensation payments.

Mr. Long and I continued our tour into the alleyways snaking back behind the district road, where pavement turned to red earth. Little by little, Mr. Long said, these alleys would be paved, cleaned up. As it stood, private spaces around homes and public pathways spilled into each other, and the pathway we were on passed through an impromptu café with low plastic chairs where we approached a group of men, some wearing loose T-shirts, some bare-chested, who were sitting there smoking, joking, and drinking coffee. As we approached this café, Mr. Long seemed ready to turn in the other direction, unprepared as he was to narrate what looked at first glance like indigent, unemployed loafers. But then one of the men called us over, excited.

"Who is this?" he yelled out to Mr. Long, pointing to me.

When Mr. Long relented and explained that I was a student from the United States interested in the daily life of people in Hóc Môn, the man stood up.

"I am a king here!" the man said to me, his clothes torn and falling off his back but his spirits upbeat, a huge grin stretching cheek to cheek. *In America people work all the time, they don't have time for coffee.*[7] The man was obviously underemployed, as were many men in Hóc Môn, yet he argued, jokingly to be sure, but also with conviction, that he was better off than other people with more material possessions and money. Money and material wealth, he continued, mean nothing without *time*. He tugged on his rag of a shirt and laughed. He had very little material wealth, but he had enough to eat and enough to buy coffee and sit with his friends and relax.

He moved his outstretched hands around him in a circular swath, taking in the little alleyway like a king encompassing his domain. "I am a king!" He went on to explain how little work he had to do to maintain his existence, how *thoải mái* life was, that is, how relaxed, unencumbered. He had been born and raised in Hóc Môn, he said. His family had a home, enough food to eat. And he had *time*. He had no designs of leaving for America or for downtown Ho Chi Minh City. Everyone who went to those places chasing success always complained that they only worked, that they *had no time to drink coffee*. Thanks to this, the city itself was *phức tạp,* complicated, having sacrificed sociality for the sake of making money.

Long had expected to be embarrassed by these men who seemed to be loafing in the café, but "the king" ended up extolling the basic point he had been struggling to make with the other two business people; that it was all right to live in Hóc Môn, that the people were content with the pace of change. But the reasons for this were unexpected, and they had to do with *time-orientation* that prioritized sociality rather than the accumulation of money alone.

The Time Value Calculus

As "the king" described it, Vietnamese and American lifestyles stand in something of an inverse relation to each other. Stereotypically, Americans have plenty of things to enjoy but little free time to enjoy them; Vietnamese have plenty of time but few things to enjoy. Yet more and more Vietnamese are coming to realize that the equation is gradually becoming more favorable for an increasing number of people who have a minimum amount of land and income. Certainly they do not possess the level of material opulence present in the United States, but they are gradually achieving new standards of material comfort, and the average person has access to a larger number of goods than before. All the while, the average Vietnamese still claims to have much more free time than the average American. So the crude equation that balances time against material comfort is turning more and more toward the advantage of the Vietnamese lifestyle.

One might imagine an equation, a kind of time value calculus underscoring happiness:

$$\text{(material comfort)} \times \text{(free time)} = \text{happiness}$$

This equation cannot, of course, be calculated in any sort of mathematical sense, because the numbers for the abstract concept *material comfort* can be only hypothetical conjectures. Furthermore, the concept *free time* cannot be taken for granted because the very time that one accepts as free time in Vietnam is hardly a universal category of free time. For example, the lazy, carefree extended time that one spends drinking coffee after a trip delivering corrugated metal from one spot on the highway to another spot on the highway may indeed indicate a more relaxed attitude toward work than would be seen in the average American corporate lawyer or in a Vietnamese American who toils in a nail salon. But the drinking of coffee may well be seen as part of the job itself, for the laborer drinks coffee while waiting for another job. Furthermore, the worker may not technically be working for very many hours of the day, but he or she is prepared to work at almost any time during the course of the day. This idea of a time value calculus is complicated by the fact that "work" and "free time" cannot so easily be distinguished in Vietnam as a whole and in Hóc Môn in particular.

Although people may be "sitting around drinking coffee," they are not necessarily unemployed. In fact, drinking coffee is intimately connected to the act of finding work. Therefore, the Vietnamese idea of time usage dramatically differs from the idea of wage labor we have come to take for granted in the West. But this does not mean that people will not work for a wage.[8]

The owners of streetside businesses both inside and outside the city have a similarly blurred relationship to "work time" and "free time." Even when they are working, they remain at home and spend much of their working time actually engaged in household business such as cooking, cleaning, planting flowers, arranging furniture, and raising children. Vietnamese work, in this sense, cannot be extracted from the home life Westerners typically associate with their free time. Conversely, home life can never be fully separated from work in Vietnam. If one wishes to leave home for a holiday or even a trip to the seaside, for example, the prerequisites of business create a very real obstacle. One cannot simply lock the door and go to the beach. Someone must stay home to receive customers and protect the shop. The rhythm of daily life must follow the rhythm of work life, even though one can ostensibly consider oneself one's own boss.

Land, Labor, and the Time Orientation of Social Reproduction

Despite their differences, the two shop owners and "the king" in the café shared one common feature: all three of them demonstrated a temporal orientation to everyday action that prioritized their ability to reproduce themselves as social persons above all else.[9] That is, they did not conceive of work primarily in terms of labor calculated in terms of clock time; they conceived of work in terms of what was necessary to reproduce their household and themselves as members of that household. The noodle vendor worked out of the front of his home, and the business he ran contributed directly to the reproduction of his household. Indeed his household *is* the restaurant, and the restaurant *is* the household. For him there was no separation of work and residence, no separation of leisure and work. The shop owner also worked out of the front of her home, and the sales she made were directly related to her ability to maintain her household itself. The king relaxed in the cafe, which was not far removed from the front of his home, which blended into the alleyway of his neighborhood. All three had enough land to satisfy their basic living requirements, and their spaces of work, leisure, and residence were combined in a relatively circumscribed place. All of these people subordinated clock time to another sense of time, to "social time" construed in terms of time spent cultivating social relations and linked to the patrilineal ideal of reproducing a bounded patrilocal family unit. Work time and social time fused, and working directly contributed to the household.

None of these individuals were "peasants," but they shared something with the ideal peasant family described in ethnographic literature. Ignoring, for a moment, the notion that peasants engage in agricultural activity, Scott points out that most depictions of peasant labor processes emphasize a central feature of a peasant household: "unlike a capitalist enterprise, it is a unit of consumption as well as a unit of production."[10] The two vendors exemplify this idea; the home is where they work, where they produce the means for reproducing themselves. It is also where they consume. Nevertheless, they are engaged in economic transactions that are clearly capitalist in nature. From this it is clear that a so-called peasant indifference to clock time extends beyond the subsistence-oriented agricultural peasant. This time orientation is not as much based on agricultural production as it is intricately connected to social relationships on a very localized level; it depends not as much on indifference to the clock as on deference to the time of social reproduction, the time required to reproduce the ideal of a patrilocal unit located within a bounded space of land. The ability to function outside of the clock depends on a form of reproducing the means of production (the laborers themselves) that subordinates the strict concept of wage labor to the more basic idea of reproducing the social unit. If one's work and home are combined in one place, it is entirely possible that the units of consumption and production are contained in one place, even if the kind of production is a simple economic transaction of buying cheap and selling dear (selling housewares), taking raw materials and transforming them into a product (making soup), or applying one's labor to random tasks (performing casual labor). At root, there is a fundamental similarity between these forms of exchange and the forms of exchange carried out by peasants, and this similarity is based on relations of time and space in which work and leisure, labor and social life all blend into each other. The accumulation of capital is not a means in itself but is a subset of the totality of the socially construed labor of reproducing the family unit.

In the examples given earlier, the most salient point of concern shared by the two people running businesses had to do with the "productivity" of their land. The Chinese noodle vendor was quite satisfied with how events had turned out for him. The shop owner was concerned about her frontage space. The spatial position of each of them along this district road allowed for a certain combination of work and residence. The heavy traffic in front of their homes made them ideal places for business. Their spatial position made it possible to work where they lived.

As for the king, even though he himself would often work outside his home, he also spoke in an idiom of security based on the fact that his family had a home. He was able to relax because he had attained a minimum subsistence level that secured his ability to reproduce his role as a social person without the constant need to generate new income. But unlike the other two, he had a home that was not in such a spatially advantageous position because it was tucked away in the alleyway, so he and his family members would not be able to make money from his front door. Yet his insistence that he did not need to subordinate himself to a regimented form of clock time in which there is no time to drink coffee indicated the degree to which he prioritized social relations over the accumulation of capital. And although he was not working at the precise moment when we met him, he was not in fact unemployed.

The king was engaged in casual labor, what Vietnamese men designate with the phrase "Có việc gì, làm việc đó" (Whatever work there is, I do that work). This is a common form of labor prized by local men, a form of labor in which they are always ready to work and yet constantly at leisure. If someone wanted to dig a large ditch, transport some dirt, or build a home, he could simply stop by the café and announce the job available, and the men at the café would debate the relative merits of the job, decide whether the compensation seemed adequate, and then be ready to work immediately. If a job seemed suitable, they might not even finish their coffee before setting off to begin, hopping on their motorbikes before even putting out their cigarettes. The labor is "casual," but men like the king are also constantly on call, ready to roll. They are ready to work as long as a certain set of conditions is met.

The conditions determining whether a local resident will or will not work reveal the degree to which land still underscores relations to labor time, even in cases in which workers are willing to work outside of the household unit of consumption. For this kind of labor to remain casual, a local resident like the king requires that two key criteria be satisfied: (1) he must already have housing and a minimum level of subsistence, and (2) the labor must not permanently alter his subjective relationship to *free time;* that is, it must not deprive him of his ability to remain relaxed, *thoải mái.* Because of the stability created by the satisfaction of a minimum subsistence, a man in these circumstances can easily refuse work based on the failure of such work to satisfy his demand for autonomous control of his free time. But all of this seems impossible. How can someone work without fundamentally altering his relationship to free time? Are not work and free time fundamentally different concepts? How can one have both?

The Relationship of Space to Time Use

One can simultaneously work and have free time by integrating the very concept of labor into one's social life; the distinction between work and leisure disappears because both are subsumed under the general concept of being able to reproduce oneself as a social person. This is clearest in a classic peasant household, in a shopfront, or in a family restaurant operating out of the home. The full unity of work, family, and leisure can be achieved in time only when the space of work and leisure are one and the same and when work itself is conceptualized as a social relationship rather than a strict exchange of labor. One cannot combine work and leisure when they are in separate places because one cannot be in two places at the same time.

But when a male laborer like the king does work, he most certainly sells his labor, and he obviously leaves his home and goes off to work for someone when he agrees to do a job in exchange for a wage. Even if he judges the kind of work against what he will get for it, and even if he maintains control over his autonomy for the greater part of his social life, at the moment he accepts a job he effectively sells his labor as an abstract commodity. He temporarily enters a relation of production based on the wage construed in terms of the working day. But in so doing he does not enter any form of contract that will *permanently* commodify his labor. This is where temporal oscillation becomes important. Once this job is finished, he can return to his preferred state of being *thoải mái,* of relaxing. Yet the important point is that his ideal state prioritizes the ideal of sociality. He works just enough to reproduce the means of being *thoải mái.* He will certainly not take a steady factory job, because by doing so he would fully give up the possibility of being at home or structuring the temporality of his labor on terms that prioritize sociality above work itself. In order for him to negotiate this oscillation between the two poles of work and home, he must stand somewhere between both of them, in a place that is simultaneously home oriented and work oriented.

The café solves this problem by serving as a site of mediation among leisure, work, and home. The café itself is very "local" in the sense that it serves people in the immediate vicinity, and the familiarity of the scene implies a social connection through which the very idea of work must pass. In a certain sense, people like these men in the café are simultaneously at home and at work, even though objectively they are really in neither of those places. When an offer of work is made in the café, the men will discuss among themselves the relative merits of the labor, confer about the compensation offered, ask for more money, and decide how many of them will go (or, if only one of them is needed, they will decide who should go based on an understanding of who most needs the job). Often, if the person looking to hire help is relatively familiar to the group, these discussions will not be necessary; a generally fair amount of compensation will be expected, anywhere from 30,000 *đồng* (US$2) to 60,000 *đồng* (US$4) for a day's work.

Even though money is exchanged, the implicit understanding remains that this is a temporary foray into the zone of capitalist labor but not a wholesale renunciation of a socially construed relationship of social production. When the work is done, the men will go back to being *thoải mái.* In the larger social sense, then, this whole process recalls what Chayanov called "non-Capitalist economic systems," supplemented by but not wholly subsumed by capitalist conceptions of commodified labor. Chayanov himself used this concept to describe peasant economies as part of "a very wide area of economic life . . . based, not on a capitalist form, but on the completely different form of nonwage family economic unit. Such a unit has very special motives for economic activity and also a very specific conception of profitability."[11] In this case, although the king will be working for a wage, it will be a wage calculated not in terms of hours worked but in terms of the larger unit of a day's labor, which can itself vary and includes resting during the middle of the day. His labor does not fully extract him from social relations and temporality based around the café and the ideal of the patrilocal home but rather serves as a temporary move into commodified labor time that will be followed by a return to the temporal cycle of socially construed production measured in terms of the family cycle, immediate needs, and how much the family needs to reproduce itself.

In the family production unit that underlies the great majority of peasant economies, the most important category of income stems from family *labor product.* This means that the transformation of means of production into product stems wholly from the labor of family members rather than from labor bought and sold as a commodity. In a classic peasant economy, the combination of land and family labor with very little external input should be enough to reproduce the social relations of the family. But in this case, the king is not a subsistence peasant; his family has labor, but land is scarce, as are other inputs. There is enough land to reproduce the requirements of patrilocal *residence* but not enough to meet the *subsistence needs* of the family; the king's family owns a compound in the alleyway but no family fields. To meet their subsistence needs, then, members of this family have to work for money, which can be converted into subsistence through the purchase of food and other goods. Although members of the family must occasionally sell their labor as a commodity, they do so for a temporally restricted period, based on a subjective evaluation of the kinds of jobs they will or will not take based on a subjective interpretation of how much effort they are willing to expend. Unlike the classic Marxist definition of commodified labor in full-fledged capitalism, which reduces the value of labor to a universal unit of socially necessary labor time translated into a wage, these men evaluate the value of their labor in terms of both wage labor and what

Chayanov calls "self-exploitation," a concept construed in terms of how hard people will work in relation to the ratio of family need to available family labor:

The amount of the labor product is mainly determined by the size and composition of the working family, the number of its members capable of work, then by the productivity of the labor unit, and—this is especially important—by the degree of labor effort—the degree of self-exploitation through which the working members effect a certain quantity of labor units in the course of the year.[12]

The subjective value, and hence the minimum value, of labor itself is based not only on a quantitative relationship of money but also on the subjective relationship of the members of a household to the work itself as well as to a subjective evaluation of household needs. If the household does not need much, the worker is in a position to refuse work. It is this subjective evaluation that Chayanov speaks of when he refers to the all-important "degree of self-exploitation."

"The degree of self-exploitation," Chayanov explains, "is determined by a peculiar equilibrium between family demand satisfaction and the drudgery of labor itself."[13] The conditions that determine both what constitutes family demand and the drudgery of labor relate to the number of mouths to feed in the family, the number of working-age producers in the family, the family's access to markets, and commodity prices, as well as the quality and price of the land.[14] The volume of production in family-based production is intimately tied to the composition of the family, but the effort to achieve maximum production is also linked to the subjective evaluation of the relative importance of what this labor adds to the satisfaction of the family's needs.

At the café, the king and his friends subjectively compare the marginal utility the work will give to their respective family resources against the perceived "drudgery of labor" represented by the work itself. To understand this instantaneous subjective evaluation of what counts as socially acceptable work for these men in the café, it helps to consider a certain kind of work that local men in cafés will not do, barring extreme circumstances. They will not work in a local factory. Even though it might offer a more stable wage, the "drudgery of labor" in a factory exceeds the subjective, unwritten threshold of how much they will subordinate themselves to a form of labor that compromises their ability to reproduce themselves as social persons.

Factory Labor and the Negotiation of Spatiotemporal Oscillation

For local men and women in Hóc Môn contemplating the idea of engaging in local factory labor, the drudgery of labor in industrial work outweighs the marginal increase in wages they might gain from this work. On one level, the reason for refusing factory work might be simply attributed to the desire to differentiate oneself from "poor laborers." To be sure, many long-time residents of the outer-city districts insist that factory work is base, dirty work. More important than the symbolic associations linked to factory labor, however, are the specifics of the labor process. In Hóc Môn, as in other outer-city districts, the people who work in factories predominantly come from outside the area—migrants mainly coming from the Mekong Delta, from the southern central regions (such as Quảng Ngãi), and from as far away as northern Vietnam.[15] According to Đặng Nguyên Anh, at least 10,906 migrants went to Hóc Môn from other provinces between 1994 and 1999.[16] Therefore, these jobs are largely filled by former "peasants" who came from structurally marginalized positions in the countryside and who, in striking contrast to assumptions about "peasant temporality," most fully subordinate themselves to the temporal discipline of capitalist production within the factories.[17] Working in a factory is a form of labor that requires a fundamental separation of work and home, which these laborers have enacted fully through labor migration. The worker must leave home and work in the factory according to a set schedule of hours.

Because the vast majority of the people who will work in these factories come from outside of Hóc Môn, they do not have land or housing in the area. They must pay to sleep in rented cubicles, which they share with other migrant laborers. For the most part, they are separated from their families, having come from other regions with the express purpose of earning a cash income, part of which they use to pay their own expenses and part of which they (hope to) send home to family members in their hometown or province. As Lê Bạch Dương writes, many Vietnamese migrant households "have to absorb the full costs of subsistence and social reproduction, turning only to the wages on which they become dependent. With low wages and insecure jobs, many cannot meet the required expenses. They absorb the costs through tolerating poverty, enduring poor health conditions, and accepting privatization of public goods in general."[18] Factory workers, in contrast to locals who refuse factory work, subordinate the time of social reproduction to work time. Under ideal circumstances, this kind of work is construed as a temporary fix for financial struggles back home. Many such workers also see this work as part of an act of temporal oscillation—they have shifted into the phase of submission to the clock in order to accumulate capital resources, which can later be reinvested in their home area. This foray into the strict discipline of capitalist work is just a moment in the larger oscillation between spatiotemporal modes. Factory labor is seen by many as something they are willing to do for a while in order to earn a wage before returning to the alternate temporal ideal of "social time" construed in terms of social reproduction of the family unit in a bounded, patrilocal space back home.

A factory worker in Hóc Môn earns between 600,000 *đồng* (US$40) and 1,000,000 *đồng* (US$66) per month, and because most of the workers are from out of town, most of them have to pay for their own accommodations at rates that hover around 50,000 *đồng* per month. Small, rudimentary, unpainted brick rooms rent for 200,000 *đồng* per month, and the typical worker will share such a space with three others, with four to a room. Although the wage is low, it is not necessarily lower than the total monthly income of local people who refuse to work in the factory. The main difference is the relation of space and time. The factory worker has wholly subordinated family time and space to the time and space of the factory.

The cubicles migrant workers rent (see Figure 6) offer little more than places to sleep and to lock their belongings. These cubicles are too hot in the daytime, and workers are loath to hang around them too much because they will need to use their fans to cool the superheated tin-roofed rooms and they do not want to spend their savings on electricity. In short, they have come to Hóc Môn in order to work, not to hang around or spend time in their rented quarters; otherwise they would never have left where they came from. In this temporal space dissociated from the temporal space of social relations where they came from, they fully commit to the temporality of capitalist labor and production.

The degree to which factory workers fully commit themselves to the temporal demands of the factory labor process and the accumulation of wages became clearest to me one day when I went to join some factory workers at the Chisan textile factory during their daily lunch break. I arrived just past noon at the cafeteria run by a local family that lived across from the factory. This was the time that the workers typically got off for

FIGURE 6. Migrant labor housing. Hóc Môn district.

lunch, and the company had contracted with the family to provide lunches for the workers. Because this was the only time to catch up with workers, I would join them for lunch discussions, paying 3,000 *đồng* (ca. US$0.20) for the standard plate of rice, a piece of pork, fried tofu, or fried fish, egg custard, and an alternating soup.

When I arrived this time, almost everyone was gone. Cường, a thirty-three-year-old man from Vĩnh Long (in the Mekong Delta) who worked as a fabric cutter, was sitting alone. He explained that there had been an electrical blackout in the neighborhood all morning. During blackouts, the industries all shut down and the workers are "allowed to rest" *(cho nghỉ)*. This euphemism for resting has an obvious double meaning, similar to that of the English term for workers who are "let go." When workers say they have been allowed to rest, it really means that they have not been invited to work that day. And these workers are all there to work, not to rest, at least not during this portion of the day. Their entire living situation is structured around working as much as possible. On top of "resting," they are also not fed. According to Cường, when the workers rest they are not given food.

The few people resting at the lunch place were all sweating in the heat, trying to take advantage of the slight breeze passing through the wide-open space in the outdoor dining room, chatting with the owner of the restaurant, taking turns in the few hammocks hanging toward the back of the area. Our conversations were lethargic, punctuated by complaints: "Nóng quá! Không ngủ được!" (It's too hot to sleep!).

In this case, this rest from work arrived specifically at a moment when the workers certainly could not rest. Even if they wanted to rest, the power outage itself meant that the electric fans in their sleeping cubicles would not work even if they chose to use them. With no way to sleep in their rented cubicles, which had become hot boxes in the midday sun, they sat aimlessly, not working and yet unable to rest. They were resting restlessly, looking for a way to escape from this unplanned rest from work. Without work, there was absolutely nothing to do.

Spatiotemporal Oscillation and Social Reproduction

Because most of these workers come from rural areas, they accept employment in these harsh circumstances because it offers them an opportunity to raise capital in ways not possible in the economically depressed regions they come from. Their ideal, however, is to return to their home regions. Even though they completely subordinate themselves to the time discipline of factory labor, the ideal is to support the reproduction of social relations back home through this accumulation of capital. In terms of their larger household-based labor process, they go outside in order to send money back to the inside. In large degree, the majority of people working in the factories are described as coming from peasant backgrounds, where their ability to generate capital is limited by the strict economic imbalances of rural and urban Vietnam. Although the stereotypical dichotomy of peasant and urbanite assumes that peasants follow the natural rhythms of the agricultural cycle, paradoxically it is recent migrants from the rural areas who are most vulnerable to the clock-based time discipline of the factory.

In contrast, the Hóc Môn locals largely refuse to submit to this temporal orientation of factory discipline. If anyone maintains a temporal orientation divorced from clock time, it is the Hóc Môn locals, who prefer to take casual labor or to work out of their homes. But it is precisely the locals who can claim to be much more urban than those "peasant" outsiders from the countryside who come to work in factories. As a result, the difference between time orientations confounds the strict differentiation between peasant time and urban time that stereotypes would lead one to expect. Instead, time orientation is linked to one's position vis-à-vis one's household, construed as a unit defined and bounded by its relationship to a stable, typically patrilocal, plot of land. Within Hóc Môn, the primary distinction between local laborers and nonlocal laborers depends on this separation of work and home. "The king" refuses to work in local factories because he has a home. People from outside of Hóc Môn have mostly come to work and establish only the most superficial social relationships with local residents. As a result, the king is able to oscillate between home-oriented temporal notions of social reproduction and outward-oriented temporal notions associated with wage labor. In this confluence of competing and complementary time disciplines, the practical ability to negotiate these different temporal schedules is the ultimate clue to successful "articulation" of the new economic relations in Vietnam and also provides a clue to how social actors navigate the merging of time disciplines and the real experience of social change.

The temporal oscillation of nonlocal factory laborers working in Hóc Môn is reproduced among people from Hóc Môn as well, albeit at a different level. The family of the housewares vendor encountered earlier provides a clear example. Although her own household-based labor process escaped the regulatory rhythm of the clock, this was not the case for her children, who had all gone abroad as export workers. The children, who are Hóc Môn locals working abroad, are thus structurally on a par with the migrants who have come to Hóc Môn from other provinces. Just like internal migrants who come to the city from rural provinces, people who go abroad as export laborers also make a fundamental break from their place of residence. Like the internal migrants, they send most of their wage back to their family home, thus making it possible to reproduce the household as a spatially localized residence organized according to a labor process unsubordinated to clock time. The utter and complete subjugation to the clock while working abroad, then, is conceived of as a temporary movement outside of time designed to perpetuate the possibility for the social reproduction of the family in forms not wholly subjugated to the clock. Rather than orchestrating a permanent move to embrace clock time, people oscillate between industrial labor discipline in the world outside and an idealized form of labor and work that prioritizes the social reproduction of the household, conceived of as the inside.

Going abroad and sending money home is temporal oscillation realized.[19] There is always the risk, however, that temporary forays into the space-time of industrial capitalism will become permanent, that the worker will become wholly enslaved to the temporality of labor separated from the home. The very real risks involved can be seen in the large numbers of prostitutes from the Mekong Delta, textile workers who never actually make enough to send home, or abused export laborers who are tricked out of wages and forced to stay as some sort of indentured laborers in the foreign country, unable to send remittances back to the family unit.[20] Such cases represent temporal oscillation interrupted.

These relations of production contradict the simple binary distinction between country and city that depicts them as distinct spaces identified with their own respective time orientations. More precisely, everyday time orientation is itself contextually nested within a larger temporal cycle that oscillates spatially between the inside and the outside. Time orientation is never fully rural or urban; it oscillates according to the social relationships people develop within the place where they live and the place they come from. These relationships, in turn, may depend on how long they have lived there, larger trajectories of social movement, their general "status," and their access to constant capital, especially land and inputs. In general terms, subjugation to the clock develops most intensely with the split between residence and labor, the split between work and leisure, and the dismantling of social connections that integrate work with social relations. The ability to resist complete subordination to the clock and to imagine alternative trajectories of time outside of the linear time frame of progress toward modernization and development rests not on a strict division between country and city but on the division between people who have access to the means of reproducing themselves as social persons *in space* and those who do not.

The fundamental distinction between those who will work in local factories and those who will not rests on access to land in the district where they have migrated to work. Those who will work in a factory are either landless or, if they do come from households that have land back in their hometown, come from provinces where their ability to generate income from their family plots of land is seriously compromised.[21] They are mostly recent migrants to the area. Those who refuse this kind of work are either long-term residents of Hóc Môn who have the security of their families and some household space to fall back on or migrants to the area who have been able to secure some land for themselves in Hóc Môn.

An important difficulty emerges for those who have land now. For land is a scarce resource: not everyone who now has land through their families can be guaranteed of this in the future. As a result, time discipline changes within a family in response to objective transformations in the household over time. Thus, even in families that appear to show a marked indifference to clock time, the children often undergo a transformation in the ideal of unbounded time and must often accept the clock as a guiding force in their lives.

Kinship, Accumulation, and Spatiotemporal Oscillation

Time orientation is thus tied into the strategies people fashion in order to reproduce themselves as ideal social persons. This, in turn, is linked to their relation to space. In the Vietnamese notion of kinship discussed in Chapter 1, the "inner realm" of the patriline *(bên nội)* is often idealized as the primary means of reproducing the social unit. The patriline is bounded in space and can be traced backward deep in time (measured in terms of lineage depth), which means that the *ideal* family is able to accommodate successive generations with patrilocal residence in a relatively circumscribed space around the larger patrilineal family. Although the prevalence of alternative family structures confounds this ideal, the idea of powerful families still depends on the notion of a long history that can be traced through time and located in space.

The anthropologist Phan Thị Yến Tuyết, for example, traces the unique family worshiping practices of several established Ho Chi Minh City families as a way of establishing the historical importance of the city itself. In the process, she celebrates those families with the longest histories. One of these is the Nguyễn family, whose members "left their mark" by establishing villages in Quảng Trị and Quảng Nam provinces before establishing themselves in what is now Ho Chi Minh City. "All told," writes Tuyết, "the history of this Nguyễn family is longer than 520 years, spanning approximately 20 generations." She also glorifies the Trần Công lineage, "also with a depth encompassing 500 years, also 20 generations . . . having come to [live in] our Ho Chi Minh City for these past several hundred years."[22] Looking at the family altars, the shrines, and the ancestral rites of such established families allows Tuyết to argue that

Vietnamese in the southern region have retained an important sense of rootedness:

Only by looking back on the lineages of Vietnamese migrants coming into the south of the country to open up cultivated land *(khai phá)* can one see the truly extremely great, highly precious, pride-worthy manner in which these migrants displayed fierce vitality and indomitable will in preserving their family cultural spirit. It was precisely through the traditions of "living and dying together," "drinking water remembering the source" *(uống nước nhớ nguồn)*, "paying respect to ancestors" that these Vietnamese migrants were able to break fresh ground *(khẩn hoang)* in the South despite hardship, fatigue, and the disturbances of war. They still did not abandon or "stray from their inherent duty," did not lose their source, lose their roots. They upheld the sincere folk wisdom that "trees have roots, water has a source, people have lineage ancestors" *(cây có cội, nước có nguồn, con người có tổ tiên dòng tộc)* that the Vietnamese people especially cherish.[23]

Although the southern rites of ancestral worship may differ from the northern and central ones in several respects, Tuyết argues that they provide evidence of a kind of cultural continuity in the south over the "last three hundred years."[24] This argument highlights the ways in which many people continue to idealize lineage depth as a key index of family cohesion.

Over time, however, maintaining a lineage in space becomes increasingly difficult, because the material realities of space restrict the ability to reproduce this spatially bounded patrilineal descent group. (In fact, this is highlighted by the great Nguyễn and Trần families, cited earlier, which obviously left their place of origin.) In practice, many people retain an idealized view of the long patriline rooted in a homeland at the same time that they develop a more pragmatic relationship to the actual family structures and social relations around them. For example, my neighbors, who had moved to Hóc Môn from Huế over the course of the past fifteen years, expressed a more ambivalent relation to their roots. On the one hand, they would sometimes get together and sing songs about the banks of the perfume river in Huế, their homeland. And when one of them would strum out the lines of the famous song "Quê hương" (Homeland) a sense of excitement would overtake the group. He would sing the chorus with a dramatic flare:

Quê hương mỗi người chỉ một   Homeland . . . only one each
Như là chỉ một Mẹ thôi   Like having one Mother

Quê hương nếu ai không nhớ	Homeland. . . . One who forgets
Sẽ không lớn nổi thành người	Won't become a person

These last lines would come out in a kind of teary lament, a wistful, drawn-out wail of "Quê H-ư-ơ—ng . . . ," followed by a truncated collapse into ". . . only one." He would swallow the final heavy accent of the word "một" (one), eyes closed in a grimace that made it seem that he was swallowing tears along with the word and the idea of a singular home. And then he would end the song thus: "Whoever forgets their homeland cannot become a person" *(thành người).*

On the other hand, these neighbors had a saying that conveyed a completely different sentiment altogether: "Gia đình xa không bằng láng giềng gần" (A distant family cannot compare with close neighbors). Here the homeland is relinquished in order to foster close relations in the place where people actually live. Thus, despite the ideals, in most families there is simply not enough land to continually subdivide among successive generations. Practical adjustments have to be made to the patrilineal ideal. Although the bounded family plot of land remains an ideal, people need to turn elsewhere for the means of reproducing the social unit. It is exactly this which is transforming the face of contemporary Hóc Môn, because the debate about what kind of work people are willing to do is also a debate about what counts as socially necessary labor time, which is connected to the practical exigencies of what people need to do in order to reproduce the family unit and how they will get land to support new generations of the family at a time when land is growing scarce and land prices are rising.

Spatial Changes in the Outer-City House

One solution to this problem of land scarcity is to change the architecture of the family home, to divide and subdivide a family plot in order to accommodate more members of a patrilocal kin group (see Figures 7 and 8). This solution appears throughout Hóc Môn. This is one reason that people with homes along roads often build upward, adding additional levels when the ability to build outward is closed off by the shoulder of the road. Homes further removed from the highway often have more space in the family plot. But surrounding homes also prohibit expansion outward. In these cases, people build inward, in a form of localized involution that uses up all available space on a family plot. But architectural

FIGURE 7. Subdivision on a single family plot. A husband and wife stand in front of the home they built as a patrilocal residence for their son and his wife on their family plot. The older family home can be seen in the background. Hóc Môn district.

solutions cannot compensate for the land crunch indefinitely. And when a bounded place in space cannot be continually reproduced, people turn toward the alternate form of kinship affiliation, the "non-male-oriented" kinship structure that Luong describes as "un-bounded in space."[25] Thus socially necessary labor time depends on shifting concepts of what is necessary to reproduce the social unit, which is itself dependent on the availability of land for productive activity of various types as well as a minimum amount needed for the reproduction of the patrilocal household.[26] A kinship idiom that is unbounded in space facilitates the accumulation of capital but threatens the reproduction of the spatially bounded social unit.

The problem of land and space in Hóc Môn is therefore intimately related to the temporal orientation of work and labor. Work that requires a separation of home and workplace often offers a steady, predictable wage calculated in terms of the working day. But it requires one to work outside the home. The economic transformations associated with Vietnam's pathway of development is mostly associated with increasing the opportunities for the kind of work that produces an income derived from labor according to the clock. Subsistence agriculture is not enough to

FIGURE 8. Subdivision of the family plot through building upward. Hóc Môn district.

support families where land is scarce and where other inputs necessary to social reproduction (such as schooling, health care, and transportation) are monetized. The fact that this kind of labor is separated from the place of residence itself offers an opportunity to transcend the limitations of the household production unit, allowing one to accumulate capital without a significant amount of land. And although a social person needs enough land to reproduce the social unit (that is, enough space for eventual new households), wage labor offers a form of escape from the limitations of the household production unit.

As Luong has described with respect to terms of person reference, Vietnamese kinship (especially in the south) tends to shift between two conceptualizations of kinship and social relations depending on circumstance.[27] Just as people shift between patrilineal (bounded in space) and bilateral (unbounded in space) models of the family lineage *(họ),* they also shift between notions of temporal action that are centered on the local family unit and emphasize work at home and orientations to temporal action that lead them to work outside of the family.

This does not mean that people permanently forsake one form of family organization for another. More precisely, they oscillate between them, attempting to gain the advantages of both forms of spatiotemporal social organization. Tôn Nữ Quỳnh Trân describes kinship relation in terms of a cyclical process of family formation.[28] People shift away from close kinship ties during times of transformation and then eventually return to the patrilineal ideal in times of consolidation. She identifies two factors associated with urbanization that impinge on kinship relations. First, newly urbanizing areas have mostly new immigrants with few family relations located in the new area. When they immigrate, such individuals submit themselves to basic tasks of material accumulation. With limited social networks, such people have little ability to concentrate on the idea of cultivating their lineage, and lineage obligations may even seem burdensome or threatening to people who are struggling to earn enough money to survive day to day. Furthermore, urbanization raises the price of land and leads to competition and struggle among members of a household. However, a second stage in family relations follows thereafter. As time goes by and the family's position within the new environment stabilizes, family members begin to consolidate and share their resources with each other, and then they begin to focus inward on the lineage. They start to write their family genealogies, organize annual rituals, cultivate family grave sites, build temples to ancestors *(miếu),* and so on. The shifting relationship between inside and outside, viewed through the lens of different ways of imagining kinship affiliations, is thus not unidirectional; it emerges within historical transformations of the social landscape that take place over time.

Limits of Land and Temporary Wage Labor

A family with large amounts of land can accommodate a new family within its compound. But after several generations, the family will not be able to do this anymore. A family with little or no land will have to move somewhere in order to find a bounded space where they can reproduce the family unit. Social reproduction of the household involves creative solutions and leads to situations in which households in Hóc Môn often exhibit multiple temporalities and members living under the same roof engage in several modes of production, often side by side. The mother of one family told me of her roots in Nam Định province and how she and her husband were orphans who worked the land as members of an agricultural collective before moving to Kiên Giang province in the Mekong Delta, where they worked as laborers on another person's farm. After that, because of heavy flooding in the region, they decided to move to Hóc Môn, where they could have a better chance of making a living and where they were finally able to buy a small house as well as some land for themselves and their nine children. The parents are rice farmers, and the whole family contributes with supplementary sideline work as well. The husband is primarily unemployed, but helps with the labor in the fields when necessary; the twenty-year-old daughter works in Củ Chi in the Fuji Film factory; the ten-year-old son walks along the highway selling lottery tickets at restaurants, cafés, and individual homes; and the rest of the family supplements this income by caning bamboo chairs on a piecework basis. With nine children, the parents do not sell the rice they farm but use most of it to feed the family itself. Neither rural nor urban, the family combines multiple spatiotemporal strategies under one roof in a largely successful attempt to reproduce itself as a social unit.

Temporal Oscillation and the Kinship Mode of Production

In this way, labor choices do not represent once-and-for-all resistance from or acquiescence to clock-oriented labor. Instead they are intimately connected to efforts centered around reproducing the social person, which ideally requires the reproduction of the patrilineal unit within a bounded space on land. But with land scarcity, single-pronged solutions become impossible and people oscillate between multiple modes of spatiotemporal organization. Although the patrilineal, patrilocal ideal of the household remains strong, the production of a social person within a household often requires both a spatially bounded form of reproduction and a spatially expansive form of reproduction—a distinction that corresponds to the reproduction of an insular patrilineal kinship lineage and the expansion outward into a bilateral model that more readily enables creative forms of labor. As land becomes more and more scarce and as the drudgery of labor produced through processes of involution yields fewer and fewer returns, people will begin to seek out other opportunities.

This labile process reproduces structures by transcending them, proceeding as a movement of social oscillation, stretching out to bilateral networks and regressing to patrilineal cocoons. Capital accumulation often occurs in the wide swath of extended kin in the *ngoại* realm, and social reproduction occurs within the localized *nội* realm. The infamous practice of constructing fake marriages in order to acquire foreign visas serves as a paradigmatic example. The idea, of course, is that a wife married out into a foreign land will generate new possibilities to generate capital that will ultimately be able to support the family back home. In quite simple terms, this shows the process of temporal oscillation and the opposition between accumulation and reproduction of the patriline through the extension of bilateral ties. In a purely patrilineal model, the daughter would be lost to the family that bore her. But the very idea of marrying a daughter out in order to generate new gains for the inside implies that she will be making a sacrifice for the family and that she will be sending money back, which itself implies an expectation that her new family will maintain important ties with her natal family. The idea of a woman's family investing US$20,000 in a fake marriage with a foreigner makes it clear that these bilateral ties constitute very practical connections with real material effects.

Such tactical forms of spatiotemporal oscillation depend both on the primacy of inside relations as well as the recognition that the inside is inherently limited. In simple spatial terms, households will not be able to subdivide their land indefinitely and reproduce themselves within the bounded compound of the family unit. Spatially, they have to look outward to a larger conception of social space, and temporally this transforms their understanding of how they can organize their own action in terms of time. It is not surprising, then, that younger members of households sometimes employ new conceptions of space that in turn change their conception of time and labor. Young people entering the work force are increasingly drawn to the city, where they see the sacrifice of time now as an investment in a kind of future stability. But this, of course, comes at a cost. The cost is the forced separation of work and home. But as land becomes more scarce, this separation is itself necessary in order to develop the resources necessary to eventually purchase the land needed to reproduce a household. Rather than seeing new work patterns as a complete denial of socially embedded conceptions of reproduction, they may be productively understood as moments within a larger process of temporal oscillation. Young laborers oscillate between the idea of subordinating themselves to work outside the home and the ideal of eventually reproducing the spatially bound, self-reproducing household. For now, young people will work outside the home in an effort to rebuild the possibility of combining work and residence. The now is sacrificed for a future that, oddly enough, reproduces "traditional" patterns of patrilocal residence.

One twenty-two-year-old female student who lived in Hóc Môn but traveled by motorbike to school in the city (a one-and-a-half-hour round trip) explained that she invested her time in study with the implicit hope that she could create a future. But she also spoke at length about the importance of relaxing and having fun, a concept Vietnamese designate with the particularly evocative term *đi chơi* (to play). She was describing the two extreme poles that designate the boundaries of sociotemporal oscillation. She turned to a proverb: "Học không chơi đánh rơi tuổi trẻ, chơi không học đánh mất tương lai" (All study, no play, lose your youth; all play, no study, lose your future).[29] The ability to successfully negotiate these two temporal frames is the key to success in contemporary Vietnam. The ability to do so is a reflection and a source of power and prestige. To play, *đi chơi,* really signifies an accumulation of social prestige fashioned out of social relations, and it is incompatible with the pure accumulation of money. Indeed, it may very well entail the consumption or frivolous expenditure of resources. But such consumption and expenditure is really a kind of input into the production of the social person. Work or study is posed as the antithesis of play; they are forms of accumulation ultimately linked to the accumulation of capital and symbolic capital out in the wider world. (It is not surprising that study is most often linked to a future-oriented practical profession tied in with foreign ideas; studying English and, increasingly, Japanese, for example, translates directly to work.) Navigating these opposing extremes is analogous to the movement between a future-oriented outside *(ngoại)* realm associated with accumulation, and a tradition-oriented inside *(nội)* world associated with long-standing social relations rooted in bounded space. The ability to oscillate between them with facility is the ultimate recognition of one's power in the world. It signifies a command of all time and space.

The Power of Spatial and Temporal Mobility

In this chapter I have shown how the idealized separation of the country and the city becomes realized in everyday action through the oscillation between them. In and of themselves, these idealized categories of space and time appear fixed. But as Bachelard so cogently warns, the fixity of such "obvious geometry" risks obscuring more complex relationships.[30]

Yet Bachelard's philosophical critique itself obscures the important social fact that categories of inside and outside do indeed persist in today's Vietnam. Combining philosophical skepticism about the fallacy of geometrical reductionism with the realities of everyday practices that reproduce these very structures of opposition has revealed that the ideal categories of inside and outside are not as much depictions of reality as social fields upon which intense and creative social maneuvers can constitute and generate forms of practical power that thwart structures by playing with them. The ideal "power" in the categories of rural and urban becomes realized only in social action when social actors manipulate these categories in order to acquire, consolidate, or increase their status positions and material advantages in relation to other social actors. The manipulation of the meaning of space and time becomes a key mechanism by which to carve a space for social action in the world. But to move between different orientations to space and time it is necessary to create and maintain the idea that there are different dimensions of space-time in the first place. To toggle back and forth between the country and the city or between the inside and the outside, one must have these oppositions to toggle between. By constructing a notion of "peasant time" and "urban time" people create the idea of distinct spatiotemporal worlds that can be crossed with certain powerful effects. The next chapter shows how the construction of the Trans-Asia Highway quite concretely manifests the political and social effects of this manipulation of temporal and spatial relations. On the Trans-Asia Highway, ideal concepts of space become so real you can watch them being built; you can feel them, ride on them, even crash into them.

Part III

Realizing the Ideal

5. The Road to Paradise
Building the Trans-Asia Highway

> Giao thông là mạch máu của mọi việc. Giao thông tắc thì việc gì cũng
> khó. Giao thông tốt thì việc gì cũng dễ dàng.
> Traffic is the blood vessel of all work. Traffic stops and work is burden.
> Traffic flows and work is easy.
>
> —Attributed to Hồ Chí Minh

Road Burns

When he pulled up to the café Lam Sơn a few weeks after his accident, Ba Ven appeared as a silhouette against the steady traffic of motorbikes, buses, and dump trucks passing to and fro on the half-finished section of the Trans-Asia Highway behind him. Framed by the rectangular screen of bright sun where the café opens to the road, he took a few long minutes to park his motorbike, a baggy thin shirt several sizes too large billowing around him, light passing through the fabric, a shadow outlining his body within. He carefully dismounted, his motions slow and cautious, his leg making a stiff, exaggerated arc over the seat of the bike before he limped inside. As he stepped out of the glare into the café, an odd smirk on his face revealed the twisted combination of laughter and deep sadness often seen in people cursing their own misfortune. His confident swagger of earlier days had been transformed into a limp, he had a scab of dried blood beneath his left nostril, and he wore his shirt hanging loose like a shawl, trying to cover himself from the sun without touching his skin.

I asked what had happened. He answered: "Xuyên Á!" The Trans-Asia Highway, the *Xuyên Á,* had happened. Ba Ven opened up his shirt and revealed a left arm encrusted with dried blood and torn skin. Underneath his loose shirt the entire left side of his body was covered with huge scabs that ran along his leg and up to his shoulder, entirely shredded by road burn. Oddly, almost impossibly, he smiled and laughed out a sigh: "Tai nạn," accident.

From November 1999 to December 2003, an ambitious project by the Vietnamese Ministry of Transportation, supported with a US$100 million loan from the Asian Development Bank (ADB) and US$44.7 million from the Vietnamese government, slowly transformed National Highway 22, leading northwest out of Ho Chi Minh City, into the Vietnamese portion of the Trans-Asia Highway. Part of the larger economic integration plans of the Association of Southeast Asian Nations regional trade organization, this international roadway will eventually connect Ho Chi Minh City with the Cambodian capital, Phnom Penh, and continue to Bangkok, in Thailand. ADB Senior Project Engineer John Cooney aptly summarized the macroeconomic and regional political significance of the highway project at the November 15, 1999, groundbreaking ceremony as, "a very positive signal . . . that the sub-region has taken the first steps to becoming a more closely integrated economic area."[1] Deputy Prime Minister Nguyễn Tấn Dũng linked economic exchange and infrastructure development directly to politics when he said, "The highway marks the promotion of friendly and cooperative relations between [the] governments and peoples of the Association of Southeast Asian Nations (ASEAN) member countries, and between Cambodia and Vietnam, in particular."[2]

Although few local residents seem to care or talk about the effect the road will have on "friendly relations" with the people of Cambodia, many people living in the outer-city districts along the route near Ho Chi Minh City do see the highway project as a symbol of social progress and transformation. Not only does the highway promise the gradual integration of Vietnam into the world economy, from a local perspective it especially seems to promise the transformation of formally rural areas like Hóc Môn into vital satellites of the increasingly prosperous city. When discussing the highway directly, people emphasize progress and development, how the highway will bring jobs, ease traffic congestion, and cut down the travel time from the suburbs to the city. When asked directly how they feel about the new road project cutting through their community, few people contest what they see as the obvious benefits of fresh cement and pavement: at the very least it will be nice to have a modern road, something new. In this sense, the highway stands for Saigon's cutting edge, the forward progress of a move into the future.[3]

Yet such optimism obscures another tendency that emerges when people discuss the highway in a less direct fashion. For people also seem detached from the road, describing its construction as one might describe the unfolding of fate. To be sure, most people do indeed marvel at the progress of the road as a successful work of man and even as an example of the successful development policy of "the party" and the Vietnamese government; the road is something to be proud of. But they also seem to see it as something outside of themselves, something uncontrollable and unpredictable. Whether it will be good or bad, they have little role in the shape the road will take. And in off-the-cuff comments they bemoan the troubles the road brings: the difficulty of crossing it, the noise and the dust created by speeding trucks carrying loads of dirt for Saigon construction projects from the outer districts, the unpredictable pace of the construction project, the construction debris strewn about haphazardly, the loss of business brought about first by construction and the loss of places to park and finally by the fact that the road is made for moving, not for stopping. Highway travelers do not stop to buy coffee and supplies on their way anymore; they just go. And people talk of death and danger on the road: the accidents, the near-misses, the specter of ever-present death.

These two seemingly contradictory ways of describing the effects of the Trans-Asia Highway upgrade as it wends its way through Hóc Môn provide a poignant example of how the powerful lure of perfection and order overshadows the equally real yet less glamorous backside of everyday experience. As Ba Ven went on to explain how he slipped on a sandy stretch of roadway while driving fast along a straight stretch of road, he described his accident on the highway as an unfortunate turn of events brought on by his own tendency toward recklessness and high-speed driving. From his words it seemed that he accepted blame for himself, but his initial reaction—his look, his impossible laugh, his actions—really implied that *it was the Xuyên Á that had happened to him.* Because of the sloppy construction work, the cement blocks and building debris scattered across the road, the poor planning, and the lack of signage, it was no surprise to hear him explain that it was a slippery patch of sand in the middle of the road that had contributed most to his fall. Slipping in sand or crashing into scattered construction debris is the backside of development: these tragedies mark the imperfect reality of the perfect plan.

The highway shows the confrontation of perfect visions of progress with the messy realities of development in practice. Although the road as ideal offers the promise of an imagined temporal jump into a future paradise, the road as reality also brings along a host of spatiotemporal transformations that often conflict with the spatial organization of social relations on Saigon's edge. Whereas National Highway 22 served both as a roadway through Hóc Môn and as a central axis around which much of the public community space in Tân Thới Nhì was organized, its new incarnation as the much faster Trans-Asia Highway cuts the commune into disconnected parts nearly as decisively as it links those parts with other places.

In this chapter I begin with a description of the particular role roads play in Vietnamese social space, showing how roads in Vietnam have formed an important yet largely undertheorized element in the social organization of space that needs to be added to accounts of Vietnamese village morphology. Scholars interested in the "Vietnamese village" need to consider the way that roads themselves often constitute an important organizing principle around which village society now organizes.

Yet the rapid pace of road construction and the contemporary Vietnamese zeal for infrastructure development, modernization, and urbanization also make it unrealistic to describe contemporary roads as a fixed grounding point in the concrete realities of spatial organization. Just as plans are made, loans are taken out, houses are relocated, and families along the road shift their patterns of life, so do the "concrete realities" of the material world shift in accordance with the realization of modernization plans, development schemes, and the everyday practices of people as they make use of the space. The concrete is literally being poured as we speak, and the social world and the concrete world emerge in what Hy Van Luong has called in another context a "dialogical restructuring" of each other.[4] Therefore, any analysis of the road as a social space is never finished because the road itself emerges from a set of social relations on Saigon's edge that the road itself helps to produce. The transformation of social space that comes about with the introduction of new types of roads traces a cybernetic feedback loop in which the spatial and temporal changes that come with new road technology profoundly affect local social organization. This, in turn, happens at the very same time that the final shape of the road emerges from social negotiations and power plays centered on the social and cultural control of space and time. Space-time changes road changes space-time changes road.

Individual social actors rarely have the luxury to step outside of their daily relationships, and they cannot constantly track the range of social relations and power plays that inform this loop of mutually inflecting transformations. Perhaps for this reason, many people describe the progress of the road as it wends its way through their community in abstracted, idealized forms. In such descriptions the social relations immanent in the road project disappear from immediate view, and the concrete and pavement seem to flow with an almost human agency; the road takes on a life of its own. This is not to say that people are mystified, in the sense that they have no idea what is happening; everyone understands the obvious fact that the road is an artifact of human endeavor that exists only because people are creating it. Yet trying to define who exactly those people are proves difficult and leads to vague abstractions. Although the road winds through social space, it changes that social space in ways that the social actors living there cannot always readily identify. Therefore, the road stands as an iconic marker of similar abstractions that are transforming contemporary Vietnamese society in opaque, indescribable ways. The road—like "the party," "the state," "the people," and slogans such as "Investment," "Development," "Urbanization," and "Modernization"— obviously plays a central role in social transformation. Yet the most convenient way to talk about it is in glowing ideal terms, because reality proves impossible to fully grasp and leaves one floundering in speculation and unanswered questions.

Strangely, the ideal of the road as an autonomous thing endowed with social agency of its own *appears* more concrete than all the real social activities that produce it, because the sociality embedded in the roadway proves intertangled with it and confused by its movement through multiple levels of action and discourse (see Figure 9). Nevertheless, a road has no life of its own; it is social only as a place where people live, as a technology for moving people, as a project, and as a part of the economic and political strategies of the region. So although the easiest and most common way to conceptualize the road is as a thing, this chapter emphasizes the social processes that have produced it and give it meaning. The very material presence of this road gives it the illusion of a pure reality contained wholly within itself. This ideal conception of reality assumes that one can find concrete meaning in the concrete, but it often fails to account for the shimmering chimeras of often contradictory social action that give the road its meaning, that change the road's meaning, that built the road, and that must now confront the road as part of the social landscape itself. This road is a thing human beings themselves have made but now confront as an alien agent acting upon them.

FIGURE 9. The partially completed Trans-Asia Highway, Xuyến Á. Hóc Môn district.

All the Road's a Stage:
Watching Social Action on National Highway 22

The café Lam Sơn near the Lam Sơn intersection offers a convenient place to stop for a moment and have a look at this road where Ba Ven had his accident. As in many Vietnamese roadside cafés, the owners of the Lam Sơn have arranged the seating so that the entire front entrance forms something of a large rectangular window onto the world moving past. They have set up low-to-the-ground folding metal lawn chairs with woven nylon seats and arranged them in twos behind small wooden tables. All of the chairs face the entrance, as seats in a theater face the stage or the silver screen. If the café owners show a bootleg copy of a dubbed foreign film or if gamblers and fans fill the café for a soccer match, patrons may turn their tables toward the television screen to the left of the entrance, but the tables always start out facing the rectangular entrance as if it were a movie screen showing the everyday performance of social life on the road outside. Cafés like this one represent the ultimate centers of male social space in contemporary Vietnam, and the men there come to see and be seen. They face the road, for that is where the (social) action is.

People coming from each direction pull up off the road on their motorbikes and line them up in front of the café. The space of the café opens up in a way that allows patrons to see and be seen by people passing by on the road outside. This imaginary film screen formed by the front door actually projects social action in two directions. It mediates the outside world with the inside world, creating a link between the social spaces of the street and the café. Riding past the open front of the café is like riding past a social magnet or tractor beam; if one sees or is seen by an acquaintance while riding past, one must stop, even if it is only for a moment to give an excuse for why one cannot stop longer.

The motion of traffic on the road in front collides with the motion in and out of the café, creating an eddy, a traffic pattern that moves in many directions, punctuated by abrupt turns, as drivers going in both directions veer off the road in order to dismount and park their own bike next to the others before taking a seat on one of the low chairs facing the road. When people must get back on their way, they mount their motorbike and drive immediately along the shoulder of the road without waiting, moving in the direction they wish to travel without regard for the "legal" direction of traffic. They continue in the direction they want to go, waiting for gaps in the traffic, and then eventually merge diagonally forward and across into something of an unmarked but reasonably spaced "lane" that heads the way they want to go. This is not seen as rude; it is the normal way to move into traffic. On the Highway 22 this poses little problem, because people tacitly recognize the shoulder of the road as a space of multidirectional traffic, to be shared with pedestrians and bicycles. One can easily move against the traffic, hugging the shoulder until there is space to cross over to the other side and join the flow moving in the same direction. There is nothing "wrong" with going the wrong way down a street if one is near the shoulder. In fact, that is what the shoulder is for. This type of movement through space on and off of the road is seen not only in front of the café Lam Sơn but in front of other cafés, sundries stores, beer joints, roadside noodle shops, sandwich shops, construction material and motorbike repair shops, restaurants, karaoke bars, furniture stores, woodworking shops, cooking gas dealers, houses (which often double as one or more of the other establishments), and alleyways (which often lead to more fronts of houses).

The shoulder of the road provides a sort of interface zone between the parallel motion of linear traffic along the road and the perpendicular movement required to move into and out of storefronts, alleyways, feeder roads, and other attractions that lie off of the main road. In this way, the shoulder allows the road to function as a social space by directing movement across the road's own path and by softening the abrupt linearity of movement along a line and facilitating horizontal movement across it. It offers the possibility of being on the road without moving along it, of looking across it rather than simply up and down it. It allows one to face the opposite side of the road and to recognize that opposite side as part of a singular social space united with the side one stands on. It allows one to stop, start, turn around, go backward, cross over, and switch sides in the ways required for social interaction. Aided by this multiuse shoulder, the road itself forms a link between its opposite shoulders, where storefronts and homes face each other across a swath of social space.

The road and the spaces along it produce each other as important social spaces of encounter and interaction. The constant movement and the variable speeds of traffic along the road create a critical mass of potential face-to-face encounters with customers, family members, friends, and others in a way that gives social visibility to the multiuse homes and places of business along the road. At the same time, the road realizes its potential as a social space only because of these places along the shoulder and the horizontal movement that crosses it. Unlike a lonely road across an empty landscape that has very little capacity to foster social interaction, Highway 22 realizes its potential as a social space because of the demographic space it passes through—because it passes through places with people. Although incessant disruptions to its linear flow may frustrate planners intent on cutting down travel time between places across the region, these disruptions are themselves the very signifiers of place that give relevance to that very movement. Disruption in flow due to cross-flow traffic is the surest sign that one has reached a social space of any relevance in Vietnam.

It Travels to Itself: The Road as Social Space

Although the scholarly literature has given particular importance to how the geospatial organization of Vietnamese villages conditions general patterns of social organization and social behavior, the central importance of roads as key social spaces has received only indirect treatment.[5] Before being upgraded into a faster, wider, more modern highway, National Highway 22 in Hóc Môn was not simply a small road in need of widening.

Instead it was a multiuse feature of the local landscape that formed a central axis for the organization of social space. More than just a pragmatic technology of linear movement between points on a line, the road served as a spatial link between its two sides as much as a link between places along it. One might productively imagine the road surface as something of an elongated plaza or central square, interrupted but never wholly bisected by traffic passing through its center.[6] Although the center of a closed corporate village community described in the ethnographic literature might be characterized by the importance of a fixed center of communal space, the most important communal spaces in many Hóc Môn communes are consolidated along the roadway itself. In large part, the central part of the commune or the village *(xã)* of Tân Thới Nhì in Hóc Môn surrounds the hamlets *(ấp)* that stretch out along the length of the communal roadway, with nodes of congestion forming around key spots that shift according to the time of day and are segregated by porous unwritten hierarchies of age, gender, class, and status. The road is not just a vehicle between places; in many of the outer-city districts, the road and "the place" are one. A purposeful road leads from place to place, from village to village, for example. In this case, the road leads to itself. In Tân Thới Nhì, to go to the road is to go to the heart of the "village."

Facing the Road/Facing the Front: The Road in Village Morphology

Many scholars have warned against conflating the prototypical "northern Vietnamese village" with some ideal standard or universal form of the "traditional Vietnamese village."[7] Even Gourou, whose work many once cited as evidence of this traditional "closed corporate" village community introverted and contained within itself "behind the bamboo hedge," saw this Red River Delta village form only as one among many highly diversified village forms.[8] One of the most striking and clearly articulated arguments for important differences in village morphology appears in Hickey's description of Khánh Hậu village in Long An province, which he describes as laid out along the length of the rivers and canals of the Mekong Delta. Rather than a contained space encircled by a village gate or hedge, Khánh Hậu was linear and elongated. For political and cultural as well as geographic and environmental reasons, the spatial organization of Vietnamese communities simply does not reproduce in carbon copy fashion the idealized standard of the primordial Red River village—or any other idealized standard, for that matter.[9] Moving away from the congested fringe of the city into the further reaches of Hóc Môn district, communities and groupings of people united under the administrative classifications of communes *(xã)* and hamlets *(ấp)* begin to organize along the elongated shape of the road. They are linear in much the same way as Hickey described Khánh Hậu, but they follow the road instead of rivers or canals.

This tendency to cluster near the road is not surprising when one considers the importance of streets and roads in Vietnamese public life. The Vietnamese language itself reveals this importance in the interchangeability of the spatial terms *mặt đường* and *mặt tiền. Mặt đường* means "facing the road." *Mặt tiền* quite simply means "front-facing." In describing property, facing the front and facing the road always signify the same thing. Furthermore, the Vietnamese word for a piece of property facing a roadway has an illuminating mistranslation. *Mặt tiền* can be mistakenly read as "facing money" based on a translation of its two component phonemes, *mặt* (face) and *tiền* (money). The double meaning, although not acceptable as a proper translation of the term, nevertheless quite conveniently summarizes why such property commands the highest value in rental and real estate markets.[10] The road literally represents money and economic opportunity. The main public social action in contemporary Vietnam takes place on the street, and if one has front- or road-facing property one's front door opens onto a world of social interaction and exchange. One finds the most people on the front, on the street, and if one's doors open to the front, they are open for business.[11]

The road does not cut *through* social space; the road *is* social space. The high value of front-facing property shows the importance of the space in almost quantifiable terms. People literally capitalize on this prominent position within visible social space. Living along the road allows many people to more effectively convert property into both real capital and symbolic capital. This is true in the city as well as in the countryside. In the city, urban involution creates a proliferation of front-facing property.[12] In the outer-city districts, the road creates a pseudo-urban corridor of services, modern shops, and homes. But unlike in the city, this urban corridor has no urban backside to it. Stretched out in a line, the backside turns to clay-covered red dirt roads that always remain muddy in the rainy season and rutted with bone-dry grooves in the dry season.

In contrast to these side roads, the highway not only represents high-value real estate but also symbolizes the forms of social and cultural capital associated with modernity and progress.[13] People living along the red-earth roads must confront the daily nuisances of underdevelopment and poverty.[14] By contrast, people living along the highway look out on a pseudo-urban corridor of modern infrastructure, more modern homes, bustling traffic, and a wide variety of services not unlike the ones to be found in the city itself. If one stands on the highway, one cannot see the dirt roads running behind it. The view is not much different from that one might have on a large boulevard in some of the inner-city districts like Tân Bình, Bình Thạnh, or parts of Districts 3, 5, and 10.

Classic models of urban morphology clearly describe the demographic character of urban expansion as characterized by "a tendency for an urban centre of high density to be surrounded by rings of lower population density."[15] As these urban cores reach their limits, however, urban expansion becomes "centrifugal" in the way that it expands outward around the rural–urban boundary zones. Although this general model seems to hold true for Ho Chi Minh City and most large Southeast Asian cities, the concrete forms of outward urban expansion always intersect with geographical, cultural, and historical particularities of each city. In the late 1960s McGee showed how intense rural–urban migration coupled with poor infrastructure, inadequate public transportation, and the lack of a sustainable economic base led to specific problems of suburban development in post–World War II Southeast Asian cities where an emerging middle class commingled with marginalized squatter settlements on the rural fringe. In Vietnam, postwar patterns of middle-class emigration and the emergence of universal poverty, coupled with the enclave mentality of the post–*đổi mới* middle class have created a slightly different situation. As new class divisions emerge through trade opportunities, an increasingly prosperous class of small traders tends to own most of the roadside property, while the poor live in the network of dirt roads concealed behind the face of the pseudo-urban corridor. So although one can describe a scene as McGee does—with the modern homes of the emerging middle class rising next door to the dilapidated shacks of rural migrants—social space is also hierarchically organized and stratified in terms of access to the road.

The road itself is simultaneously historical and cultural. The current historical moment—in which the promise of industrialization, modernization, and the celebration of urbanization resonate across ideological rifts in Vietnamese society—helps situate the importance of the pseudo-urban "core" that extends in a linear fashion along the length of the road. Although it takes on the appearance of a geographical fact, the road both is born out of the social and cultural orientation to space and helps reproduce that orientation. The social significance of *mặt tiền* property adds meaning and value to the road, and the presence of the road contributes to the spatial orientation of the property. This, in turn, transforms the morphology of the "traditional village" on the outskirts of town. Populations do not simply gather around points in the center of the city and radiate outward like concentric circles of decreasing density. Strips of population density also follow the roads that lead out of town. This is seen in the way that services and homes cluster around the highway as it runs through Tân Thới Nhì commune on the northern edge of Hóc Môn district, bordering Củ Chi.

Because of this corridor along the road, even after one moves quite far into the "rural" outer districts of the Ho Chi Minh City administrative zone, one discovers that a distinctly "urban" flavor remains along the highway's edge. The so-called bamboo hedge is replaced by an urban facade, a stage set of modernity that goes one row deep. The physical characteristics of these urban filaments extending outward from the city are intricately linked with the symbolic and practical organization of socially and culturally significant space both along the road and behind it. As one moves off the road into the spaces behind it, one sees that the homes and businesses radiate out from this linear space like a linear gradient of decreasing density extending into the network of red-earth roads leading to fields, workshops, factories, and garden plots that one finds behind the road.

Back in the Xóm

Most people refer to the area behind the road as the *xóm,* a word that has both administrative and colloquial meanings. Administratively, *xóm* means "subhamlet" and stands for the smallest administrative unit in a village. But in administrative practice, this category is rarely used, having been replaced by the more operational neighborhood associations *(tổ dân),* each headed by a locally elected *tổ trưởng*. The *tổ trưởng* is the direct liaison between the neighborhood association and the head of the village People's Committee, *trưởng ấp*. Yet in everyday conversation, people still refer to the area behind the road as the *xóm* because of the way it resembles a neighborhood. Yet this is not a romanticized image of a neighborhood, because in popular usage this term conveys a slightly derogatory sense. For the most part, the *xóm* to which people refer is an accumulation of inward-looking private compounds, a neighborhood only in the sense that it represents a cluster of homes. Houses in the *xóm* are private spaces with little extralocal interaction between families.

Indeed, despite the close proximity of homes in the *xóm,* many people there expressed a sense of alienation from and mistrust of their neighbors. For the most part, the private happenings of individual households remain contained within the household itself, a situation that sometimes produces a sense of fear in the *xóm.* Information about the nonpublic activities of other residents travels mainly through gossip and speculation. Unidentifiable sources of social problems are attributed to abstract suspicions and vague assumptions about what other people might be doing outside of public view.

Yet even back in the *xóm,* the densest groups of houses lie along the red-earth roads. Again, a variant of linear involution repeats itself along the internal neighborhood roads. Smaller cafés, smaller sundries shops, and even smaller markets line these inner roads. The red-earth roads themselves branch off into smaller alleys *(hẻm)* and pathways *(đường mòn).* Viewed from the perspective of public significance, the different types of social space produce a hierarchy of ever-reducing levels of social openness that is almost directly related to the width of the road or the amount of human traffic on the road. The main road is the most public, followed by the paved feeder roads, the red-earth roads, the *hẻm,* and finally the pathways, which are the most private. Although there are indeed many interesting places in the network of red-dirt roads "back in the *xóm,*" all roads lead to the highway, which, despite its linear form, operates as the center of social life.

Public Performance on the Road

The central position of the social space that opens out onto the main thoroughfare is not purely economic. It also forms a central part of the public social landscape, a space that often stands in direct contrast to the hushed privacy of space in the *xóm.* In addition to its functional role as a space of movement, it serves most importantly as a site of public performance. It brings people out of the private space of their homes in the *xóm* and allows them to perform the public acts of sociality required to maintain a sense of community. So instead of trying to classify the village of

Tân Thới Nhì in terms of the reductionist differentiation of the "closed" northern village and the "open" southern village so often reproduced in the ethnographic literature, we must acknowledge that it comprises both closed and open spaces. The main open, public space is provided by the highway running through it. People use the public space of the road to perform their social obligations.

Social action on this "front-stage" space of the road entails a whole set of social relations and appropriate behaviors that identify people as members of the community. For men this can mean simply joining groups of other men at one of the multiple cafés on the road. Or it might mean joining a group of men to *nhậu,* a word that specifically describes the act of drinking, eating food, and conversing all at once. These occasions provide a space for people to sit and share stories, tell jokes, and buy each other coffee, beer, or food in socially significant ways. These public appearances helps diffuse the suspicion that develops when people remain completely closed off in the private space of the home. They also solidify the idealized notions of a gendered division of labor ordered around the male role as social networker and the female role as head of the home, guardian of finances, and marketeer. Furthermore, the networking and public camaraderie in the cafés and beer joints puts many of the local men in the community in a network of casual labor and employment that sets them off from migrant workers from other regions.[16] These spaces of public performance contribute to the performance of what Harvey describes as "Place," in this case a local place with a hierarchy of belonging and access to particular forms of work and opportunity reserved for locals.[17] The string of public places with doors open to the road makes this public appearance possible.

The road also provides a space for the public performance of ritual in the more traditional sense. Especially on auspicious days on the ritual calendar, travelers on the road must share space with ritual processions and gatherings associated with weddings, funerals, community hall celebrations, and Buddhist ceremonies (see Figures 10a and 10b). In the unwritten code of social behavior, regardless of what the lawbooks say, rites of passage always have the right of way on the roadway. And it is important that the wide-open space of the road provides not only a public outdoor place that can accommodate important rituals but also a space that is highly *visible,* for an important part of the ritual process

FIGURE 10A. Funeral procession on the Trans-Asia Highway. Hóc Môn district.

FIGURE 10B. Another view of the funeral procession on the Trans-Asia Highway seen in Hóc Môn district.

specifically requires that people be *seen* performing it. The ritual must be public. And the best place to be seen is on the road.

Social Space and the Time of "the Market"

The social exigencies of ritual performance can impede more practical matters of movement through space. As Vietnam moves increasingly toward the market rationalism of commodity-based exchange and the cost–benefit framework for evaluating social life, these impediments to transit seem to hinder economic development. Traffic slowdowns translate to lost efficiency and increased transit costs. They limit the feasibility of industrial processing zones located on the suburban fringes and lead to increased production costs that undermine Ho Chi Minh City's edge in attracting foreign direct investment. Although labor remains cheap on the rural–urban interface, the headaches of transport limit the expansion of capital into these areas.

However, it is precisely the social performance of the market itself that creates the conditions for limits to market expansion; much of the social performance that takes place on the highway emerges in dialogical relationship to the expansion of the market itself. Anthropologists have convincingly shown that social life and economic activity are embedded within each other.[18] In Vietnam more specifically, Malarney and others have suggested that đổi mới and economic growth have spurred an increase in public ritual activity.[19] Furthermore, many of the processes and developments often associated with the global themselves produce a sense of local place.[20] In a study of the peasant labor process in Wesley, a banana-producing village in Dominica, Trouillot observed that the greatest sense of village community emerged at the sites of mediation where the village opened up to the outside world. Otherwise isolated households actually become a "local village" when people meet in mediating spaces such as post offices, banana-boxing plants, and shops where goods from outside the village are sold: "Wesley people meet themselves at the heart of Wesley primarily because here is where they meet the rest of the world."[21] The same pattern occurs on the highway that runs through Tân Thới Nhì; the community finds its most identifiable sense of self on the highway's edge, at the very space where it intersects with the regional and national network of communication and exchange.

The social relations of the highway and of the village produce each other. The same process that increases the economic importance of traffic on the highway also increases the social importance of the highway as a space for public performance. Clearly, the increase in the number of travelers on the highway represents a highly visible and material development of economic growth; this traffic consists of people carrying goods to and from the market, children going to school, transport trucks and worker buses moving to and from the building and manufacturing sectors in the outer-city districts and in the city itself. A quick look at the road reveals how engaged people are in business opportunities and jobs that require them to go places on the road, often in quite impressive vehicles. Whatever the variable growth numbers might say, the economy seems to be *moving*. And as a result, the very social practices of public performance and display that create a roadblock to this movement along the road are themselves at least partially produced by that self-same economic recovery. It takes money to pay for the big funerals and weddings spilling out onto the road, the community hall festivals, the events that draw big crowds, and the displays of bravado in drinking beer and Hennessey that put increasing numbers of drunken men on the road in increasingly expensive vehicles.

The Trans-Asia Highway project seeks to create an economic windfall by clearing traffic congestion in and out of the city. But this very process produces its own contradiction, because economic booms fill the streets. In order to prevent the tendency for the rate of profit to fall, capitalist growth depends on the constant willingness of the consumer to go out and buy things.[22] In the same way that the greatest public performance of vibrant capitalism might be seen at the crowded shopping mall,[23] in the case of Tân Thới Nhì the vibrancy of the emerging market economy contributes to the performance of place at the roadside market. And paradoxically, as the Tân Thới Nhì market realizes itself as a place to buy and sell, it starts to cut off the very road that has contributed to its prosperity. In the mornings, when the pace of selling is most fervent, a semicircle of buyers and sellers gathers by the entrance to the marketplace. Impromptu bicycle and motorbike parking lots extend onto the surface of the roadway, and the mass of people surges outward into the lanes of traffic, which slows and compresses into a thin line trying to squeeze through the bottleneck thus formed. Motorbikes snake through, and cars and trucks have to honk to clear a path. The market thrives because of its position along the highway, the self-same highway it cuts off with its success. The market bites the road that feeds it.

Destruction and Reconstruction: The Double Edge of Development

Yet the road bites back. The continuing expansion of the road, once a site of mediation where the village met itself, demands the obliteration of the local space it has helped to produce. Directed by urban, regional, political, and economic planners; financed by the government and the Asian Development Bank; and supported at least ideally by large sectors of the population, the Trans-Asia Highway upgrade seems poised to conquer the chaos of local social performances that block the smooth passage of the road. The quaint, romantic notion of roadside activity—of markets spilling into the roadway, motorbikes and bikes moving every which way with goods lashed on, and peasants riding their bicycles to market, hobbling alongside tourist buses and earth movers—does not hold much currency in the framework of development articulated by the government slogan "Công nghiệp hóa, Hiện đại hóa đất nước" (Industrialize, modernize the country). Roadside bottlenecks are a pain in the neck for planners and peasants alike. These unfortuitous meetings of traffic and social life are often frustrating, full of hassle, unpleasant, and at times deadly. They look like chaos, and at least publicly, most people want order.[24]

The highway project purports to deliver such order. The plans for the future appear dreamlike; they soothe the pain of the everyday with colorful drawings of modern landscapes, clean lines, and orderly demarcations of space zoned according to usage and populated by happy people moving effortlessly about. Highway plans avoid the problem of social space by imagining space *asocially,* in wholly materialist terms. But even road building itself is a socially and culturally embedded process. As the road wends its way through social space, the very material acts of land clearance (which in real terms means tearing down homes and relocating people who live in the way), grading, pouring concrete, building road dividers, constructing drainage systems, and laying asphalt prove to be social at every turn. It is also useful to consider the construction of the road itself as a public performance of the state's attempts to transform and "modernize" Vietnam. Like other public performances, this one takes place on the road, the quintessential social space.

Magazines and newspapers often run front-page pictures of pavement rollers preparing new sections of highway (see Figure 11). Flying the Vietnamese flag on imported heavy machinery enacts the symbolic union of the Vietnamese government with foreign capital and the people it claims to represent. Construction displays the policies of *đổi mới* in visible, material terms that assert the benefits of state policy as tangible fact. And during the road-building process people seemed to enjoy watching many aspects of this material transformation. As the machines passed through Tân Thới Nhì, small crowds would often gather to watch important phases of the project (such as the laying of new tarmac or the completion of a traffic overpass). People came out of their shops and houses

FIGURE 11. Pavement roller preparing the Trans-Asia Highway. Hóc Môn district.

to watch when the machines came to lay a carpet of new asphalt. The process itself quickly transformed the dusty and potholed surface of the road into a smooth surface, glistening with the wet black color of fresh tar, perfectly dust free. As the machines steamed slowly past, literal before and after pictures unfolded before the crowd. In this context, when the fresh pavement flows, the ideal starts to look very real and tangible. The pleasure of fresh tarmac strikes most Vietnamese observers as an aesthetic experience, a tangible visual performance of *hiện đại hóa* (modernization). The road, most people said, was "đẹp" (beautiful).

Social activity continues on the road throughout the construction process. As grading and paving proceeded on one side of the road running through Tân Thới Nhì, the other side remained a space of mixed-use traffic and public gathering. In the cooling part of day just before sunset, people would come outside and walk back and forth along the road, sitting at times along the recently installed line of two parallel concrete barriers that would eventually form a traffic median when the road was finished. In these early evening periods, the edge of "the eel" *(con lươn),* as they called this long snake of cement, was just the perfect height for sitting and chatting in the open air of the road's wide swath of space.

I would often have short conversations with our landlord's grand-father, a white-haired patriarch who liked to walk out with his cane to the middle of the road and sit on the median and watch people walk past. On one of these occasions he said I looked "văn minh" (civilized) because I was wearing a button-up shirt tucked into long pants. As we sat along the median, he looked at the unfinished road and lamented, "Vietnamese people are not civilized." He continued by explaining what Vietnam had to do to catch up with the rest of the world. It needed things like this highway expansion in order to modernize, and he was looking forward to the road's being finished because it might make people act more civ-ilized. Others concurred. Not only *đẹp,* the road was *văn minh* as well.

But fresh tarmac quickly dries, and within days the road became dusty again. When both sides of the road opened, no one sat on the median, and the space between the two concrete barriers that form the eel began to serve as a long, linear garbage pit.

This peculiar public performance of state-guided modernization dif-fers from other social performances on the road: it erases the very stage it plays upon. It specifically seeks to modernize the social elements of this type of mixed-use road out of existence. The performance of road construction, in ways analogous to the ritual process, engineers a social transformation, a movement through stages of social life recast as stages in the modernization process. In this context the ritual process assumes the historicized idioms of socialist modernism (with its teleology of forward progress through the stages of socialism) and of capitalist development (led by the international lending institutions with their own teleology of progressive economic development). In this ritual analogue, the road construction turns the residents along its pathway into liminal initiands. In their state of *communitas,* they remain uniform in their befuddlement about the shape the future will take, waiting for their reaggregation into a newly defined place within the social-spatial and social-temporal hier-archy of Ho Chi Minh City.

The process of converting Highway 22 into a section of the Trans-Asia Highway is making the road more modern and more amenable to orderly traffic patterns. At the same time, the road itself is becoming in-creasingly antisocial. The Tran-Asia Highway is going places, but to get there requires a movement out of one configuration of social space and into another. The new highway enacts a separation between the social world of those people who want to sit on the edge and the liminal world of those subsumed by motion down its path. Once completed, the passage will become the site of a daily, regenerating *auto-route de passage* designed to constantly reinforce a new set of social hierarchies and social relations mapped out in new configurations of time and space. Rather than the center of space, the new form of the road marks the margin, a space between spaces, a *limen.*

The Road as "Antisocial" Space

The liminal zone is dangerous. While building the road through Tân Thới Nhì with limited resources, workers were often forced to leave large U-shaped concrete blocks out in the middle of the unfinished section of highway (see Figure 12). They worked with their bare hands and had only one cement mixer and set of metal molds in which to pour cement. Once the molds were filled and the concrete was set, the workers needed heavy machinery with hydraulic arms to move the big blocks into position. But with the backhoe being used by another crew to dig the long

FIGURE 12. Concrete U-shaped blocks. During construction of the Trans-Asia Highway, blocks like these were placed in the ground to form a drainage line along the shoulder of the highway. After the concrete was poured, the blocks were left to dry in the sun, scattered dangerously about the road until it was time to put them into position. Hóc Môn district.

trenches alongside the road, the only way they could keep the work moving was to pour the cement, remove the molds, move a bit down the road, and let the concrete dry in place.

Those concrete blocks were the immediate reason I found myself attending a funeral one sad evening in Hóc Môn. Thành, edgy as usual, tried to laugh away tragedy. The deceased, he said, was probably drunk like all the other men riding their motorbikes home late most evenings. *Ngu quá!* Stupid!

The men mourning the deceased were certainly drunk at his funeral. They were all laughing and telling jokes. They were passing the shot glass around, taking turns at the *rượu đế* rice wine. Someone explained that they had to act "happy" in this way to "divide the sadness," *chia buồn.* They were laughing hard—working at it, really. The deceased had smacked right into a concrete U. That is how he had died. Thành said he must have been drunk, but it did not seem right to ask at the funeral with his young children and his widow present.

Who knows if the deceased was drunk or not? He was not the only one to die that year on the Xuyên Á, dubbed the "highway of death" by one newspaper and a "nightmare" by another.[25] Remember Ba Ven? He almost died in his accident. Phúc and Tân got clipped from behind when they made the turn at the Lam Sơn intersection. Thành's son skidded out on gravel up by the An Hạ canal. Mr. Tý's son had those scrapes on his head, and months later they were still paying installments for the other man's motorbike. Mr. Tý's son had smashed into it, but he swore it was not his fault. Over the Vietnamese Independence Day holiday everyone was talking about a group of children and a woman who were run down from behind by a jeep.

As the highway became more efficient as a people mover, formerly social space became increasingly antisocial space. The space of the road increasingly blocked horizontal movement across its path and divided the space it cut through. The most disturbing evidence of this transformation was the funerals of people who had died on the road. Evidence also emerged in newspaper headlines and sensationalist stories:

Constructing the Trans-Asia Highway: Heart-rending. . . . Clever is the one who can cross the road!

Trans-Asia Highway Project: Many Deadly Traffic Accidents Due to Construction[26]

The pleasure of concrete quickly became a guilty pleasure. The new and improved, more modern, faster highway has a double edge—the cutting edge and the edge that cuts.

Although the murderous tendency of the highway may be the surest sign of its increasingly antisocial quality, there are a range of less dramatic examples that express this change in different ways. In interviews with people living along the road through Tân Thới Nhì that were conducted before the crews had finished both sides of the road, a woman wondered what might happen if the project included a concrete median. She had been on the recently upgraded road from Ho Chi Minh City to Vũng Tàu and knew that medians made it nearly impossible to cross the road. Breaks in the medians were so few and far between that people physically removed parts of the medians, creating extrememly dangerous crossing zones.

For the past five years this woman had been running a building supply store specializing in imported tiles, high-end fixtures, decorative moldings, and ironwork, in addition to general construction materials like the ubiquitous Vietnamese bricks and bags of cement. With her husband and four children she lived behind the store in a two-year-old, two-story home built in the current middle-class fashion of sloped tile roofs and multiple balconies. The house stood behind the business as a model of what progress and economic development might bring, especially when combined with the modern construction materials available in her store. The business was doing quite well, employing two northerners and five local Hóc Môn residents. Although the rapid pace of building had obviously been good for businesses like hers, she also worried about the potential of the road to disrupt the very business it facilitates. The road leading to Vũng Tàu was too fast, she explained by way of comparison. No one wants to stop and buy goods. The divider down the middle of the road makes it difficult for people traveling one direction to cross over to the other side. Widening the road also eliminates parking on the shoulder, making it difficult to load the large vehicles that stop to pick up building supplies.

This seller of construction materials said she would wait and see. She explained that no one was sure exactly how much the government would decide to widen the road, how high the actual road surface would end up being. It was pointless and indeed risky to try to act in advance because these kinds of projects have a history of changing without notice, regardless of what the plans might indicate.[27]

This example illuminates the persistent double sense of what the road will bring and what it might take away. It brings people into closer contact with distant social spaces, but it also transforms the very spaces it cuts through. Furthermore, the road seems to grow and change according to unidentifiable bureaucratic whims; new phases of construction proceed without warning. Few people could predict what the road through Tân Thới Nhì would look like when it was finished because they have no say in the process. They have to wait before they make improvements to their own homes because they cannot predict how much the road will be raised. They do not know if there will be a sidewalk or not. If they build too soon, they may be forced to tear down a section, because the raised road surface might be higher than their doorway, making it impossible to control runoff water in the rainy season. So although it may be easy to say from a theoretical perspective that the road is a social project built by people, the hierarchies of power and authority that organize the social relations of decision making and access to information make it impossible for local residents to reach the people building the road or see the plans those people have in their heads. The social production of the road seems about as connected to the people as "the government" itself, about as easy to grasp and identify as the ideal concepts of development or modernization.

One woman who practiced traditional Oriental medicine out of the front of her home explained that she was not so concerned about how the road project would affect her own business, because she had an established base of patients who came specifically for the kind of treatment she offers. They continued to come for visits even after the project sliced off the front twenty-two meters of her property. Yet she added that she could not really form any other opinions about the road project, because there was no way to tell what it would look like when it was done. She had seen a story about it in a 1996 issue of the *Tuổi Trẻ* newspaper but had never heard anything else since. It is difficult to know what to expect, she said, turning to the experience of land compensation as an example. She had been promised compensation for twenty-two meters but received payment for only seventeen because the government claimed the additional land as its own.[28] And even though her direct income was not affected by the project, she expressed a silent resignation that no one would know the end result until all was said and done.[29]

A man working in a large roadside workshop that glues and presses hardwood veneers onto plywood boards described this sense of not knowing with a combination of worried foreboding and idealized hope. On the one hand, he pointed out what might happen if the road was widened any further. He would lose a large portion of his work space as well as the space to park and load vehicles. Knowing more about the road project could really help people plan the future of their businesses or the way they work on their own homes, he said, pointing to a crack forming on the top corner of one of the obviously new houses built on the property. Houses needed to be built stronger now, he explained, because the increased traffic on the road shakes the earth and makes them fall apart more easily. He also pointed out that houses needed to be built up off of the ground because water running off of the road during the rainy season would come inside houses built at street level. If one built too soon, as his family had done, one risked building too low or too high. And the foundation might shift so cracks would develop in one's house. So people felt left in the dark, not sure how the project would proceed, and as a result, unsure how to proceed with their own projects.

And those were not the man's only concerns. He explained that Hóc Môn had been "a lot more fun in the old days." The new highway had spoiled the peacefulness of the area. For young people, he said, the building of the road was great because it would connect them with emerging opportunities in Saigon. But for old people, he continued, it was a threat to their peacefulness and tranquility, forcing them to go to the countryside *(về quê)* when they reach a certain age. The transition from country into city on Saigon's edge was marked for this man by a loss of peacefulness and a sense of indeterminacy.

With all this talk about the negative consequences of the road, I asked the man in the workshop if he thought there was a negative side to development. This direct question prompted a change in his narrative. He stopped his critical stance and made a point of saying that he "must say 'thank you' regarding development," because if it was his duty to express a sense of gratitude to those responsible. He then added that "investing in Vietnam is really great."[30]

In this discussion the speaker artfully compartmentalized his reservations about the road project and yet remained positive and idealistic about the general idea of development and about the road project as a symbol of that larger process. The point was not that the road was perfect in and of itself but that somehow the ideas of development and investment were themselves important social realities. Indeed, both development and investment are extremely real elements of the social landscape of contemporary Vietnam. Although they are clearly concepts, people act on them as if they were material realities. In this framework, the abstract concept of development can persist despite the cracked concrete reality of the brand-new houses already crumbling with the rumble of the road. Development as a thing has a perfect quality that obscures the material imperfections of the road that claims to stand for it. The road represents both an ideal concept and a material object.

In the same way that abstract concepts such as development take on a magical, seemingly objective existence as things, the road-building process appears less like a project that social beings work to create and more like an autonomous creature with a will or an agency of its own. The widening of the highway ritually severs the very connection of the road to the society it runs through. One can skin one's knee on it, hit one's head on it with great force, crash into a wall, skid out. But the social relations that produce the road seem to disappear from view. The subjectivity of the road substitutes for the subjective ability of people living alongside it to influence its progress.

The median that snakes down the middle of the road shows what happens when the road begins to appear solely as a thing and functions less and less as an integral part of social space. The median obviously serves to control movement, to order traffic and keep people on the correct side of the road. In very real ways, however, the eel dividing the two sides of the road has become a marker of antisocial space, a linear refuse pit filled with litter, a place to quickly get across but never to linger. The following disturbing scene taken from my field notes demonstrates the degree to which the eel has become a space outside of social structure:

Friday, 10 May 2002: At about 7:30 a.m., on the way up to purchase *xôi* [sticky rice] at the Tân Thới Nhì market, I noticed that a large crowd of about a hundred people had gathered around the median of the highway, just past the Lam Sơn intersection. They were blocking traffic, peering into the median space between the two sides of the road.

As I rode closer toward the crowd, I saw my friend Tuấn, who was coming in my direction, apparently leaving the scene. "What happened?" I asked. "Someone was murdered. Whacked on the head with a piece of wood," he said, miming the motion of someone hitting someone from behind with a heavy object. "His head has been severed." He then continued on his way. As I rode past the scene, I asked a random onlooker what happened: "He was shooting heroin. They found him there this morning." Through the spaces between the crowd gathered around, between the legs of people craning their heads to get a view, I could see a woven mat placed over the spot in the ditch around which everyone congregated. A teenage boy sat squatting near the spot, clutching something, his face red with tears.

Later that day I asked the head of police what had happened. "Tai nạn" [Accident], he said, avoiding any details. I said someone told me the person had been murdered or that it had been a drug overdose, and he said he wasn't sure, they were "investigating" it. He would only reveal that the person was not from this *xã,* but came from *xã* Tân Hiệp.

A young boy selling lottery tickets also said that the man was not from here. He had heard that the man was murdered and dumped by the side of the road. The man's family had last seen him two days ago, when the man had gone to celebrate a death anniversary. Rumor held that he was into drugs, and that he had been killed and deposited by the road sometime in the night before being discovered around 6 a.m. this morning.[31]

Several days before the appearance of this body, I had nearly stepped on a dead dog while trying to cross the road. It had been stuffed in a bag, which had been thrown into the median only a few hundred meters from the scene just described. The median, located precisely in the center of a road that once served as a center of social action, now cuts off social space and has become a dead zone in the middle of a liminal *auto-route de passage* reserved for movement *between* social spaces. It is no longer part of the structural order of social space itself.

Transforming Time through Space

Although the immediate space of the road itself might now seem liminal, even antisocial in ways, it remains part of social life. The spatiotemporal dimensions of this social life, however, have changed. The road unifies the experience of socially construed space and time in precisely the way that people now collapse the concepts "how long" and "how far" into a single conceptual category. How far is Tân Thới Nhì commune in Hóc Môn from District 1 in downtown Saigon? According to taxi meters (which, of course, measure both time and spatial distance), it is almost precisely eighteen kilometers away, and the ride costs between 100 thousand and 120 thousand *đồng* (US$6.70–8.00); it is one or two hours by bus depending on one's fortune with stops, traffic, and transfers and how long the drivers want to wait for a full load of passengers; it is forty-five minutes by car in normal traffic and thirty minutes to an hour by motorbike. The section of road is always eighteen kilometers long, but how long it takes to travel it depends on traffic (time of day), the weather (time of year, because rainy-season puddles and mud slow traffic to a bottleneck), the daring of the driver, and the speed of one's vehicle. People in Saigon say that Hóc Môn is "xa lắm" (very far). To emphasize the distance, they cite not kilometers but traffic and the infamously dangerous road construction on the Trans-Asia Highway and the main roads that lead out to connect it with the city.

The builders of the Trans-Asia Highway, of course, hope the finished road can reduce the physically oppressive feeling of distance by cutting down on the time it takes to move from point to point on the highway.[32] In this way, it effectively "transforms time though space."[33] For the people of Hóc Môn, the prospect of magically moving closer to the center of the city seems to offer a solution to the crisis of their liminal position on Saigon's edge. On the edge now, they often describe the spatial transformation of the road as a pathway into the future, a future that they describe in terms of a spatial repositioning of their district from the suburbs to the inner city—from *ngoại thành* to *nội thành*. Yet the same thing that changes the amount of time it takes to move down the road also changes the amount of time it takes to get across the road. Thus places on the other side of the road effectively become farther away at the same time that places along the length of the highway become effectively closer. Hóc Môn moves closer to Ho Chi Minh City but farther away from itself. To bring Hóc Môn closer to Saigon, the road must be widened. But there are houses on the side of the road. People live where they want the traffic to flow. Building roads may seem a base, material concern. But with people involved, such building itself enters a social and political space of its own.

The Road to Paradise

Outside of my ethnographic prodding, most people I spoke with avoided overt reflection on the tense social and political changes the road might bring. Instead they most often found themselves watching the construction and the traffic passing by late in the day, sitting on the unfinished blocks of U-shaped concrete that lined the highway, on the concrete "eel" that would form a divider through the center of the road once both sides were finished. Their sitting on the construction materials along the unfinished road may well have been the last meaningful social relationship between the road and those who live alongside it. Even these last places to sit and watch the road builders work were being swallowed up into the shoulder of the road. The U-shaped blocks would soon be connected, forming a long drainage channel at the edge of the road, buried in the ground, topped off by a concrete lid.

But the road is political precisely because it represents a transformation of the spatial and temporal order of life on Saigon's edge. It fundamentally alters pathways of movement, linking distant places together and cutting places on either side of the road off from each other. This development privileges the movement back and forth between the inside of the city and the outside of the city. Fraught with power, the road generates new opportunities for those who straddle realms of life both inside and outside the city—those who work in the city but live on the outside or who live on the inside but run industries or engage in land speculation on the outside. It largely compromises the lives of many who get in the way of this transformation. As I have shown, reactions to the road project are ambiguous and rife with contradictions. The power of the road, like Hóc Môn itself, emerges from the way in which people use it to transcend time and space. The danger of the road comes when powerful actors use it in an attempt to transcend other people's mode of existence.

The political context within which the road construction must be seen extends beyond Hóc Môn itself. Various sectors of the Vietnamese government, guided by the Ministries of Transportation and Communication, Public Security, and Construction, have pragmatic goals as they struggle to keep up with the increasing levels of traffic in and out of the city by instituting a material and legal apparatus that takes its most visible form in things like the new multilane roads with designated lanes for different kinds of traffic. The roads are separated by dividers that attempt to transform the social spaces of roads into orderly people movers. However, the linear directional movement of these new roads that move from point A to point B comes into direct conflict with the forms of social movement that actually exist in the social spaces where the planners lay them down.

The social dynamics of movement on the roads that lead out of central Saigon demonstrate this conflict between local conceptions of social space and the efficiency-minded technical conception of traffic emanating from on high. An example from the main road leading out to the Eastern suburbs, passing through the heavily populated working-class Bình Thạnh district, puts this into clear relief. As the newspaper *Tuổi Trẻ* reported, "From the Hàng Xanh traffic circle, turning onto Điện Biên Phủ street and leading up towards the Saigon bridge, there is a place that the people living on both sides of the road call the 'road to paradise.'" At this spot countless people ride their motorbikes across a space where they have removed the concrete dividers that separate the two sides of the road with traffic flowing in different directions. In this collective effort to save time by illegally cutting across the road, up to three accidents occur at the spot each day. A small altar has been erected at the spot, but "the people crossing the street see it as a normal matter of course."[34]

Further examples from Hóc Môn show that traffic planning and road construction in Vietnam are a double-edged sword best articulated by the double meaning implicit in this "road to paradise." The road leads to the paradise that comes after death as well as the imagined paradise of modernity offered by the development of a modern city infrastructure.[35] On paper, such a road epitomizes the triumph of traffic planning, another one in a string of successful projects completed. Yet for the people who use it, the road, like modernization itself, symbolizes both death and rebirth at once. The road seems to offer a vision of social progress at the same time that it demonstrates the alienating effects of planning as it separates people from the very social forms they supposedly make up.

Government-level planners, as well as most people in direct conversation, pose the question of traffic as a simple binary choice between chaos and control, between the unpredictability of everyday action and the assertion of order through material construction and disciplinary control. Yet in the actual process of building roads and enforcing traffic order, "the social" always returns. The materialist vision of infrastructure development, planning, and traffic control in Ho Chi Minh City starts by engineering roads and then seeks to engineer people to fit them. This is more than a metaphor. This is how the Vietnamese government articulates the problem of traffic though its own legal and practical division of labor. And although people may constantly seek to subvert new forms of traffic control and regulation in their everyday actions, their conception of what the modern highway can offer closely mirrors the official government position. It is only when people are thinking about other things—

"Why don't people stop at our café anymore? Why is it so hard to get to the other side of the road?"—that they begin to comment on the changes the road brings along with it.

The positive material changes brought about by the road are quite clear and easy to see. The negative consequences, by contrast, most often appear as accidents, the results of individuals' poor driving skills rather than the disconnect between social conceptions of space and the play of power that puts these roads right through the heart of social action. If a person drove a car through the heart of a major walking street in a town's main square, society would punish that person for reckless driving. Yet somehow if a society builds a highway through its own central social space it can call the project development and write off the ensuing deaths as accidents.

Chaos, Control, and Social Meaning

Although the desire to solve the problem of traffic accidents resonates across all levels of Vietnamese society, many people articulate traffic problems as something removed from society. On the streets they joke that traffic follows the "law of the jungle" *(luật rừng)*. In the government, traffic is seen as a problem associated with rudimentary infrastructure and the lack of a proper consciousness among the people. Both of these interpretations hinge on a notion of traffic as antisocial, chaotic in the ways it does not correspond to any meaningful set of social categories. In the case of Ba Ven's accident, the Xuyên Á simply *happened*. The social processes that made the Xuyên Á happen were not immediately apparent.

On some level, this makes complete sense. In order to define what he called meaningful "social action," Max Weber did the same thing when he called up the image of two bicyclists colliding on the street: "A mere collision of two bicyclists may be compared to a natural event. On the other hand, their attempt to avoid hitting each other, or whatever insults, blows, or friendly discussion might follow the collision, would constitute 'social action.'"[36] Here Weber distinguished between the kind of action that responds to socially understood norms of interaction between people and the kind of action that occurs by accident. But after looking at traffic patterns during the upgrading of the highway through Hóc Môn, this example of colliding bicyclists takes on a new and important twist. This is because the threat of the accident—the threat of the unintended, meaningless, asocial collision—has itself become a subject of social concern. The problem Weber deemed natural originates in the realm of the social: traffic accidents, caused by the chaos on the streets, represent part of a larger social problem that requires social intervention. The people who get into accidents while breaking traffic rules on the road to paradise do so in specifically social ways. As people said in the earlier example of the accidents at the spot in the road where the concrete barrier has been removed, such accidents are a "normal matter of course"; it is socially understood that people will cross the road in such a spot.

It does not take a wise old social scientist like Max Weber to make us realize the difference between meaningful action and accidents. Yet it also does not take much to make us realize that traffic accidents cannot be simply dismissed as asocial. At Hàng Xanh the road was built, the barrier was removed, and people cross it en masse. In Hóc Môn, when someone crashes into a U-shaped block for the drainage system, the fact is that someone has left that block on a part of the road that people expect to be able to ride down without slamming into things. Even though accidents are not meaningful actions in the sense that they convey intended messages between social actors, they cannot be divorced from the social. Because who makes the infrastructure? People do. More generally, a society composed of people does.

From a purely anthropological perspective, traffic on the highway thus emerges as a form of social experience through the interplay of structural form and practical action. A simple observation makes this clear: the structure of traffic constrains the navigation of space, yet the navigation of space informs and builds the structure of traffic. People create the pathways they drive on through the very act of driving, but the roads people drive on direct the pathways people follow.

Therefore, traffic depicts the very same dynamic between the individual and society that has long captivated anthropologists in their study of culture. Like culture, traffic is made by people; there can be no traffic without human beings. Also like culture, traffic constrains the movements people make. Human beings thus confront traffic as constituent members of this larger whole, and they also, fantastically, confront this whole as if it were something outside of them, something larger than them, something beyond their control. The road is at once a social space and an *apparently* antisocial space, but it is always manmade. Movement through traffic is thus simultaneously conscious and unconscious, something like the *habitus* described by Pierre Bourdieu. Produced by the people who make it up, the structure of traffic is like the coral reef of old-time anthropological metaphors.

But unlike the *habitus,* which produces its structures out of a magical dialectic with structure itself, and unlike the coral reef, which has no people, traffic is so obviously constituted by human action that it can stand as an even more powerful visual representation of society. Seen from above, the circulating lights of individual motorbikes represent a mass of individual identities subsumed into the dazzling electric light parade of the social whole. Those are all real people down there, and this whole is somehow made up of them. And like society, this light show represents a paradoxical, multivalent face of contradictory possibilities: in the flowing lights we see realization as well as estrangement; we see routes of passage as well as blockages, liberation and confinement, order as well as chaos. Individual riders on their motorbikes, taxi drivers and their passengers, truck drivers delivering goods to Saigon from the provinces, NGO workers, businesspeople and international functionaries in their chauffeured minivans and SUVs, tour buses, cyclos, motorized three-wheeled carts, and city buses all compete as individuals trying to make space in this immanently social scene that confronts them on the level of appearances as a material world through which to navigate.

In the confrontation with traffic as thing, the social nature of traffic splits into its mystified form, where the interrelation of structure and action become temporarily divorced from each other on the level of appearances. In this moment of disarticulation and cognitive detachment, the product of social interaction and the movement of bodies through social space becomes reified as a thing, a thing that confronts the social actor as an alien presence comparable to a natural disaster. The people who confront it remain only vaguely aware of its social origins, seeing traffic as an alienating antisocial space. Traffic, thus mystified, appears as something outside of society. We see this with the altars on the side of the road, as if traffic could be controlled by appeasing the spirits of those who have died on the road. For the people who give traffic its very flow, the chaotic potential of traffic floats into the misty realm of religion and the unexplainable. Traffic happens.

But this is not only about some abstraction called society. The social relations that produce new forms of time and space include power-laden relations of politics and money as well. In the conception of traffic that emanates from on high in the Ministry of Transportation and the Ministry of Construction's Institute for Urban Planning, this immanently social relation called traffic is reified as a material entity to be corrected through material transformation. The structure of traffic is seen not as a matter of social structure but as a matter of infrastructure.

Materialist Visions of Chaos and Control

The government takes an explicitly materialist approach to controlling chaos, this social thing that no one can make sense of. By this I mean that central planners emphasize the material problem of traffic infrastructure first and focus on social transformation only later, as a corollary to material change. The construction of roads becomes the motor for the construction of society.

To see this, let us turn to the Ministry of Construction, whose 1999 publication articulates the role of the Institute of Planning in the process of urbanization:

The goal of developing urban Vietnam is prompted by the general goal of developing the country from now until 2020 [which is to] "Give all energy to strive *(phấn đấu)* to turn the country into an industrialized country with a modern material and technical base, a sound economic structure, advanced relations of production appropriate to the development level of the productive forces, elevated material life and spirit, a solid national security, rich people, a strong country, and an equal and civilized society."[37]

In this description, the material development of urban infrastructure precedes and creates the possibility for the transformation of both the material life and the spirit of the people. In this context, "spirit" does not refer to religious life but implies something closer to the idea of the collective spirit, intellect, or sensibility of the people, a collective consciousness engendered by relations of production. This materialist conception of social consciousness makes a facile connection between the division of labor and the level of civilization in functionalist, Durkheimian terms that emphasize collective progress toward the same goal. Such an approach fails to account for the kinds of differences that might make one want to cross the road rather than ride straight down it. The materialist assumption is clear: if we make the road straight, people will ride straight on it.

The head of the Ministry of Construction continued to explain that "the general goal of urban development throughout the country until 2020 is to . . . play a role in properly realizing the two strategic duties of building socialism and defending the country, [as well as] pushing for industrialization and modernization of the country."[38] All of these tasks are linked through the idiom of construction. The Ministry of Construction not only focuses on constructing an urban infrastructure but hopes that by doing so it will literally lay the foundation for a particular form of urban society appropriately linked to the construction of socialism. Urban space will create urban minds; civilized roads, civilized people.

This same text later turns specifically to traffic as the primary concern in a section headed "Development Direction of the Basic Urban Technical Infrastructure."[39] Developing a sound urban traffic regime requires setting aside enough land for traffic (which the writers of the text set at 20 to 30 percent of the total land in the "big" urban areas), fully working out the road network in the urban areas, reorganizing traffic patterns, establishing policies for the reduction of traffic congestion, clearing up congested traffic intersections, adding stoplights and traffic signs, and "liberating the center of the roads and the sidewalks" *(giải phóng lòng đường, vỉa hè)*.[40] So here we see the Ministry of Construction with its historical-materialist interpretation of how to build up to socialism. Its subsidiary organ, the Institute of Planning, depicts traffic planning as one of the more important aspects of building a civilized urban-based Vietnamese society.

Part of the solution is thus clearly material, involving the physical "liberation" of the roads and sidewalks in a language that echoes that of socialist revolutionary victory as the ultimate act of liberation through military force. But of course the liberation of the roads, much like the grand liberation of 1975, is dialectically linked to the liberation of people, an essentially spiritual conception of social transformation that is unavoidably linked to material progress. So the Ministry of Construction links its own project to a larger strategy of social transformation. As used, the word for construction, *xây dựng,* deploys its full double meaning, the strict meaning of building a house or modern infrastructure and the metaphorical yet penetrating notion of building a society, of "building socialism" *(xây dựng XHCN)*.[41]

This double meaning both prioritizes the role of the Ministry of Construction and inadvertently identifies its own limits. On the one hand, construction is linked to the construction of a socialist society. Yet on the other hand, even in the decidedly materialist approach to traffic offered by the ministry, the material transformation of the traffic problem itself butts heads with the problem of "the social." Moving through these descriptions of physical transformations that must be enacted in order to build an idealized urban space, the section of the ministry's text on traffic eventually encounters the social beings within. This realization of the social first appears with an emphasis on the need for stoplights and signs, objects that mediate the material infrastructure of the road with meaningful signifiers designed to interact with social beings. The section culminates in a call to "propagandize and make widespread knowledge and laws about traffic," a simple call with far-reaching implications.[42]

With this fallback onto propaganda, the materialist notion of constructing a socialist society meets its match. Even though the construction of infrastructure claims a primary role in constructing social consciousness, builders still need to propagandize and build consciousness. Building roads alone is not enough. The baton is passed to other organs of the government that specialize in social engineering, such as the Ministry of Culture and Information. The problem of traffic always returns to what Nguyễn-võ Thu-hương, applying the work of Nicholas Rose and Foucault to the Vietnamese governing apparatus, has called the problem of "governing the social."[43]

Nguyễn-võ describes a division of labor in the Vietnamese state apparatus, a division that is both practical and marked by political factions that compete for control in the governance and control of social life. Such a division also emerges when it comes to controlling traffic, as evidenced by a recent governmental decision detailing exactly how to implement several aspects of the Traffic Law.[44] This document, aimed primarily at allocating different tasks among the various ministries, shows how the problem of the social increasingly supplements the materialist thrust of the general project of urbanization. The roles of the Ministries of Transport and Communications, Public Security, National Defense, Finance, Construction, Health, Labor, War Invalids and Social Welfare and the various People's Committees are defined in terms of building and implementing traffic infrastructure as well as enforcing the laws. These are mainly materialist approaches based on construction and discipline. They focus on the physical interaction of people with the environment. Yet in addition the Ministry of Culture and Information and the Ministry of Education and Training are given the tasks of teaching the people about traffic, of making the notion of traffic resonate as a part of the collective conscience.

Two sets of mechanisms emerge for implementing the new regimes of traffic. One is highly material, based on constructing the infrastructure of traffic and ensuring that people correctly use that infrastructure. These mechanisms build the straight roads and make sure people ride straight along them. The other set of mechanisms is ideological, designed to change minds, to make people conform naturally to the forms of traffic as if they were one and the same with their own desire. Their job is to make the people *want* straight roads.

The social has reappeared. And it does not always conform to the materialist assumptions about how the physical world will mold the minds of men. Behind the search for smoothly flowing traffic lurks a civilizing mission.[45] In 2003 this mission was made explicit in the program called the Year of Order and Civilized Urban Lifestyles *(Năm trật tự kỷ cương, nếp sống văn minh đô thị),* a projection of social idealism that found an important outlet in the renewed emphasis on traffic control. This rubric promoting an ideological notion of urban civilization reacted to a whole nest of traffic-related issues, including a campaign to stop illegal motorbike racing among Ho Chi Minh City youths and attempts to reduce the number of congested traffic areas by 30 percent, to eliminate delays of more than thirty minutes, and to reduce the number of accidents by 10 percent.[46] Linked publicly to the idea of hosting the Southeast Asia Games, the stress on urban civility emphasized a modern face of Vietnam before the world, coopting the nationalist pride associated with hosting an international sporting event in order to legitimize new conceptions of social control and order. The rules included cleaning up the streets and fining people for throwing trash, dressing poorly in public, and urinating or sleeping in public spaces. But the general transformation expected by the cultural emphasis on civilization proved disappointing, and the Ministry of Culture and Information recommended that the authority to enforce the rules be extended to the local ward level.[47] All these "uncivilized" problems were still rampant by mid-2003, and the only way to control them was by more effectively issuing citations and collecting monetary fines.

The campaign for urban civilization is a propaganda campaign exactly because it does not resonate with the social practices of everyday life on the streets of Vietnam. So rather than look at traffic as emerging from the way in which people navigate the streets, the ministerial division of labor begins with infrastructure and then moves to shape the people to fit that infrastructure through what the ministry calls "propaganda plans" enforced by punitive measures.[48] Transforming space and time on Saigon's edge not only works in the world of symbols and ideals; it entails heavy-handed ideology and material force as well. As I show in the next chapter, the connections between the spatialized power of road building and the material and symbolic relations of rural and urban are quite intimate. The quest to civilize is not only about traffic and infrastructure; it represents a concerted attempt to rework the relationship between the urban and the rural, privileging the powerful inside in an idiom of linear history in which rural life must be transcended by urban forms of progress. These propaganda plans, in turn, framed in an idiom of development, attempt to mediate the social with the built material environment by flattening the various dimensions of Vietnamese society into a singular collective conscience.

But, most pressingly, as Ba Ven almost found out that day that the Xuyên Á happened to him, it is not only consciousness that is being flattened on the road to paradise as it wends its way through Saigon's edge.

6. The Problem of Urban Civilization on Saigon's Edge

> At present many of the rules of conduct and sentiment implanted in us as an integral part of one's conscience, of the individual super-ego, are remnants of the power and status aspirations of established groups, and have no other function than that of reinforcing their power chances and their status superiority.
>
> —Norbert Elias, *The Civilizing Process*

Shocking Shorts

While conducting fieldwork in Hóc Môn's Tân Thới Nhì commune, I undertook a series of interviews with elderly household heads in order to collect local histories and to learn about the transformations of spatial and social relations in the district. Hoping to follow the ethical protocols of research and to maintain an air of openness with the local district and commune authorities, I agreed to conduct these interviews with members of the commune's Old People's Association and to present a list of my questions to officials from the local branch of the Fatherland Front.

The Fatherland Front is Vietnam's "official mass organization," a sort of umbrella organization for groups like the Peasant's Association, the Women's Association, the Veteran's Association, and this one, the Old People's Association. According to the Vietnamese Constitution, the Front "and its member organizations constitute the political base of people's power." A sort of state-sponsored apology to the idea of civil society, it is designed to promote the formation of social groups as long as their ideas are "unified" and "legitimate."[1] The Constitution adds, "The Front promotes the tradition of national solidarity [and] strengthens the people's unity of mind in political and spiritual matters."[2]

Cadres from the Front reviewed the questions I gave them, then provided me with a list of appropriate people to interview. They accompanied me on several of the interviews to ensure that I actually asked the questions I had prepared. Mr. Chinh, the head of the Fatherland Front in Tân Thới Nhì, suggested that I take two cans of sweetened condensed milk and a kilo of sugar to present as a gift to each of the interviewees. I repeated the phrase he used to describe the gift as I would a mantra, because it sounded like the first line of a folk poem: "Hai hộp sữa một ký đường" (Two cans milk; one kilo sugar). Everyone smiled, nodded, and repeated the phrase as I did. "Two cans milk; one kilo sugar," said ông Thao, the head of the Old People's Association. "Two cans milk; one kilo sugar," repeated anh Tương, the vice-head of the Fatherland Front.[3] They explained that it was an old tradition to offer these gifts when visiting elderly people in the countryside. It reenacted a relation of exchange in which refined urban industrial products are delivered to old people in the country without access to such goods. I also said I would take my camera along and take some pictures so I could give the people I visited framed enlargements as a gift. Everyone agreed that this was a good idea, because these people do not have many photos of themselves. Then, in a set of eight interviews carried out in this spirit of unity, openness, and exchange, with these members of the Fatherland Front interjecting at opportune moments during the interviews, my informants told me a good deal about the glory of industrialization and modernization and the wonders of urbanization.

The formulaic structure of this format appeared in the following inter-action between our group of interviewers and an eighty-year-old farmer who described his return to Hóc Môn after 1975. During the American War, he had worked as a taxi driver in Saigon, after which he took up the government's offer to farm a piece of land along the An Hạ canal in Hóc Môn. When he started to describe how difficult the time was, the attendant added that this was because of the false postwar economy. "After Liberation," another attendant explained, "people didn't have any work and the government granted people as much land as they could work." There was no mention of any coercion among people "encouraged" to leave the cities to farm land in the New Economic Zones. The interviews skirted the issue of collectivization and postwar economic difficulties and focused more on positive elements of modernization and change.[4]

In retrospect, the interviews themselves were mostly a front for the Fatherland Front, with the attendants constantly interjecting qualifications to keep the stories in line with official notions of progress. One interviewee wrote his responses in advance and simply read from a carefully crafted essay about progressive development guided by the light of government policies. The whole setup constructed a field of inquiry that reinforced the narrative of "unity of mind" among my informants and gave a sense of popular support for government programs. The story was one of simple people on the rural margins of the city supporting but also gradually benefiting from the modernizing programs of the Communist Party. Like the canned milk and refined sugar we gave the interviewees, rural products and people are converted into their fullest potential when transformed by urban industrial science.

In one interview, a seventy-year-old man recently retired from a life of rice and commercial farming described the advantages of the urban transformation in Hóc Môn this way:

In the past Vietnamese people did not yet live the urban lifestyle and the people were very dull witted *(dốt nát)*, completely dim headed *(ngu muội)*, and not very wise *(khôn ngoan ý thức)*, but now Viet Nam . . . now the Vietnamese nation has been modernized . . . now the country has made Viet Nam advance forward into modernization, which I think has really been a big change for people and for a refined and courteous life *(cuộc sống thanh nhã)*. Without the fear of strenuous work and difficulty, people can advance the popular level of cultural standards *(dân trí)*.[5]

The answers to my questions displayed a kind unity of mind that really made it difficult to learn anything from these interviews. As is common in ethnographic research, the most interesting information came when the recorder was shut off. With these interviews in particular, the structure surrounding the whole interview process—rather than the interviews alone—told the story.

After the interviews were finished, I showed the photographs I had taken of the old people to Mr. Chinh. He smiled at the gesture and then looked carefully at the framed enlargements, expressing pleasure for the most part as he went through them. But he stopped short when he saw the final photograph: "Who is this? He was not on the list. And why is he wearing shorts? That is impolite *(không lịch sự)*." The original, preselected interviewee had become ill, and an alternate person had been chosen at the last minute. Apparently Mr. Chinh was not informed of this change. He was visibly displeased. He kept repeating two things: this man was someone he had not vetted, and he was wearing shorts. He kept repeating this out loud: *How could anyone pose for a picture in shorts?*

As Mr. Chinh described it, this man in shorts was "not polite." But there was more to his reaction than a simple concern about *politesse* and decorum. The shorts indicated that this man was too informal in what was supposed to be a formal interview. The shorts indicated a lack of advance preparation. Mr. Chinh must have wondered if this man in shorts could have possibly represented the unity of mind these interviews had been intended to demonstrate. All of this was coded in the statement that this man was impolite.

Peasants' Headaches and Double Meanings

Mr. Chinh's reaction recalled something Grant Evans points out in his book *Lao Peasants under Socialism*. He writes that "the persistence of peasant society has been a constant headache for communist governments in the twentieth century. The peasantry are an uncomfortable reminder to communist leaders of the underdeveloped nature of their economy and society and of their precocious attempt to 'bypass capitalism.'"[6] In many ways, contemporary Vietnamese socialism supports the claim Evans makes here. Perhaps Mr. Chinh was shocked to encounter a peasant in what is supposed to be a "postpeasant" era guided by the themes of industrialization, modernization, and urbanization.

But this is not the whole story. Peasant headaches are coupled with reverence and nostalgia. Vietnamese nationalist narratives also claim that the nation was formed in the name of the peasantry, and people still idealize rural life as a symbol of cultural purity, creating a tenuous double symbolism regarding the relationship between urban society and rural Vietnam. Lisa Drummond and Mandy Thomas, for example, point out that the current increase in rural–urban migration comes "at a time when the image of rural life resonates increasingly strongly as a site of the nostalgic imagination."[7] Despite the fact that urban incomes far surpass those of the countryside, they argue that the "alienation" of urban life leads many people to create a romantic view of rural life in which "rural images . . . project a sense that the countryside is the repository of traditional values, national identity, that life in the village is more peaceful and that relationships there are based upon emotion rather than money."[8] This is certainly true. Images of rural Vietnam constantly remind observers of the imagined purity of rural origins. In this sense, "the rural" works as a kind of escapist pain reliever for distinctly *urban* headaches.

But ultimately the symbolic reverence of rural society persists only insomuch as it reinforces a sense of urban righteousness and a hierarchical sense of rural and urban difference. For example, the whole purpose of these interviews was to learn about how these older people understood the change from rural to urban society taking place in this formerly agricultural district on the edge of the city. Mr. Chinh was not shocked by the idea that the man I had interviewed was a peasant. After all, it had been Mr. Chinh's idea to take milk and sugar to the interviews. But this very gesture implied the subordination of these elderly interviewees to urban paternalism. The structure of the gift was designed to invoke tradition and implied that these old people had no access to such things. That was precisely the point, to establish a hierarchical relation of giving and receiving. We would arrive as intellectuals with this gift of urban progress. They would accept the gift, and in their words they would tell stories that showed appreciation for the urban message. But ultimately, the story required the voice of these people to give it authenticity; their stories would legitimize their acceptance of the urban message. This produced a contradiction: a subordinated rural voice was required to say that these people hoped to transcend rural life. The interviews themselves were designed to show how the rural fringe of the city was superseding its own outdated relations of production. That is why Mr. Chinh was not shocked by the encounter with a peasant per se but focused instead on how the man presented himself. Dressed in shorts, he posed a threat to the social message of urban behavior as an emergent form of "civilized" comportment.[9]

The Paradox of Peasant-Based Revolution in Vietnam

This complex relationship between urban idealism and rural attitudes is not new. Compare Mr. Chinh's reaction with the writings of another man named Chinh, Trường Chinh, the author, with Võ Nguyên Giáp, of *The Peasant Question,* published between 1937 and 1938. At one point in this classic treatise, a document that attempts to establish the Indochinese Communist Party as *the* party of peasant revolution, they proclaim that "the peasants of Indochina know that the most essential thing is *to have confidence in oneself.*"[10] But in that very same text the authors explain that peasants "have many prejudices. They have been indoctrinated for so long that they think they are not exploited. They are grateful to the people who exploit them, and consider themselves the servants of the landlord. This is extremely dangerous!"[11] So much for confidence.

The Peasant Question identifies a two-part problem. First of all, people who exploit the peasantry are bad: "All of these people dance and feast on the sweat and tears of the peasant. The rich live in luxury, competing for wealth and honors made possible by the peasant's labor."[12] Second, the peasants are unfortunately mystified: "The unlucky and simple-minded peasants accept their wretched fate because they do not understand the cause of their misery."[13] The solution proposed is to be found in the intellectual vanguard, which claims to empower the peasants with confidence, which can be done by clearing their minds of superstition and making them understand the power they hold as a collective mass.[14]

As it emerged in the 1930s, the Vietnamese revolutionary narrative of a worker-peasant revolution took on the following basic structure, conveniently paraphrased by the late Cornell professor Huỳnh Kim Khánh:

You are poor and miserable; but you do not have to be poor any longer. You are poor not because of anything you did or failed to do, not because of Fate or bad luck. You are poor and you are exploited, and you are going to be poor and be exploited, because of the existing economic and political conditions; because of the French, the notables, and the landlords.

You do not have to be poor. The conditions that make you poor can be changed. They are going to be changed and you are going to help change them. Whether you are aware of it or not, what will happen is that you are going to make a revolution. Those who rule over you and keep you poor and miserable will be overthrown. By the revolution you can eliminate once and for all the exploitation of man by man; you can enter into a socialist society, in which you can be your own master.[15]

Overtly, this narrative structure forges an affinity with the peasant base of Vietnamese society, but it does so in a way that constrains acceptable peasant ambition, always articulating the interests of the peasantry in terms of communist ideology and modernization theory. Anything else is "dangerous" at worst, misguided at best.[16]

This relationship persisted through time and war. For example, Nguyễn Khắc Viện, the eloquent wartime spokesman for Vietnamese socialism to Western audiences, argued that "the peasants' struggle for their rights weaves in and out of Vietnamese history like a piece of red thread."[17] But there was also a red thread running through his summary of the socialist revolution's narrative of peasant consciousness. Namely, he suggested that peasants have power, but it is an uneducated, misguided power. Reflecting on events that had transpired in 1961, Dr. Viện described the need to correct peasant superstition with an anecdote about a well in a village: "A health team arrived in a village with the mission of sinking a well so that the residents would no longer use a large pond for their drinking water. Some time thereafter, the inhabitants filled the well and returned to using the same pond."[18] Why did they do that, he asks? Apparently a child died soon after the new well was put in, and "it was rumored that the death was the fault of the well, that the underground dragon was taking its revenge against the people."[19] Underground dragons! Typical peasants! *Nhà quê!* As he describes it, the relationship of rational science to the peasantry was quite necessarily one of mind managing muscle. Socialist science, he argued, would conquer superstition.[20]

Urban Solution / Urban Problem:
Công Nghiệp Hóa, Hiện Đại Hóa, Đô Thị Hóa

Behind all the rhetoric of solidarity with the peasantry, it is easy to note a tendency in Vietnamese communist theory to prioritize urban intellect.[21] Patricia Pelley notes this in the way Party historians vacillated in their story about rural and urban relations:

The hierarchy that initially privileged peasants was far from absolute. When it was reversed, peasants, once regarded as the life blood of revolution, as the source of all that was pure and authentic, suddenly appeared ignorant, superstitious, and on the verge of political reaction. . . . Cities generally, but especially Hanoi, figured as estimable centers. Likewise urban dwellers became civilized, open not to superstition but committed to science; they were urbane and politically progressive rather than passive or reactionary.[22]

Pelley rightly describes this as a narrative reversal, but it is not exactly a surprise to see this. Such reversals are inherently part of the theory; they form a key part of the Vietnamese socialist conception of how peasants relate to urban-based modes of rationality.

In addition to the exaltation of the peasantry, then, another story runs like a red thread through the images of Vietnamese socialism: the story of how rural society will be transformed by the anticipated rise of industrialization, modernization, and eventually urbanization. The collectivization of agriculture, for example, began with the call for a more equitable distribution of land among the peasantry. But this transformation in agricultural relations was not simply an end in itself. It was part of the strategy to achieve socialism by creating the basis for a move to industrialization without passing through the stage of advanced capitalism.[23]

Later, many outside observers cited the failure and eventual dismantling of agricultural collectives in the 1980s as evidence of the party's

misguided policies regarding the economy.[24] In response, official histories of the period cite the ability of reform-minded visionaries within the
party to recognize the potential of the peasant-based "household mode
of production" and to adapt policy in accordance with the will of the
people.[25] Subsequently, in the early 1990s, the increased productivity of
agriculture and the resumption of agricultural exports were used to chart
the development of Vietnam and, paradoxically, to provide evidence of
the party's own ability to guide economic development. Thus, in 1995 the
General Secretary of the Communist Party, Đỗ Mười, could provide the
following narrative account of the preceding fifteen years of change:

> The renovation initiated and led by our Party in the past years also regards
> the countryside as the main ground and agriculture as a breakthrough. Directive
> No. 100 of the secretariat (4th session) and Resolution No. 10 of the Political
> Bureau (6th Session) are two great landmarks which made a very important
> contribution to create a turning point on the path to development of agriculture
> and rural areas in our country. Carrying out this renovation line over the past
> few years, our agriculture has recorded encouraging results, mainly because the
> productive forces in rural areas have been liberated to an important extent, and
> the great potentialities of the peasantry have been promoted.[26]

Taking the apparent paradox of peasant resistance head on, the revised
party narrative asserts its own leadership in these times of change and
once again sides with the peasantry. "These achievements," Mười continues, "are due to the fact that the Party's line of renovation has summed
up the creative experience of the masses and conforms to the social laws
and the people's hearts."[27] Adjustments to the narrative of socialist development have thus led to a reinterpretation of the timing and shape of
change in such a way that the advanced stages of capitalism are incorporated into the historical move to socialism.[28] Still, in this new version
of the story, the party manages to use the notion of peasant interests to
secure for itself a vanguard role in guiding the nation.

But this triumph of the agricultural economy was not a vindication
of a peasant mode of production for the sake of the peasantry. Rather, it
was used as evidence that Vietnam was advancing steadily toward industrialization and modernization. Thus, on the one hand the party leadership
claimed to emphasize the importance of agriculture, but on the other hand
agriculture always remained a basis for socialist industry rather than an
end in itself.[29]

So the notion that peasants can form the impetus for social transformation at the same time that urbanization represents the pinnacle of socialist development cannot be simply understood as a "reversal" or even a contradiction. It is actually quite consistent in its vacillations.[30] Those very moments when rural agricultural producers recognize their central role in society are shown as evidence for an immanent transformation away from rural relations of production. Just as collectivization signals the inevitable end of agricultural oppression, the increase in grain production signals the coming of economic development and industrialization. Ideally, rural self-consciousness and success will lead to self-transcendence.

But the photos of the man in shorts challenged the official narrative. The year was 2002, and Mr. Chinh could not stop muttering about this man standing in front of a relatively new home, who was economically well off and who in his interview had expressed unqualified support for government development programs. But the wind symbolically whipped up from the fields behind him, and Mr. Chinh could not get over the fact that he was wearing shorts.

Urban Charms and Urban Ills

In Vietnamese urbanization texts, Vietnamese history is supposed to move in a straight path from a rural society toward one based on rational, scientific, urban social relations. The thesis of a book about ancient Vietnamese cities argues that modern urbanization will solve a problem that the ancient Vietnamese model of urban development never could. With the new form of urbanization, Vietnamese society will be able to transcend the agricultural basis of the economy. Even though many ancient cities were built to satisfy defined administrative and economic goals, and even though they often were built around a central citadel, the authors claim that precolonial Vietnamese cities were always subordinated to agricultural society. They point to nineteenth-century maps of relatively developed urban centers like Thăng Long–Hà Nội, which reveal rice paddies right in the middle of the urban center.[31] This is posed as a problem.

The authors of these urbanization texts go on to argue that the "function of history" *(chức năng lịch sử)* is to lead to a true form of urbanization, a more civilized form of urbanization in which country and city are kept separate.[32] The strict separation of country and city is the profound innovation of the modern era, they say, the real boon of true "urbanization."

The function of history unfolds like the Hegelian cunning of reason. And the subjectivized *list der vernuft* wears a shirt and tie, not a rural *áo ba ba*—and most certainly not shorts.

Here is what a 1999 textbook, *Quản lý đô thị* (Urban Administration), written for political functionaries, has to say about the historical relationship between the country and the city:

As a society becomes more civilized, the needs of life become more developed. Within this a segment of society breaks away from agricultural production and engages in handicraft production, trade, and social administration. These people, along with their families, live grouped together in population centers with a new residence form, working and living with a high sense of specialization. That is the bud that turns into the first signs of civilized life at the first stage of humanity; it is often also called the place of urban population.[33]

With all of the social evolutionary rhetoric of Tönnies and Durkheim,[34] the book asserts that the social division of labor produces the possibility for a civilized urban society. This division of labor underscores the ability to absorb a specifically "urban" form of "modern" thought:

An urban place is a dense concentration of inhabitants, predominantly nonagricultural laborers, who live and work following the manner and lifestyle of the city. The characteristics of that lifestyle include the following traits: there is a high need for intellectual activity, an ability to rapidly engage with the civilization of humanity, and there is sufficient and appropriate investment in basic economic and social infrastructure.[35]

But a certain problem emerges. If modern urban society emerges out of a rationalized social division of labor, its very success threatens its coherence, because urban society will lure peasants away from the countryside. The division of labor requires a strict differentiation of functions, and this division will lose its coherence if all the country folk stream into the city. Among many "unsolved riddles" *(những tồn tại),* the author mentions first the problem of rural people coming to the city: "The situation of peasants being pulled from the country to the city in order to find work and to create opportunities to make a living makes the situation of social-economic disorder more serious and creates many new problems, most urgently in the management of urban traffic control."[36] This reference to traffic prefigures a whole litany of problems that will lead to a general reduction in order and discipline,[37] and may potentially devolve into lawlessness, a state in which illegal building compromises the rational use of space for industry, traffic congestion increases, and people throw garbage everywhere, in the streets and in public spaces.[38]

In conclusion, the textbook proposes that for urbanization to develop in a sound and stable fashion, it has to completely transform life from rural to urban: "Urban development that proceeds in parallel with sufficient development of the economic and social infrastructure is comprehensive urban development that completely transforms life from the country into the city, or from the old style city to the new style city, [which is] more modern, more economical, [and] more civilized."[39] This is demonstrated by the "reality of history," in which urban areas have developed with the backing of strong administrative authority: "Reality shows that the social life in the developing countries is gradually taking on an urban more than a rural character. With such reality, the urban areas are using the power of government to encroach upon *(xâm lấn),* expand into *(bành trướng),* and annex *(thôn tín)* the rural outer-city areas in order to develop industry and commerce."[40] This process of encroaching, expanding, and annexing is not depicted in a negative fashion. Instead it will lead to the full realization of Vietnam's potential:

Nowadays, Vietnam is a country with a "middle-stage" *(thế hệ trung)* transitional rural civilization. Because of that, the urbanization process has created, is creating, and in the next few decades will continue to create, many obstacles. However, when carrying out industrialization in close connection with modernization, and with applied, well-chosen advanced industry, then Vietnam has a lot of potential to close the gap in living standards in comparison with other countries in the region, and will advance toward a form of industrial civilization, just as have other countries in the ASEAN Bloc.[41]

Idealized histories of urban development thus claim that the antagonism between the country and the city will disappear. Ideally, this will be in the form of enlightened urbanization built first on the foundation of rationalized and equitable agricultural production, which represents the final goal before a complete transformation into a rational urban form that epitomizes enlightened, scientific socialist development.

The Problem of Saigon–Ho Chi Minh City

But there are some problems when the cunning narrative of reason-guided urbanization confronts the actual course of urban development, which is fraught with ambiguity and the mixture of roles. In previous chapters I looked critically at how pseudotraditional ideologies of *âm* and *dương* construct an idealized notion of the city as creating symbiotic unity through oppositions. More recent Vietnamese interpretations of rationalized city planning do much the same thing by giving the outer city a function in the larger organic whole of the city. Instead of yin and yang they turn to organic metaphors reminiscent of Western notions of urban planning that posit the city as a functional organism.

In such functionalist organic metaphors Ho Chi Minh City–Saigon appears alternately as a city of progress and again as a city threatened by the mixing of categories. Urban civilization depends on taming disorder and constantly focuses on the need to transcend mixed uses and introduce a rational division of space. The Provisional Revolutionary Government that assumed control of the city in 1975 encountered an urban environment that even Western commentators deemed "artificial." Not long after the Fall/Liberation of Saigon, William Turley wrote of urban problems that included "the concentration of hundreds of thousands of soldiers and other personnel of the former regime in the cities, exacerbating already serious problems of unemployment, order and security; and urban over-population, the symptom of an artificial distribution of population in this basically agrarian economy."[42]

One scholar has stirringly described wartime urban development in Saigon as "savage urbanization," and less provocative observers insist that postwar Saigon was faced with a form of urbanization quite at odds with the rational, enlightened form envisioned by socialism or by traditional urban planners.[43] A key problem stemmed from how the actual development of Ho Chi Minh City confounded the notion that rational urbanization requires separation and ordered interaction, a relationship of exchange, but not one of mixing, such that country and city must interact in a carefully ordered division of labor that is based on the maintenance of difference. Any cursory view of life on the edge of Ho Chi Minh City, however, reveals that the economy really functions through the blurring of such boundaries. Social life emerges through the constant flow between the country and the city in a process of mutual constitution. But this poses a problem for urban strategies that seek to keep the country and the city separated as discrete spaces that form a functional division of labor based on a clear spatial demarcation of roles.

The idea of the functional city grafts indigenous Vietnamese ideas of controlling space with different—yet strangely familiar—forms of imagining space that emerged during the French and American periods. In all of these conceptions, the outer city is taken for granted as a kind of afterthought to the inner city. Although the inner city is planned and well thought out, the outer city becomes a kind of handmaiden to the needs of the inner city.

This is not just a "Vietnamese" contradiction; the problem of the periphery recurred in various guises among the French and American plans for the city.[44] In a 1928 article penned for the journal *L'Architecture,* the French urban planner Hébrard described Gia Định province, which surrounded and encompassed the expanding colonial Ville de Saigon, as an idyllic greenbelt that would give life to the inner city: "Although Gia-dinh is the capital of a large province, it really forms a suburb of Saigon. It is a green garden city, with the pleasant homes of well-off locals."[45] Echoing the contemporary European fascination with Ebenezer Howard's popular Garden City movement, Hébrard idealized a complementary unity between country and city that would lend civilization to the countryside and preserve the freshness of the city.[46]

Yet the rural reaches of Gia Định province proved a nemesis to colonial authorities as well. Those self-same "pleasant homes of well-off locals" on the margins of the city seemed to conceal a certain mystery and danger. In 1931, for example, when visiting the anticolonial patriot Nguyễn An Ninh at his house in Hóc Môn district, the journalist Andrée Violis described an idyllic car journey to the gardenlike fringes of the city. Three Annamites with degrees in letters, natural sciences, and law drove her out to meet with Ninh, passing by "villages of earth and bamboo huts under slender clumps of coconut trees, fruit and vegetable markets, shimmering so we might say they were painted and varnished." She further marveled at the "fields of tobacco, inundated rice-fields," and of course, the classic symbol of rural innocence, "children squatting on buffalos."[47] This idyllic view of the countryside outside Saigon, however, reflected the sympathies of a journalist who supported Vietnamese nationalism, a rosy view not shared by the local gendarmes. The gendarmes quickly arrived on the scene, implored her to return to Saigon, and regaled her for her apparent failure to understand the dangers of associating with this subversive agent and for venturing into such dangerous territory. The anticolonial Francophile Ninh, it seemed, hid his activities and concealed his ambitions to undermine French authority behind the neatly trimmed hibiscus hedges of his outer-city home.

A double sense of the space outside the city as both beautiful and dangerous seems to have informed the colonial imaginary ever since the earliest occupation of Saigon. Take the observations of Lucien de Grammont, who served as director of indigenous affairs in "Thu-yen-mot" and "Hoc-môn" in 1861 (and whom you might remember from the introduction). He commented on the importance of bringing natives from the provinces under the watchful eye of the urban authorities. Despite what he described as the haphazard nature of native building practices, he argued that developing local attachment to the city had favorable security implications:

The natives, who have not always found sufficient security in the provinces, come in droves, concentrating in Saigon, and they build, as if by magic, entire streets. This new population, almost completely Christian, is not rich, and find themselves most often in our care, and the houses they build are nothing more than straw huts. Is it necessary, as I have heard, to disparage this opulence? I don't think so. In addition to the refuge it provides to many people who do not want to participate in the movements of the provinces, it also brings laborers who we always lack. Others obtain concessions around the city and populate the outskirts; many fish or bring in products from the neighboring countryside. All of them become better off little by little, making them able to improve their homes in a short while, and the city will have gained in every respect. I admit that thanks to this movement, many suspect individuals have come to hide in Saigon; but all in all, wouldn't it be better to have them under our hands than far from our surveillance?[48]

Early French officials like de Grammont expressed a tension between overurbanization and the desire to centralize habitation near the city in an effort to keep the natives within the colonial gaze. Although de Grammont anticipated the idea of the *garden city* with his ideas of locals on the fringes providing fish and provincial products, the rural reaches also appeared as a threat. It was precisely the mystery that made the rural zones around the city so intriguing and also necessitated colonial strategies of surveillance and inspection.

While stationed in Hóc Môn, for example, de Grammont was fond of taking walks, which satisfied his aesthetic and administrative impulses at once. In a section called "Beauties of Indochine" he described one such walk, on which he cut a triangular path of inspection that doubled as a pleasant promenade:

In the plain, the tributaries of large rivers pour out everywhere an inexhaustible fertility, transforming the two banks that border it into a long series of gardens. There, the Annamite homes, hidden in the folds of these natural canals, sleep in the shadows of trees, always green and laden with fruits. Several pagodas with hooked roofs or expiatory chapels sheltered by centenarian tree-trunks invite one to stop. Leaving from Hoc-môn, if you pass down just to Binh-nham on the way to Binh-ly-thòn, you will pass the admirable land called Vinh-duong. I often took this promenade, returning in the direction of Thoi-yen and Tuân-Keou. The assistant to the chief of the canton always came along with us on these excursions. I gave him a little mare which he became quite fond of. Also, it was his pleasure to go in front of us like a scout in order to announce our passage into the places we were about to visit. He often had us stop at the home of the old mayor of Binh-nhan, where we would receive a truly bygone form of hospitality. I will always retain an excellent memory of this good Pho-lieù, who so often gave me evidence of his sincere attachment.[49]

But not all his friends in the outer-city regions left such "excellent memories." According to de Grammont, a certain canton chief named Van from the Cau-an-ha district within de Grammont's jurisdiction "maintained a mask by overwhelming me with expressions of friendship" even though he turned out to be secretly allied with the anti-French insurrection.[50]

Overall, de Grammont's reflections on administrating the rural space around Saigon paint a picture of pleasure mixed with fear. At this time, the French were busy quelling resistance movements on the rural fringes, including at the Vietnamese fort at Chí Hòa (Kỳ Hòa). In addition to the dangers of insurrection, there were natural dangers of not yet civilized space. For example, de Grammont remarked on the ever-present danger of tigers: over three months in the canton of Cau-an-ha, a dozen locals had encounters with tigers, in Hoc-môn four people disappeared in several weeks, and in Thu-yen-mot eight locals were devoured in a period of several months.[51] In his eyes, the space was undeveloped, and he advocated the need for infrastructure development, namely the building of roads, as a key part of the strategy for bringing the wild environs into order.[52]

Partly an affectionate, aesthetic memoir and partly an artifact of a colonial will to power, de Grammont's text links the larger colonial imagination of space with the kinds of intimate details that Stoler has shown to be so fundamental to colonial rule.[53] The literary critic Panivong Norindr reads the "geographic romance" in Marguerite Duras's depictions of colonial Saigon in similar ways, linking the aesthetic and the political. Showing how visions of space reproduce visions of power,

Norindr reads Duras in conjunction with the tropes of colonial urbanism, a symbolically rich combination of desire and enforced order "set in binary terms . . . : white versus native, civilization versus barbarity, the city versus the country, culture versus nature, man versus woman, affluence versus poverty, colonizer versus colonized, silence versus noise are opposing terms of two interdependent systems that need and require each other to exist."[54] The French colonial urbanists of the nineteenth and twentieth centuries, despite their own well-documented differences in political and architectural predilections, were ultimately concerned with the production of a civilized urban space.[55] Although the meaning of the French colonial mission may have alternated between policies of assimilation and those of association, the idea of a functional and ordered urban center with an organic relationship to the surrounding countryside has persisted at least since Colonel du Génie Coffyn famously proposed a plan for a "City of 500,000 souls" and mapped the grids of colonial Saigon in 1862.[56] But these early plans were themselves a product of intercultural dialogue from the very beginning. Coffyn's plan was oriented in relation to a preexisting Vietnamese fortress. This fortress had itself been built according to the Vauban style. But the European-inspired construction also underscored the Vietnamese conceptualization of space divided into zones "inside the walls" *(nội thành)* and "outside the walls" *(ngoại thành),* conceptions, as I have described in previous chapters, that have come to stand for the inner city and the outer city of today.[57]

Although these anecdotes do not constitute a complete history of French colonial perceptions of space and their articulation with Vietnamese notions of inside and outside, they do indicate that the potential double meaning of the outer city, or the distinction between rural and urban, is clearly not just Vietnamese but also parallels or intersects with certain colonial precedents. A similar confluence of ideas related to security, civilization, order, and infrastructure development can be seen in recent Vietnamese discourses on civilization, and they also underscored the American-backed Saigon regimes. The colonial, postcolonial, postwar, and postrenovation socialist conceptions of urban order all struggle with the problem of the edge and how it can be reconciled with the functioning of the inner city.[58]

The space surrounding a city takes on symbolic meaning that emerges out of the distinction between an ordered center and a surrounding periphery. The flip side of order is the potential for chaos. But the idea of order shifts according to the scale at which one views the relationship of the inside and the outside or the country and the city. In the national rural–urban dichotomy of Vietnam today, the outer city also has a double meaning. On the one hand, it is part of Ho Chi Minh City, which sets it up in symbolic opposition to the rest of rural Vietnam. Yet in the inside–outside dichotomy, the outer city is rural, which sets it up in opposition to urban Saigon. These two schemes of pure binary oppositions overlap in the outer city and produce a contradictory confluence of irreconcilable symbolic meanings.

The same was true, in somewhat different ways, for the Americans during the Vietnam War. The rural fringe surrounding Saigon posed a security concern. On one occasion, while walking down a dirt back road in Hóc Môn, my companion, a former soldier who had once served in the southern Army of the Republic of Vietnam and now lived in the area, stopped short to tell me how strange it felt to be walking there with an American. He told me that I would have been dead meat walking there during the war. This had been "VC [Viet Cong] territory" by night. He said it was strange to think about this now because we were just walking along this road, without a care in the world. When I returned from fieldwork and told Vietnamese Americans who had once served alongside American soldiers that I had been living in Hóc Môn, they often recalled unpleasant memories as well, reminding me that it had been a notoriously dangerous zone where the population vacillated between support for and deep resistance to the Saigon government. They had supported "the Republic by day and the VC by night."

During the American period in Saigon, the outer-city districts functioned as strategic buffer zones. In some formerly agricultural outer-city districts this seems to have jump-started the urbanization process. In one description, the establishment of military bases near Tân Sơn Nhất airfield "transformed [the formerly outer-city district of] Gò Vấp into a protective military base for northwest Saigon,"[59] and the militarization of the district actually intensified the urbanization process by filling the buffer with military personnel, depots, and so on. In other outer-city districts like Hóc Môn, the militarization of space transformed the areas into contested no-man's zones, the kinds of places where the locals could be friends in the daytime and enemies at night.

Even Graham Greene played on the symbolism of this unknown zone on the road to Tây Ninh, which is, in fact, the same Highway 22 that cuts through Hóc Môn. In *The Quiet American,* the space along the road from Saigon to Tây Ninh (spelled "Tanyin" in the novel) is described as a dangerous space between places but not much of a place in its own right. The dark patch of road between spaces provides the perfect symbolism for a key transition in the novel when the protagonist is trapped with the "friend" he will soon betray in a mud watchtower first erected in the colonial period but now surrounded by dangerous "Viets." Not long after his friend leaves him, he finds himself with a broken leg in an empty field, alone, afraid, and vulnerable.[60]

Although vulnerable zones often appear in war and make for good scenes in novels, they confound the work of urban planners. In postwar Ho Chi Minh City, urban planners sought to transform the nonurban periphery into productive space, to switch the function from defense to production of foodstuffs. A wartime defensive stance promoted by the previous regime hewed to a new emphasis on state socialism and collective agriculture. Important decisions by the Ho Chi Minh City People's Committee and People's Assembly attempted to confront a suburban sector largely devastated by war, where infrastructure was almost nonexistent, the lives of people were unstable and fragmented, and farmers returned to fields with little else besides their hands.[61] In 1976, Directive 02/4/1976 of the Ho Chi Minh City People's Committee sought to solve the land problem in the outer-city districts, and Directive 7 (10/5/1976) sought to completely eliminate the role of "feudal" landowners, with the intention of redistributing land, especially to the 15 percent of landless peasants.

The immediate task was to convert the "vành đai trắng" (no-man's land or, literally, "clear belt"), into a "vành đai xanh," or agricultural greenbelt.[62] Initially this was accomplished through the development of infrastructure, electrification, and an attempt to build agricultural collectives on the outskirts of the cities.[63] Although the strategy of collectivization eventually failed, the organic metaphor of the outer city persisted. In 1986, just as the larger national reforms of the sixth National Party Congress were introducing the new policies of renovation *(đổi mới),* the Ho Chi Minh City Party Committee issued a new five-year plan for the city at its own fourth meeting. The plan emphasized the importance of developing agriculture in the outer-city district as a strategy to complement the industrialization of the city itself: "Investing in the outer city is truly a service to the inner city, to industry, and to the realization of the agroindustrial structure of the city," and "the outer city must clearly change in terms of economy and culture and meaningful service *(phục vụ)* to the city center."[64] Here we see unwitting echoes of de Grammont's and Hébrard's quaint idea of how a rural periphery can satisfy the functional needs of the inner city. Ultimately, even though a new generation of Vietnamese scholars have criticized the rush to collectivization in the southern region as "illogical" *(phi lô-gích),* they never question the larger assumption that the ideal city should be linked to its fringe in an organic division of labor. As Đinh Huy Liêm asks, how can one improve the productivity of the outer-city districts by introducing an urban and industrial economy of scale while encouraging the kind of intensive labor that has been demonstrated through private family production on private land?[65] How can one make the outer-city districts economically productive while at the same time preserving them as the green "lungs of the city"?[66]

In all of these iterations, the space of the outer city appears as a problem of civilization and security, a threat to order. By the close of the twentieth century, the problem of security and civilization has come full circle. In ways strangely reminiscent of the French colonial discourse of civilizing the fringes, the Vietnamese state has begun to deploy what Thongchai has called "differentiated spaces of civilization" in an attempt to reclaim a sense of order and control in a period of global fragmentation and chaos.[67] Posed against the cunning story of rational urbanization, the mixing of roles and categories poses a challenge to the story of urban development based on a discrete, spatialized division of labor. Mr. Chinh's reaction to the interviewee's shorts provides an important example of the fact that the actual transformation of the edge from country into city is not so straightforward. The mixing of country and city appears as an uncomfortable shock.

In his interview, the man in shorts told a story much as the other people did about the progressive rationalized, modernized, and industrialized urban transformation. But his very person belied the sense of a strict division of rural and urban space. His dress was an uncivilized *(thiếu văn minh)* mixture of rural and urban. In today's Ho Chi Minh City, this kind of confusion is posed as something of a crisis.

"Urban Civilization" (Văn Minh Đô Thị) and the Problem of "Urban Ruralization" (Nông Thôn Hóa Đô Thị)

According to Mr. Chinh, wearing the shorts was not polite *(không lịch sự)*. What does being polite have to do with an urban transformation? In a 1999 paper presented at an international conference on sustainable development held in Ho Chi Minh City, a scholar at the Hùng Vương People's University warned of an impending "crisis in urban manners" *(sự khủng hoảng tác phong văn minh đô thị)* about to overtake the city:

In the next few decades, at least half of the population now living in the countryside will have to move and live in the urban areas. Most definitely they will
not yet meet the standards of a civilized urban life, creating *a crisis in urban
manners*. In other words, the phenomenon of *"ruralization of the city"* will
develop, undermining urban order and discipline, urban hygiene, urban beauty,
and the civilized urban mode of interaction. In order to overcome the crisis in
urban manners, it is necessary to have concrete educational solutions regarding
civilized urban manners in Vietnam.[68]

The warning spoke of the future but located omnipresent signs of this crisis by referring to the unsavory habits of people living in the contemporary city.

The author continued in the next paragraph with some curious repetition and some everyday examples laced with an awkward temporality in which he referred to current problems in order to speak about the future:

In the next few decades, new urban areas like the new established districts in
the outer city of HCMC [Ho Chi Minh City] will be almost completely made up
of rural populations who have moved to live in urban areas. How will the inhabitants of Vietnam's urban areas acquire the lifestyle of urban order, such as
forming themselves into orderly lines—not pushing and shoving in disorderly
fashion in crowded areas at the post office, the theater, at stores, bus stations,
airports—as has been achieved today in developing Southeast Asian countries
like the Philippines? How can we make it so that people no longer relieve themselves in random fashion, or throw dead rats and dead domestic animals out into
the streets, down into rivers and canals, and at the feet of bridges . . . ? How is
it possible that urban residents will become interested in urban beauty, know
how to make the city pretty beginning right in every home, to willingly paint,
touch up, and decorate instead of hanging clothes out to dry in an untidy fashion
as they do today? How is it possible to have urban inhabitants not go shirtless
or dress frumpishly *(lếch thếch)* on the streets or use these impolite gestures in
their industrial manners and modes of work as they do today in the urban areas?

Those are the big questions that need to be answered regarding civilized urban manners in Vietnam today.[69]

In the rest of the paper the author criticized the current state of the education system and pointed out that students are not taught to respect their environment in schools.[70] To correct these flaws, the author then outlined a five-point program of education that encouraged Vietnamese people "to build an urban civility that both expresses a modern character and a Vietnamese character" that satisfies the goals outlined in a state-sponsored program called Civilized Urban Manners in Vietnam (Tác phong văn minh đô thị Việt Nam).[71] The connection the author made between education and civility is certainly not unique. For example, when a person does something impolite (or dresses frumpishly) it is not uncommon for people to exclaim that they "have no culture" *(không có văn hóa)* or that they are "undercivilized" *(thiếu văn minh).* These terms are used almost interchangeably with the idea that these people do not know anything because they have a "low level of education" *(không có học vấn).*[72] Vietnamese people commonly make this connection. Indeed, this is the same kind of culture and civility Nguyễn Khắc Viện spoke of when he imagined villagers drinking clean water from their new well, abandoning their fear of dragons and embracing science.

Let us look more closely, however, at the way the author constructed rural Vietnam as a scapegoat for the looming urban crisis. On the one hand, the problems of the city already seem present; these are the things the author cited to build the sense of moral panic. Yet on the other hand, the author repeatedly referred to a period "in the next few decades" when the city will be inundated by rural migrants. The temporality contradicts itself: it assumes, as do all the standard texts about urbanization, that urbanization is a natural endpoint in history. Urbanization will produce a civilized society because the urban relations of production are more civilized and naturally based on a rational division of labor. Yet it never deals with the main problem: how urbanization can represent the "natural" course of history if it is unable to overcome the threat of rural society.

Curious about this fear of ruralization, I took the article to one of my teachers at a local university, expecting a more sober perspective. This teacher had spent several years earning a law degree in France, was respected for his work translating Western social science texts into Vietnamese, and was generally cynical about common stereotypes. I asked him to read the article and tell me what he thought of it. I expected him to share my initial reaction, to see the scapegoating of rural Vietnamese as an escapist tactic used to avoid the more pressing problems of urban poverty and unequal access to urban citizenship. He told me a story about toilets instead.

It's true what this author says, my teacher said as he skimmed the article, *and there are examples of this problem right here at this university.* He then told me that many of the professors working in the university were basically frauds with fictitious, meaningless degrees. They were really just peasants masquerading as university professors. If I wanted proof, all I had to do was go into the faculty restrooms and look at the toilets. I would see that there are footprints on the toilet seats. The faculty are such peasants, he explained, that they think one is supposed to climb up on the rim of the seat and squat over it, as one would do in a country latrine or in the Mekong Delta, where one squats on a platform that juts out over the river so one can "feed the fish."

My teacher told me that the real crisis was more complicated than even the author of the article imagined, because people in positions of authority were still "peasants" on the inside. One cannot always tell by looking at people, because they put on a dress shirt, wear slacks, and walk around in shoes with socks. But inside, in their minds, they are still peasants to the core. As he described it, one could see this problem everywhere. *Look at the people eating in the street restaurants near the Prudential building,* he told me. *They are all dressed up in urban clothes, and they work in air-conditioned offices. But just watch them eat! They throw their bones everywhere, toss their trash in the street.* He told me that these people still had a peasant mentality. They wore the superficial uniform of urban living and moved through urban space, but they were urban imposters who still treated the city as if it was the countryside. They were city folk on the outside but still peasants on the inside.

On another occasion, during a master's-level seminar on culture and economy at the same university, the discussion erupted into a boisterous condemnation of what participants described as the remnants of a "peasant mentality" among bureaucrats in the state administration. *Do you know why there is corruption in Vietnamese politics?* one girl asked rhetorically. *Because villagers used to share work in a reciprocal fashion. When the rural cadres get any position of power, they have to honor their family obligations and pay back all the people in their social network.*

No one disputed this claim. Rural cadres were corrupted by an almost natural impulse to act this way, an impulse that had emerged from the apparent nature of village society. All of this was couched in a general discussion about cultural impediments to economic development. The class unanimously agreed that rural culture was not amenable to economic development.[73]

In this urban Vietnamese variation on the confrontation between country mouse and city mouse, country mouse is pure when he stays home in the country. But in Ho Chi Minh City, when the mouse moves from the country to the city, he turns into a rat. Let us pause for a moment and think about the words for mice.

The Vietnamese language has only one word for both mouse and rat—*chuột.* The best way to know what kind of *chuột* you are dealing with is to ask where you found it. If you found it in the rice fields of rural An Giang or Kiên Giang province, you are a lucky person, because you have found yourself a *chuột đồng,* a field mouse, which is a delicacy. If you found it in the city, watch out, for you have found a *chuột cống,* a sewer rat. If you walk into a restaurant specializing in country flavors, you can order a *chuột đồng nướng,* a grilled field mouse. If you walk into the wrong part of the city, you risk entering a neighborhood of rat-infested houses, *các nhà ổ chuột.* Where do the tasty clean mice come from? The countryside. Where do the people who live in rat-infested houses come from? The countryside.

The difference between the rat and the field mouse, as these examples indicate, is based on where it lives. The semantics of *chuột* indicate that mice belong in the fields, and they are pure and clean when they feed off rice grains. When they move to the city, they feed off waste, living in the cracks and edges of society, infected creatures of the shadowy realms hidden behind or beneath public culture. An analogous symbolic transformation occurs when the country person moves to the city and the apparent crisis of urban ruralization threatens urban civilization.

But this becomes confused by the emphasis on urban civilization. It tells the country mouse how great and civilized the city is but calls him a rat when he goes there.

Văn Minh Đô Thị

The country mouse really strikes people as a threat to this concept called *văn minh đô thị,* or "urban civilization."[74] Despite its propagandistic ring, *văn minh đô thị* seemed to resonate with the thoughts of many everyday people I met. Even the most cynical critics of government propaganda campaigns—the kinds of people who would sometimes whisper, "I hate communists" to me over their shoulder while riding motorbikes through the city—would have trouble understanding my own discomfort at the notion of "civilized urban lifestyle."[75]

But what exactly *is văn minh đô thị*? Pure definitions of the term prove elusive.[76] It sometimes refers to a particular kind of lifestyle, as one might say "wet rice civilization" or "orchard civilization."[77] In other cases, it implies an elevated sense of decorum and behavior, a mode of comportment appropriate to an urban mode of production.[78] But the best way to understand what it means is to think about the topics and words that come up alongside the term. In a 2003 interview conducted in conjunction with the twenty-eighth anniversary of the liberation of Saigon, Lê Thanh Hải, the chairman of the Ho Chi Minh City People's Committee, took the opportunity to describe the achievements of the city's program called the Year of Order, Discipline, and Civilized Urban Lifestyles *(Năm trật tự kỷ cương–nếp sống văn minh đô thị)*. The interview focused on three major issues: traffic safety, infrastructure, and the regulation of building throughout the city. The chairman explained that regaining order and discipline in those three areas will lead to *văn minh đô thị* and will make the city modern. "Recently," he told the interviewer, "the face of Ho Chi Minh City has become more ordered, civilized, clean and beautiful, open and well-ventilated, and safer than before. The leadership of the City will firmly continue these decisive measures with interagency cooperation, giving stability to the people's lives and development to a civilized and modern city."[79]

The idea of urban civilization appeared with some frequency in newspaper articles. One article focused on the problem street food posed for urban civilization. Despite the convenience and the important economic role of street food, the article cautioned, "it is necessary to solve certain problems related to its influence on urban civility, and the health of the consumers."[80] Others focused on the "civilized" image the city should try to project to foreign guests attending the Southeast Asia (SEA) Games, and still others focused on comportment and dress.[81] The discourse is not confined to Ho Chi Minh City. In Hanoi, the city passed specific regulations that threatened to fine people for a variety of uncivilized behaviors. Penalties could be incurred for going shirtless or wearing inappropriate clothing in public places, throwing garbage and disposing of waste water in the street, smoking in places where it was prohibited, relieving oneself in undesignated places, buying and selling at falsely inflated prices and cheating customers, annoying tourists by begging and selling to them, letting domestic animals roam freely, speaking vulgarly, fighting in public, causing noise that affected other people from 10 p.m. to 5 a.m., putting ads on walls, and advertising and selling goods in the roadway. Fines started at 20 thousand *đồng* (US$1.34) and ranged up to 100 thousand *đồng* (US$6.67).[82] There were similar rules in Ho Chi Minh City.

In a sarcastic article called simply "Văn minh đô thị!" (Urban Civilization!) printed in the *Tuổi Trẻ* Saturday edition's weekly "Relaxation" column, an author poked fun at the common problem of people who use public walls in the city to paint advertisements for "Cement Cutting," "Drain Cleaning," and services offering help with problems of "Weak Libido."[83] Such graffiti compromised efforts to preserve "urban civility," and the author proposed a few humorous ways to get the whole community involved in stopping this problem. The root of the problem, he explained, must be that these businesspeople lacked customers; that is why they felt compelled to paint their advertisements everywhere. The obvious solution entailed giving them business. For the cement cutters, the author proposed that city planners redesign the width of major roads at least three times so that the people living along them would have to rebuild their houses each time in accordance with the new scheme. They would have to hire cement cutters each time the roads were redesigned. Inundated with business, the cement cutters would not need to paint their advertisements on city walls anymore. The author claimed that it would not be a problem for city administrators to implement this idea: "Just give it to the planners to worry about; after all, they specialize in this." And to keep the drain cleaners working, the author urged people to start putting all their "waste" in one place instead of casting it about all over the city as they do now. Finally, to help reduce the number of ads for "weak libido," the author simply encouraged people to eat. The toxic food in Ho Chi Minh City would surely give enough people weak constitutions to keep these people busy. This sarcastic letter proved critical of both the administration and the people of Ho Chi Minh City. But it built its critique off of a clear commitment to the idea of a true *văn minh đô thị*. Behind all the sarcasm it implied that the people really need to be controlled.

A writer in Hanoi took the issue more seriously and was even inspired to write a letter to the newspaper supporting the new regulations on urban civilization. "I very much support the Hanoi People's Committee's decision about reestablishing urban civility," wrote the author. The letter not only supported the new regulations; it argued that they should be more strictly enforced. The author had been working in a foreign country, and despite an intense love for Hanoi, expressed a sense of shame and embarrassment about such uncivilized behavior.[84] The author hoped the new rules would be effectively enforced with strict penalties.

All of these discussions linked *văn minh đô thị* with order, discipline, safety, sustainability, cleanliness, beauty, openness, ventilation, stability, regulation, and development. It is *modern.* It requires law, traffic safety, infrastructure development, investment, regulation of building codes, safe food, and *decisive measures.* When the city outlined "four main goals for '2003, the Year of Order, Discipline—and Civilized Urban Lifestyle,'" the first three goals all linked civilization to a sense of urban discipline. First, officials aimed to decrease the number of traffic jams by one-third, reduce the number of traffic accidents by 10 percent, and completely eliminate the scourge of illegal racing. Second, they vowed to regain order in the building sector, eliminate illegal building, and more thoroughly deal with the people involved. Third, they sought to establish order and discipline in the system of government agencies, making sure that all the decisions issued from the upper level were also issued at lower levels and strictly carried out. The fourth goal was more ambiguous and joined all of these changes with an emphasis on civilized urban "culture" that would bring about renovations in weddings, funerals, and other cultural and civilized activities and support the services of the SEA Games.[85]

All of these concerns ultimately assume that some form of urban civilization is desirable. There is little to no debate about this. The key to achieving this goal, however, requires social intervention designed to maintain order and prevent the blurring of pure conceptual categories and spaces. In the transformation of rural and urban relations, the directionality is always clear: urbanizing the countryside is considered progressive, sustainable development; ruralizing the city, by contrast, is regressive. The idealized notion of urban living emerges from discipline and order; it is something learned and enforced. The rural mentality, by contrast, is engrained in the mind in the manner of a bad habit; it must be worked on and transformed through a process of education in order to create the conditions for urban civilization.

Symbolic Fields in a Field of Symbols

The rural–urban fringe, however, is neither rural nor urban. It is a place that lies in the middle of the urbanization process. Ideally, a person in such a district will corroborate the language of the history books, offering straightforward praise for this process as a unilateral move forward toward urban civilization. The man dressed in shorts actually did that in his interviews. He talked about the development of the area, and he specifically praised the introduction of electricity, the government's improvement of the irrigation network, and the improved transportation system. Toward the end of the interview, he added conclusively: "So life now is the best already. Compared with the old days, these days are the best ever. In the old days I thought I wouldn't even eat, but now I have plenty of things to eat. . . . In the old days you would plant some yams and have to wait six months, three months and go out to dig them up before you could eat. Now if you want to eat you just go out to the store and it's there, now it's very happy."[86] He even gave an almost evolutionary depiction of technical progress in the form of his progressive purchases of a bicycle, a mobilette, and, more recently, a modern motorbike. But despite these words, he was wearing those shocking shorts. They threatened Mr. Chinh's understanding of an urbanization process that requires "civilized urban manners" and a careful separation of rural and urban space into discrete places.

The very place where we conducted the interview confounded many received truths about orderly urban development that divides space into discrete functional units. Living on the edge of Ho Chi Minh City, this farmer structurally straddled the country and the city. By conflating the symbolism of country and city he showed that they remain connected in blurry ways that defy official attempts to organize society in discrete compartmentalized places. The farmer occupied what Victor Turner would call a liminal position between structurally opposed categories. This liminal position itself opens up a challenge to orderly, programmatic categories that divide the nation in an organic division of labor based on the functional opposition between country and city. Turner describes how such a structurally ambiguous position threatens the coherency of orthodox "programs" for ordering the world: "Without liminality, program might indeed determine performance. But, given liminality, prestigious programs can be undermined and multiple alternative programs may be generated. The result of confrontations between monolithic, power-supported programs and their many subversive alternatives is a sociocultural 'field' in which many options are provided."[87] The farmer's shorts represented the potential for structurally ambiguous aspects of reality to resurface without warning in the midst of a socially contested field of symbols. In this case, the field of symbols was an actual field, right there behind him. This structurally flexible field represented at least two possibilities. Move one way and the field might represent open space that might provide room for the expansion of the urban dream, a place for a new factory or an urban resettlement zone. Move another way and the field might represent the persistence of agriculture on the edge of the expanding city. There is plenty of what Turner calls symbolic debris and "fallout" scattered around Hóc Môn to choose from. And this farmer chose to wear shorts, which effectively "ruralized" his contested field of symbols on the edge of the city and seemed a rejection of the civilizing gift of urban order and discipline.

This is the same problem experienced with the so-called crisis of urban ruralization, or the apparent "problem" of peasants masquerading throughout the city disguised in urban clothes. It is the same reason a mouse becomes a rat. These situations subvert the potential to categorize "the people" in discrete ways; they subvert the notion of society as founded on an organic division of labor, and they undermine the assumption that urbanization is an inevitable civilizing process of progressive advancement. And this is the same problem with outer-city districts like Hóc Môn, those anomalous zones between the country and the city, where the people seem Vietnamese, speak Vietnamese, and act Vietnamese but somehow stand as a threat to the unified mind and consciousness of "the people" as well. And that is the shocking effect a pair of shorts may have when one speaks about one's changing life on the civilizing fringe of Saigon's edge.

Conclusion
What Edges Do

This, then, is the puzzle of cultural dualism on the Copperbelt: how are we to square off a well-founded suspicion of dualist models of society and culture with the ethnographic fact of a persistent sort of cultural bifurcation—one, moreover, that informants insisted on conceptualizing in terms of tradition and modernity, the old and the new, the rural and the urban?

—James Ferguson, *Expectations of Modernity*

Postmodern critics tell us today that this modernism is now finished, its creativity exhausted. Yet, I would suggest another aspect of the problem: if modernism is dying, it nevertheless remains dominant, at the very least in the third world.

—James Holston, *The Modernist City*

Productive Binaries

The story of Saigon's edge is a complex one entangled with the story of urban transformation; dramatic changes in the Vietnamese political and economic orientation to socialism, capitalism, and global integration; and the legacy of the Vietnamese Revolution and its changing trajectory in the postwar and postrenovation period. In telling this complex story about life on the fringes of Ho Chi Minh City, however, nearly all of my Vietnamese informants, companions, friends, passing acquaintances, and even local social science research colleagues turned to binary spatial and temporal idioms for imagining the world as a set of rural versus urban and inside versus outside oppositions. Their version of the story seemed to favor simplification over engaging with the complexity of everyday life that marks contemporary Vietnam. In this book, based on accounts people told me of their lives in the outer-city district of Hóc Môn, I have shown how this reliance on binary schemes for explaining the world produced stories that were full of dreams and unspeakable silences as well.

In one sense, the opposition between country and city and between inside the city and outside the city produced a felicitous dream of order and meaning, an understandable world made "legible" by the way it could conform to a notion of progress and development. Indeed, a profoundly beautiful set of images appears when one closes one's eyes and imagines the pure stereotypes of rural and urban Vietnam; it is a harmonious place combining tradition and modernity, a place where social life appears to fruitfully combine intellectual verve and idyllic rural serenity. In another, less agreeable sense, this framework for knowing and understanding the world seemed to compress reality into overly neat conceptual categories that often obscured a great deal of practical social life. At best, some people did not fit into these schemes. At worst, some people were actively excluded, silenced, forgotten.

In simple strokes, people explained Ho Chi Minh City to me as if viewing snapshots of pure social and spatial types through the lens of a postcard photographer's camera: there are inner-city districts and outer-city districts; there are urban areas and rural areas; different kinds of people (should) live in those different places. Despite the rapid transformation of the material landscape that would have seemed to confound such simple binary categories, idealizations of inside versus outside and rural versus urban consistently framed the way my informants described and imagined social space on the anomalous fringes of Ho Chi Minh City. As I have shown, however, these modes of viewing the world cannot be dismissed as simply wrong or derided as evidence of false consciousness. The camera never lies. Rather, it represents the world in particular ways, leaving much beyond the frame. These modes of representation are, as I explained in early parts of this book and elaborated with examples throughout, more productively understood as idealizations forged in a process that Herbert Marcuse has called "the absorption of ideology into reality."[1] They are "ideological" in that they represent ideals; they are not illusions, however, but simply provide another way of explaining and presenting social reality, with their own unique but always very real social effects.

Although there are certainly other ways of describing social space, these categories represent profoundly important social facts that are themselves key parts of the social world that I set out, as an ethnographer, to study. To dismiss them would have meant dismissing my informants, ignoring their words, and ultimately producing my own set of binary truth claims that arrogantly opposed the ethnographer's real truth against the informant's imaginary truth. In his work on the Zambian copperbelt,

James Ferguson confronted a similar theoretical and methodological challenge. In experiences that resonate directly with my own, Ferguson encountered informants who persistently offered him "dualist" frameworks for explaining rural–urban relations that seemed to reproduce what he had been trained to see as largely outmoded anthropological theories of linear social evolution and discredited theoretical paradigms of static, unchanging rural–urban processes. Ferguson confronted this dilemma with a combination of critical skepticism and sensitivity that mirrors the approach I have taken in the case of Hóc Môn. Like Ferguson, I have attempted to show that "the narrative of an emerging urban modernity set against the dark background of a static rural tradition is a myth, but to say this is not to be done with the matter. On the contrary, myths are socially and cosmologically productive; in this sense, they require to be analyzed, and not just refuted."[2]

The driving purpose of this book has been to show the key role these "myths" of pure rural and urban difference play in social life. They do something. I have shown that, despite what I or other observers might see as their drawbacks, these binary categories enable people to craft spaces of meaningful social action within which they can carve out opportunities in their lives. The possibilities presented by life on the edge of purely conceived binary oppositions prove to be both full of potential and full of risks. Reproducing notions of rural versus urban lifestyles and stereotyping the meaning of inner-city versus outer-city districts puts people on the edge in the fullest sense. Living on the edge of the city, which also represents living in between pure categories, Hóc Môn residents risk falling off the categorical edges of symbolic precipices; they risk a form of marginalization that conceals or elides their place in and essential contributions to the larger society in which they live. In more material terms, they risk being pushed to the margins of social life, often excluded from the economic advantages associated with Vietnam's rapid economic development, cheated out of their land by urban land speculators, derided as uneducated or uncivilized remnants of an imagined Vietnamese past, and ignored by urban planners who see the urban fringe as a handmaiden to the city center.

But people on the edge are surprisingly active in the production of this risk-taking social edginess. Edginess often puts these same residents on the cutting edge of opportunity as well. They are not wholly disenfranchised but often find meaningful potential in the spaces that lie between official categories. Life outside the gaze of state power can be refreshingly liberating. Yet there can be no liberating "space between" on the outside or on the edge if there is no normative space to give these liminal positions meaning in the first place. In the first part of the book I showed that Hóc Môn residents negotiated life on the edge in ways that parallel the way Vietnamese households negotiate the contradictions of patrilineal kinship. Ideally, Vietnamese households strive to reproduce a male-oriented system of kinship, strictly organized around spatiotemporal conceptions of inside and outside. In practice, however, they often cultivate bilateral, non-male-oriented ties of kinship, and social actors simultaneously reproduce a patrilineal model of kinship as they transgress it.[3] Their oscillation between alternative models produces a sense of power that enables social actors to extend their influence outward across social space without relinquishing the ability to consolidate it in a spatially bounded unit. In the same way that households oscillate between inside and outside to produce effects of power, Hóc Môn residents oscillate between "the inside" and "the outside" of the city to turn a seeming space of marginality into an edgy space of potential. As I showed in Part II of the book, the ability to oscillate between idealized modes of supposedly rural and urban lifestyles offers alternatives to the time discipline of factory life and wage labor, allows one to capitalize on different regimes of value, and offers a challenge to unidirectional models of development.

This oscillation is not always successful, of course, and the play of politics and economic constraints always impinges on a person's ability to negotiate these parameters of action. But the space within which the residents of Hóc Môn struggle to craft productive and meaningful lives remains defined in many ways by the orderly categories they have inscribed on the idealized landscape. People can oscillate between the rural and the urban and the inside and the outside only because these concepts exist in the first place. Their movements have the capacity to take on the socially specific meanings they do because there are socially constructed notions of differentiated space across which people can move. In a world divided into rural versus urban and inside versus outside spaces, people do not just move around; they move productively and with intent, from meaningful place to meaningful place.

Throughout the book I have emphasized the lives and stories of real people as they navigate and oscillate across dynamic structural spaces that are imbued with abiding cultural meanings and political-economic values. I have evoked the structural constraints and conditions that make such movement possible, but I have also emphasized experiences and attitudes that reveal that social edginess is as much a sensibility and an experience of being as it is a structural condition. Social edginess, as I described it, is like a smile forced out of a grimace, the act of "sucking the soapberry and calling it sweet." Living in a space that is simultaneously full of potential and rife with inequality, the people of Hóc Môn are edgy, and this edginess offers both power and the threat of social exclusion.

To live on the edge of the city, as I show more concretely in the third part of the book, is to live not only in a material world with special challenges but in a world forged out of concepts and social meanings. These concepts and meanings transform the way people experience the material world, and the material world, thus transformed, also transforms the space within which social concepts take on meaning. Space and meaning codetermine each other in a dynamic social world. On Saigon's edge, this world is explicitly framed in dialogue with ideas of discrete rural and urban spaces mapped onto the city plan in terms of inside and outside. It is framed by infrastructure projects that both work within and transform existing conceptual relations of space-time. And it is forged in terms of notions of progress and change that are themselves conditioned by the lingering expectations of Vietnam's own narrative of peasant revolution, which purports to help rural folk transcend their own material conditions through the celebration of an urbanization process directed by enlightened urban intellectuals. These ideas, in turn, resonate with both male-centered and non-male-centered Vietnamese kinship idioms, which offer spaces of negotiation within otherwise top-down structures of patriarchal authority. And all of these negotiations take place within a world in which the Vietnamese landscape has undergone profound material transformations and where the very terms rural and urban have accrued complex symbolic associations linked to the history of the Vietnamese Revolution, subsequent wars for national liberation, postwar experiments in agricultural collectivization, the post–reform era promise of urban development, and the new demands of global capital.

Theorizing Vietnamese Folk Structuralism

Understanding the way social actors deploy their edginess within a wider field of meaningful binary oppositions that they simultaneously transgress and reproduce has important consequences for anthropological theory, urban studies, and the way we think of contemporary Vietnamese socialism. As I have shown throughout the book, both recent anthropological theory and critical urban studies have productively challenged explanatory models organized around binary oppositions and other simplifying schemes. Offering important and wide-ranging critiques of expert knowledge and showing how modernist schemes often fail to account for local social diversity and everyday practices, a host of studies have encouraged a renewed emphasis on how people actually use space in creative, unanticipated ways. Like most contemporary anthropologists, I have been invigorated by the critical move away from structuralist oversimplification of the sort that tends to shoehorn all social life into external models imposed by outside researchers onto social life. But these critiques have largely avoided the challenge of understanding why these models persist outside of academia itself. My own research on Vietnamese conceptions of urban space revealed what might be called a persistent Vietnamese "folk structuralism" that explains society through binary oppositions quite similar to those cast aside by poststructuralist theory. Thus, although recent trends in academic scholarship and new innovations in urban studies invite a healthy skepticism about these kinds of simplistic binaries, a key problem remains: local informants repeat these binaries with astounding regularity. To dismiss these binaries as false would be to ignore a fundamental element of the social landscape. Regardless of whether external observers choose to see them as accurate, they do something.

Furthermore, a new binary has emerged in the rush to critique structuralism's reliance on overly simplistic binary oppositions and in the unsparing critique of modernist modes of architecture, planning, urban design, and social theory. The very notions of poststructuralism and postmodernism (along with post-socialism, to which I will turn in a moment) have introduced their own binaries. The *post* in these theories, like many of the binaries and simplifications they critique, is itself a marker of a linear trajectory, not unlike an evolutionary model of intellectual development. As the apex of a newly constructed hierarchy of knowledge, these intellectual posts, perhaps unwittingly, start looking like self-congratulatory signposts on a long road to intellectual truth. Once the rest of the world becomes modern, critical theory, always seeking to be a step ahead, becomes postmodern. Everything preceding the *post* is relegated to the past as so many ways of old thinking, quaint ideas no longer relevant. In this sense, the very hubris of moving beyond previous intellectual trends dooms the *post*s to repeat the problems they claimed to move beyond in the first place. The more one tries to apply these theoretical paradigms, the more one begins to feel like a dog chasing its own tail or, to follow the *post* metaphor again, a lost driver unwittingly circling back along the same road: "Haven't I seen that *post* before?"

The more I confronted the dilemma of thinking through Vietnamese binary categories using contemporary critical theory, the more I came to see parallel forms of intellectual hubris in both. First I struggled with the striking sense that critical theory has relegated structuralism and the very notion of binary oppositions to the theoretical past in much the same way that Vietnamese thinkers have relegated the countryside to the social past of Vietnamese life. This showed that contemporary critiques of binary oppositions were themselves binary oppositions. More important, it also revealed that these theoretical paradigms, which have so significantly critiqued the ways anthropological knowledge often assigns "the other" to the past, themselves risk relegating Vietnamese thinking—with its adherence to discredited binaries, its insistent modernism in the postmodern world, and its refusal to abandon socialism—to the past as well. As Hardt and Negri argue, postmodern theory is as much a symptom as an explanation of new relations of power emerging in the new globalized form of governmentality they call "Empire."[4] And as an American anthropologist working in a country that my own country once endeavored to bomb back into the Stone Age, the risk that academic work will turn into an extension of empire can never be underestimated. Postmodern critiques were important, but they also fell into the very traps they critiqued.

A dog can chase its tail for only so long. Lost drivers eventually rethink their route and get on with the business of going where they need to go. Instead of imagining theory as a march toward the pinnacle of knowledge, I have taken a different approach, seeing theory as a collection of ideas appropriate to different aspects of a more comprehensive analysis. In studying Vietnamese notions of rural–urban relations, I discovered that there is still much to be gained from structuralist method as a means to understand the role these persistent binaries play in organizing social action in the world. Indeed, critical debate itself often requires oppositional discourse lest it always resign itself to consensus. I also realized that there is much to be gained from being skeptical of such methods and attending to those elements of social life that fall through the cracks. In the end, this book is both structuralist and critical of the reductions structuralist thought produces.

Similar theoretical flexibility is also essential to thinking through Vietnamese socialism and the modernist vision that underscores it. For, like Vietnamese "folk structuralism" and its insistence on binary models no longer in favor in Western theory, Vietnamese socialism and modernism also risk appearing as relics in an intellectual curio cabinet, more easily critiqued and dismissed than understood. Like the binary categories of rural–urban relations that I have studied in this book, Vietnamese modernism and socialism are most definitely not things of the past, and they also entail intellectual tendencies toward simplification that require both critique *and* understanding.

Postmortem Modernism and the Problem of "Late Socialism"

The critique, as always in anthropology, comes easiest. In many ways, I would argue that the challenges facing modern Vietnamese socialism have less to do with its socialism than with its uncritical commitment to modernism. By modernism I mean a set of intellectual, bureaucratic, and social commitments to truth, reality, and social problems that locates agency solely in "the interventions of the prince (state head) and the genius (architect planner)."[5] In Vietnam, this modernism emerged from the genealogical tradition of French sociotechnical intellectuals described by Rabinow,[6] shares attributes with the revolutionary Leninist "Marxist modernism" described by Donham,[7] and has persisted in the postcolonial and postwar era in ways that parallel the rise of "technopolitics" and social expertise described by Mitchell.[8] The experts who have emerged express a profound desire and hope to improve the world, but often, wittingly or unwittingly, compress that world for the sake of governance. Such modernist impulses often obscure as much as they reveal. They resort, as Scott has shown, to "seeing like a state" and, in the process, end up not seeing a great deal of the diversity that makes society work. In the Vietnamese case, modernist expertise is also infused by an intellectual genealogy that mixes Marxism, Leninism, Durkheimian functionalism, and Chinese neotraditionalisms, which together maintain a special claim to seeing reality and "true" Vietnamese culture in terms of functional models.[9] This blend of Durkheimian and Marxist modernism cherishes elements of the world consistent with organic metaphors of solidarity and collective consciousness and rigorously seeks to rectify or dispense with any elements that might be linked to social "anomie," or what the Vietnamese call "social evils." Vietnam is a clear example of James Holston's assertion that, despite the important critiques of postmodern theory, "if modernism is dying, it nevertheless remains dominant, at the very least in the third world."[10] In a world where critical theory pronounces modernism dead, the vibrant modernism of Vietnam today is not simply post but postmortem, a postmortem modernism that survives after the so-called death of modernism in the West.

The persistence of this postmortem modernism in spite of postmodern critiques forces a simple question: what does modernism have to offer that makes it so resilient in Vietnam? To understand its resilience, it is important to remember that early modernists, perhaps relishing the thrill and potential of "modernity," hoped to improve the world they lived in. The modernist avant-garde of the early twentieth century first emerged from leftist European circles hoping to eliminate the distinction between the prince and the people. Theirs was a utopian modernist plan designed to free human beings from the shackles of history and culture that have bound them to archaic forms of hierarchy and inequality. But the failure of modernism was lodged in its own intellectual egoism; modernism denied agency to the very people it claimed to liberate. In seeking to liberate the masses through expert design, the masses were unwittingly placed in a subordinate role to those very experts who contrived to design the world on their behalf.

This is quite similar to the way Vietnamese revolutionaries conceived (and contemporary experts still conceive) of the peasantry. But this impulse is not just "Vietnamese" or "communist." This impulse also underscored the logic of the French civilizing mission, the American "experts" who first arrived in Vietnam as advisors and "nation builders," and the history of capitalist "creative destruction" across the globe. Thus, although it is easy to critique the way contemporary Vietnamese socialism paradoxically links "building socialism" with the top-down force of all of its centrally planned development projects, it is impossible to attribute this to socialism alone. It is just as easy to read a certain irony into American nation-building strategies that combined infrastructure development with bombing sorties and defoliation. That the paradoxes of "building socialism" also produce a similar kind of building through destruction indicates that these two building efforts share something that transcends them both. The shared failure of all these idealistic schemes stems from the fact that they attempted to escape the inequalities of the modern world through methods that ended up endowing self-styled omniscient leaders and planners with a blank slate from which to design their new world. But in attempting to erase the horrors of history, they often erased history and context itself, often in quite violent or inequitable ways. On paper, the blank slate made it seem possible to remake the world. But one cannot have a blank slate when there are people involved. In this way, modern Vietnamese socialist utopians were much like modern utopians from other camps. But it was ironic that they, as Marxists, managed to forget Marx's key lesson: man makes the world but not always in the ways he himself had dreamed. They have internalized Hegel's musing on the cunning of reason, but they seem to have misunderstood Marx's critique, founded in the philosophy of praxis.

But these critiques themselves reveal part of the modernist promise as well. Simplification, as I discovered with the idealized images of rural and urban ideal types, can offer a beautiful vision of a perfect society, an orderly society that works. And in a world where a great many things do not always work and are not always beautiful, it is not much of a stretch to imagine why large numbers of people cling to ideals and why they might be willing to risk so much in the hope of attaining a dream. One need not agree that these simplifications are in fact appealing. But it is not so difficult to understand why some people would find them so.

The hubris of modernism echoes the double edge of modernity itself, a condition in which a world so full of potential also threatens to unleash great destruction. To see the relationship between the modernist impulses within Vietnamese socialism and the condition of modernity that inspires it, it helps to compare Marshall Berman's famous definition of modernity with Vietnamese statements about culture that emerged not long after the August Revolution. Berman writes: "To be modern is to find ourselves in an environment that promises us adventure, power, joy, growth, transformation of ourselves and the world—and, at the same time, threatens to destroy everything we have, everything we know, everything we are."[11] In November 1945, Nguyễn Hữu Đang and Nguyễn Đình Thi wrote something quite similar. In a tract titled "A New Culture," they explicitly acknowledged that the new transformative adventure of building socialism was intimately connected with destruction: "As in other spheres, the task of construction in the cultural arena has to begin with destruction: for a new culture to develop, it needs a cleared piece of land that contains no vestiges of feudalism or colonialism."[12] Like so many simplifying schemes, this vision promised excitement and transformation. It also contained the seeds of no uncertain violence and destruction. In Vietnam today, the potentials offered by renovation and global integration produce a similar mixture of excitement coupled with threat. As I have detailed in so many cases throughout this book, development is always double edged and is often accompanied by acts of destruction. Every new road to paradise comes with social transformation, houses raised to make space for more asphalt. The modern moment in Vietnam has not disappeared. As an informant rhetorically asked me and I related in chapter 1, "How can one have development without suffering?"

The Vietnamese commitment to modernism, like commitments to modernism elsewhere, entails deep political choices. But it also offers possibility and excitement for many of those involved; it is a classic modern moment. The anthropologist Philip Taylor has written extensively about the Vietnamese search for modernity and the contested alternatives to modernity that emerge on the fringes of official discourse. He describes a cacophony of voices that emerge in the quest to define what modernity might bring and thus reveals part of the excitement and promise of the future so prevalent in today's Vietnam. But Taylor also sensitively critiques the top-down impulses that often silence nonofficial versions of modernity, asserting, quite significantly, that modernity can, and does, exist outside the plans of experts.[13] As Mary Beth Mills has described it in Thailand, Vietnamese modernity operates "as a powerful field of popular discourse and cultural production. The meanings and practices of modernity constitute a discursive arena through which people make claims or express ideas concerning themselves and their society, and about which they may or may not agree."[14] In Vietnam, as in the Thailand described by Mills, "discourses on modernity permeate much of everyday life. People from all parts of the country and of diverse class backgrounds are familiar with and employ a language of modernity in order to discuss and at times critique directions of social and cultural change."[15] Thus, although modernity can be teleological, and the modernist belief in simplifying schemes can at times be rigid and unyielding, this belief also has the potential to engender conversation and exchange in more complex ways than we sometimes imagine. In my interactions with Vietnamese everywhere, this excitement has always been omnipresent.

There is a pulse to life, an energy that underscores every new advance, every new infrastructure project. New bridges become the centerpiece of karaoke videos, tall buildings grace calendars, and urbanization never ceases to provoke awe and fill people with national pride.

But there is also trepidation. Taylor has rightly noted that the (both local and foreign) modernist princes guiding Vietnamese policy in this fruitful moment of modernity are not always committed to letting the full range of expression emerge. Although modernity itself can lead to a wide range of competing discourses and opens itself to a wide range of what Dilip Gaonkar has aptly called "alternative modernities," the modernist project that remains so strong in Vietnam is often disturbingly dismissive of alternative voices.[16] It grips this modern moment with the strength of a two-pronged fork. One prong of modernism claims to catch hold of modernity itself, seemingly crossing ideological divides and resonating with a wide range of aspirations from different social groups in ways that few other intellectual projects can. For example, a modernist commitment to the importance of a central prince's ability to change the world underlies the ideas of both the old socialist hardliners and the emerging middle class in Vietnam. Both of these groups have very different ideas about what economic or political pathway Vietnam should follow. But they seem to agree on one thing: "experts" should lead the way. The other prong of modernism, however, seems sharpened to a violent point, for the experts themselves control the terms of discourse, policing the conversation instead of seeking input and listening to alternative voices. And as Taylor has shown, these experts often fail to recognize how wonderfully modern so many of the people whom they seek to modernize already are.

To be sure, the ambitious plans proffered by modernist expert know-it-alls are often beautiful. But their practices are often destructive as well. And, more important, they often maintain a disdainful stance toward the messy realities that muddle up their orderly models. Places like Hóc Môn do not fit into these schemes. They must be eradicated or drawn to one side in a system of black-and-white, either/or positions. The same could be said for a host of complex problems, all cast in terms of good and bad in slogans such as these: "Industrialize, Modernize the Nation!" "Urbanize the Rural Zones!" "Eradicate Corruption and Social Evils!" "Traffic, Begone!"

The promise of modernist schemes is that they claim to harness the potential of modernity, to direct human action toward self-perfection.

Their problem is that they often fail to do so, as often as not directing human action toward the destructive dark side of modernity. Modernist projects thus parallel the binary systems of life on Saigon's edge, creating spaces of potential but often devolving into spaces riven with despair. The double edge of both Saigon's edge and modernism underscores the current state of Vietnamese socialism as well. Infinitely creative and often quite reflexive and adaptable to change when conducted on its own terms, Vietnamese socialism is also quick to suppress challenges and critical discourse.

Too Early for "Late Socialism"

Subtleties and niceties suffer under modernist schemes in which the politics of either/or reign. In the spring of 2004, when several Vietnamese colleagues from the Institute of Culture and Information Studies in Hanoi were applying for permission to attend a symposium I organized at Cornell University, they politely asked if we might change the name of the event. They explained that the title, Vietnamese Late Socialism: The Politics of Culture in Contemporary Vietnam, was making it difficult to obtain permission to leave the country in order to attend. Higher-ups in the administration saw the word "Late" in the title as a veiled attempt to pronounce the premature death of Vietnamese socialism. (It was not intended as such.) They read the word "Late" in the same way we might read it when one says, "The *late* Hồ Chí Minh," as a prefix for someone or something that has passed on.

Originally I saw the use of "Late Socialism" as a way to avoid the problem of using the term "Post-socialism"—which clearly deals with the period after the end of socialism—while trying to reckon with contemporary manifestations of socialism in today's highly integrated "late capitalist" and "post-Fordist" global economy. Surely Vietnamese socialism today is dramatically different than it was during the period of land reforms and the collectivization of agriculture or when price subsidies, contract quotas, and ration tickets organized exchange. Li Zhang, speaking of late socialism in China, describes it as "a unique historical moment at which the Chinese economic system has largely shifted to a capitalist mode of production mixed with reduced state-managed production, while the political-legal system remains largely dominated by one-party rule."[17]

Late socialism still strikes me as the most appropriate term to use in the Vietnamese case as well. Classical socialism scoffs at the market and sees imperialism and globalization as the final contradictions of the tendency for the rate of profit to fall. According to classic socialist interpretations, expanding capitalist markets across the globe only staves off the eminent collapse of a production regime founded on unsustainable practices. In order to avoid the inherent crisis of overproduction, capitalist imperialists take over the world and make the world's people into slaves of consumption and production. Late socialism, in fundamental contrast to the classic socialist rejection of such imperialist market economies, has a market orientation. These forms of socialism—market socialism and classical anticapitalist socialism—may share a common historical ancestor, but they are by no means the same thing.

This brings us back to the modernist connection. The one thing that unites the previous form of Vietnamese socialism with the contemporary market-oriented socialism of today is a staunch belief in the possibility for rational human planning to pave the way to a better future. In short, today's socialism, like the socialism of the early Vietnamese Worker's Party, is modernist. In today's version of Vietnamese socialism, almost every critique of capitalism has been abandoned. The one key element that remains is the modernist commitment to forward-marching progress guided by a vanguard of experts. Modernism cuts across the ideological divide that for socialists once made the devil out of trade and saw murder in the market and for capitalists equated socialism with the death of freedom. In fact, modernism cuts across a great majority of the ideological divides in twentieth-century Vietnamese history. And in the Vietnam of today, a belief in modernism is the great tie that makes it possible for the World Bank to talk to communists. All of these people, groups, and organizations believe in the great promise of modernism—the promise that people can improve the world through a conscious attempt to move *forward,* guided by experts.

The cadres' critique of the term *late socialism* proved prescient. A more precise term might very well be *modern Vietnamese socialism,* with emphasis on the *modern.*

There is certainly good reason to maintain a healthy skepticism of both modernism and socialism. But how do we understand their persistence? We might take a lesson from Vietnamese folk structuralist categories that appear as rigid and fixed binary oppositions on the surface but open up complex pathways of oscillatory social action in everyday practice. Despite their simplifying tendencies, Vietnamese modernism and socialism have the potential to be much more dynamic than they might seem. I have already shown how, despite its rigidity, modernism is itself quite flexible, allowing seemingly opposed groups from opposite ends of the ideological spectrum to unite around the idea of improving the world. Recent developments in Vietnamese socialism indicate a similar flexibility, which is otherwise obscured by a seemingly rigid adherence to formal, seemingly inflexible categories.

The Vietnamese Transition to a "Market Economy with a Socialist Direction"

In stereotypically rigid form, Article 4 of the Constitution of the Socialist Republic of Vietnam clearly describes the role of the Communist Party within the political regime: "The Communist Party of Vietnam, the vanguard of the Vietnamese working class, the faithful representative of the rights and interests of the working class, the toiling people, and the whole nation, acting upon the Marxist-Leninist doctrine and Ho Chi Minh's thought, is the force leading the State and society." The Vietnamese state remains publicly committed to fulfilling the goals of the revolution. Yet in practice, *đổi mới* ("change to the new" or "renovation") has been the key watchword in Vietnamese politics and society for over twenty years. An official publication, *A Selection of Fundamental Laws of Vietnam,* opens with a foreword whose very first lines explain the official position of the National Assembly. These words precede a reprint of the Constitution cited earlier: "In 1986, Vietnam started the course of *doi moi* (renovation) of the country, implementing the open-door policy and building a multi-sectoral economy operating in accordance with the market mechanism under the State's regulation."[18] In official terms, then, the Vietnamese Communist Party guides the transition toward a market-based economy. Alongside the writings of Marx, Lenin, and Hồ Chí Minh, one might find World Bank publications, stock listings, reports on banking reform, market analyses, and an application—recently approved—for entry into the World Trade Organization (WTO). The Vietnamese government calls this a "market economy with a socialist direction" *(Kinh tế thị trường định hướng XHCN),* and it has strongly advertised this new direction with official pronouncements and state visits.

In June 2005, for example, Prime Minister Phan Văn Khải became the highest-ranking Vietnamese official to visit the United States in the thirty years since the end of the Vietnam War. His mission: to ask President George W. Bush "to help his nation join the World Trade Organization."[19] In addition to meeting with Bush at the White House, the prime minister also met with the presidents of Harvard and MIT and traveled to Seattle, Washington, where he met with Bill Gates at the Microsoft campus and toured an airplane factory with executives from Boeing.[20] During his trip, Prime Minister Khải published an op-ed piece in the *Washington Times* entitled "Vietnam on the Path of Reform," in which he spelled out his government's stance toward the global economy:

We are also accelerating the building of the institutions of a market economy eliminating favoritism, striving for greater liberalization, transparency and consistency, all of which are critical to meet the demands of economic integration.

Foreign-invested and private enterprises play an increasingly important role in generating growth and employment. The success in expanding relations with other countries, including the United States, Europe, and Asia have deepened Vietnam's integration into the global economy.[21]

Vietnamese-American protesters in the United States, however, offered a more critical assessment of this visit. Some demonstrators in Seattle "gathered on downtown streets, shouting 'Down with communists,' and calling for an end to political and religious persecution in Vietnam. Some held signs that read 'Khải is another Saddam Hussein.'"[22] For such critical observers, Vietnam's transition to the market economy appeared an act of opportunism. They regarded Vietnamese leaders as self-interested powermongers attempting to dip into the money pot of global capital without relinquishing their tight grip on political relations within the country. Adherents to this perspective hold that although the state hopes to benefit from the capital inflow associated with the free market, it maintains authoritarian control at home. It uses laissez-faire economics to support a regime that refuses to "just let things happen" with much else; despite its professed willingness to "meet the demands of economic integration," the state continues to lay down the law and struggles to remain the one and only "force leading the State and society." Central to this critique among protesters is a straightforward question: How can the state be capitalist and communist at once? How can the Communist Party of Vietnam guide the nation's entry into the WTO? The idea behind such a critique is simple: A state cannot be two opposite things at once. Once again, the problem of folk binaries returns. Only this time, the Vietnamese socialists are the ones blurring boundaries with their capitalist socialism, and the outside critics are the ones trying to shoehorn them into the simple carica-ture of a big, bad, evil communist government posed against a rational and just democracy.

Clearly the critics put forth their own binaries. But in the process they have also revealed precisely how the apparent binary between cap-italism and socialism in Vietnam operates; it works not so much as an either/or choice but as a space of potential oscillation. But although this oscillation itself might reveal the ways in which state bureaucrats seek to hold onto power, it also reveals the way they seek to carve out a space for Vietnam within the contemporary global order. Oscillating between these two poles enables an otherwise marginalized nation to hold onto two forms of power, maximizing the advantages of both. This practice, as the critics suggest, may prove dangerous to some. But it also proves dynamic and powerful as well.

This vision of seemingly rigid Vietnamese socialists pragmatically oscillating between socialism and capitalism returns us to the lessons of Hóc Môn district. On many different levels, Hóc Môn also embodies the uncomfortable position of sitting between two irreconcilable symbolic positions. As I have described it throughout this study, Hóc Môn is both rural and urban at once. It is an outer-city district within the Ho Chi Minh City metropolitan region. In this sense, it sits between two symbolically opposed worlds, just as Vietnam is both socialist and increasingly orga-nized around the global capitalist market economy. Like Vietnam as a whole, Hóc Môn struggles to be "both/and." This struggle, as I have shown, is both full of risks and full of potential. It appears to reproduce rigid structures, but great creativity bursts forth from within those seem-ingly rigid parameters.

Prime Minister Khải's visit brings us back to Hóc Môn in more con-crete ways as well. A quick glance at the landscape reveals the impor-tance of and the challenges presented by the foreign-invested enterprises Khải mentioned in his piece for the *Washington Times*. Korean and Tai-wanese joint-venture factories producing mostly garments and shoes, as well as webbing and metal products, line feeder roads that jut into for-merly agricultural hamlets. These are surrounded by hastily erected dor-mitories and canteens built by local families on their ancestral properties in order to supplement their incomes housing and feeding the Vietnam-ese labor force that has come to the area from the poorest north, central, and Mekong Delta provinces in order to find work. A large Fuji film plant sits in Củ Chi district, just across Hóc Môn's largest remaining swath of rice fields on the northwest side of the An Hạ canal, which forms the district border. The construction of the Vietnamese spur of the Trans-Asia Highway through Hóc Môn recalls Khải's plug for increased integration into the world economy. The highway itself is part of a concerted effort to integrate Ho Chi Minh City with the larger ASEAN regional economy. In addition to connecting the city with the rest of Southeast Asia, the widening of the highway serves to improve transport between the largely land-locked outer-city industrial zones and the international shipping ports along the Saigon River. The highway also serves the legions of Hóc Môn locals who increasingly find employment in the inner city.

Although Hóc Môn is called a rural district *(huyện)* and although the administrative subdivisions within it are called villages *(xã)* and hamlets *(ấp),* it is certainly not an example of an isolated village community. I have used the case of Hóc Môn in order to provide a more detailed understanding of how different Vietnamese people in structurally different social positions experience the Vietnamese transition to a market economy in different ways. And just as we can only understand Hóc Môn as a place embedded within the larger transition that Prime Minister Khải described, it is also true that we can understand this transition only by attending to places like Hóc Môn.

In this work I have attempted to use the tools of a native discourse in order to unravel that discourse and show what it reveals, what it masks, and also what it does. The Vietnamese oppositions of the country versus the city and the inside of the city versus the outside of the city are quite similar to the binary oppositions once fashionable in structuralist anthropology. I have thus found it useful to use a structuralist method as a first step in my hopes of describing the logic of an idealized mode of describing the world. But I also use this method to show the limits of this way of seeing the world. It is clear that the truth it produces is only partial and that it masks a whole other order of reality. Yet it is not false. Entangled with idealized conceptions of spatial order are practices, strategies, and socially embedded negotiations that play off of the ideal in order to make a space for everyday life. The ideal world is a pure system divided into country and city. The practical world of everyday life lurks in the space that lies tangled in its midst. That space is Hóc Môn, neither country nor city but uncomfortably both.

Notes

Introduction

1. Following anthropological convention, names of individuals in the text have been changed to protect their identities.

2. Davis, *Planet of Slums.*

3. Orwell, *The Road to Wigan Pier,* 109.

4. Lê Như Hoa, *Quản lý văn hoá đô thị trong điều kiện công nghiệp hoá hiện đại hoá đất nước,* 4; Chae, "Contemporary Ho Chi Minh City in Numerous Contradictions."

5. Keesing, "Theories of Culture Revisited"; Roseberry, *Anthropologies and Histories.*

6. Nader, "Controlling Processes," 1–11.

7. Nguyễn-võ Thu-hương, *The Ironies of Freedom.*

8. Williams, *The Country and the City.*

9. Ibid., 1–2.

10. Wood, *The Origin of Capitalism,* 53.

11. Polanyi, *The Great Transformation.*

12. Werner and Bélanger, *Gender, Household, State;* White, "Alternative Approaches to the Socialist Transformation of Agriculture in Postwar Vietnam"; Kerkvliet, "State–Village Relations in Vietnam"; Kerkvliet, "Land Struggles and Land Regimes in the Philippines and Vietnam during the Twentieth Century"; Kerkvliet, *The Power of Everyday Politics.*

13. This is therefore not a simple question of a failed "socialist" form of production being supplanted by a more natural or inevitable form of "capitalist" enterprise. In Vietnam, as in many of the postsocialist economies of Eastern Europe, the most successful communists are often also very successful capitalists. Compare, for example, the case of post-Soviet Kazakhstan with that of Vietnam. Gainsborough, *Changing Political Economy of Vietnam;* Nazpary, *Post-Soviet Chaos,* 33, 44.

14. Saskia Sassen and David Harvey both show how the production of "place," or of distinctive notions of territorial difference, has become intensified at the very time that globalization seems to obliterate territorial distinction and local differences. See Harvey, *The Condition of Postmodernity,* 271; Sassen, *Cities in a World Economy,* 24.

15. Williams, *The Country and the City,* 7.

16. Ferguson, "The Country and the City on the Copperbelt," 141–45.

17. Ibid., 152.

18. Roseberry, *Coffee and Capitalism in the Venezuelan Andes.*

19. Kearney, *Reconceptualizing the Peasantry.*

20. Gupta, "Peasants and Environmentalism," 325.

21. Guha, *The Unquiet Woods.*

22. Huang, *The Peasant Economy and Social Change in North China,* 307.

23. Pelley, *Postcolonial Vietnam;* Ninh, *A World Transformed.*

24. Goldstein, *The Spectacular City.*

25. Caldeira, *City of Walls;* Caldeira, "Fortified Enclaves: The New Urban Segregation"; Davis, "Fortress Los Angeles"; Low, "Urban Fear"; Low, "The Edge and the Centre."

26. Murray, *Taming the Disorderly City,* 39–41.

27. Li Zhang, *Strangers in the City;* Holston, *Insurgent Citizenship;* Holston, "Spaces of Insurgent Citizenship"; Leaf, "Vietnam's Urban Edge."

28. District boundaries often change to accommodate demographic shifts and increased population densities. As of 2008, the city has 19 inner-city districts and five outer-city districts. The two newest districts are Tân Phú (formerly part of Tân Bình) and Bình Tân (formerly part of Bình Chánh).

29. "Special Use land" refers to government-occupied land, including a walled-in military training camp that was off limits to the general population and to researchers.

30. Huỳnh Văn Giáp, "Một số vấn đề đặt ra trong tiến trình đô thị hóa nông thôn huyện Hóc Môn," 64–66, 64.

31. These official figures come from Lê Hoang ("Bản đồ Thành phố Hồ Chí Minh") and are corroborated by Huỳnh Văn Giáp *(Xây dựng và phát triển nông thôn trong chiến lược CNH—HĐH của 2 huyện Bình Chánh và Hóc Môn TP. HCM),* 18. These statistics (like most official figures in Vietnam) should be used with caution. For example, the seemingly simple figure depicting the area of the district appears different in different places. In addition to the figure of 109.5 square kilometers that I have cited, another source (Tôn Nữ Quỳnh Trân, *Văn hóa làng xã)* gives the area of the district as 156.1 square kilometers, and another gives 16,952 hectares, which is equal to 169.52 square kilometers! Unfortunately, I did not measure the district myself.

32. Districts 5 and 11 have total populations of 210,708 and 239,318, respectively. But these roughly similar total populations are squeezed into areas more than twenty times smaller. District 5 has an area of 4.1 square kilometers and district 11 covers roughly 5 square kilometers.

33. When citing informants directly I have used the conventional style of quotation marks and indented long quotations, thus demarcating either recorded interviews or direct transcriptions of what people said. In other instances, where it was impossible to immediately write down or record a conversation and hence to faithfully reproduce the exact words of the informant, I have *italicized* the text to indicate that I have paraphrased them in a form that remains as true to what was said as possible but is not an actual transcription of the words spoken.

34. For more on village names in early Hóc Môn, see Nguyễn Đình Đầu, *Nghiên cứu địa bạ Triều Nguyễn;* Nguyễn Đình Đầu, "Địa lý lịch sử Thành phố Hồ Chí Minh"; and Tôn Nữ Quỳnh Trân, *Văn hóa làng xã,* 57.

35. See Tôn Nữ Quỳnh Trân *(Văn hóa làng xã)* for an academic discussion of the name and ThangbomVN *(Hóc hay Hốc?)* for an online discussion thread that corroborates her view.

36. Grammont, *Onze mois de sous-préfecture en Basse-Cochinchine,* 94.

37. Ibid., 93.

38. Ibid., 94.

39. Đinh Huy Liêm, "Chuyển biến của kinh tế nông hộ và kinh tế hợp tác trong nông nghiệp ngoại thành Thành phố Hồ Chí Minh, 1975–1994," 118.

40. Huỳnh Văn Giáp, "Xây dựng và phát triển nông thôn trong chiến lược CNH—HĐH của 2 huyện Bình Chánh và Hóc Môn TP. HCM," 30.

41. Many of the Karaoke rooms were secret because they provided illicit sexual services to clients in the darkened private rooms.

42. Ibid., 24.

43. Cadière, *Croyances et pratiques religieuses des Vietnamiens.*

44. For more on such pilgrimages, see Taylor, *Goddess on the Rise.*

45. Huỳnh Văn Giáp, "Xây dựng và phát triển," 29.

46. Huỳnh Văn Giáp, "Một số vấn đề," 64–66, 65.

47. Taylor argues that by emphasizing the confusion of history while paying careful attention to the historical specificities that emerge from the material traces available in the archive, scholars can avoid the trap of falling into the narrative service of nationalism. When the past "stops confusing us, we can be sure that we have understood it into something dangerous." See Taylor, "Surface Orientations in Vietnam," 954, 974.

48. Pelley, *Postcolonial Vietnam,* 115.

49. Ninh, *A World Transformed,* 165.

50. Although Ninh seems to see this as a specifically "communist" phenomenon, Western notions of culture followed a similar trajectory. Around the same time that the Vietnamese formed the Ministry of Culture, the famous American interpreter of culture, Clifford Geertz, was in Indonesia conducting fieldwork that would later inform his *Religion of Java.* And the anthropologist Gerald Hickey was employed by a consulting arm of the U.S. military to conduct ethnographic research into popular village culture, later published as *Village in Vietnam.*

51. Ninh, *A World Transformed,* 168.

52. Trần Ngọc Thêm, *Cơ sở văn hóa Việt Nam,* 11.

53. Ibid., 54–55.

54. Jamieson, *Understanding Vietnam,* 15–16.

55. Bui Hoai Mai, "Introduction," 7.

56. Vietnamese nationalism often conflates the themes of legends with the historical foundations of the nation, fashioning mythical themes into evidence of a persistent cultural essence founded in the crucible of the earliest mythical kingdoms. Former Prime Minister Phạm Văn Đồng, for example, cites this and other legends of the Hùng kings as evidence of an inherently Vietnamese political system that unites family, village, and country from ancient times until the present day. Such legends, he argues, reflect the deep themes of a long national history "seen through the creative eyes of the poetic-minded masses" *(Culture and Renovation,* 8–9).

57. Certeau, *The Practice of Everyday Life,* 94–95.

58. Scott, *Seeing Like a State,* 103–46.

59. Certeau, *The Practice of Everyday Life,* 95.

60. Wolf, *Peasant Wars of the Twentieth Century.*

61. Nguyen Cao Ky, *How We Lost the Vietnam War;* Scott, *Weapons of the Weak,* 5.

62. McAlister and Mus, *The Vietnamese and Their Revolution.*

63. Herzfeld, *Anthropology through the Looking-Glass,* 4.

64. Turner, "Value, Production, and Exploitation in Non-capitalist Societies," 1.

1. Bittersweet Transitions

1. For more on the "Uprising of the Eighteen Areca Garden Villages," see Sơn Nam, "18 Thôn Vườn Trầu," 161–77; Huỳnh Minh, *Gia Định xưa,* 245–49; and Lê Quốc Sử, "Đất nước và con người (18 Thôn Vườn Trầu)."

2. For a description of the execution, see Hội đồng chỉ đạo biên soạn Lịch sử Khởi nghĩa Nam kỳ, *Lịch sử Khởi nghĩa Nam kỳ,* 502–3.

3. VnExpress, "Mua đất vùng Ngã Ba Giồng."

4. See Đoan Trang, "Khu đô thị Tây Bắc Tp.HCM," 1, 14, and H. G., "TPHCM: Đề nghị thu hồi 6000ha đất," 6.

5. The brownish-yellow peel of the soapberry *(bồ hòn, Sapindus mucosossi Gaertn)* contains 19 percent saponin, and sources claim that Vietnamese people used it to wash clothes before the advent of soap. For a description of the bitter fruit and the phrase "Ngâm bồ hòn làm ngọt," see Hữu Ngọc, *Từ điển văn hóa,* 99.

6. The revolutionary tract "Đường kách mệnh" was penned by Hồ Chí Minh at the revolutionary headquarters of the Thanh Niên organization in Canton and serialized in the newspaper *Thanh Niên* between 1925 and 1927. See Huỳnh Kim Khánh, *Vietnamese Communism,* 67. Here Đường Cách Mạng Tháng Tám leads from Hóc Môn to Ho Chi Minh City, but it is a common street name in cities throughout Vietnam.

7. Low, "Spatializing Culture."

8. Harvey, "The City as Body Politic," 33.

9. Compare this with Douglas, *Purity and Danger,* 99.

10. As Bourdieu puts it regarding the attempt to objectively depict space, "The science which claims to put forward the criteria that are most well founded in reality would be well advised to remember that it is merely recording a *state* of the struggle over classifications." Bourdieu, *Language and Symbolic Power,* 223 (italics in original). But as Anderson, in *Imagined Communities,* and Thongchai, in *Siam Mapped,* have argued, the science of mapping often represents a strategic claim to represent reality, an active force within a struggle over classifications.

11. Burlat describes the symbolic meaning of the Ho Chi Minh City master plans in further detail. Regarding the imagined function of the beltway, her observations here concur with my own. See Burlat, "Processus institutionnels et dynamiques urbaines," 218.

12. In Vietnam's administrative system, the word *huyện* also signifies the separate districts of the largely rural provinces throughout Vietnam. A *huyện* in Vietnamese

political usage therefore identifies a rural space, and the usage of the two terms *quận* and *huyện* ostensibly divides the urban administrative zone into a purely urban center and a rural periphery.

13. Nguyễn Đình Đầu, *From Saigon to Ho Chi Minh City: 300 Year History,* 20.

14. See, especially, McGee, "The Emergence of *Desakota* Regions in Asia."

15. Trần Ngọc Thêm, *Cơ sở văn hóa Việt Nam,* 124.

16. Ibid., 122; Lê Văn Chưởng, *Cơ sở văn hóa Việt Nam,* 154.

17. Quoted in H. Đ. and T. A., "Không thể tiếp tục quản lý đô thị như quản lý các làng, xã," 1.

18. Burlat describes the "power" of this ideal representation: "The master plan does not offer mastery over the evolution of a process, but offers up an ideal image, which has the role of promoting its own creation." Burlat, "Processus institutionnels et dynamiques urbaines," 217.

19. Lê Văn Chưởng, *Cơ sở văn hóa,* 154; Nguyễn Ngọc Châu, *Quản lý đô thị;* Toan Ánh, *Làng xóm Việt Nam;* Trần Ngọc Thêm, *Cơ sở văn hóa,* 122; Viện Sử học, *Đô thị cổ Việt Nam.*

20. Toan Ánh, *Làng xóm Việt Nam,* 57.

21. For an insightful essay on this poetic form, see Huỳnh Sanh Thông, *An Anthology of Vietnamese Poems,* 8–11.

22. See Hickey, *Village in Vietnam,* and compare it with Redfield, *The Little Community.* For a critical overview of these perspectives, see Kearney, *Reconceptualizing the Peasantry.*

23. Toan Ánh, *Làng xóm Việt Nam,* 57.

24. Taylor, "Poor Policies, Wealthy Peasants."

25. The specter of unchecked urban expansion and the image of the overweight rich person have emerged as parallel tropes in the critique of the nefarious effects of contemporary change in Vietnam. Pham Thu Thuy describes a trend in political cartoons that focus on the rotund bodies of corrupt officials. The image offers a way to pose a critique without naming specifics: "Instead of exposing graft and corruption as a problem brought on by the lack of accountability and transparency in the current political systems, cartoons tend to concentrate on a group of unnamed and faceless 'bad individuals' at whose door are laid most of the country's difficulties." Pham Thu Thuy, "Speaking Pictures," 101.

26. Nguyễn Văn Tài, *Di dân tự do,* 59.

27. Abrami and Henaff, "The City and the Countryside"; Trần Hồng Vân, *Tác động xã hội của di cư tự do;* Gubry, Hong, and Le Van Thanh, *Les chemins vers la ville;* Parenteau, *Habitat et environnement urbain au Việt-nam.*

28. Nguyễn Văn Tài, *Di dân tự do,* 85.

29. Ibid., 87.

30. Ibid., 87, 88.

31. McGee, "The Emergence of *Desakota* Regions in Asia."

32. Ibid., 7.

33. Ginsburg, "Preface," xiii–xiv; Sassen, *Cities in a World Economy.*

34. Many people also exploit the "internal edges" of the city along canals. Urban involution and the subdivision of space within the city proceed at the same time that

the physical edges of the city move outward in space. For studies on these internal edges, see Burlat, "Processus institutionnels et dynamiques urbaines"; Nguyen Van Dua, "Urban Development in Ho Chi Minh City"; Waibel, "The Production of Urban Space in Vietnam's Metropolis"; Waibel et al., "Housing for Low-Income Groups in Ho Chi Minh City"; and Wust, Bolay, and Thai Thi Ngoc Du, "Metropolization and the Ecological Crisis."

35. McGee and Robinson, *The Mega-Urban Regions of Southeast Asia,* ix.

36. See Davis, *Planet of Slums;* Goldstein, *The Spectacular City;* and Li Zhang, *Strangers in the City.*

37. McGee, "The Emergence of *Desakota* Regions," 17–18.

38. Nguyễn Văn Tài, *Di dân tự do,* 101.

39. Mumford, *The City in History,* 486.

40. A *café ôm,* which translates literally as a "hugging café," is a darkened café where female servers sit next to male patrons, often holding their hands and caressing them in exchange for "tips."

41. Luong, *Discursive Practices and Linguistic Meanings.*

42. Ibid., 5.

43. Ibid., 7.

44. Ibid., 48.

45. Ibid., 63–69.

46. Ibid., 64.

47. Hirschman and Vu Manh Loi, "Family and Household Structure in Vietnam," 231.

48. Other forms of evidence also show that people genuinely seek to solidify their affective ties with both inside and outside kin. In an interview, a famous singer, Thùy Dung, explained her relationship with her husband and his family: "The thing I have been most afraid of until now was that I wouldn't be accepted in the heart of my husband's mother, but now I am completely at ease because I know both the inner and outer sides of the family love me." VnExpress, "Thùy Dung." An overseas Vietnamese reader sent a letter to the same newspaper about how he misses Vietnam during the lunar year holiday. "I sit here in an office in a small town in California, reading these lines of news from VnExpress and can't hold back my tears. I don't miss home, don't miss my father or my mother, because both my inner and outer lineages have settled in America, but I miss my homeland . . . really miss it." Huey Truong, "Tết đến, tôi càng thấy nhớ quê hương."

49. Malarney, *Culture, Ritual and Revolution in Vietnam,* 161.

50. Ibid., 162–63.

51. Fruitful comparisons can be made with the work of Margery Wolf, who describes a similar contradiction in Chinese kinship based on her research in rural Taiwan and also locates strategies that thwart the ideal patriline without fully dismantling it. Wolf, "Child Training and the Chinese Family," 42, and Wolf, *Women and the Family in Rural Taiwan.* See also Sangren, *History and Magical Power in a Chinese Community,* 41–43.

52. Fruitful comparisons can be made with Turner, "Social Complexity and Recursive Hierarchy."

53. For similar observations, see Turner, "Social Body and Embodied Subject," and Butler, "Performative Acts and Gender Constitution."

54. Butler, "Performative Acts," 272 (italics in original).

55. Nguyễn-võ Thu-hương, "Governing the Social," 97.

56. Ibid., 114.

57. Ibid., 117–18.

58. Compare Marx, "The Real Basis of Ideology," with Butler, "Performative Acts."

2. Power and Exclusion on the Edge

1. VnExpress, "Ô nhiễm nguồn nước do nghĩa địa tự phát"; VnExpress, "Nhiều hộ dân TP HCM đang uống nước từ nghĩa địa."

2. Phúc Huy, "TP.HCM: Nỗi lo . . . nhà siêu mỏng."

3. T. Đ., "Nhà nghỉ ven đô—điểm hẹn của các cặp tình nhân."

4. Lê Văn Hải, "Nạn rải đinh đã về Hóc Môn."

5. The term is from Bourdieu, who critiques anthropological analyses that rely on the objective description of rules and codes and desperately turn, in Bourdieu's words, to simplifying "maps" of culture. Bourdieu, *Outline of a Theory of Practice,* 1.

6. Jacobs, *The Death and Life of Great American Cities,* xvii.

7. McGee, "The Emergence of *Desakota* Regions in Asia," 17. McGee has thoughtfully coined the now popular term *désakota* to mediate between the two oppositions with a synthetic term that combines the Bahasa Indonesian words for village *(désa)* and city *(kota).* From an anthropological perspective, however, this term fails to show the ways in which local actors experience this new kind of space as a fundamentally incongruous meeting of two pure opposites. In the Vietnamese language, the country and the city cannot be combined into a composite term; such a term would come across as strange and incongruous.

8. Scott, *Seeing Like a State.*

9. Hebdidge, *Subculture, the Meaning of Style.*

10. Author's field notes, 2002.

11. Douglas, *Purity and Danger,* 41.

12. Durkheim, *The Division of Labor in Society,* 291–309.

13. Douglas, *Purity and Danger,* 99.

14. Tsing, "From the Margins," 279.

15. Author's field notes, 2002.

16. He also did not speak of the solid waste produced by cutting leather, rubber soles, and fabric for the shoes. The dirt road surrounding the factory was covered with rubber cut-outs left over from making insoles.

17. The exploitation of the rural fringe to attract foreign investment is actually the very lure that leads to the demise of this space as rural space. Factory owners are eager to tap into cheap rural space, but it is exactly those factories that end up displacing rural space. From the perspective of land investors, this very process amounts to an investment strategy; investors commonly purchase land when it is zoned for agricultural uses and sit on it until it is rezoned for more valuable urban land use.

This investment strategy is nicely described by Annette Kim in *Learning to Be Capitalists*, 38–41.

18. The power of such expectations found a parallel in the way my partner, Isabella, experienced Hóc Môn as a stifling environment where people expected her to stay home while I, the male ethnographer, roamed about the district talking to people and going out with friends. It always presented something of a dilemma when I insisted that she join us at the male table or that she be included in a round of drinking.

19. Rather than oppose the study of material need against a less "real" study of culture and symbol, Terence Turner argues that we view social relations as "a totality of internally related entities, which consists of an internally motivated process of activity by human actors who *reflexively produce the needs and values that constitute the subjective goals of their activity as part of the same process through which they produce the objective means of satisfying and attaining them.*" Turner, "Production, Value, and Structure in Marx," 3 (italics in original).

20. Lefebvre, *The Production of Space*, 27.

21. Compare this with James Scott's assertion that state programs that attempt to render social space and social life "legible" also render certain social elements invisible. Simple conversations with everyday people living in Hóc Môn made it clear that seeing the landscape in terms of the rural and urban dichotomy was not simply a problem of "seeing like a state" but entailed a wider, more pervasive sense of describing the world using received categories.

22. Author's field notes, 2002.

23. Ibid.

24. Ibid.

25. This is, effectively, a description of the labor theory of value inherent in capitalist production. For a coherent description of Marx's concept and how surplus value emerges from the application of human labor, see Foley, *Understanding Capital*, 32–34.

26. See Wallerstein, *The Modern World-System;* Wallerstein, *The End of the World as We Know It;* and Gundar Frank, *Capitalism and Underdevelopment in Latin America.*

27. Bourdieu, *Language and Symbolic Power*, 98–111.

3. Future Orientations in the Country of Memory

1. This pun rests on the multiple meanings of the term *cất*, which can mean "lift, raise"; "set off, take off" (as in setting off on a voyage); "relieve" (as in to relieve someone of his or her position); "abate" (as in an illness); "lay by, store"; and "buy up a whole contingent of goods for reselling." Thus the term *xây cất* literally means "to raise a structure." Viện Ngôn ngữ học, *Từ điển Việt-Anh*, 178. But when the two elements of the compound are separated by the term "in order to" *(để mà)* the meaning changes completely and the term literally means something like "build in order to set aside for oneself a whole contingent of goods for reselling" *(xây để mà cất).*

2. Hue-Tam Ho Tai, ed., *The Country of Memory.*

3. For an important critique of anthropological depictions of "social time" since Durkheim, see Gell, *The Anthropology of Time.*

4. Gell quite carefully makes the case for the universality of time while upholding the possibility of culturally specific orientations to time. Indeed, logically speaking, there can be no understanding of relativity without a standard form against which divergences are themselves contrasted. Gell, *The Anthropology of Time,* 316.

5. Dilthey, "Awareness, Reality," 149.

6. Ibid., 150.

7. Saint Augustine, "Time and Eternity," 263.

8. Harvey sees the annihilation of space through time as a key transformation of global capitalism. Harvey, *The Condition of Postmodernity,* 217, 255, chap. 17 passim. The concept is from Marx, who wrote in the *Grundrisse* about "circulation time" as the "natural barrier" to the realization of labor time. Marx, *Grundrisse,* 539.

9. Greenhouse, *A Moment's Notice,* 1.

10. Leach, "Two Essays Concerning the Symbolic Representation of Time," 135 (italics in original).

11. Elias, "Time and Timing," 254.

12. Greenhouse, *A Moment's Notice,* 47–48.

13. See Wolf, *Peasants;* and Wolf, *Peasant Wars of the Twentieth Century.*

14. Pelley, *Postcolonial Vietnam,* 168.

15. Appadurai, "The Past as a Scarce Resource"; Bloch, "The Past and the Present in the Present."

16. On the production of a peasant "other," see Kearney, *Reconceptualizing the Peasantry.*

17. Quoted in Gell, *The Anthropology of Time,* 64.

18. For a critique of the impossible logic underlying this position, see Gell, *The Anthropology of Time,* 64–66; for this problem of "temporal othering" in anthropology writ large, see Fabian, *Time and the Other.*

19. See Munn, "The Cultural Anthropology of Time."

20. Author's field notes, 2002.

21. This discussion with the cucumber farmer was very typical of these kinds of encounters in the fields, which tended to turn on these simple enumerations of how many hours farmers spent working each day and how many harvests they had per year.

22. On this concept, see Chayanov et al., *The Theory of Peasant Economy.*

23. Hoskins, *The Play of Time.*

24. Author's field notes, 2002.

25. This refers to a Kohler brand generator. For an illuminating discussion about Vietnam's "Kohler Revolution," see Biggs, "Motorized Mekong."

26. Author's field notes, 2002.

27. Eliade, *The Sacred and the Profane;* Levi-Strauss, "Time Regained."

28. The traditional Vietnamese system of time reckoning, for example, is organized according to the *can chi* system of counting years in terms of heavenly stems *(thiên can)* and earthly branches *(địa chi).* These two systems thus consist of an unequal number of elements cycling at the same rate. As a result, they are able to

mark time in the form of binomial "dates" in a cycle that starts at Giáp-Tí, the first cycle of twelve years, and then restarts every sixty years when the two sets meet again at Giáp-Tí. Although it is certainly cyclical in some respects, this time orientation also moves forward in a linear direction.

29. For the formula, see Trần Ngọc Thêm, *Cơ sở văn hóa Việt Nam,* 78–79.

30. The speaker was a twenty-three-year-old girl from Hóc Môn who studies and works on the side. Author's field notes, 2002.

31. The speaker was a forty-eight-year-old Hóc Môn woman who sells goods in the market. Author's field notes, 2002.

32. The speaker was a twenty-nine-year-old male beef-noodle soup vendor from Hóc Môn. Author's field notes, 2002.

33. Munn, "The Cultural Anthropology of Time."

34. Bakhtin, *The Dialogic Imagination;* Basso, "Stalking with Stories."

35. For example, although the cyclical calendar may express important elements of symbolic meaning, these interpretations of the meaning of time rest upon a whole concept of authority and legitimacy. The ritual specialist or fortune-teller *(thầy bói)* can interpret these calendars because of ritual authority derived from a grasp of the technology of time, convincing performance, and confirmed success. But so can specialists who manipulate the so-called Western calendar. Even on a national level, we can see how Western dates acquire symbolic meaning through state rituals. April 30, 1975, or "Liberation Day," for example, has important symbolic meaning, but this meaning is derived from a certain form of power and authority.

36. Pelley, *Postcolonial Vietnam,* 167.

37. Quoted in ibid., 23.

38. Pelley, *Postcolonial Vietnam,* 43.

39. For an analysis of how the decisions made in this period show a generalized confidence in the linear model of history as a set of stages leading toward socialism, see Duiker, *Vietnam since the Fall of Saigon,* 14–31.

40. See Turley, "Urban Transformation in South Vietnam."

41. Ibid., 624.

42. Đoàn Thanh Hương, *Lược sử 300 năm Sài Gòn,* 8.

43. Author's field notes, 2002.

44. Greenhouse, *A Moment's Notice,* 82.

45. Ibid., 83 (italics in original).

46. Author's field notes, 2002.

47. Described in Young, *The Vietnam Wars,* 113.

48. The relative pace of productive activity, for example, is commonly measured in terms of time. The GDP, for example, is measured in terms of yearly gross domestic product. Five-year plans, production quotas, and so on, are also clearly temporal measures.

49. Taylor, *Fragments of the Present,* 11.

50. Rigg, *Southeast Asia,* 122; Williams, *The Country and the City.*

51. Johannes Fabian critiqued this process of "othering" in his critical account of how anthropology typically assigns ethnographic subjects to a temporal space outside of contemporary history. Interestingly, Philip Taylor shows (in *Fragments of*

the Present) how Vietnamese themselves effectively divide their own society into two sets of "others" divided by alternate relations to tradition and modernity.

52. Taylor, *Fragments of the Present,* 23–55; Robert, "'Social Evils' and the Question of Youth in Post-War Saigon."

53. Nguyễn-võ Thu-hương, "Governing the Social," 119.

54. Ibid., 122.

55. Taylor, *Fragments of the Present,* 9.

56. Ibid., 21.

57. Ibid., 85.

58. Trouillot, *Silencing the Past.*

59. Kirsch, "Feasting and Social Oscillation."

4. Negotiating Time and Space

1. The concept of social oscillation derives from the work of Leach as reworked by Kirsch. Kirsch, "Feasting and Social Oscillation"; Leach, *Political Systems of Highland Burma.* Although their work focuses on upland groups in Southeast Asia, their conceptual model applies well to a large number of social circumstances in which seemingly opposed models of social structure oscillate in pendulum-like movement between seemingly contrasting forms of social organization. For an important analysis concerning the space of transcendence produced in between the structural poles in symbolic systems, see Terence Turner, "Transformation, Hierarchy and Transcendence."

2. On the concept of "reproducing the social person" see Turner, who explains that "the relevant categories of value must be defined in each case in relation to the specific processes of social production of the society in question, and what counts as social production must be defined in relation to the relevant categories of social value" (18). Value can still be defined in terms of *socially necessary labor time,* but it must not be conflated with labor time in the restricted sense of labor calculated in terms of hours and minutes. Instead we need to emphasize the more generalized notion of time as that which is socially required to reproduce the social being and the family. Turner, "Value, Production, and Exploitation in Non-capitalist Societies."

3. Harvey, "Between Space and Time," 419.

4. Bachelard, *The Poetics of Space,* 211.

5. Munn, *The Fame of Gawa,* 9.

6. Bachelard, *The Poetics of Space,* 216.

7. The idea of drinking coffee came up quite often as a point of comparison between the United States and Vietnam. Drinking coffee in a café represents a particularly salient form of leisure that is contrasted to a vision of America devoid of leisure. Readers will be interested to compare this with the chapter "They Don't Sit around in Cafes Here, Do They?" in Nguyễn Quí Đức's poignant memoir of immigration to North America, *Where the Ashes Are.*

8. Ever since the publication of Sahlins's *Stone-Age Economics,* anthropologists have argued that equating wages with production often obscures more complex, nonmonetized forms of productive social life. Recently Phillip Taylor has applied

similar insights to the Vietnamese context, showing that rural people often live lives that are much "richer" than many observers recognize. Emphasizing morality, alternative modernities, and rural cosmopolitanism—all components of what anthropologists would see as the production of the total social person—Taylor writes that "rural people have come to enjoy a standard of living that is often not captured in conventional development indicators." Taylor, "Poor Policies, Wealthy Peasants," 6. The same might be said for many residents living on the rural–urban margins who have fashioned innovative spatiotemporal worlds full of meaning and alternative conceptions of socially constituted value.

9. Turner, "Production, Value, and Structure in Marx."

10. Scott, *The Moral Economy of the Peasant*, 13.

11. Chayanov, *The Theory of Peasant Economy*, 1.

12. Ibid., 6.

13. Ibid.

14. Ibid., 11.

15. Lương Văn Hy, "Thành phố Hồ Chí Minh," 174–75.

16. Đặng Nguyên Anh, "Di dân và đô thị hóa bền vững ở Hà Nội và Thành phố Hồ Chí Minh," 338.

17. Ong, *Spirits of Resistance and Capitalist Discipline;* Thompson, "Time, Work Discipline and Industrial Capitalism."

18. Lê Bạch Dương and Robert Bach, "Market Reforms, Social Protection and Rural–Urban Migration," 71.

19. As I explained in previous chapters, Luong's work shows that there are flexible possibilities inherent in the system of inclusive and exclusive person reference. Invoking the historical past of a lineage can represent a strong claim to land. Extended bilateral kin networks can extend a family's roots over wide swaths of space, enabling people to claim a certain degree of what Munn calls "fame" across space, even if these links cannot be traced far back in time. People will refer to family in America in order to extend their supposed influence beyond the bounded limits of a small community—yet these familial connections are often tenuous at best, reaching to the furthest ends of a highly extended bilateral network of kin and even fictive kin.

20. Bélanger and Wang, "International Migrant Workers from Vietnam," 177.

21. It is important to differentiate between having land in the home region and gaining access to land at the destination. Lương Văn Hy notes, for example, that very few of the migrant households coming to Ho Chi Minh City from Quảng Ngãi province are actually landless. Their situation is contrasted to that of households coming from Long An province, where there are greater disparities among those with and those without agricultural land. Lương Văn Hy, "Di dân từ nông thôn ra thành thị ở Việt Nam," 439. What this indicates is that the relation of land to willingness to work specifically depends on having land in the area where one works. For those who have land in their hometown, the temporary foray into factory labor itself can be construed as part of this process of spatiotemporal oscillation in which they generate income outside of their ancestral homeland but nevertheless retain important financial and social connections with those on the inside of their kin groups back home.

22. Phan Thị Yến Tuyết, "Một số hình thức thờ cúng tổ tiên của các dòng họ cư dân Việt tại Thành phố Hồ Chí Minh," 393–94.

23. Ibid., 393.

24. Ibid., 394.

25. Luong, *Discursive Practices and Linguistic Meanings,* 49–50.

26. Rey ("The Lineage Mode of Production") and Meillassoux *(Maidens, Meal, and Money)* have made similar arguments about the need for a broader view of production that accounts for alternate modes, such as the "lineage mode of production." Feminist scholars such as Rose critique the dominant paradigm employed in analyzing class-based resistance to capitalist development, which "centers working-class formation on artisanal and skilled workers engaging in organized political protest" (Rose, "Class Formation and the Quintessential Worker," 135). Class formation and resistance cannot be understood without accounting for the diversity expressions in everyday life and escaping the paradigm of the "quintessential worker," whose subjectivities are paradigmatically understood "as being constituted by work itself" (138). All of these points expand our understanding of production and obliterate the distinction between public and private labor by emphasizing instead the realm of production and reproduction of the social person.

27. Luong, *Discursive Practices and Linguistic Meanings,* 49–69.

28. Tôn Nữ Quỳnh Trân, "Quan hệ dòng tộc trước chuyển động đô thị hóa tại thành phố Hồ Chí Minh."

29. Author's field notes, 2002.

30. Bachelard, *Poetics of Space,* 211.

5. The Road to Paradise

1. Saigon Times, "The Start of Mammoth Projects."

2. Ibid.

3. I conducted an initial survey into attitudes and perceptions about the highway between February and March 2002. To do this I walked along the highway, moving door to door for approximately one month to discuss the building project with residents living along the highway and to chat with individual household members. Most conversations took several hours each, and I could typically conduct only two or three per day. The survey data were supplemented by participant observation in the community throughout the entirety of 2002.

4. Luong, "The Marxist State and the Dialogic Re-stucturation of Culture in Vietnam."

5. Hickey points out the importance of the road in his *Village in Vietnam* but then focuses on a more traditional ethnography of the village world as a contained unit of study. The spatial relation of the road to the organization of the village itself remains undertheorized. Contemporary Khánh Hậu, the site of his study, however, is clearly dependent on the road, and much of its spatial arrangement follows the road in the same way that Hickey describes it as following the river.

6. Although the Trans-Asia Highway project recalls the auto routes Augé has productively described as "non-places," roads like Highway 22 retain many of the

qualities Setha Low attributes to urban plazas in that they, too, are meaningful public spaces that host a wide variety of social action. Augé, *Non-places;* Low, *On the Plaza.*

7. Gourou, "Les paysans du delta tonkinois"; Graw, "Nam Tien and the Development of Vietnamese Regionalism"; Grossheim, "The Impact of Reforms on the Agricultural Sector of Vietnam"; Hickey, *Village in Vietnam;* Kleinen, "Village as Pretext"; Kleinen, "Is There a Village Vietnam?"; Rambo, "A Comparison of Peasant Social Systems of Northern and Southern Vietnam."

8. For a detailed discussion of several types of villages in the Red River Delta, see Gourou, "Les paysans du delta tonkinois," 224–72. Although Gourou does try to create a system of classifying villages, he never assumes that there might be a single prototypical form. Even his system of classifying villages produces six major types, each with variants of its own.

9. As Kleinen abruptly puts it, "the village" is a "pretext." My description of village morphology along the roadway in Tân Thới Nhì is not meant, however, to say that there is no such thing as a bamboo hedge in Vietnam. By pointing to the importance of the road in the contemporary organization of social space on the suburban fringe, I simply invite regional comparison and also hope to point out the ways in which regional and national conceptions of spatial organization intersect with a local concept of social space.

10. It is tempting to insist on this mistranslation to account for the apparent value of the front-facing property, but my Vietnamese friends and colleagues vociferously refuse to participate in such silliness.

11. This obvious fact seems surprisingly overlooked in descriptions of the social organization of Vietnamese cities, towns, and villages. Focusing on the internal structure of the village as an isolated world, the outward orientation of the community has often been seen as an intrusion of the outside world. Rambo and Jamieson *(Cultural Change in Rural Vietnam)* tried to use this schema as a way of extending Eric Wolf's ("Closed Corporate Peasant Communities") idea of the closed corporate community to describe the difference between North and South Vietnam. But this leads to an ultimately reductionist thesis that the "closed" villages of the north were naturally inclined toward communism, while the "open" southern villages were more naturally inclined to the open economy of the global market.

12. See Burlat, "Processus institutionnels et dynamiques urbaines."

13. For similar associations of roads with modernity, also replete with ambivalence and linked to transformations in spatiotemporal consciousness, see Pina-Cabral ("Paved Roads," 719) and Roseman ("How We Built the Road"). For a critical review of what trends toward "automobility" might do to social life, see Sheller and Urry ("The City and the Car").

14. Houses on the road almost invariably have flush toilets, direct access to running water, and cement driveways. They are often multistory and of more solid, recent construction. Houses behind the road may exhibit these characteristics, but the number of homes with pit toilets, exposed drainage, and temporary construction increases dramatically.

15. McGee, *The Southeast Asian City,* 106.

16. See chapter 4 for a detailed account of the role cafés play in labor and time orientation.

17. Harvey, *The Condition of Postmodernity.*

18. In "Objet et méthodes de l'anthropologie économique," Godelier thus emphasizes a holistic anthropological viewpoint that "forbids description of the economic without showing its relation to the other elements of a social system" (56) and that attempts to show how economic activity is organically linked with other political, religious, and cultural activities (60). This economic anthropology effectively began as the anthropological extension of Karl Polanyi's emphasis, in *The Great Transformation,* on how economies are embedded in social relations. See also Wilk, *Economies and Cultures.*

19. The literature on contemporary ritual practices in Vietnam is extensive. For a useful start, see Endres, "Engaging the Spirits of the Dead"; Fjelstad and Hien, *Possessed by the Spirits;* Kleinen, *Facing the Future, Reviving the Past;* Kwon, *After the Massacre;* Malarney, *Culture, Ritual and Revolution in Vietnam;* Malarney, "Weddings and Funerals in Contemporary Vietnam"; Taylor, *Goddess on the Rise;* Taylor, *Modernity and Re-enchantment.*

20. Bestor, "Supply-Side Sushi"; Bestor, *Tsukiji;* Sassen, *Cities in a World Economy.*

21. Trouillot, *Peasants and Capital,* 205.

22. Marx first identified this as the main contradiction of capitalism. Rather than describing it as a contradiction, however, economists see it as a measure of a healthy economy. In either view, the basic point holds: capitalist development requires consumers. But this is the contradiction of the highway. Consumers take up space. They cause traffic jams. But efficient production, especially in the planning schemes of contemporary Vietnam, requires the easy flow of goods.

23. The glum descriptions of post-1975 Vietnam before its slow road to economic recovery often emphasized the emptiness of the streets and the lack of people in the public markets.

24. In chapter 6 I provide a more thorough discussion of the conflation of "order" with modernization, progress, development, and "civilization."

25. VNS, "Trans-Asia Highway Becomes Nightmare for Southern Vietnamese."

26. Tự Trung, "Công trình đường Xuyên Á"; Tự Trung and Thanh Tòng, "Đường Xuyên Á đang thi công."

27. Author's field notes, 2002.

28. The size of her property was reduced from forty-two by seven meters to a much smaller twenty by six meters.

29. Author's field notes, 2002.

30. Ibid.

31. Ibid.

32. In 2006, with much of the Vietnamese section upgraded, it took about two hours by bus to travel eighty kilometers to the border post at Mộc Bài. From Bavet on the Cambodian side to Phnom Penh it took anywhere from eight to ten hours to travel roughly twice the distance.

33. The concept, as used in urban studies, is described by David Harvey, who

builds from Marx's notion of the annihilation of space through time. (See chapter 3, note 8.)

34. Tuổi Trẻ, "Đường lên thiên đàng."

35. For an interesting comparison, see Masquelier's trenchant analysis of how Niger's National Route 1 possesses both hopes and malevolent demons representing a history of violence. Masquelier, "Road Mythographies."

36. Weber, *Sociological Writings*, 3.

37. Bộ Xây dựng, *Quy hoạch xây dựng các đô thị Việt Nam*, 38.

38. Ibid.

39. Ibid., 52.

40. Ibid., 53.

41. Ibid., 38.

42. Ibid., 53.

43. Nguyễn-võ Thu-hương, "Governing the Social," 1–11.

44. The text of the decision, numbered 14/2003/NĐ-CP and issued on February 19, 2003, provides a detailed summary of the idealized ministerial division of labor; see Chính phủ Việt Nam, "Nghị định của Chính phủ quy định chi tiết thi hành một số điều của Luật Giao thông đường bộ."

45. For the full text of these decisions of the prime minister, see Thủ Tướng Chính Phủ, "Quyết định số 195/2001/QĐ-TTg Ngày 26-12-2001 của Thủ tướng Chính phủ về việc thành lập Ban chủ nhiệm Chương trình phòng, chống tai nạn, thương tích," and "Quyết Định Số 197/2001/QĐ-TTg Ngày 27-12-2001 của Thủ tướng Chính phủ về việc phê duyệt Chính sách Quốc gia phòng, chống tai nạn, thương tích giai đoạn 2002–2010." These decisions itemize the cross-ministerial work and mass mobilization that need to be done to engage the people in a general movement against accidents and injuries.

46. Như Trang, "TPHCM sẽ chấm dứt nạn đua xe trong năm nay."

47. Nghĩa Nhân, "Đề nghị cho cấp phường xử lý vị phạm nếp sống văn minh."

48. Chính phủ Việt Nam, "Nghị định của Chính phủ quy định chi tiết thi hành một số điều của Luật Giao thông đường bộ," 20.

6. The Problem of Urban Civilization on Saigon's Edge

1. Mass organizations like the Fatherland Front are mechanisms for co-opting mass participation in ways that promote popular support for the party rather than political pluralism. See Turley and Selden, *Reinventing Vietnamese Socialism*, 259–60.

2. The role of the Fatherland Front is described in Article 9 of the Vietnamese Constitution.

3. Author's field notes, 2002.

4. Ibid.

5. Ibid.

6. Evans, *Lao Peasants under Socialism*, 65.

7. Drummond and Thomas, *Consuming Urban Culture in Contemporary Vietnam*, 7.

8. Ibid., 8.

9. For an important parallel in China, see Anagnost, *National Past-Times,* where she describes a civilizational discourse in post-Mao China that focuses on peasant bodies and articulates civilization as a "lack" that explains China's failure to modernize (86).

10. Truong Chinh and Vo Nguyen Giap, *The Peasant Question,* 14 (emphasis in original).

11. Ibid., 25.

12. Ibid., 7.

13. Ibid.

14. The riddle of how a mainly urban leadership can negotiate the proper balance between rural might and urban light recurs throughout the history and development of Vietnamese socialism. See Ninh, *A World Transformed;* Woodside, *Community and Revolution in Modern Vietnam;* Woodside, "Peasant and the State in the Aftermath of the Vietnamese Revolution"; Duiker, *The Communist Road to Power in Vietnam.*

15. Huỳnh Kim Khánh, *Vietnamese Communism,* 103.

16. Debates at the time were much more complex than Khánh implies in retrospect, but many urban Vietnamese did fear the consequences of a revolution that would give too much power to what they considered uneducated peasants. See Marr, *Vietnamese Tradition on Trial,* 378–87.

17. Nguyen Khac Vien, *Tradition and Revolution in Vietnam,* 20.

18. Ibid., 140.

19. Ibid.

20. Shaun K. Malarney provides extended discussions on the socialist campaigns against superstitions. Note especially how the "cultural and ideological revolution" of the revolutionary period *(cách mạng tư tưởng và văn hóa)* was associated with the ideas of progress *(tiến bộ)* and novelty associated with the "new," epitomized by the campaigns for both "New Ways" *(nếp sống mới)* and "New Life" *(Đời sống mới).* Malarney, "Ritual and Revolution in Viet Nam"; Malarney, *Culture, Ritual and Revolution in Vietnam,* 52–64.

21. Huỳnh Kim Khánh explains that "the urban petite-bourgeoisie . . . had thought of themselves and others in their social stratum as suitable postindependence leaders. Contemptuous of 'rural hicks' *(nha que)* and 'Coolies' (that is, the urban proletariat), they could not conceive of an active political role for these people, who constituted more than 90 percent of the Vietnamese population at the time." Huỳnh Kim Khánh, *Vietnamese Communism,* 161.

22. Pelley, *Postcolonial Vietnam,* 139–140.

23. Duiker, *Sacred War,* 135–139.

24. The literature on decollectivization is extensive. For useful introductions to key issues, see especially Beresford, "Household and Collective in Vietnamese Agriculture"; Fforde, *The Historical Background to Agricultural Collectivisation in North Vietnam;* Fforde, *The Agrarian Question in North Vietnam;* Fforde and De Vylder, *From Plan to Market;* Kerkvliet, *State–Village Relations in Vietnam;* Kerkvliet, "Land Struggles and Land Regimes in the Philippines and Vietnam during the Twentieth

Century"; Kerkvliet, *The Power of Everyday Politics;* Quang Truong, "Agricultural Collectivization and Rural Development in Vietnam"; Watts, "Agrarian Thermidor."

25. Most explanations for the introduction of the production contract system in 1981 and the subsequent 1988 policy that made households independent economic units assert that there was some sort of natural inclination or trend among farmers to spend more energy and time working their own household plots than they spent working the collective plots. Party policy changes, these explanations posit, were thus reactions to the state of affairs naturally at work in Vietnamese household production. See Chử Văn Lâm, *Hợp tác hóa nông nghiệp Việt Nam;* Vo-Nhan-Tri, "Party Politics and Economic Performance."

26. Do Muoi, *Vietnam,* 44.

27. Ibid., 45.

28. Vasavakul, in "Vietnam," convincingly describes this recasting of the national narrative as an attempt to reestablish waning state legitimacy.

29. Tran Thi Que, *Vietnam's Agriculture,* 7.

30. The history of decollectivization in the south shows the persistence of such vacillation. During the 1980s many southern farmers were boycotting the collectives, abandoning their land and even killing their livestock. See Ngo Vinh Long, "Some Aspects of Cooperativization in the Mekong Delta." Although total food production for the first five-year plan had increased over 6 percent, this did not keep up with the population increase of over 9 percent for the same period. Per capita production was falling, not rising. Vo-Nhan-Tri, "Party Politics and Economic Performance," 80. But despite the lack of success, the third five-year plan for 1981–85, announced at the Fifth Congress of the Communist Party in 1982, maintained the goal of "basically completing agricultural cooperativization of the southern provinces" (Lê Duẩn, quoted by Vo-Nhan-Tri, 83).

31. Viện Sử học, *Đô thị cổ Việt Nam,* 10.

32. Ibid., 38.

33. Nguyễn Ngọc Châu, *Quản lý đô thị,* 5. This evolutionary stance is far from isolated. In the book *Văn hóa trong Quá trình Đô thị hóa ở Nước ta hiện nay* (Culture within Our Country's Current Urbanization Process), Trần Văn Bính writes that urbanization is "the process of moving from the country into the city, moving from a low form of civilization to a higher form of civilization" *(chuyển từ một nền văn minh thấp sang một nền văn minh cao hơn)* (9). This very sentence, in turn, is cited with approval in Lê Văn Năm's book *Nông dân ngoại thành Thành phố Hồ Chí Minh trong tiến trình đô thị hóa* (10), indicating the wide currency of such thinking.

34. Susan Bayly's important essay "French Anthropology and the Durkheimians in Colonial Indochina" charts the emergence of this intellectual tradition in Indochina, perhaps explaining why rural–urban relations become theorized as a clear move from *gemeinschaft* to *gessellschaft,* or from organic to mechanical solidarity.

35. Nguyễn Ngọc Châu, *Quản lý đô thị,* 5–6.

36. Ibid., 30.

37. Ibid., 31.

38. For other versions of this same argument, see chapter 5.

39. Nguyễn Ngọc Châu, *Quản lý đô thị,* 38.

40. Ibid., 66.

41. Ibid., 68.

42. Turley, "Urban Transformation in South Vietnam,"607.

43. The quote is from the title of an essay by Quach Thanh Tam-Langlet, "Saï-gon, capitale de la République du Sud-Viêtnam (1954–1975) ou une urbanisation sauvage." See also Duiker, *Vietnam since the Fall of Saigon,* 13–15; Goodman and Franks, "The Dynamics of Migration to Saigon, 1964–1972"; Thrift and Forbes, *The Price of War;* Turley, "Urban Transformation in South Vietnam."

44. The urban space of central Saigon–Hồ Chí Minh City has developed out of a succession of settlement strategies built up, layerlike, by successive cultures, regimes, and political administrations. Vietnamese, French, Japanese, Chinese, Soviet, and American conceptions of urban space have all participated in the long historical transformation of the ethnic Khmer village of Prei Nokor into what we now know as contemporary Hồ Chí Minh City. See Nguyễn Đình Đầu, "Địa lý lịch sử Thành phố Hồ Chí Minh"; Nguyễn Đình Đầu, *From Saigon to Ho Chi Minh City.*

45. Hébrard, "L'urbanisme en Indochine,"40.

46. For a critical view of Howard and the Garden City Movement, see Kolson, *Big Plans,* 99–109.

47. Viollis, *Indochine S.O.S.,* 14–23. For English sources on the dynamic life of Ninh, see Henchy, "Performing Modernity in the Writings of Nguyễn An Ninh and Phan Văn Hùm"; Hue Tam Ho Tai, *Radicalism and the Origins of the Vietnamese Revolution;* Marr, *Vietnamese Tradition on Trial.* Both a Francophile and an anticolonial activist, Ninh confounded simple binaries, to the extent that Léon Werth, who met him during a visit to Saigon in 1924, could claim at one moment, "I am with a European. His name is Nguyen An Ninh" and then later state that Ninh also represented the "spirit of the Annamese." Werth, *Cochinchine,* 131, 143.

48. Grammont, *Onze mois de sous-préfecture en Basse-Cochinchine,* 101.

49. Ibid., 139.

50. Ibid., 299.

51. Ibid., 219.

52. Ibid., 93–94.

53. Stoler, *Carnal Knowledge and Imperial Power.*

54. Norindr, *Phantasmatic Indochina,* 115.

55. See especially the work of Wright, who, in *The Politics of Design in French Colonial Urbanism,* describes the ways in which colonial architecture reflected different styles of colonial politics in the French period.

56. Despite superficial transformations of the surface features of the city, this original network of grids underscored subsequent colonial plans for the basic shape of the developing city. See Burlat, "Processus institutionnels et dynamiques urbaines," 67–70.

57. Malleret, "Éléments d'une monographie des anciennes fortifications et citadelles de Saïgon"; Peycam, "Saigon, des origines à 1859."

58. The idea of the Vietnamese *thành* may be compared with the French idea of the *bourg,* for example.

59. Trần Văn Điệu, "Những vấn đề đặt ra trong quá trình đô thị hóa Quận Gò Vấp—Thành phố Hồ Chí Minh," 102.

60. Greene, *The Quiet American,* 83–84, 89–114.

61. Đinh Huy Liêm, "Chuyển biến của kinh tế nông hộ và kinh tế hợp tác trong nông nghiệp ngoại thành Thành phố Hồ Chí Minh," 76.

62. Ibid., 74, 76–77.

63. As Warwick Anderson shows, the focus on infrastructure, hygiene, and development has always been a classic element of the "civilizing mission." Anderson, *Colonial Pathologies.*

64. Quoted in Đinh Huy Liêm, "Chuyển biến," 118.

65. Ibid., 157.

66. Ibid., 157–58.

67. Thongchai Winichakul, "The Quest for *'Siwilai,'*" 537.

68. Hãn Nguyên Nguyễn Nhã, "Các biện pháp giáo dục cụ thể về tác phong văn minh đô thị tại Việt Nam," 67 (emphasis in original).

69. Hãn Nguyên Nguyễn Nhã, "Các biện pháp giáo dục cụ thể về tác phong văn minh đô thị tại Việt Nam," 67.

70. The text also laments that parents cannot be counted on to enforce urban values in their children's education because they are mainly concerned with basic education and their children's test scores. After all, the author claims, older people themselves often do not have a sense of urban civil manners in the first place. The author continues by citing Central Decision V of the Communist Party of Vietnam, which focuses on building an "advanced culture" and a "warm and friendly" national identity. Ibid., 69.

71. Ibid., 71. The text continues by describing a new program announced by the National Assembly in 2000, which first established an annual commemorative celebration called the Day for Building Civilized Urban Manners *(Ngày xây dựng Tác phong văn minh đô thị Việt Nam).* Second, the Ministry of Education instituted the program Civilized Urban Manners in Vietnam *(Tác phong văn minh đô thị Việt Nam)* into the preschool, primary, and middle-school curricula. Third, authorities at all levels were encouraged to develop policies to promote popular education about civilized urban manners and also to develop punishments to enforce infractions of civilized urban manners. Fourth, the Fatherland Front was encouraged to participate. And fifth, the mass organizations and media outlets were encouraged to publish and disseminate the contents of the programs throughout the country. Ibid., 71–73.

72. The English definition of *học vấn* is "knowledge *(gained from study),* culture." Viện Ngôn ngữ học, *Từ điển Việt-Anh,* 335. Both the official and the popular way to refer to one's level of education is to refer to one's "level of culture," *trình độ văn hóa.* The first term in the compound words for culture and civilization, *văn hóa* and *văn minh,* is the borrowed Han-Viet word *văn,* which means "letters" (in the same sense that we use the Latin prefix *liter-* to construct words such as *literature, literate,* and *literati).*

73. For an important critique of this kind of conclusion, see Philip Taylor, who persuasively shows that rural Vietnamese lead "modern, engaged, and sustainable" lives, which typical development practitioners have trouble seeing. Taylor, "Poor Policies, Wealthy Peasants," 7.

74. Philip Taylor, writing in less metaphorical terms, claims to have experienced similar reactions: "Many urban professionals have complained to me about the unplanned ruralization of the city and the consequent deterioration in the order, civility, and morality of their neighborhoods and public places." Taylor, "Poor Policies, Wealthy Peasants," 14.

75. As an anthropologist, I found the idea of civilization an uncomfortable reminder of French colonialism and its infamous *mission civilizatrice.* My friends in Ho Chi Minh City and in Hóc Môn, however, found it one of those ideas they seemed to share with the People's Committee.

76. As Anagnost shows for the parallel Chinese concept of *wenming,* one may trace the (re)emergence of the term to East Asian intellectual practices of "innovative classicism," in which Chinese classical concepts were reinscribed backward to China via Japanese thinkers during the Meiji restoration. Anagnost, *National Past-Times,* 27, 80. For the movement of such concepts into Vietnam, see Woodside, *Community and Revolution in Modern Vietnam,* 54. As these authors show, the meaning of *văn minh* cannot simply be reconstructed by tracing where it comes from. The meaning emerges in how it is used. Thongchai argues a similar point in his discussion of how late nineteenth- and early twentieth-century urban Siamese intellectuals appropriated and transformed the Western concept of civilization into the Thai neologism *siwilai.* Despite the obvious linguistic connection to the Western concept, the concept also encouraged a localizing impulse celebrating an emerging sense of Thai national identity *at the same time* that it indexed Thai fascination with Western ideas. Thongchai Winichakul, "The Quest for '*Siwilai,*'" 529. Peter Perdue, writing of China, is equally perceptive when he asks: "How does our understanding of the civilizing mission change upon recognition that the civilizing mission is as Chinese a marker as it is a European one?" Perdue, quoted in Stoler, McGranahan, and Perdue, *Imperial Formations,* 18.

77. In December 2003, contributors to the Viet Nam Studies Group listserv engaged in a lively debate about the best way to translate the concept of *văn minh;* is it civilization, lifestyle, culture, "the Way," or, more simply, life? The discussion circled around the different uses of the term people have encountered in practice and how any one translation would essentially petrify the meaning of this complex of meanings. Vietnam Studies Group, *Translation Stumper* (on the concept of văn minh).

78. Bradley, in "Becoming *Van Minh,*" describes how, in 1920s Vietnam, *văn minh* discourse fashioned a "radical" critique that broke with the Confucian past, encouraged democratization, and offered a liberating impulse to anticolonial movements. But the liberating potential of this discourse also contained a seed of repression. Benedict Anderson has shown how the unifying consciousness of nationalism that makes anticolonial movements possible in one moment can often turn into a stultifying, homogenizing form of nationalism in another. In the same way, the idea of a Vietnamese form of *văn minh* that proved liberating in the 1920s casts "the people" as lacking *văn minh* in the present era.

79. Đoan Trang, "Chủ tịch UBND Lê Thanh Hải."
80. Lê Thanh Hà, "Để đảm bảo an toàn cho thức ăn đường phố."
81. Thi Ngôn, "TP: Tháng cao điểm."

82. Nghĩa Nhân, "Cởi trần ra phố mới chỉ bị nhắc nhở."

83. Xuân Giang, "Văn minh đô thị!"

84. Trinh Tuan Hai, "Cởi trần ra đường bị phạt là rất hợp lý."

85. Đoan Trang, "Chủ tịch UBND TP.HCM Lê Thanh Hải."

86. Author's field notes, 2002.

87. Turner, *Dramas, Fields, and Metaphors,* 14.

Conclusion

1. Marcuse, *One-Dimensional Man,* 11.

2. Ferguson, *Expectations of Modernity,* 85.

3. Luong, *Discursive Practices and Linguistic Meanings.*

4. Hardt and Negri, *Empire.*

5. Holston, *The Modernist City,* 11.

6. Rabinow, *French Modern.*

7. Donham, *Marxist Modern.*

8. Mitchell, *Rule of Experts.*

9. Bayly, "French Anthropology and the Durkheimians in Colonial Indochina"; Nguyễn-võ Thu-hương, *The Ironies of Freedom.*

10. Holston, *The Modernist City,* 93.

11. Berman, *All That Is Solid Melts into Air,* 15.

12. Quoted in Ninh, *A World Transformed,* frontispiece.

13. Taylor, *Fragments of the Present;* Taylor, *Modernity and Re-enchantment;* Taylor, "Poor Policies, Wealthy Peasants."

14. Mills, *Thai Women in the Global Labor Force,* 14.

15. Ibid.

16. Gaonkar, *Alternative Modernities.*

17. Li Zhang, *Strangers in the City,* 312.

18. Vietnam, *A Selection of Fundamental Laws of Vietnam.*

19. Reichman, "Vietnamese Leader to Meet With Bush."

20. Bodeen, "Vietnamese PM to Talk Business in U.S."

21. Phan Van Khai, "Vietnam on the Path of Reform" (punctuation as in original).

22. Woodward, "Protests Decry Vietnam Leader's U.S. Trip."

Bibliography

Abrami, Regina, and Nolwen Henaff. "The City and the Countryside: Economy, State and Socialist Legacies in the Vietnamese Labour Market." In *Reaching for the Dream: Challenges of Sustainable Development in Vietnam,* ed. Melanie Beresford and Tran Ngoc Angie. Singapore and Copenhagen: Institute for Southeast Asian Studies and Nordic Institute for Asian Studies Press, 2004.

Anagnost, Ann. *National Past-Times: Narrative, Representation and Power in Modern China.* Durham, N.C.: Duke University Press, 1997.

Anderson, Benedict. *Imagined Communities: Reflections on the Origin and Spread of Nationalism.* New York: Verso, 1991.

Anderson, Warwick. *Colonial Pathologies: American Tropical Medicine, Race, and Hygiene in the Philippines.* Durham, N.C.: Duke University Press, 2006.

Appadurai, Arjun. "The Past as a Scarce Resource." *Man* (n.s.) 16 (1981): 201–19.

Augé, Marc. *Non-places: Introduction to an Anthropology of Supermodernity.* London: Verso, 1995.

Augustine. "Time and Eternity." In *The Confessions.* New York: Vintage, 1998 [397].

Bachelard, Gaston. *The Poetics of Space.* Boston: Beacon, 1994 [1964].

Bakhtin, M. M. *The Dialogic Imagination.* Austin: University of Texas Press, 1981.

Balaize, Claude. *Villages du Sud Viet-Nam.* Paris: L'Harmattan, Recherches Asiatiques, 1995.

Basso, Keith. "Stalking with Stories: Names, Places, and Moral Narratives among the Western Apache." In *Text, Play and Story,* ed. E. Bruner. Proceedings of the American Ethnological Society, 1984.

Bayly, Susan. "French Anthropology and the Durkheimians in Colonial Indochina." *Modern Asian Studies* 34, no. 3 (2000): 581–622.

Bélanger, Danièle, and Hong-zen Wang. "International Migrant Workers from Vietnam." In *Market Transformation, Migration and Social Protection.* Hà Nội: Thế Giới, 2008.

Beresford, Melanie. "Household and Collective in Vietnamese Agriculture." *Journal of Contemporary Asia* 15, no. 1 (1985).

Berman, Marshall. *All That Is Solid Melts into Air: The Experience of Modernity.* New York: Verso, 1983.

Bestor, Theodore. "Supply-Side Sushi: Commodity, Market, and the Global City." *American Anthropologist* 103, no. 1 (2001): 76–95.

———. *Tsukiji: The Fish Market at the Center of the World.* Berkeley: University of California Press, 2004.

Bhabha, Homi K. "Of Mimicry and Man." In *The Location of Culture.* New York: Routledge, 1994.

———. "Sly Civility." *October* 34 (1985): 71–80.

Biggs, David. "Motorized Mekong." Paper presented at a conference of the Association for Asian Studies, April 6–9, 2006, San Francisco.

Bloch, Maurice. "The Past and the Present in the Present." *Man* (n.s.) 12 (1977): 278–92.

Bộ Xây dựng [Ministry of Construction]. *Quy hoạch xây dựng các đô thị Việt Nam* [Master Building Plans for Vietnam's Urban Areas]. Hà Nội: Xây Dựng, 1999.

Bodeen, Christopher. "Vietnamese PM to Talk Business in U.S." *Washington Post,* June 17, 2005.

Bourdieu, Pierre. *Language and Symbolic Power.* Cambridge, England: Polity Press, 1991.

———. *Outline of a Theory of Practice.* Cambridge, England: Cambridge University Press, 1977.

Bradley, Mark P. "Becoming *Van Minh:* Civilizational Discourse and Visions of the Self in Twentieth-Century Vietnam." *Journal of World History* 15, no. 1 (2004): 65–83.

Bray, Francesca. *The Rice Economies: Technology and Development in Asian Societies.* Berkeley: University of California Press, 1994.

Brook, Timothy, and Hy Van Luong, eds. *Culture and Economy: The Shaping of Capitalism in Eastern Asia.* Ann Arbor: University of Michigan Press, 1999.

Bui Hoai Mai. "Introduction." In *Two Cakes Fit for a King,* ed. Nguyen Nguyet Cam and Dana Sachs. Honolulu: University of Hawaii Press, 2003.

Burlat, Anne. "Processus institutionnels et dynamiques urbaines dans l'urbanisation contemporaine de Ho Chi Minh Ville (1988–1998): Planification, production, gestion des 'secteurs d'habitat.'" Thèse de doctorat en urbanisme et aménagement, Université de Lyon II, 2001.

Butler, Judith. "Performative Acts and Gender Constitution: An Essay in Phenomenology and Feminist Theory." In *Performing Feminisms: Feminist Critical Theory and Theatre,* ed. Sue-Ellen Case. Baltimore: Johns Hopkins University Press, 1990.

Cadière, Léopold. *Croyances et pratiques religieuses des Vietnamiens.* 3 vols. Paris: École Française d'Extrême-Orient, 1958 [1944].

Caldeira, Teresa Pires do Rio. *City of Walls: Crime, Segregation, and Citizenship in São Paulo.* Berkeley: University of California Press, 2000.

———. "Fortified Enclaves: The New Urban Segregation." In *Cities and Citizenship,* ed. James Holston. Durham, N.C.: Duke University Press, 1999.

Certeau, Michel de. *The Practice of Everyday Life.* Berkeley: University of California Press, 1984.

Chae, Suhong. "Contemporary Ho Chi Minh City in Numerous Contradictions: Reform Policy, Foreign Capital and the Working Class." In *Wounded Cities: Destruction and Reconstruction in a Globalized World,* ed. Jane Schneider and Ida Susser, 227–48. New York: Berg, 2003.

Chatterjee, Partha. *The Nation and Its Fragments: Colonial and Postcolonial Histories.* Princeton, N.J.: Princeton University Press, 1993.

Chayanov, A. V., Daniel Thorner, Basile H. Kerblay, and R. E. F. Smith. *The Theory of Peasant Economy.* Homewood, Ill.: American Economic Association, 1966.

Chính phủ Việt Nam [Government of Vietnam]. "Nghị định của Chính phủ quy định chi tiết thi hành một số điều của Luật Giao thông đường bộ" [Governmental Decision Regulating the Details for Implementation of Several Articles of the Traffic Law]. Chính trị Quốc gia, Hà Nội, 2003.

Chử Văn Lâm. *Hợp tác hóa nông nghiệp Việt Nam* [Agricultural Collectivization in Vietnam]. Hà Nội: Sự Thật, 1992.

Coffyn. "Plan for a City of 500,000 Souls." In *Saigon: Mistress of the Mekong,* ed. Anastasia Edwards. New York: Oxford University Press, 2003.

Đăng Nguyên Anh. "Di dân và đô thị hóa bền vững ở Hà Nội và Thành phố Hồ Chí Minh" [Migration and Sustainable Urbanization in Hanoi and Ho Chi Minh City]. In *Đô thị hóa và vấn đề giảm nghèo ở Thành phố Hồ Chí Minh* [Urbanization and the Issue of Poverty Reduction in Ho Chi Minh City], ed. Mạc Đường, Nguyễn Thế Nghĩa, and Nguyễn Quang Vinh. Thành phố Hồ Chí Minh: Khoa Học Xã Hội, 2005.

Davis, Mike. "Fortress Los Angeles: The Militarization of Urban Space." In *Variations on a Theme Park: The New American City and the End of Public Space,* ed. Michael Sorkin. New York: Hill and Wang, 1992.

———. *Planet of Slums.* New York: Verso, 2006.

Dilthey, Wilhelm. "Awareness, Reality: Time and the Understanding of Other Persons and Their Expressions." In *The Hermeneutics Reader,* ed. Kurt Mueller-Vollmer. New York: Continuum, 1997 [1926].

Đinh Huy Liêm. "Chuyển biến của kinh tế nông hộ và kinh tế hợp tác trong nông nghiệp ngoại thành Thành phố Hồ Chí Minh, 1975–1994" [The Transformation of the Agricultural Household Economy and the Collective Economy in Ho Chi Minh City's Suburban Agriculture, 1975–1994]. Thesis, Viện Khoa học Xã hội, tại Thành phố Hồ Chí Minh, 2001.

Do Muoi. *Vietnam: New Challenges and New Opportunities.* Hanoi: The Gioi, 1995.

Đoàn Thanh Hương. *Lược sử 300 năm Sài Gòn–Thành phố Hồ Chí Minh: 1698–1998* [300 Years of Saigon-Ho Chi Minh City History: 1698–1998]. Thành phố Hồ Chí Minh: Trẻ, 1999.

Đoan Trang. "Chủ tịch UBND Lê Thanh Hải: Xây dựng Tp.HCM thành một đô thị văn minh, hiện đại" [Ho Chi Minh City People's Committee Chairman Lê Thanh Hải: Building Ho Chi Minh City into a Civilized and Modern Urban Center]. *Tuổi Trẻ,* May 1, 2003, 3.

———. "Chủ tịch UBND TP.HCM Lê Thanh Hải: 'Mọi trường hợp cố tình vi phạm xây dựng đều phải đập bỏ'" [Ho Chi Minh City People's Committee Chairman Lê Thanh Hải: All Intentional Cases of Illegal Building Need to Be Demolished], *Tuổi Trẻ,* February 12, 2003.

———. "Khu đô thị Tây Bắc Tp.HCM: Động lực để tăng tốc nền kinh tế thành phố." [The Northwest Ho Chi Minh City Urban Zone: A new motive force to speed up the City economy.] *Tuổi Trẻ,* October 2, 2002, 1, 14.

Donham, Donald. *Marxist Modern: An Ethnographic History of the Ethiopian Revolution.* Berkeley: University of California Press, 1999.

Douglas, Mary. *Purity and Danger: An Analysis of the Concepts of Pollution and Taboo.* New York: Routledge, 1991 [1966].

Drummond, Lisa and Mandy Thomas, ed. *Consuming Urban Culture in Contemporary Vietnam.* London and New York: RoutledgeCurzon, 2003.

Duiker, William J. *The Communist Road to Power in Vietnam.* 2nd ed. Boulder, Colo.: Westview, 1996 [1981].

———. *Sacred War: Nationalism and Revolution in a Divided Vietnam.* New York: McGraw-Hill, 1995.

———. *Vietnam since the Fall of Saigon.* Updated edition. Monographs in International Studies, Southeast Asia series, 56A. Athens: Ohio University Center for International Studies, 1989.

Durkheim, Émile. *The Division of Labor in Society.* Translated by W. D. Halls. New York: Free Press, 1984 [1893].

———. *The Elementary Forms of Religious Life.* Translated by Karen Fields. New York: Free Press, 1995 [1912].

Eliade, Mircea. *The Sacred and the Profane.* New York: Harvest Book, 1957.

Elias, Norbert. *The Civilizing Process.* Cambridge, Mass.: Blackwell, 1994 [1939].

———. "Time and Timing." In *On Civilization, Power, and Knowledge,* ed. Stephen Mennell and Johan Goudsblom. Chicago: University of Chicago Press, 1998.

Endres, Kirsten. "Engaging the Spirits of the Dead: Soul Calling Rituals and the Performative Construction of Efficacy." Paper presented at the conference Modernities and Dynamics of Tradition in Vietnam, Binh Chau, Vietnam, December 15–18, 2007.

Evans, Grant. *Lao Peasants under Socialism.* New Haven, Conn.: Yale University Press, 1990.

Fabian, Johannes. *Time and the Other: How Anthropology Makes Its Object.* New York: Columbia University Press, 1983.

Ferguson, James. "The Country and the City on the Copperbelt." In *Culture, Power, Place: Explorations in Critical Anthropology.* Durham, N.C.: Duke University Press, 1997.

———. *Expectations of Modernity: Myths and Meanings of Urban Life on the Zambian Copperbelt.* Berkeley: University of California Press, 1999.

Fforde, Adam. *The Agrarian Question in North Vietnam, 1974–1979: A Study of Cooperator Resistance to State Policy.* Armonk, N.Y.: M. E. Sharpe, 1989.

———. The Historical Background to Agricultural Collectivisation in North Vietnam: The Changing Role of "Corporate" Economic Power. Revised edition. Department of Economics, Birkbeck College, University of London, 1983.

Fforde, Adam, and Stefan De Vylder. *From Plan to Market: The Economic Transition in Vietnam.* Transitions—Asia and Asian America. Boulder, Colo.: Westview, 1996.

Fjelstad, Karen, and Nguyen Thi Hien. *Possessed by the Spirits: Mediumship in Contemporary Vietnamese Communities.* Ithaca, N.Y.: Cornell University Southeast Asia Program, 2006.

Foley, Duncan K. *Understanding Capital: Marx's Economic Theory.* Cambridge, Mass.: Harvard University Press, 1986.

Gainsborough, Martin. *Changing Political Economy of Vietnam: The Case of Ho Chi Minh City.* New York: RoutledgeCurzon, 2003.

Gaonkar, Dilip. *Alternative Modernities.* Durham, N.C.: Duke University Press, 2001.

Gell, Alfred. *The Anthropology of Time: Cultural Constructions of Temporal Maps and Images.* Oxford, England: Berg, 1992.

Ginsburg, Norton. "Preface." In *The Extended Metropolis: Settlement Transition in Asia,* ed. Norton Ginsburg, Bruce Koppel, and T. G. McGee, xii–xviii. Honolulu: University of Hawaii Press, 1991.

Glewwe, Paul, Nisha Agrawal, and David Dollar, eds. *Economic Growth, Poverty, and Household Welfare in Vietnam.* Regional and Sectoral Studies. Washington, D.C.: World Bank, 2004.

Godelier, Maurice. *L'idéel at le matériel.* Paris: Fayard, 1984.

———. "Objet et méthodes de l'anthropologie économique." *L'Homme* 5, no. 2 (1965): 32–91.

Goldstein, Daniel M. *The Spectacular City: Violence and Performance in Urban Bolivia.* Latin America Otherwise. Durham, N.C.: Duke University Press, 2004.

Goodman, Allan E., and Lawrence M. Franks. "The Dynamics of Migration to Saigon, 1964–1972." *Pacific Affairs* 48, no. 2 (1975): 199–214.

Gourou, Pierre. "Les paysans du delta tonkinois: Étude de geographie humaine." *Publications de l'École Française d'Extreme-Orient* 27 (1936).

Grammont, Lucien de. *Onze mois de sous-préfecture en Basse-Cochinchine.* Paris: J. Sory, 1863.

Gramsci, Antonio. *Selections from the Prison Notebooks.* New York: International Publishers, 1980 [1971].

Graw, Steve. "Nam Tien and the Development of Vietnamese Regionalism." Thesis, Cornell University, 1995.

Greene, Graham. *The Quiet American.* London: Penguin, 1973 [1955].

Greenhouse, Carol. *A Moment's Notice: Time Politics across Cultures.* Ithaca, N.Y.: Cornell University Press, 1996.

Grossheim, Martin. "The Impact of Reforms on the Agricultural Sector of Vietnam: The Land Issue." In *Vietnamese Villages in Transition,* ed. Bernhard Dham and Vincent J. Houben. Passau, Germany: Passau University Department of Southeast Asian Studies, 1999.

Gubry, Patrick, Vu Thi Hong, and Le Van Thanh. *Les chemins vers la ville: La migration vers Hô Chi Minh Ville à partir d'une zone du delta du Mékong.* Paris: Éditions KARTHALA, 2002.

Guha, Ramachandra. *The Unquiet Woods: Ecological Change and Peasant Resistance in the Himalaya.* Expanded paperback edition. Berkeley: University of California Press, 2000.

Gundar Frank, Andre. *Capitalism and Underdevelopment in Latin America.* New York: Monthly Review Press, 1967.

Gupta, Akhil. "Peasants and Environmentalism: A New Form of Governmentality?" In *Postcolonial Developments: Agriculture in the Making of Modern India,* 291–329. Durham, N.C.: Duke University Press.

Gupta, Akhil, and James Ferguson, eds. *Anthropological Locations: Boundaries and Grounds of a Field Science.* Berkeley: University of California Press, 1997.

Gurvich, G. *The Spectrum of Social Time.* Dordrecht, The Netherlands: Reidel, 1961.

H. Đ. and T. A. "Không thể tiếp tục quản lý đô thị như quản lý các làng, xã" [Cannot Continue Administering Urban Areas in the Same Way as Administering Villages and Communes]. *Tuổi Trẻ,* July 27, 1995, 1.

H. G. "TPHCM: Đề nghị thu hồi 6000ha đất xây dựng Khu công nghiệp-dân cư Tây Bắc TPHCM" [Ho Chi Minh City: Proposal to Appropriate 6000 ha to Build the Northwest Industrial–Residential Zone]. *Tuổi Trẻ,* April 24, 2003, 6.

Hãn Nguyên Nguyễn Nhã. "Các biện pháp giáo dục cụ thể về tác phong văn minh đô thị tại Việt Nam" [Concrete Educational Procedures for the Urban Lifestyle in Viet Nam]. Paper presented at Hội thảo quốc tế: Phát triển đô thị bền vững, vai trò của nghiên cứu và giáo dục [International Conference: Sustainable Urban Development, the Role of Research and Education], Thành phố Hồ Chí Minh, March 9–12, 1999.

Hardt, Michael, and Antonio Negri. *Empire.* Cambridge, Mass.: Harvard University Press, 2000.

Harms, Erik Lind. "Saigon's Edge: Transforming Time and Space on Ho Chi Minh City's Rural–Urban Margin." Dissertation, Cornell University, Ithaca, N.Y., 2006.

Harvey, David. "Between Space and Time: Reflections on the Geographical Imagination." *Annals of the Association of American Geographers* 80, no. 3 (1990): 418–34.

———. "The City as Body Politic." In *Wounded Cities: Destruction and Reconstruction in a Globalized World,* ed. Jane Schneider and Ida Susser, 25–46. New York: Berg, 2003.

———. *The Condition of Postmodernity.* Oxford, England: Basil Blackwell, 1989.

———. *The Limits to Capital.* Chicago: University of Chicago Press, 1982.

Hebdidge, Dick. *Subculture, the Meaning of Style.* London: Methuen, 1979.

Hébrard, Ernest. "L'urbanisme en Indochine." *L'Architecture* 41, no. 2 (1928): 33–49.

Henchy, Judith. "Performing Modernity in the Writings of Nguyễn An Ninh and Phan Văn Hùm." Dissertation, University of Washington, Seattle, 2005.

Herzfeld, Michael. *Anthropology through the Looking-Glass: Critical Ethnography on the Margins of Europe.* Cambridge, England: Cambridge University Press, 1987.

Hickey, Gerald C. *Village in Vietnam.* New Haven, Conn.: Yale University Press, 1964.

Hirschman, Charles, and Vu Manh Loi. "Family and Household Structure in Vietnam: Some Glimpses from a Recent Survey." *Pacific Affairs* 69, no. 2 (Summer 1996): 229–49.

Hội đồng chỉ đạo biên soạn Lịch sử Khởi nghĩa Nam kỳ [Steering Committee for Compiling the History of the Southern Uprising]. *Lịch sử Khởi nghĩa Nam kỳ* [History of the Southern Uprising]. Hà Nội: Chính Trị Quốc Gia, 2002.

Holston, James. *Insurgent Citizenship: Disjunctions of Democracy and Modernity in Brazil.* Princeton, N.J.: Princeton University Press, 2008.

——. *The Modernist City: An Anthropological Critique of Brasília.* Chicago: University of Chicago Press, 1989.

——. "Spaces of Insurgent Citizenship." In *Cities and Citizenship,* ed. James Holston, 155–73. Durham, N.C.: Duke University Press, 1999.

Holston, James, and Arjun Appadurai. "Cities and Citizenship." In *Cities and Citizenship,* ed. James Holston, 1–18. Durham, N.C.: Duke University Press, 1999.

Hoskins, Janet. *The Play of Time: Kodi Perspectives on Calendars, History, and Exchange.* Berkeley: University of California Press, 1997.

Huang, Philip. *The Peasant Economy and Social Change in North China.* Stanford, Calif.: Stanford University Press, 1985.

Hue-Tam Ho Tai, ed. *The Country of Memory: Remaking the Past in Late Socialist Vietnam.* Berkeley: University of California Press, 2001.

——. *Millenarianism and Peasant Politics in Vietnam.* Cambridge, Mass.: Harvard University Press, 1983.

——. *Radicalism and the Origins of the Vietnamese Revolution.* Cambridge, Mass.: Harvard University Press, 1992.

Huey Truong. "Tết đến, tôi càng thấy nhớ quê hương" [I Miss My Homeland Even More during Tet]. *VnExpress.net,* January 27, 2004.

Hữu Ngọc. *Từ điển văn hóa cổ truyền Việt Nam.* [Dictionary of Traditional Vietnamese Culture]. Hà Nội: Thế Giới, 2002.

Huỳnh Kim Khánh. *Vietnamese Communism.* Ithaca, N.Y.: Cornell University Press, 1982.

Huỳnh Minh. *Gia Định xưa* [Old Gia Định]. Thành phố Hồ Chí Minh: Thanh Niên, 2001 [1973].

Huỳnh Sanh Thông, ed. *An Anthology of Vietnamese Poems: From the Eleventh through the Twentieth Centuries.* New Haven, Conn.: Yale University Press, 1996.

Huỳnh Văn Giáp. "Một số vấn đề đặt ra trong tiến trình đô thị hóa nông thôn huyện Hóc Môn" [Issues Emerging in the Process of Urbanizing the Countryside in Hoc Mon District]. *Tập san khoa học Xã hội và Nhân văn* [Social Sciences and Humanities Review] 12 (1999): 64–66.

——. "Xây dựng và phát triển nông thôn trong chiến lược CNH—HĐH của 2 huyện Bình Chánh và Hóc Môn TP. HCM [Building and Developing the Countryside during the Campaign to Industrialize and Modernize the Districts of Binh Chanh and Hoc Mon]. Báo cáo khoa học [Scientific Report]. Thành phố Hồ Chí Minh: University of Social Sciences and Humanities, 2001.

Jacobs, Jane. *The Death and Life of Great American Cities.* New York: Modern Library, 1993 [1961].

Jamieson, Neil L. *Understanding Vietnam.* Berkeley: University of California Press, 1993.

Kearney, Michael. *Reconceptualizing the Peasantry.* Boulder, Colo.: Westview, 1996.

Keesing, Roger. "Theories of Culture Revisited." In *Assessing Cultural Anthropology,* ed. Robert Borofsky. New York: McGraw-Hill, 1994.

Kerkvliet, Benedict J. Tria. "Land Struggles and Land Regimes in the Philippines and Vietnam during the Twentieth Century." Wertheim Lecture Series 40. Amsterdam: Center for Asian Studies, 1997.

————. *The Power of Everyday Politics: How Vietnamese Peasants Transformed National Policy.* Ithaca, N.Y.: Cornell University Press, 2005.

————. "State–Village Relations in Vietnam: Contested Cooperatives and Collectivization." Centre of Southeast Asian Studies, Monash University, Melbourne, Australia, 1993.

Kim, Annette. *Learning to Be Capitalists: Entrepreneurs in Vietnam's Transition Economy.* New York: Oxford University Press, 2008.

Kirsch, A. Thomas. "Feasting and Social Oscillation: Religion and Society in Upland Southeast Asia." Ithaca, N.Y.: Cornell University Southeast Asia Program, 1973.

Kleinen, John. *Facing the Future, Reviving the Past: A Study of Social Change in a Northern Vietnamese Village.* Singapore: Institute of Southeast Asian Studies, 1999.

————. "Is There a Village Vietnam?" In *Vietnamese Villages in Transition,* ed. Bernhard Dham and Vincent J. Houben. Passau, Germany: Passau University Department of Southeast Asian Studies, 1999.

————. "Village as Pretext: Ethnographic Praxis and the Colonial State in Vietnam." In *The Village in Asia Revisited,* ed. Jan Breman, Ashwani Saith, and Peter Kloos, 353–95. Delhi: University of Oxford Press, 1997.

Kolko, Gabriel. *Vietnam: Anatomy of a Peace.* London: Routledge, 1997.

Kolson, Kenneth. *Big Plans: The Allure and Folly of Urban Design.* Baltimore, Md.: Johns Hopkins University Press, 2001.

Kwon, Heonik. *After the Massacre: Commemoration and Consolation in Ha My and My Lai.* Berkeley: University of California Press, 2006.

Landes, David S. *Revolution in Time: Clocks and the Making of the Modern World.* Cambridge, Mass.: Harvard University Press, 1983.

Lê Bạch Dương and Robert Bach. "Market Reforms, Social Protection and Rural–Urban Migration." In *Market Transformation, Migration and Social Protection.* Hà Nội: Thế Giới, 2008.

Le Duc Thuy. "Economic Doi Moi in Vietnam " In *Reinventing Vietnamese Socialism: Doi Moi in Comparative Perspective,* ed. William S. Turley and Mark Selden. Boulder, Colo.: Westview, 1993.

Lê Hoang. *Bản đồ Thành phố Hồ Chí Minh* [Map of Ho Chi Minh City]. Thành phố Hồ Chí Minh: Bản Đồ, 2000.

————. *Thành phố Hồ Chí Minh* [Ho Chi Minh City]. Thành phố Hồ Chí Minh: Trẻ, 2000.

Lê Như Hoa. *Quản lý văn hoá đô thị trong điều kiện công nghiệp hoá hiện đại hoá đất nước* [Managing Urban Culture in the Circumstances of Industrializing and Modernizing the Nation]. Hà Nội: Viện Văn hoá và Văn hoá–Thông tin, 2001.

Lê Quốc Sử. "Đất nước và con người (18 Thôn Vườn Trầu)" [Country and People (The 18 Betel Garden Villages)]. Self-published pamphlet, Thành phố Hồ Chí Minh, n.d.

Lê Thanh Hà. "Để đảm bảo an toàn cho thức ăn đường phố" [To Ensure the Safety of Street Food]. *Tuổi Trẻ,* September 14, 2003.

Lê Văn Chưởng. *Cơ sở văn hóa Việt Nam* [Vietnam's Cultural Basis]. Thành phố Hồ Chí Minh: Trẻ, 1999.

Lê Văn Hải. "Nạn rải đinh đã về Hóc Môn" [The Plague of Spreading Nails Has Returned to Hóc Môn]. *Tuổi Trẻ*, February 28, 2003.

Lê Văn Năm. *Nông dân ngoại thành Thành phố Hồ Chí Minh trong tiến trình đô thị hóa* [Ho Chi Minh City's Outer City Peasants in the Urbanization Process]. Thành phố Hồ Chí Minh: Tổng hợp Thành phố Hồ Chí Minh, 2007.

Leach, Edmund. *Political Systems of Highland Burma: A Study of Kachin Social Structure.* Boston: Beacon, 1964 [1954].

————. "Two Essays Concerning the Symbolic Representation of Time." In *Rethinking Anthropology.* London: Athlone, 1961.

Leaf, Michael. "Vietnam's Urban Edge: The Administration of Urban Development in Hanoi." *TWPR* 21, no. 3 (1999): 297–315.

Lefebvre, Henri. *The Production of Space.* London: Blackwell, 1991 [1974].

Levi-Strauss, Claude. "Time Regained." In *The Savage Mind.* Chicago: University of Chicago Press, 1966.

Li Zhang. *Strangers in the City: Reconfigurations of Space, Power, and Social Networks within China's Floating Population.* Stanford, Calif.: Stanford University Press, 2001.

Logan, William S. "Hanoi Townscape: Symbolic Imagery in Vietnam's Capital." In *Cultural Identity and Urban Change in Southeast Asia,* ed. Marc Askew and William S. Logan, 43–70. Victoria, Australia: Deakin University Press, 1994.

Low, Setha M. "The Edge and the Centre: Gated Communities and the Discourse of Urban Fear." *American Anthropologist* 103, no. 1 (2001): 45–58.

————. *On the Plaza: The Politics of Public Space and Culture.* Austin: University of Texas Press, 2000.

————. "Spatializing Culture: The Social Production and Social Construction of Public Space in Costa Rica." *American Ethnologist* 23, no. 4 (1996): 861–79.

————. "Urban Fear: Building the Fortress City." *City & Society* 9, no. 1 (1997): 53–71.

Luong, Hy Van. "'Brother' and 'Uncle': An Analysis of Rules, Structural Contradictions, and Meaning in Vietnamese Kinship." *American Anthropologist* 86 (1984): 290–315.

————. *Discursive Practices and Linguistic Meanings: The Vietnamese System of Person Reference.* Philadelphia: John Benjamins, 1990.

————. "The Marxist State and the Dialogic Re-stucturation of Culture in Vietnam." In *Indochina: Social and Cultural Change,* ed. David Elliot. Claremont, Calif.: Claremont McKenna College, 1994.

————. *Revolution in the Village: Tradition and Transformation in North Vietnam, 1925–1988.* Honolulu: University of Hawaii Press, 1992.

Lương Văn Hy. "Di dân từ nông thôn ra thành thị ở Việt Nam: Câu chuyện của hai miền đô thị hóa và vấn đề giảm nghèo" [Migration from the Country to the City in Vietnam: A Tale of Two Urbanizing Regions and the Problem of Poverty Reduction]. In *Đô thị hóa và văn đề giảm nghèo ở Thành phố Hồ Chí Minh* [Urbanization and the Issue of Poverty Reduction in Ho Chi Minh City], ed. Mạc Đường, Nguyễn Thế Nghĩa and Nguyễn Quang Vinh. Thành phố Hồ Chí Minh: Khoa Học Xã Hội, 2005.

———. "Thành phố Hồ Chí Minh: Vấn đề tăng trưởng kinh tế, di dân và đô thị hóa" [Ho Chi Minh City: Issues of Economic Growth, Migration, and Urbanization]. In *Đô thị hóa và văn đề giảm nghèo ở Thành phố Hồ Chí Minh* [Urbanization and the Issue of Poverty Reduction in Ho Chi Minh City], ed. Mạc Đường, Nguyễn Thế Nghĩa and Nguyễn Quang Vinh. Thành phố Hồ Chí Minh: Khoa Học Xã Hội, 2005.

Malarney, Shawn Kingsley. *Culture, Ritual and Revolution in Vietnam.* London: RoutledgeCurzon, 2002.

———. "Ritual and Revolution in Viet Nam." Dissertation, University of Michigan, Ann Arbor, 1993.

———. "Weddings and Funerals in Contemporary Vietnam." In *Vietnam: Journeys of Body, Mind, and Spirit,* ed. Nguyen Van Huy and Laurel Kendall, 173–95. Berkeley: University of California Press, 2003.

Malleret, Louis. "Éléments d'une monographie des anciennes fortifications et citadelles de Saïgon." *Bulletin de la Société des Études Indochinois, Saïgon* (1935).

Marcuse, Herbert. *One-Dimensional Man.* Boston: Beacon, 1964.

Marr, David G. *Vietnamese Tradition on Trial: 1920–1945.* Berkeley: University of California Press, 1981.

Marr, David G., and Christine P. White, eds. *Postwar Vietnam: Dilemmas in Socialist Development.* Ithaca, N.Y.: Cornell Southeast Asia Program, 1988.

Marx, Karl. *Grundrisse.* New York: Vintage Book, 1973.

———. "The Real Basis of Ideology, Division of Labour: Town and Country." In *The German Ideology.* New York: International Publishers, 1978 [1846].

Masquelier, Adeline. "Road Mythographies: Space, Mobility, and the Historical Imagination in Postcolonial Niger." *American Ethnologist* 29, no. 4 (2002): 829–56.

McAlister, John T. Jr. and Paul Mus. *The Vietnamese and Their Revolution.* New York: Harper & Row, 1970.

McGee, A. T. *The Southeast Asian City.* London: G. Bell and Sons, 1967.

McGee, T. G. "The Emergence of *Desakota* Regions in Asia: Expanding a Hypothesis." In *The Extended Metropolis: Settlement Transition in Asia,* ed. Norton Ginsburg, Bruce Koppel, and T. G. McGee. Honolulu: University of Hawaii Press, 1991.

McGee, T. G., and Ira M. Robinson. *The Mega-Urban Regions of Southeast Asia.* Vancouver: University of British Columbia Press, 1995.

Meillassoux, Claude. *Maidens, Meal, and Money: Capitalism and the Domestic Community.* Themes in the Social Sciences. Cambridge, England: Cambridge University Press, 1981.

Mills, Mary Beth. *Thai Women in the Global Labor Force.* New Brunswick, N.J.: Rutgers University Press, 1999.

Mitchell, Timothy. *Rule of Experts.* Berkeley: University of California Press, 2002.

Mumford, Lewis. *The City in History.* New York: Harcourt, Brace & World, 1961.

Munn, Nancy D. *The Fame of Gawa.* Cambridge, England: Cambridge University Press, 1986.

———. "The Cultural Anthropology of Time: A Critical Essay." *Annual Review of Anthropology* 21 (1992): 93–123.

Murray, Martin J. *Taming the Disorderly City.* Ithaca, N.Y.: Cornell University Press, 2008.

Nader, Laura. "Controlling Processes." *Essays on Controlling Processes: Kroeber Anthropological Society Papers* 77 (1994): 1–11.

Nazpary, Joma. *Post-Soviet Chaos.* London: Pluto Press, 2002.

Nghĩa Nhân. "Cởi trần ra phố mới chỉ bị nhắc nhở" [Go Shirtless Out into the Street and Only Get Reminded]. *VnExpress.net,* September 3, 2003.

———. "Đề nghị cho cấp phường xử lý vi phạm nếp sống văn minh" [Recommend Giving the Ward Level Authority to Process Urban Lifestyle Violations]. *VnExpress.net,* October 6, 2003.

Ngo Duc Thinh. "Len Dong: Spirits' Journeys." In *Vietnam: Journeys of Body, Mind, and Spirit,* ed. Nguyen Van Huy and Laurel Kendall, 253–72. Berkeley: University of California Press, 2003.

Ngo Vinh Long. *Before the Revolution: The Vietnamese Peasants under the French.* Cambridge, Mass.: MIT Press, 1973.

———. "Some Aspects of Cooperativization in the Mekong Delta." In *Postwar Vietnam: Dilemmas in Socialist Development,* ed. David G. Marr and Christine P. White. Ithaca, N.Y.: Cornell Southeast Asia Program, 1988.

Nguyen Cao Ky. *How We Lost the Vietnam War.* New York: Stein & Day, 1984.

Nguyễn Đình Đầu. "Địa lý lịch sử Thành phố Hồ Chí Minh" [Historical Geography of Ho Chi Minh City]. In *Địa lý văn hóa Thành phố Hồ Chí Minh* [Cultural Geography of Ho Chi Minh City]. Thành phố Hồ Chí Minh: Thành phố Hồ Chí Minh, 1998.

———. *From Saigon to Ho Chi Minh City: 300 Year History.* Thành phố Hồ Chí Minh: Land Service Science and Technics Publishing House, 1998.

———. *Nghiên cứu địa bạ Triều Nguyễn: Gia Định* [Cadastral Registers Study of the Nguyễn Dynasty: Gia Định]. Thành phố Hồ Chí Minh: Thành phố Hồ Chí Minh, 1994.

———. *Tổng kết nghiên cứu địa bạ Nam Kỳ Lục Tỉnh* [Completed Cadastral Registers Study of the Six Southern Provinces]. Thành phố Hồ Chí Minh: Thành phố Hồ Chí Minh, 1994.

Nguyễn Đình Lạp. *Ngoại ô* [The Outskirts]. Hà Nội: Văn Hóa Thông Tin, 1997 [1941].

Nguyen Khac Vien. *Tradition and Revolution in Vietnam.* Berkeley: Indochina Resource Center, 1974.

Nguyễn Ngọc Châu. *Quản lý đô thị* [Urban Administration]. Hà Nội: Xây Dựng, 2001.

Nguyễn Quí Đức. *Where the Ashes Are.* Reading, Mass.: Addison-Wesley, 1994.

Nguyen Van Dua. "Urban Development in Ho Chi Minh City: Strategy and Solution." Paper presented at the conference City Development Strategies: From Vision to Growth and Poverty Reduction, Hà Nội, November 24–26, 2004.

Nguyen Van Huy and Laurel Kendall. *Vietnam: Journeys of Body, Mind, and Spirit.* Berkeley: University of California Press, 2003.

Nguyễn Văn Tài. *Di dân tự do Nông thôn–thành thị ở Tp. Hồ Chí Minh* [Spontaneous Rural–Urban Migration in Ho Chi Minh City]. Thành phố Hồ Chí Minh: Nông Nghiệp, 1998.

Nguyễn Văn Tiệp et al. *Sự thích ứng của cư dân ven đô Thành phố Hồ Chí Minh với những biến đổi kinh tế—xã hội trong quá trình đô thị hóa: Trường hợp Tân Tạo* [The Adaptation of Residents on Ho Chi Minh City's Urban Fringe to the Social and Economic Transformations of the Urbanization Process: The Case of Tan Tao]. Ho Chi Minh City: Đại học Quốc gia Thành phố Hồ Chí Minh Trường Đại học KH-XH & NV, 2001.

Nguyễn Xuân Oánh. *Đổi Mới: Vài nét lớn của một chính sách kinh tế Việt Nam* [Doi Moi: Some Important Features of one of Vietnam's Economic Policies]. Thành phố Hồ Chí Minh: Thành phố Hồ Chí Minh, 2001.

Nguyễn-võ Thu-hương. "Governing the Social: Prostitution and Liberal Governance in Vietnam during Marketization." Dissertation, University of California, Irvine, 1998.

———. *The Ironies of Freedom: Sex, Culture, and Neoliberal Governance in Vietnam.* Seattle. University of Washington Press, 2008.

Như Trang. "TPHCM sẽ chấm dứt nạn đua xe trong năm nay" [Ho Chi Minh City Will Bring the Evil of Motorbike Racing to an End This Year]. *VnExpress.net,* February 27, 2003.

Ninh, Kim N. B. *A World Transformed: The Politics of Culture in Revolutionary Vietnam, 1945–1965.* Ann Arbor: University of Michigan Press, 2002.

Norindr, Panivong. *Phantasmatic Indochina: French Colonial Ideology in Architecture, Film, and Literature.* Durham, N.C.: Duke University Press, 1996.

Ong, Aihwa. *Spirits of Resistance and Capitalist Discipline: Factory Women in Malaysia.* Albany: State University of New York, 1987.

Orwell, George. *The Road to Wigan Pier.* Harcourt Brace & Co., 1958.

Parenteau, René, ed. *Habitat et environnement urbain au Viêt-nam: Hanoi et Hô Chi Minh-Ville.* Paris: Éditions Karthala, 1997.

Pelley, Patricia M. *Postcolonial Vietnam: New Histories of the National Past.* Durham, N.C.: Duke University Press, 2002.

Peycam, Phillipe. "Saigon, des origines à 1859." In *Saigon, 1698–1998: Architectures/Urbanisme,* ed. Lê Quang Ninh and Stéphane Dovert. Ho Chi Minh City: Nha Xuat Ban Thanh Pho Ho Chi Minh, 1998.

Pham Thu Thuy. "Speaking Pictures: *Biem Hoa* or Satirical Cartoons on Government Corruption and Popular Political Thought in Contemporary Vietnam." In *Consuming Urban Culture in Contemporary Vietnam,* ed. Lisa Drummond and Mandy Thomas. New York: RoutledgeCurzon, 2003.

Phạm Văn Đồng. *Culture and Renovation.* Hà Nội: Thế Giới, 2002.

Phan Thị Yến Tuyết. "Một số hình thức thờ cúng tổ tiên của các dòng họ cư dân Việt tại Thành phố Hồ Chí Minh" [Aspects of Ancestor Worship among Viet Migrant Lineages in Ho Chi Minh City]. In *Sài Gòn—TP.Hồ Chí Minh thế kỷ XX* [20th-Century Ho Chi Minh City]. Thành phố Hồ Chí Minh: Trẻ, 2000.

Phan Van Khai. "Vietnam on the Path of Reform." *Washington Times,* June 21, 2005.

Phúc Huy. "TP.HCM: Nỗi lo . . . nhà siêu mỏng" [Ho Chi Minh City: Worried Feelings . . . Super Thin Houses]. *Tuổi Trẻ,* December 10, 2004.

Pina-Cabral, João de. "Paved Roads and Enchanted Mooresses: The Perception of the Past among the Peasant Population of the Alto Minho." *Man* 22, no. 4 (1987): 715–35.

Polanyi, Karl. *The Great Transformation: The Political and Economic Origins of Our Time.* Boston: Beacon Hill, 1944.

Popkin, Samuel. *The Rational Peasant.* Berkeley: University of California Press, 1979.

Porter, Gareth. *Vietnam: The Politics of Bureaucratic Socialism.* Politics and International Relations of Southeast Asia. Ithaca, N.Y.: Cornell University Press, 1993.

Quach Thanh Tam-Langlet. "Saïgon, capitale de la République du Sud-Viêtnam (1954–1975) ou une urbanisation sauvage" [Saigon, Capitol of the Republic of South Vietnam (1954–1975), or a Savage Urbanization]. In *Péninsules Indochinoises, études urbaines.* Paris: L'Harmattan, 1991.

Quang Truong. "Agricultural Collectivization and Rural Development in Vietnam: A North/South Study (1955–1985)." Dissertation, Free University of Amsterdam, 1987.

Rabinow, Paul. *French Modern: Norms and Forms of the Social Environment.* Chicago: University of Chicago Press, 1989.

Rambo, A. Terry. "A Comparison of Peasant Social Systems of Northern and Southern Vietnam: A Study of Ecological Adaptation, Social Succession and Cultural Evolution." Dissertation, University of Hawaii, 1972.

Rambo, A. Terry, and Neil L. Jamieson. *Cultural Change in Rural Vietnam: A Study of the Effects of Long-term Communist Control on the Social Structure, Attitudes, and Values of the Peasants of the Mekong Delta.* New York: Southeast Asia Development Advisory Group of the Asia Society, 1973.

Redfield, Robert. *The Little Community: Viewpoints for a Study of a Human Whole.* Chicago: University of Chicago Press, 1955.

Reichman, Deb. "Vietnamese Leader to Meet with Bush."*Washington Post,* June 21, 2005.

Rey, Pierre Philippe. "The Lineage Mode of Production." *Critique of Anthropology* 3 (1975): 27–79.

Rifkin, Jeremy. *Time Wars: The Primary Conflict in Human History.* New York: Touchstone, 1987.

Rigg, Jonathan. *Southeast Asia: The Human Landscape of Modernization and Development.* New York: Routledge, 1997.

Robert, Christophe. "'Social Evils' and the Question of Youth in Post-War Saigon." Dissertation, Cornell University, Ithaca, N.Y., 2005.

Rose, Sonya. "Class Formation and the Quintessential Worker." In *Reworking Class,* ed. John Hall, 1997.

Roseberry, William. *Anthropologies and Histories: Essays in Culture, History, and Political Economy.* New Brunswick, N.J.: Rutgers University Press, 1989.

———. *Coffee and Capitalism in the Venezuelan Andes.* Austin: University of Texas Press, 1983.

Roseman, Sharon. "'How We Built the Road': The Politics of Memory in Rural Galicia." *American Ethnologist* 23, no. 4 (1996): 836–60.

Sahlins, Marshall. *Stone-Age Economics.* Chicago: Aldine, 1972.

Saigon Times. "The Start of Mammoth Projects: The Trans-Asia Highway Will Facil-
itate Regional Transport and Cooperation." *Saigon Times Magazine,* March 29,
2000.

Sangren, P. Steven. *History and Magical Power in a Chinese Community.* Stanford,
Calif.: Stanford University Press, 1987.

Sassen, Saskia. *Cities in a World Economy.* Thousand Oaks, Calif.: Pine Forge
Press, 1994.

Sayer, Derek. "Ideal Superstructures." In *The Violence of Abstraction.* Oxford, England: Blackwell, 1989.

Schneider, Jane, and Ida Susser, eds. *Wounded Cities: Destruction and Reconstruction in a Globalized World.* New York: Berg, 2003.

Scott, James. *The Moral Economy of the Peasant.* New Haven, Conn.: Yale University Press, 1976.

———. *Seeing Like a State: How Certain Schemes to Improve the Human Condition Have Failed.* New Haven, Conn.: Yale University Press, 1998.

———. *Weapons of the Weak: Everyday Forms of Peasant Resistance.* New Haven,
Conn.: Yale University Press, 1985.

Sheller, Mimi, and John Urry. "The City and the Car." *International Journal of
Urban and Regional Research* 24, no. 4 (2000): 737–57.

Sơn Nam. "18 Thôn Vườn Trầu" [The 18 Betel Garden Villages]. In *Bến Nghé xưa*
[Old Ben Nghe]. Thành phố Hồ Chí Minh: Văn Nghệ, 1992.

Stoler, Ann Laura. *Carnal Knowledge and Imperial Power: Race and the Intimate
in Colonial Rule.* Berkeley: University of California Press, 2002.

Stoler, Ann Laura, Carole McGranahan, and Peter Perdue. *Imperial Formations.* Advanced Seminar Series. Santa Fe, N.M.: School for Advanced Research Press, 2007.

T. Đ. "Nhà nghỉ ven đô—điểm hẹn của các cặp tình nhân" [Hotels on the Urban
Fringe—Where Lovers Meet]. *VnExpress.net,* August 24 2003.

Tana, Li. *Peasants on the Move: Rural–Urban Migration in the Hanoi Region.* Singapore: *Institute of Southeast Asian Studies,* 1996.

Taylor, Keith W. "Surface Orientations in Vietnam: Beyond Histories of Nation and
Region." *Journal of Asian Studies* 57, no. 4 (1998): 949–78.

Taylor, Philip. *Fragments of the Present: Searching for Modernity in Vietnam's
South.* Honolulu: University of Hawaii Press, 2001.

———. *Goddess on the Rise: Pilgrimage and Popular Religion in Vietnam.* Honolulu: University of Hawaii Press, 2004.

———. *Modernity and Re-enchantment: Religion in Post-revolutionary Vietnam.*
Singapore: Institute of Southeast Asian Studies, 2007.

———. "Poor Policies, Wealthy Peasants: Alternative Trajectories of Rural Development in Vietnam." *Journal of Vietnamese Studies* 2, no. 2 (2007): 3–56.

———. "Social Inequality in a Socialist State." In *Social Inequality in Vietnam and
the Challenges to Reform,* ed. Philip Taylor, 1–40. Singapore: *Institute of Southeast Asian Studies,* 2004.

ThangbomVN. 2003. "Hóc hay Hốc?" [Hoc or Hoc?]. In *Đặc trưng phố rùm* [Spe-
cifics Forum]. http://dactrung.net/phorum/printable.aspx?m=34643&mpage=5.
Accessed 2006.

Thi Ngôn. "TP: Tháng cao điểm: 'Vì TP văn minh—chào đón SEA Games 22'" [City: Peak Month: "For the Civilized City—Greeting the 22nd SEA Games]. *Tuổi Trẻ,* November 17, 2003.

Thomas, Mandy. "Out of Control: Emergent Cultural Landscapes and Political Change in Urban Vietnam." *Urban Studies* 34, no. 9 (2002): 1611–24.

Thompson, E. P. "Time, Work Discipline and Industrial Capitalism." *Past and Present* 38 (December 1967): 56–97.

Thongchai Winichakul. "The Quest for *'Siwilai'*: A Geographical Discourse of Civilizational Thinking in the Late Nineteenth and Early Twentieth-Century Siam." *Journal of Asian Studies* 59, no. 3 (2000): 528–49.

———. *Siam Mapped: A History of the Geo-Body of a Nation.* Honolulu: University of Hawaii Press, 1994.

Thrift, Nigel, and Dean Forbes. *The Price of War: Urbanization in Vietnam: 1954–1985.* London: Allen & Unwin, 1986.

Thủ Tướng Chính Phủ [Prime Minister]. "Quyết định số 195/2001/QĐ–TTg Ngày 26-12-2001 của Thủ tướng Chính phủ về việc thành lập Ban Chủ nhiệm Chương trình phòng, chống tai nạn, thương tích" [Prime Minister's Decision no. 195/2001/QĐ–TTg 26 December 2001 on the Establishment of a Directory Committee for the Program to Prevent and Fight against Accidents and Injuries]. In *Luật Giao thông đường bộ biển báo và các văn bản hướng dẫn thi hành* [Law on Traffic and Signage and the Acts Related to Guiding Their Implementation]. Hà Nội: Giao Thông Vân Tải, 2002 [2001].

———. "Quyết Định Số 197/2001/QĐ–TTg Ngày 27-12-2001 của Thủ tướng Chính phủ về việc phê duyệt Chính sách Quốc gia phòng, chống tai nạn, thương tích giai đoạn 2002–2010" [Prime Minister's Decision no. 197/2001/QĐ–TTg 27 December 2001 on the Approval of National Policies to Program to Prevent and Fight against Accidents and Injuries for the Period 2002–2010]. In *Luật Giao thông đường bộ biển báo và các văn bản hướng dẫn thi hành* [Law on Traffic and Signage and the Acts Related to Guiding Their Implementation]. Hà Nội: Giao Thông Vân Tải, 2002 [2001].

To Duy Hop. "Some Characteristics of the Changing Social Structure in Rural Vietnam under Doi Moi." *Sojourn* 10, no. 2 (1995): 280–300.

Toan Ánh. *Làng xóm Việt Nam* [The Vietnamese Village]. Thành phố Hồ Chí Minh: Thành phố Hồ Chí Minh, 1999.

Tôn Nữ Quỳnh Trân. "Quan hệ dòng tộc trước chuyển động đô thị hóa tại thành phố Hồ Chí Minh" [Kinship Relations in the Face of Ho Chi Minh City's Urban Transformation]. In *Sài Gòn–TP.Hồ Chí Minh thế kỷ XX* [Saigon–Ho Chi Minh City in the 20th Century]. Thành phố Hồ Chí Minh: Trẻ, 2000.

———. *Văn hóa làng xã: Trước sự thách thức của đô thị hóa tại Thành phố Hồ Chí Minh* [Village Culture Facing the Challenge of Urbanization in Ho Chi Minh City]. Thành phố Hồ Chí Minh: Trẻ, 1999.

Trần Hồng Vân. *Tác động xã hội của di cư tự do vào Thành phố Hồ Chí Minh trong thời kỳ Đổi Mới* [The Social Impact of Spontaneous Migration into Ho Chi Minh City during the Doi Moi Period]. Thành phố Hồ Chí Minh: Khoa Học Xã Hội, 2002.

Trần Ngọc Thêm. *Cơ sở văn hóa Việt Nam* [Vietnam's Cultural Basis]. Thành phố Hồ Chí Minh: Giáo Dục, 1999.

Tran Thi Que. *Vietnam's Agriculture.* Singapore: Institute of Souteast Asian Studies, 1998.

Trần Văn Bính. *Văn Hóa trong quá trình Đô thị hóa ở nước ta hiện nay* [Culture within Our Country's Current Urbanization Process]. Hà Nội: Chính Trị Quốc Gia, 1998.

Trần Văn Điệu. "Những vấn đề đặt ra trong quá trình đô thị hóa Quận Gò Vấp— Thành phố Hồ Chí Minh" [Problems Arising in the Process of Urbanizing Go Vap District in Ho Chi Minh City]. In *Làng xã ở Châu Á và ở Việt Nam* [Villages in Asia and Vietnam]. Thành phố Hồ Chí Minh: Thành phố Hồ Chí Minh, 1995.

Trinh Tuan Hai. "Cởi trần ra đường bị phạt là rất hợp lý" [It Makes Sense to Fine People for Going Shirtless Out on the Street]. *VnExpress.net,* August 15, 2003.

Trouillot, Michel-Rolph. *Peasants and Capital: Dominica in the World Economy.* Baltimore: Johns Hopkins University Press, 1988.

———. *Silencing the Past: Power and the Production of History.* Boston: Beacon, 1995.

Truong Chinh and Vo Nguyen Giap. *The Peasant Question.* Translated by Christine Pelzer White. Ithaca, N.Y.: Cornell University Southeast Asia Program, 1974 [1937–38].

Tsing, Anna. "From the Margins." *Cultural Anthropology* 9, no. 3 (1994): 279–97.

Tự Trung. "Công trình đường Xuyên Á: Nhiều tai nạn giao thông chết người do thi công" [Trans-Asia Highway Project: Many Deadly Traffic Accidents Due to Construction]. *Tuổi Trẻ,* October 25, 2003.

Tự Trung and Thanh Tòng. "Đường Xuyên Á đang thi công: Đoạn trường . . . ai có qua đường mới hay!" [Constructing the Trans-Asia Highway . . . Clever Is the One Who Can Cross the Road!]. *Tuổi Trẻ,* October 2, 2002, 6.

Tuổi Trẻ. "Đường lên thiên đàng" [The Road to Paradise]. *Tuổi Trẻ,* May 30, 2002, 11.

Turley, William S. "Urban Transformation in South Vietnam." *Pacific Affairs* 49, no. 4 (Winter1976): 607–24.

Turley, William S., and Mark Selden. *Reinventing Vietnamese Socialism: Doi Moi in Comparative Perspective.* Boulder, Colo.: Westview, 1993.

Turner, Terence. "Production, Value, and Structure in Marx: New Interpretations of the Central Concepts of Marxian Political Economy and Some Implications for Anthropology." Paper presented at the Annual Meeting of the American Anthropological Association, Denver, 1984.

———. "Social Body and Embodied Subject: Bodiliness, Subjectivity and Sociality among the Kayapo." *Cultural Anthropology* 10, no. 2 (1995): 143–70.

———. "Social Complexity and Recursive Hierarchy in Indigenous South American Societies." *Journal of the Steward Anthropological Society* 24, no. 1–2 (1997): 37–60.

———. "Theses on the Form of a Marxian Anthropology." 1985.

———. "Transformation, Hierarchy and Transcendence: A Reformulation of Van Gennep's Model of the Structure of Rites de Passage." In *Secular Ritual,* ed. S. F. Moore and B. Meyerhoff, 53–70. Amsterdam: Van Gorcum, 1977.

———. "Value, Production, and Exploitation in Non-capitalist Societies." Paper presented at the Culture and Historical Materialism symposium at the Annual Meeting of the American Anthropological Association, 1984. Denver.

Turner, Victor. *Dramas, Fields, and Metaphors: Symbolic Action in Human Society.* Ithaca, N.Y.: Cornell University Press, 1974.

———. *The Forest of Symbols: Aspects of Ndembu Ritual.* Ithaca, N.Y.: Cornell University Press, 1967.

Vasavakul, Thaveeporn. "Vietnam: The Changing Models of Legitimation." In *Political Legitimacy in Southeast Asia: The Quest for Moral Authority,* ed. Muthia Alagappa. Stanford, Calif.: Stanford University Press, 1995.

Viện Ngôn ngữ học. *Từ điển Việt-Anh* [Viet–English Dictionary]. Thành phố Hồ Chí Minh: Thành phố Hồ Chí Minh, 1997.

Viện Sử học. *Đô thị cổ Việt Nam* [Vietnam Ancient Cities]. Hà Nội: Uỷ Ban Khoa Học Xã Hội Việt Nam, 1989.

Vietnam, Socialist Republic of. *A Selection of Fundamental Laws of Vietnam.* Hanoi: Thế Giới, 2001.

Vietnam News Service. "Trans-Asia Highway Becomes Nightmare for Southern Vietnamese." *Việt Nam News,* April 14, 2004. Originally published in *HCM City Women,* April 12, 1).

Vietnam Studies Group. 2003. Translation Stumper (on the concept of văn minh). In *Archives of Previous Discussions on the VSG Email Discussion List,* ed. Judith Henchy. University of Washington Libraries. http://www.lib.washington.edu/SouthEastAsia/vsg/elist_2003/Translation%20stumper.html. Accessed 2006.

Viollis, Andrée. *Indochine S.O.S.* Paris: Gallimard, 1935.

VnExpress. "Mua đất vùng Ngã Ba Giồng" [Buying Land in the Giồng Triple Intersection Area]. From an article in Sài Gòn Tiếp Thị. *VnExpress.net,* March 2, 2002.

———. "Mua đất vùng Tân Xuân–Bùi Môn" [Buying Land in the Tan Xuan–Bui Mon Area]. *VnExpress.net,* March 3, 2002.

———. "Nhiều hộ dân TP HCM đang uống nước từ nghĩa địa" [Many families in Ho Chi Minh City Are Drinking Water from Cemeteries]. *VnExpress.net,* July 20, 2002.

———. "Ô nhiễm nguồn nước do nghĩa địa tự phát ở TP HCM" [Spontaneously Built Cemeteries Pollute Water Sources in Ho Chi Minh City]. *VnExpress.net,* May 27, 2003.

———. "Quy hoạch chi tiết quận Thanh Xuân" [Zoning the Details of Thanh Xuân District]. *VnExpress.net,* May 16, 2001.

———. "Sắp có đô thị xanh ven sông Sài Gòn–Rạch Tra" [Soon to Have a Green Urban Zone on the Edge of the Saigon River–Tra Canal]." *VnExpress.net,* September 22, 2002.

———. "Thùy Dung: 'Nghệ thuật không phức tạp hơn ngành khác'" [Thuy Dung: "Art Is No More Complicated than Any Other Profession"]. *VnExpress.net,* October 3, 2004.

Vo-Nhan-Tri. "Party Politics and Economic Performance: The Second and Third Five-Year Plans Examined." In *Postwar Vietnam: Dilemmas in Socialist Development,* ed. David G. Marr and Christine P. White. Ithaca, N.Y.: Cornell Southeast Asia Program, 1988.

Waibel, Michael. "The Production of Urban Space in Vietnam's Metropolis in the Course of Transition: Internationalization, Polarization and Newly Emerging Lifestyles in Vietnamese Society." *Trialog* 89, no. 2 (2006): 43–48.

Waibel, Michael, Ronald Eckert, Michael Bose, and Volker Martin. "Housing for Low-Income Groups in Ho Chi Minh City: Between Reintegration and Fragmentation." *ASIEN* 103, no. April (2007): 59–78.

Wallerstein, Immanuel Maurice. *The End of the World as We Know It: Social Science for the Twenty-first Century.* Minneapolis: University of Minnesota Press, 1999.

———. *The Modern World-System.* Studies in Social Discontinuity. New York: Academic Press, 1974.

Watts, Michael. "Agrarian Thermidor: Rural Dynamics and the Agrarian Question in Vinh Phu Province, Vietnam." Berkeley: Institute of International Studies, University of California, 1995.

Weber, Max. *Sociological Writings.* Edited by Wolf Heydebrand. *The German Library,* Vol. 60. New York: Continuum, 1999.

Werner, Jayne, and Daniele Belanger. *Gender, Household, State: Doi Moi in Viet Nam.* Ithaca, N.Y.: Cornell University Southeast Asia Program, 2002.

Werth, Léon. *Cochinchine.* Paris: Éditions Viviane Hamy, 2005 [1926].

White, Christine Pelzer. "Alternative Approaches to the Socialist Transformation of Agriculture in Postwar Vietnam." In *Postwar Vietnam: Dilemmas in Socialist Development,* ed. David G. Marr and Christine P. White. Ithaca, N.Y.: Cornell Southeast Asia Program, 1988.

Wilk, Richard R. *Economies and Cultures: Foundations of Economic Anthropology.* Boulder, Colo.: Westview, 1996.

Williams, Raymond. *The Country and the City.* New York: Oxford University Press, 1973.

Wolf, Eric. "Closed Corporate Peasant Communities in MesoAmerica and Java." *Southwestern Journal of Anthropology* 13 (1957).

———. *Peasant Wars of the Twentieth Century.* New York: Harper & Row, 1969.

———. *Peasants.* Englewood Cliffs, N.J.: Prentice-Hall, 1966.

Wolf, Margery. "Child Training and the Chinese Family." In *Family and Kinship in Chinese Society,* ed. Ai-li S. Chin and Maurice Freedman. Stanford, Calif.: Stanford University Press, 1970.

———. *Women and the Family in Rural Taiwan.* Stanford, Calif.: Stanford University Press, 1972.

Wood, Ellen Meiksins. *The Origin of Capitalism.* New York: Monthly Review Press, 1999.

Woodside, Alexander. *Community and Revolution in Modern Vietnam.* Boston: Houghton Mifflin, 1976.

———. "Peasant and the State in the Aftermath of the Vietnamese Revolution." *Peasant Studies* 16, no. 4 (1989).

Woodward, Curt. "Protests Decry Vietnam Leader's U.S. Trip." *Washington Post,* June 19, 2005.

Wright, Gwendolyn. *The Politics of Design in French Colonial Urbanism.* Chicago: University of Chicago Press, 1991.

Wust, Sébastien, Jean-Claude Bolay, and Thai Thi Ngoc Du. "Metropolization and the Ecological Crisis: Precarious Settlements in Ho Chi Minh City, Vietnam." *Environment and Urbanization* 14, no. 2 (2002): 211–24.

Xuân Giang. "Văn minh đô thị!" [Urban Civilization!]. *Tuổi Trẻ,* April 3, 2004.

Young, Marilyn B. *The Vietnam Wars: 1945–1990.* New York: HarperPerennial, 1991.

Index

ADB (Asian Development Bank), 155–56, 171

agency and Trans-Asia Highway, 155, 157, 159, 185

agriculture/farmers, 11, 210; agricultural distribution centers and, 14; historical past and, 102–3; industrial, 6, 10; land use and, 18, 72, 245n17; linear time and, 98, 99, 100–101, 102; mixed-use spaces and, 30, 44–46; modernization and, 13–14; peasant-based production contract system and, 200, 256n25; social hierarchical contradictory models and, 201, 256n30; socialist time and, 107; social reproduction and, 130; "social time" and, 98–100, 101–3, 114, 247n21; urbanization effects on, 9–10

âm/dương (yin/yang) complementary oppositions, 21–22, 39, 41–42, 203–4, 241n56

Americans. See United States/Americans

Anagnost, Ann, 259n76

"antisocial" space, 175–81, 253n28

ấp (hamlets) subdivisions, 9, 17, 163–64, 238

ASEAN (Association of Southeast Asian Nations), 156, 203, 238

Augustine, 92–93

Bachelard, Gaston, 121, 122, 123, 150–51

Bà Điểm commune, 16, 29, 33, 58, 62, 89

being behind/catching up, 112–13

Berman, Marshall, 230

bồ hòn (soapberry) metaphor, sucking the, 31–35, 46, 225, 242n5

Bourdieu, Pierre, 84, 186, 242n10, 245n5

Butler, Judith, 55

cafés, 71–72, 127, 129, 132–33, 160, 168, 244n40, 246n18, 249n7

catching up/being behind, 112–13

Certeau, Michel de, 22–25

Chayanov, A. V., 133–35

China, 8, 106, 228, 233, 244n51, 255n9, 259n76

city "walls and streets": thành phố, 37, 38, 52, 240; thành thị, 37

civility/civilization/civilized (văn minh), 174, 211–13

"civilized urban lifestyle"/urban intellectuals. See civilizing rhetoric; inner-city districts

civilizing rhetoric, 193, 259n76; country/city categories and, 13, 229; education and, 213, 258n70; security/civilization problem and, 11, 203–11, 205–8, 209, 229, 257n47, 257n55, 257n56; socialist policies and, 199; spatial transformations and, 189–92; traffic and, 191, 254n45; "urban civilization" and, 215–18, 259nn74–78; urban civilization on Saigon's edge and, 195–96, 197,

210, 212–15, 255n9, 258n63, 258nn70–72
clock time. *See* linear time
coffee-drinking customs, 127, 129, 249n7. *See also* cafés
Communist Party (the party): Fatherland Front and, 107, 193–94, 254n1, 258n71; historical past and, 103–7; progress and, 103–4, 107–8, 111–14; social change and, 104, 125; teleology of socialist policies and, 108, 110; urbanization and, 105–6
công nghiệp hóa (industrialization). *See* industrialization
country/city categories (rural/urban ideal), 2, 19–25, 37–40, 39, 237, 241n50, 242n12, 243n18; civilizing rhetoric and, 13, 229; factory labor force and, 139; Ho Chi Minh City/Saigon and, 2–4, 30, 37–40, 38–39, 242nn10–12, 243n18; ideal representations and, 5, 215, 222; identity construction and, 5, 24–25; industrialization and, 40; material world and, 5, 24–25, 225; power/exclusion on the edge and, 61, 62; productive binaries and, 221–23; rural-to-urban migration and, 42–43, 48; Saigon's edge and, 2, 9–11; social edginess and, 2, 36; social experiences and, 2, 5, 6, 24–26, 77, 83, 84; social hierarchies and, 115–16, 199–201, 248n51, 255n21, 256n25, 256n28, 256n30; socialist policies and, 241n50; social production and, 7; social space and, 5, 77, 222–23, 246n21; "social time" and, 116–19; spatiotemporal oscillation and, 121–23, 150, 224; state/nation and, 40–41, 199–201; *Tân Thới Nhì* and, 17; universal particularity of, 5–6, 5–9, 8–9, 239nn13–14; urban civilization on Saigon's edge and, 201–3, 211, 256nn33–34; urbanization and,

29–30, 37–49, 242nn10–12, 243n18. *See also* peasant ideal representations
culture and education level *(văn hóa),* 21, 213, 258n72
cyclical time, 101–3, 124, 247n28, 248n35

đất hoang (wasteland), 3, 18, 53, 106
Davis, Mike, 3
désakota (rural-urban interface zones), 44, 63, 65, 77, 245n7
despair/opportunities, 30, 64–69, 79–80, 82–85, 128
destruction/reconstruction: and spatial transformations, 171–82, 184–85, 229–32
development *(phát triển):* being behind/catching up/promise of, 114–16; double edge of, 171–75, 184–85, 231, 253n28; future-oriented trajectory of, 24, 90–91, 114–16; historical past and, 104–5; Ho Chi Minh City/Saigon and, 106, 205, 208, 257n44, 257n56; infrastructure and, 44, 47–48, 112–13, 165, 184–92, 202–3; linear time and, 107–8; peoples' agreement/disagreement about progress and, 111–12; social edginess and, 24; social hierarchies and, 115–16; socialist policies and, 104, 105–6, 229–30; socialist time and, 103–7; "social time" and, 90, 91, 93; teleology of, 174; urbanization and, 105. *See also* Trans-Asia Highway
Dilthey, Wilhelm, 92
District 12, inner-city, 9, 34, 42
đổi mới (renovation and political/economic reforms in 1986), 111, 165, 170, 200, 210, 235
đô thị hóa (urbanization). *See* urbanization
Douglas, Mary, 61, 68
Durkheim, Émile, 68, 188, 202, 228

economics: about activities, 14–17, 241n41; peasant-based production contract system and, 200, 256n25; renovation and political/economic reforms in 1986 and, 111, 165, 170, 200, 210, 235; Saigon's edge/double edge and, 47–49, 233; social edginess and, 68–79; social networking and, 74–75, 168, 246n18; space/spatial relationships and, 78, 79–84. *See also* market economy with socialist direction

edge, the, 4–5, 55–59, 114, 221–25. *See also* Saigon's edge; social edginess

education, 21, 69–70, 71–73, 213, 258n70, 258n72

education level and culture *(văn hóa)*, 21, 213, 258n72

Elias, Norbert, 96, 193

emigrant laborers overseas, 140–41, 250n19

Evans, Grant, 196

everyday realities. *See* social experiences

exclusion/power on the edge. *See* power/exclusion on the edge

factory labor force, 135–42, 237–38

farmers. *See* agriculture/farmers

Fatherland Front (the Front), 107, 193–94, 254n1, 258n71

Ferguson, James, 7, 221, 222–23

fieldwork, 15, 89, 193–95, 251n3

folk structuralism theorization: late socialism and, 233–35; market economy and, 236–37; modernism and, 228–33; postmodernism and, 226–27, 229; poststructuralism and, 226; productive binaries and, 225–26, 232–33; structuralism and, 227–28

French colonialism, 1, 11, 29, 104, 106, 205–8, 229, 257n47, 257n56

future-oriented trajectory of development, 24, 90–91, 114–16

future/past social oscillation, 85, 91

Gell, Alfred, 89, 92, 247n4

gendered space. *See* men/gendered male space; women/gendered female space

Gia Định province, 11, 205

globalization, 3–4, 229, 235–37, 239n13

Gourou, Pierre, 163, 252n8

Grammont, Lucien de, 11–12, 14, 26, 206–7, 211

greenbelt space, 14, 29, 30, 53, 205, 210

Greenhouse, Carol, 96, 108

Gurvich, G., 98, 99

hamlets *(ấp)* subdivisions, 9, 17, 163–64, 238

Hanoi, 8, 64–65, 105, 199, 216, 218

Harvey, David, 36, 94, 122, 168, 239n14, 247n8, 253n33

Hébrard, Ernest, 205, 211

Herzfeld, Michael, 25

Hickey, Gerald, 163, 164, 241n50, 251n5

Highway 22: modernization and, 174; roads and, 158, 162–64, 168, 251n5; social action observed on, 160–62; social space in village organization and, 162–63, 251n6; "social time" and, 90; transformation of, 155–56, 158. *See also* roads; traffic; Trans-Asia Highway

historical past: agriculture and, 102–3; Communist Party and, 103–7; development and, 104–5; edge in, 11–13, 18–19, 241n17; future/past social oscillation and, 85, 91; material world and, 104–5: progress and, 105; social change and, 6; socialist policies and, 105; social oscillation and, 118–19; "social time" and, 90, 92, 97, 102–3; southern Vietnam and, 117; space/time relationships and, 117–18; urbanization and, 29, 34, 106–7, 242n6

Hồ Chí Minh, 155
Ho Chi Minh City People's Committee, 210–11, 216
Ho Chi Minh City/Saigon, 37–38, 42, 105–6; country/city categories and, 2–4, 30, 37–40, 242nn10–12, 243n18; development and, 106, 205, 208, 257n44, 257n56; districts and, 9, 240n28; economic paradox of edge and, 48–49; greenbelt spaces and, 210; inside/outside categories and, 1–2, 37–38, 242n11; kinship relations with inside/outside idiom and, 51, 52–53, 244n48, 244n51; mixed-use spaces and, 45–47; security/civilization problem and, 203–11, 205, 209, 257n47, 257n55, 257n56; socialist policies and, 105–6; social oscillation and, 1; space/spatial relationships and, 37, 51, 52–53, 242nn10–11, 244n48, 244n51; urbanization/stretched ideal and, 42–43, 243n25; yin/yang complementary cultural system and, 39, 41–42. See also Hóc Môn district; Saigon's edge; urban civilization on Saigon's edge
Hóc Môn district: description of, 9–11, 18–19, 237–38, 240nn28–29; history of, 31–32; map, 12; modernization and, 13–16; social oscillation and, 1; statistics, 9–10, 240nn31–32. See also Ho Chi Minh City/Saigon; Tân Thới Nhì
Holston, James, 8, 221, 229
huyện ngoại thành (outer-city districts). See outer-city districts
Huỳnh Kim Khánh, 198, 255n21
Huỳnh Văn Giáp, 18, 110, 197, 240n31

ideal representations, 222; country/city categories and, 5, 215, 222; inside/outside categories and, 2–4, 18–19, 72–73, 222, 245n17;

power/exclusion on the edge and, 25, 62–63, 79, 84, 245n5; Saigon's edge and, 2; social edginess and, 25, 30, 35, 36, 84; social experiences and, 22–23, 26, 50, 62–63. See also peasant ideal representations
identity construction, 5, 24–25, 55–57
industrialization (công nghiệp hóa), 15–16; country/city categories and, 40; peoples' agreement/disagreement about progress and, 107–8, 112; socialist policies and, 194, 196, 199–201; urban civilization on Saigon's edge and, 203, 211; urban morphology and, 165
infrastructure development, 44, 47–48, 112–13, 165, 184–92, 202–3. See also development; Trans-Asia Highway
inner-city districts (quận nội thành): country/city categories and outer-city relationships with, 40–41; edge production and outer-city relationships with, 57; greenbelt spaces and outer-city relationships with, 14, 205; modernity and outer-city relationships with, 118; outer-city districts separated/linked with, 53–55; outer-city relationships with, 2, 37; outer-city separated/linked with, 53–55; productive binaries and outer-city relationships with, 223; Saigon's edge and outer-city relationships with, 209–11; space/spatial relations and outer-city relationships with, 75; urban civilization on Saigon's edge and, 209–11, 220; urban expansion and outer-city relationships with, 113. See also inside/outside categories
inside/outside categories, 5, 237; gendered female space and, 72, 78; Ho Chi Minh City/Saigon and, 1–2, 37–38, 242n11; ideal representations of,

2–4, 18–19, 72–73, 222, 245n17; identity construction and, 5, 55–57; marriages and, 73–76; material world and, 5, 225; power/exclusion on the edge and, 73–76; productive binaries and, 221–22; Saigon's edge and, 2; social edginess and, 2, 76; social experiences and, 2, 49–50; social hierarchies and, 52, 54, 81–83; social oscillation and, 1; social space and, 5, 222–23; space/spatial relationships and, 75–76; spatial transformations and, 38; spatio-temporal oscillation and, 121–23, 125, 151, 224; state/nation and, 5; Tân Thới Nhì and, 73; urbanization and, 34, 113; wartime notions of, 13. *See also* inner-city districts; kinship relations with inside/outside idiom; outer-city districts

Jamieson, Neil, 21–22, 252n11

kinship relations, 51–53, 73–74, 225. *See also* patrilineal ideal; patrilocal residence; social hierarchies
kinship relations with inside/outside idiom, 2, 225, 244n48; Ho Chi Minh City/Saigon and, 51, 52–53, 244n48, 244n51; limits of land for social reproduction and, 147–49; patrilineal ideal and, 49–53; patrilocal residences and, 50–53, 148; social edginess and, 36; spatiotemporal oscillation for production and, 146–50, 244n51, 250n19; urbanization and, 49–53

labor force: emigrant laborers overseas and, 140–41, 250n19; factory, 135–42, 237–38; labor theory of value and, 81–82, 246n25; labor/time orientation of social reproduction and, 129–35, 139–40, 145–46, 168;

social reproduction and, 131, 132, 139–40, 145–46, 148, 149–50; temporary wage, 131, 132, 139–40, 146, 148, 149–50
labor theory of value (M-C-M' relationship), 81–82, 246n25
labor/time orientation of social reproduction, 129–35, 139–40, 145–46, 168
land/time orientation of social reproduction: space/time relationships and, 128, 130–32, 134, 140, 144–45, 251n26; spatiotemporal oscillation and, 121, 123, 141, 145–46, 250n21
land use, 14; agriculture/farmers and, 18, 72, 245n17; front facing property and, 166, 252n11; limits of land for social reproduction and, 147–49; mixed-use spaces and, 44–46; rights for, 15, 43, 80, 111, 123, 126–27, 141–42, 250n21
late socialism, 233–35
Leach, Edmund, 96, 249n1
Lê Bạch Dương, 136
linear time: agriculture/farmers and, 98, 99, 100–101, 102; development and, 107–8; emigrant laborers overseas and, 141; farmers and, 98, 99, 100–101, 102; progress and, 103; social action and, 96–97, 103; social change and, 123; "social time" oscillation with, 123–25, 151; urban expansion and, 113
Li Zhang, 8, 233
Long An province, 9, 13, 29, 33–34, 163, 250n21
Lương Văn Hy, 49–51, 158, 250n21

Malarney, Shawn Kingsley, 53, 170, 255n20
marginalization/ marginal space, 2–4, 24, 46, 48–49, 68–69, 85
market economy with socialist direction: factory labor force and, 237–38;

folk structuralism theorization and,
236–37; socialist policies and, 4,
47, 200, 256n28; space/time relationships and, 158, 169–71, 253n18,
253n22, 253n23; state/nation and, 4,
235–38; Trans-Asia Highway and,
169–71, 238, 253n18, 253n22,
253n23

marriages with inside/outside categories, 73–76

Marx, Karl, 59, 134, 228, 253n22

material transformations. *See* spatial
transformations

material world: chaos/order control
interpretations and, 184, 188–92;
country/city categories and, 5, 24–
25, 225; historical past and, 104–5;
inside/outside categories and, 5,
225; interpretations of, 105, 172,
184, 188–92, 225

mặt tiền (front-facing) property, 164

McGee, A. T., 165

McGee, T. G., 44–46, 63, 65, 245n7

M-C-M' relationship (labor theory of
value), 81–82, 246n25

megaurban type of urbanization, 45–46

men/gendered male space: cafés and,
71–72, 160, 168, 244n40, 246n18;
marriages with inside/outside
categories and, 73–76; political
decision-making and, 71–72;
social networking and, 74–75, 168,
246n18. *See also* kinship relations

mixed-use spaces, 4, 45–46; agricul-
ture/farmers and, 30, 44–46; Ho Chi
Minh City/Saigon and, 45–47; land
use and, 44–46; power/exclusion on
the edge and, 61–64; spatial transformations and, 46; urbanization
and, 29–30, 38, 43–49, 243n34

modernism, 174, 221, 227–35

modernity: definition of, 230; double
edge of, 233; infrastructure development and, 184; late socialism

and, 234–35; productive binaries
and, 223; "social time" and, 85, 91–
94, 109, 116–17, 118; southern
Vietnam and, 117; *văn minh* and,
174, 211–13

modernization *(hiện đại hóa):* agricul-
ture/farmers and, 13–14; Highway
22 and, 174; Hóc Môn district and,
13–16; progress and, 93; socialist
policies and, 229–30, 232, 234; Tân
Thới Nhì and, 14–18; Trans-Asia
Highway and, 172–73, 184; wasteland versus, 3

movement dynamics, 45, 48–49, 81–
82, 93–96, 103, 112–13

myths/mythmaking, 3, 9, 22–25, 91,
101, 223, 241n56, 255n20

Nader, Laura, 5

National Highway, 22, 34, 90, 155–56,
158, 160–63, 174, 251n6. *See also*
roads; Trans-Asia Highway

nation-state. *See* state/nation

neighborhood area behind road *(xóm),*
166–67

Nguyễn An Ninh, 205, 257n47

Nguyễn Đình Thi, 230–31

Nguyễn Hữu Đang, 230–31

Nguyễn Khắc Viện, 198–99, 213,
255n16

Nguyễn Văn Tài, 42–43, 47–48

Nguyễn-võ Thu-hương, 5, 8, 58, 115–
16, 190

Ninh, Kim, 8, 20–21, 241n50

non–clock time. *See* "social time"

nông thôn hóa đô thị (urban ruralization), 212–15, 258nn70–73

northern Vietnam, 45, 65, 89, 136, 163,
168, 252n11

North Vietnam, 8, 23, 64–65, 105, 199,
216, 218. *See also* Vietnam

opportunities/despair, 30, 64–69, 79–
80, 82–85, 128

order/chaos control, 184–92, 202–4, 208–9, 211–12

Orwell, George, 1, 3

otherness/othering, 69, 248n51

outer-city districts *(huyện ngoại thành)*, 1, 2, 9, 38, 42; country/city categories and inner-city districts relationships with, 40–41; edge production and inner-city districts relationships with, 57; factory manager/outer-city official story, 69–73, 245n16; green-belt spaces and inner-city districts relationships with, 14, 205; house/family home spatial relationships and, 144–47; inner-city districts relationships with, 2, 37; inner-city districts separated/linked with, 53–55; modernity and inner-city districts relationships with, 118; productive binaries and inner-city districts relationships with, 223; Saigon's edge and inner-city districts relationships with, 209–11; space/spatial relations and inner-city districts relationships with, 75; urban civilization on Saigon's edge and, 209–11, 220; urban expansion and inner-city districts relationships with, 113. *See also* inside/outside categories

paradise: and Trans-Asia Highway (Xuyên Á), 157–58, 184, 192, 231

party, the (Communist Party). *See* Communist Party

patrilineal ideal: despair/opportunities and, 65; kinship relations with inside/outside idiom and, 49–53; power/exclusion on the edge and, 73; social experiences and, 32; social production and, 148–49, 224, 244n51; social reproduction and, 130; space/spatial relationships and, 75–76; spatiotemporal

oscillation and, 142–44, 146–49, 224, 244n51

patrilocal residence, 73, 130, 134, 140, 142, 144–46, 148–50, 149

peasant-based production contract system, 200, 256n25

peasant ideal representations, 23–24, 215; nostalgia and, 58, 115, 196; peasant-based production contract system and, 200, 256n25; peasant-based revolution paradox and, 197–99, 225, 255n9, 255n14, 255n16, 255n20. *See also* country/city categories (rural/urban ideal)

Pelley, Patricia, 8, 97, 99, 103, 104–5, 199

Phan Thị Yến Tuyết, 142–43

phát triển (development). *See* development

place/spaces: cafés, 132, 133, 160, 168, 244n40, 246n18; on the edge, 4–5; greenbelt space, 14, 29, 30, 53, 205, 210; performance of, 168; production of, 122, 239n14

political decision making, 71–72

politics: of time orientation, 91–93, 247n4; of Trans-Asia Highway (Xuyên Á), 156, 172, 182–83. *See also* socialist policies; state/nation

postmodernism, 221, 226–27, 229

poststructuralism, 226

power/exclusion on the edge: about, 61, 63, 64, 67, 84–85; country/city categories and, 61, 62; despair/opportunities and, 64–68, 79, 83–85; ideal representations and, 25, 62–63, 79, 84, 245n5; inside/outside categories and, 73–76; kinship relations and, 73–74; marginalization and, 2, 69; M-C-M' relationship and, 81–82, 246n25; mixed-use spaces and, 61–64; outer-city official/factory manager story and, 69–73, 245n16; patrilineal ideal and, 73; patrilocal residence and, 73; social edginess and, 24, 36, 68–79, 84; social hierarchies and, 80–83; space as social process and, 63–64; space/spatial relationships and, 76–84, 246n19, 246n21; spatial transformations and, 67, 81

productive binaries, 4, 9, 22–25, 101, 221–25. *See also specific productive binaries*

progress: Communist Party and, 103–4, 107–8, 111–14; construction rate and, 89, 246n1; historical past and, 105, linear time and, 103; marginal space and, 3; modernization and, 93; mythmaking by state/nation and, 3, 91, 255n20; peoples' agreement/disagreement about, 104–12; productive binaries and, 225; socialist time and, 91, 103–4; "social time" and, 90, 91, 104, 107–8, 111–14; urbanization and, 105, 112

public performances, 58, 167–69, 170, 172–74; Trans-Asia Highway and, 167–69, 170, 172–74

"real time." *See* linear time

reconstruction/destruction: and spatial transformations, 171–82, 184–85, 229–32

relaxed/unencumbered/at ease *(thoải mái)*, 128, 132–34, 150

renovation and political/economic reforms in 1986 *(đổi mới)*, 111, 165, 170, 200, 210, 235

roads, 158, 162–64, 168, 251n5. *See also* traffic; Trans-Asia Highway

Robinson, Ira M., 45

Roseberry, William, 5, 7

ruralization. *See* "urban ruralization"

rural-to-urban migration, 42–43, 48

rural/urban ideal (country/city categories). *See* country/city categories (rural/urban ideal)

rural-urban interface zones *(désakota)*, 44, 63, 65, 77, 245n7

Saigon/Ho Chi Minh City. *See* Ho Chi Minh City/Saigon; Saigon's edge; urban civilization on Saigon's edge

Saigon's edge, 2, 4; country/city categories and, 2, 9–11; despair/opportunities and, 84; double edge of, 47–49, 233; the edge and, 4–5, 114, 221–25; ideal representations and, 2; inner-city/outer-city relationships and, 209–11; inside/outside categories and, 2; middle class and, 165, 232; productive binaries and, 4, 225, 233; social experiences and, 30, 34; Trans-Asia Highway and, 156, 183. *See also* social edginess; urban civilization on Saigon's edge; urbanization

Sassen, Saskia, 239n14

Scott, James, 22–23, 63, 130, 228, 246n21

security/civilization problem, 11, 203–11, 229, 257n47, 257n55, 257n56

soapberry *(bồ hòn)* metaphor, sucking the, 31–35, 46, 225, 242n5

social action: chaos/order control of traffic and, 185–92, 202–3; Highway 22 and, 160–62; peoples' agreement/disagreement about progress and, 108–11; politics of time orientation and, 92–93; socialist time and, 103, 104–7; "social time" and, 92–93; Tân Thới Nhì and, 180, 181; teleology of, 94–96, 123; Trans-Asia Highway and, 168, 180–81

social agency, and Trans-Asia Highway (Xuyên Á), 155, 157, 159, 185

social change: Communist Party and, 104, 125; historical past and, 6; linear time and, 123; productive binaries and, 225; social edginess and,

59; space and, 90; space/spatial relationships and, 90, 102; space-time dimensions and, 92; space/time relationships and, 123, 125–28; spatiotemporal oscillation and, 140; as sweet ideal/bitter reality, 33; Trans-Asia Highway and, 158–59

social edginess, 4, 35–36; contradictory models of social hierachy and, 36; country/city categories and, 2, 36; despair/opportunities and, 30; development and, 24; economics and, 68–79; future-oriented trajectory of development and, 24; ideal representations and, 25, 30, 35, 36, 84; ideal social categories reiteration/violation and, 36; inside/outside categories and, 2, 76; kinship relations with inside/outside idiom and, 36; power/exclusion and, 24, 36, 68–79, 84; productive binaries and, 223–25; social change and, 59; social experiences and, 30, 36; social production and, 36; space/social relations and, 35, 36–37, 59; spatial transformations and, 36. *See also* Saigon's edge

social experiences, 3–4, 7; country/city categories and, 2, 5, 6, 24–26, 77, 83, 84; globalization and, 3–4; ideal representations and, 22–23, 26, 50, 62–63; inside/outside categories and, 2, 49–50; kinship relations and, 51; patrilineal ideal and, 32; Saigon's edge and, 30, 34; social edginess and, 30, 36; "social time" and, 102–3, 248n48; state/nation and, 77, 84, 246n21; as sweet ideal/bitter reality, 32–33, 34–35, 225. *See also* traffic

social hierarchies: contradictory models of, 36, 199–201, 255n21, 256n25, 256n28, 256n30; country/city categories and, 115–16, 199–201, 248n51, 255n21, 256n25, 256n28,

256n30; despair/opportunities and, 69; development and, 115–16; future-oriented trajectory of development and, 115–16; inside/outside categories and, 52, 54, 81–83; middle class and, 165, 232; power/exclusion on the edge and, 80–83; social edginess and, 36; southern Vietnam and, 115, 256n30; yin/yang complementary cultural system and, 21–22. *See also* kinship relations

socialist policies, 3–4, 6, 13; civilizing rhetoric and, 199; country/city categories and, 241n50; destruction/reconstruction and, 229–32; development and, 104, 105–6, 229–30; globalization and, 236–37, 239n13; historical past and, 105; Ho Chi Minh City/Saigon and, 105–6; industrialization and, 194, 196, 199–201; late socialism and, 233–35; market economy and, 4, 47, 200, 256n28; middle class and, 232; modernization and, 229–30, 232, 234; peasant-based revolution paradox and, 197–99, 225, 255n14, 255n16, 255n20; socialist time and, 103–7, 114; teleology of, 108, 110; "urban civilization" and, 216, 259n75. *See also* market economy with socialist direction

socialist time, 103–7, 114

social networking, 74–75, 168, 246n18

social oscillation, 1, 85, 91, 116, 118–19

social processes, 46, 63, 159

social production: country/city categories and, 7; kinship relations with inside/outside idiom and spatiotemporal oscillation for, 146–50, 244n51, 250n19; patrilineal ideal and, 148–49, 224, 244n51; social edginess and, 36; social reproduction and, 249n2; Trans-Asia Highway and, 178

social reproduction: agriculture/farmers and, 130; cafés and labor/time orientation of, 132, 168; emigrant laborers overseas and, 140–41; labor/time orientation of, 129–35, 139–40, 145–46, 168; limits of land for, 147–49; patrilineal ideal and, 130; patrilocal residence and, 130, 148–50; social production and, 249n2; space-time dimensions and, 129–32; temporary wage labor for, 149–50. *See also* land/time orientation of social reproduction

social space: "antisocial" space versus, 175–81, 253n28; inside/outside categories and, 5, 222–23; as social process, 63, 64; Trans-Asia Highway and, 170, 172, 174–75, 180, 183–85, 251n6; village organization and, 162–63, 170, 251n6. *See also* men/gendered male space; women/gendered female space

"social time," 5, 25–26, 85, 89–92, 108, 118–19, 247n3; agriculture/farmers and, 98–100, 101–2, 114, 247n21; country/city categories and, 116–19; cyclical time and, 101–3, 247n28, 248n28, 248n35; development and, 90, 91, 93; Highway 22 and, 90; Highway 22 upgrades and, 90; historical past and, 90, 92, 97, 102–3; linear time oscillation with, 123–25, 151; modernity and, 85, 91–94, 109, 116–17, 118; movement dynamics and, 96–97; peoples' agreement/disagreement about progress and, 104, 107–8, 111–14; politics of time orientation and, 91, 92, 247n4; progress and, 90, 91, 104, 107–8, 111–14; social action and, 92–93, 98; social experiences and, 102–3, 248n48; space/time relationships and, 93–94, 117–18, 130–31, 247n8; urbanization and, 91. *See also* development; linear time;

social change; "social time"; spatial transformations

southern Vietnam: despair/opportunities and, 65; factory workers and, 136; historical past and, 117; Ho Chi Minh City/Saigon as hub and, 42; modernity and, 117; patrilineal ideal and, 142–44; peoples' agreement/disagreement about progress and, 109; social hierarchies and, 115, 256n30; socialist policies and, 105–6, 117; village morphology and, 168, 252n11; wartime notions of inside/outside categories and, 13

South Vietnam, 23, 109, 252n11. *See also* Vietnam

space/spatial relationships: economics and, 78, 79–84; Ho Chi Minh City/Saigon and, 37, 51, 52–53, 242nn10–11, 244n48, 244n51; inner-city/outer-city districts relationships and, 75; inside/outside categories and, 75–76; marginal space and, 3, 24, 46, 48–49, 68–69, 85; outer-city house/family home and, 144–47; patrilineal ideal and, 75–76; power/exclusion on the edge and, 76–84, 246n19, 246n21; social change and, 90, 102; state/nation power and, 77, 246n21

space-time dimensions: labor/time orientation of social reproduction and, 129–35; productive binaries and, 225; roads and, 158; social change and, 92; social reproduction and, 129–32; space-time theory and, 125–35; spatiotemporal oscillation and, 141, 151; time value calculus and, 128–29, 249n8

space/time relationships, 94, 132–35, 247n8, 253n33; cafés and, 133; coffee-drinking customs and, 127, 129, 249n7; historical past and, 117–18; labor for wages and, 130–32;

labor/time orientation of social reproduction and, 129–35, 139–40, 145; land/time orientation of social reproduction and, 128, 130–32, 134, 140, 144–45, 251n26; land use rights and, 126–27, 141–42, 250n21; market economy and, 158, 169–71, 253n18, 253n22, 253n23; movement dynamics and, 93–94, 103; power of spatiotemporal oscillation and, 150–51; relaxed/unencumbered and, 128, 132–34, 150; social change and, 123, 125–28; social reproduction and, 129–32; "social time" and, 93–94, 117–18, 130–31, 247n8; space-time theory and, 125–35; time value calculus and, 128–29, 249n8; Trans-Asia Highway and, 169–71, 181–82, 253n18, 253n22, 253n23, 253nn32–33. *See also* spatiotemporal oscillation

spatial transformations, 7; civilizing rhetoric and, 189–92; destruction/reconstruction and, 171–82, 184–85, 229–32; infrastructure development and, 112–13; inside/outside categories and, 38; mixed-use spaces and, 46; movement dynamics and, 48–49, 95–96; power/exclusion on the edge and, 67, 81; productive binaries and, 225; social edginess and, 36; social relations and, 123, 157–58; space as social process and, 63–64; Tân Thới Nhì and, 172–73; Trans-Asia Highway and, 172–73

spatiotemporal oscillation, 121–22, 151, 224, 249n1; country/city categories and, 121–23, 150, 224; emigrant laborers overseas and, 141, 250n19; factory labor and, 135, 136–42; inside/outside categories and, 121–23, 125, 151, 224; kinship relations with inside/outside idiom

for production and, 146–50, 244n51, 250n19; labor/time orientation of social reproduction and, 145–46; land/time orientation of social reproduction and, 121, 123, 141, 145–46, 250n21; limits of land for social reproduction and, 147–49; outer-city house/family home spatial changes and, 144–47; patrilineal ideal and, 142–44, 146–49, 224, 244n51; patrilocal residence and, 130, 134, 137, 140, 142, 144–45, 148; power of, 150–51; social change and, 123; social reproduction and, 122, 139–42, 249n2; "social time"/linear time oscillation and, 123–25, 151; space-time dimensions and, 141, 151; temporary wage labor for social reproduction and, 131, 132, 139–40, 146, 148, 149–50

state/nation: contradictory models of social hierarchy and, 199–201; country/city categories and, 40–41, 199–201; inside/outside categories and, 5; market economy and, 4, 235–38; progress mythmaking and, 3, 91, 255n20; social experiences and, 77, 84, 246n21; space/spatial relationships and power of, 77, 246n21; teleology of development and, 174

structuralism, 227–28

Tân Thới Nhì: "antisocial" space and, 177, 178, 253n28; country/city categories and, 17; hamlets subdivisions, 17; history of, 11; inside/outside categories and, 73; map, 12; modernization and, 14–18; population, 15, 17; Trans-Asia Highway and, 158, 177, 178, 253n28; village morphology and, 252n9. *See also* Hóc Môn district

Tân Thới Nhì People's Committee, 15, 69–71, 125
Taylor, Keith, 19, 241n17
Taylor, Philip, 42, 115–18, 231, 232, 248n51, 249n8, 258n73, 259n74
thành phố (city "walls and streets"), 37, 38, 52, 240
thành thị (city "walls and markets"), 37
thoải mái (relaxed/unencumbered/at ease), 128, 132–34, 150
Thongchai Winichakul, 211, 259n76
time value calculus, 128–29, 249n8
Toan Ánh, 41
Tôn Nữ Quỳnh Trân, 147, 240n31
traffic: chaos/order control of, 185–92, 202–3; civilizing rhetoric and, 191, 254n45; ideology of, 155, 170–71, 174, 183–84, 191–92, 253n22; social action of, 161–62, 173, 183–88; "urban civilization" and, 216, 218. *See also* roads; Trans-Asia Highway
Trần Ngọc Thêm, 21–22, 39
Trans-Asia Highway (Xuyên Á), 26, 155–59, 182–84; "antisocial" space and, 175–81, 253n28; chaos/order control and, 184, 185–92; double edge of development in destruction/reconstruction and, 171–75, 184–85; front facing property and, 166, 252n11; Highway 22 and, 34, 90, 155–56, 158, 160–63, 174, 251n6; infrastructure development and, 165; market economy and, 169–71, 238, 253n18, 253n22, 253n23; materialist interpretations of chaos/order control and, 184, 188–92; modernization and, 172–73, 184; neighborhood area behind road and, 166–67; paradise and, 157–58, 184, 192, 231; physical dangers/effects and, 155, 157, 176–77, 184, 185, 192; politics of, 156, 172, 182–83; public performances and, 167–69,

170, 172–74; roads and, 158, 162–64, 168, 251n5; Saigon's edge and, 156, 183; social action and, 168, 180–81; social agency and, 155, 157, 159, 185; social change and, 158–59; social production and, 178; social space and, 170, 172, 174–75, 180, 183–85, 251n6; space/time relationships and, 169–71, 181–82, 253n18, 253n22, 253n23, 253nn32–33; spatial transformations and, 172–73; Tân Thới Nhì and, 158, 177, 178, 253n28; urbanization and, 34; urban morphology and, 164–66, 252n14; village morphology and, 167–68, 252nn8–11; village organization and, 170, 251n6. *See also* roads; traffic
Trouillot, Michel-Rolph, 118, 170
Trường Chinh, 197–98
Tsing, Anna, 68–69
Turley, William, 105, 204
Turner, Terence, 246n19, 249n2
Turner, Victor, 68, 219–20

"uncivilized"/unrepresentative behaviors, 10–11, 115, 211–12, 216, 218, 223
United States/Americans: coffee-drinking customs and, 127, 249n7; despair/opportunities and, 65–66, 79–80, 82, 83, 128; globalization and, 229, 235–36; kinship relations with family in, 51–52; peasant ideal representations and, 23–24; peoples' agreement/disagreement about progress and, 108–10; security/civilization problem in Ho Chi Minh City/Saigon and, 205, 209; time value calculus and, 128–29; wartime notions of inside/outside categories and, 13
universal linear time. *See* linear time
universal particularity of country/city categories, 5–6, 8–9, 239nn13–14

"urban civilization" *(văn minh đô thị)*, 212–13, 215–18, 258nn70–72, 258n71, 259nn74–78

urban civilization on Saigon's edge, 193–96, 219–20, 254n1; chaos/order control and, 202–4, 208–9, 211–12; civilizing rhetoric and, 195–96, 197, 210, 212–15, 255n9, 258n63, 258nn70–72; contradictory models of social hierarchy and, 199–201, 255n21, 256n25, 256n28, 256n30; country/city categories and, 201–3, 211, 256nn33–34; industrialization and, 203, 211; outer-city districts and, 209–11, 220; peasant-based production contract system and, 200, 256n25; peasant-based revolution paradox and, 197–99, 225, 255n14, 255n16, 255n20; security/civilization problem in Ho Chi Minh City/Saigon and, 203–11, 257n47, 257n55, 257n56; "urban civilization" and, 215–18, 259nn74–78; "urban ruralization" and, 212–15, 258nn70–73

urban intellectuals/"civilized urban lifestyle." *See* civilizing rhetoric

urbanization *(đô thị hóa)*, 33–35; agriculture/farmers, and effects of, 9–10; Communist Party and, 105–6; country/city categories and, 29–30, 37–49, 242nn10–12, 243n18; development and, 105; economic paradox of edge and, 47–49; edge production and, 55–59; expansion and, 113; greenbelt spaces and, 29, 30, 39, 53; historical past and, 29, 34, 106–7, 242n6; industries/industrial zones and, 29–30, 39; infrastructure development and, 44, 47–48; inner-city districts separated/linked with outer-city districts and, 53–55; inside/outside categories and, 29–30, 34, 113; kinship relations with inside/

outside idiom and, 49–53; megaurban type of, 45–46; mixed-use spaces and, 29–30, 38, 43–49, 243n34; peoples' agreement/disagreement about progress and, 112; productive binaries and, 225; progress and, 105, 112; rural-to-urban migration and, 42–43, 48; "social time" and, 91; stretched ideal of Ho Chi Minh City/Saigon and, 42–43, 243n25; Trans-Asia Highway and, 34; urbanization, use of term, 35. *See also* Saigon's edge

urban morphology, 164–66, 252n14

"urban ruralization" *(nông thôn hóa đô thị)*, 212–15, 258nn70–73

văn hóa (culture and education level), 21, 213, 258n72

văn minh (civility/civilization/civilized), 174, 211–13

văn minh đô thị ("urban civilization"), 212–13, 215–18, 258nn70–72, 258n71

Vietnam War, 13, 23–24, 31, 64, 106, 209

village/commune *(xã)*, 9, 15, 163–64, 238

village morphology, 167–68, 252nn8–11

village organization, and roads, 162–63, 170, 251n6

Võ Nguyên Giáp, 197–98

Vũ Hoàng Chương, 29, 43

"walls and markets," city: *thành phố*, 37, 38, 52, 240; *thành thị*, 37

wasteland *(đất hoang)*, 3, 18, 53, 106

Weber, Max, 185–86

Williams, Raymond, 5–6, 7, 8, 115

women/gendered female space: home/finances/marketing and, 73–74, 168, 246n18; identity construction and, 55–57; inside/outside categories and, 72, 78; kinship relations and,

52, 53, 225; marriages with inside/outside categories and, 73–76; outer-city official/factory manager story and, 69–73, 245nn16–17

WTO (World Trade Organization), 4, 235–36

xã (village/commune), 9, 15, 163–64, 238. *See also specific xã* (village/commune)

xóm (neighborhood area behind road), 166–67

Xuyên Á (Trans-Asia Highway). *See* Trans-Asia Highway

yin/yang *(âm/dương)* complementary oppositions, 21–22, 39, 41–42, 203–4, 241n56

Erik Harms is assistant professor of anthropology at Yale University.